BOOKS AS WEAPONS

BOOKS AS WEAPONS

Propaganda, Publishing, and the
Battle for Global Markets in
the Era of World War II

John B. Hench

CORNELL UNIVERSITY PRESS   **ITHACA AND LONDON**

First published 2010 by Cornell University Press
Printed in the United States of America

Library of Congress Cataloging-in-Publication Data

Hench, John B.
    Books as weapons : propaganda, publishing, and the battle for global markets in the era of World War II / John B. Hench.
        p. cm.
    Includes bibliographical references and index.
    ISBN 978-0-8014-4891-1 (cloth : alk. paper)
    1. World War, 1939–1945—Propaganda.   2. Propaganda, American—Europe—History—20th century.   3. Propaganda, American—Japan—History—20th century. 4. Publishers and publishing—United States—History—20th century.   5. Book industries and trade—United States—History—20th century.   I. Title.
    D810.P7E854   2010
    940.54'88673—dc22   2009048122

Cornell University Press strives to use environmentally responsible suppliers and materials to the fullest extent possible in the publishing of its books. Such materials include vegetable-based, low-VOC inks and acid-free papers that are recycled, totally chlorine-free, or partly composed of nonwood fibers. For further information, visit our website at www.cornellpress.cornell.edu.

Cloth printing   10 9 8 7 6 5 4 3 2 1

For Lea

Books cannot be killed by fire. People die, but books never die. No man and no force can put thought in a concentration camp forever. No man and no force can take from the world the books that embody man's eternal fight against tyranny. In this war, we know, books are weapons.

—President Franklin D. Roosevelt

Books do not have their impact upon the mass mind but upon the minds of those who mould the mass mind—upon leaders of thought and formulators of public opinion. The impact of a book may last six months or several decades. Books are the most enduring propaganda of all.

—Office of War Information official

The opportunity exists as it never may again for American books to have an inside track to the world's bookshelves.

—Office of War Information official

Contents

Preface

The origins of this book date back a decade, when I deliberately set out to become a book collector. I wish to emphasize the word *deliberately*. For nearly all my life I had acquired books by the hundreds—many, if not most of them, quite purposefully. I had also inherited several of my father's book collections, but they never truly became "mine," and I never built upon them. Despite such a long and deep acquaintance with books, I had never felt like a real collector. That changed, in 1999, when I decided, in the middle of one night, that I would become a collector of books and magazines published primarily for U.S. troops abroad during the Second World War.

Having been born during the war, I had always been fascinated by it, though far more by its social aspects than the history of battles. The war colored my earliest recollections growing up, particularly since my father had brought home souvenirs from his stateside service as a colonel in the army medical corps. My first visit to London, undertaken at age thirteen, just eleven years after the end of the war, aroused my curiosity as to what it must have been like to endure aerial bombardment day after day, the loss of family and friends, shortages of virtually everything (including books), and sudden attacks by V-1 and V-2 flying bombs. When I began to study history, I realized how much the effects of the war had shaped the world I lived in and how many of its consequences remained with us—the cold war, the rebuilding of Germany and Japan and their transformation into economic powers, the creation of the State of Israel and the seemingly perpetual unrest in the Middle East, and profound domestic changes such as the quest for equality and social justice for African Americans and women, and greater demand for higher education.

So a collector I became—of the down-market variety, to be sure, having made a pact with my wife that the items I acquired would be small, inexpensive, and offset by deaccessions from current holdings. The happiest surprise about my new collecting interest was that it led me to a promising research project, one that took me down paths outside early U.S. history, the field in which I was trained and with which I was associated during the third of a century I spent at the American Antiquarian Society. Still, my new research interest was in a subject field that had deeply absorbed me through all this time—the history of the book, or, to put it less abstractly, the history of printing, publishing, distribution, and reading. Through my collecting as much as through my archival research, I learned how greatly the war had affected the U.S. publishing industry and the book trades of other nations.

The artifacts I gathered included hundreds of titles in the famed Armed Services Editions series and other series of books intended to entertain and educate the troops abroad as well as hundreds of copies of miniaturized editions of *Time, Newsweek, The New Yorker,* and a couple dozen other popular periodicals. The idea for this book did not occur to me, however, until I discovered and purchased, on eBay, a book in a series called Overseas Editions, of which I knew nothing. Apparently, few other scholars or collectors knew of this series either. Finding and purchasing additional Overseas Editions—as well as exemplars of similar series such as Transatlantic Editions and Bücherreihe Neue Welt—confirmed that I had an interesting and important topic.

My collecting raised many compelling questions in my mind. What exactly were these books? Who produced them? For whom were they intended? Initial research at Princeton University Library and the National Archives in College Park, Maryland, provided some answers but prompted many more. The full story of the sponsorship of these series, it turned out, was obscured by various wartime subterfuges. Books issued by what appeared to be private publishing houses turned out to have covert government sponsorship as well. It soon became clear that these various series were intended, not for the military, but for European and Asian civilians and German and Italian prisoners of war in order to reorient their thinking as the war came to an end. These and other books, I further discovered, were designed not only to meet certain propaganda goals for the United States but also to provide the incentive and the means by which American book publishers might gain a far greater share of world markets for their products than ever before.

My long involvement with book history gave me a solid grounding and a constant reference point as I researched and wrote. I benefited from this interdisciplinary field's ability to reveal fruitful connections with—and new perspectives on—other areas of study, in this case military, political, diplomatic, and business history, and even linguistics. It was also an opportunity to contribute to the growth of a truly international perspective on the history of books. The story of the U.S. book-publishing trade's wartime experiences—the skirmishes and battles, as well as the instances of cooperation and coordination, with publishers and governments throughout the world—provides new ways of looking at the histories of the Atlantic world, the Pacific Rim, and Pan America during a period of global upheaval and the rise of U.S. military and political power.

The programs and activities covered in this book represent responses of both the U.S. government and American book publishers to a set of problems and challenges. The war provided the opportunity—even the necessity—to try to solve those problems. Accordingly, this book is organized into three parts, all centered on this theme of solving problems and meeting challenges.[1] Part 1 sets out the problems that prompted the actions described in this narrative. For the government, the challenge was to find ways to use books to "disintoxicate" the captive people after years of fascist propaganda and to generate goodwill for the United States. For the publishers, the issue was how to capitalize on both the desperate hunger for books that people in the war zones felt and the vacuum left by the diminishment of the major international publishers in order to find new markets for American books overseas. Part 2 deals with the solutions that the government and publishing trade conjured up. These included the development of post D-Day programs for what is called consolidation propaganda, using books to win the hearts and minds of civilians abroad and to make a beachhead for the products of U.S. publishing houses throughout the world. Part 3 treats the results and consequences, both short- and long-term, of these undertakings. There were many impediments to a lightning-fast conquest of the world by American books, but eventually they made their way onto the world's bookshelves, just as wartime publishers, civil servants, and military officials had envisioned.

John B. Hench
Worcester, Massachusetts

Acknowledgments

I am beholden to many individuals and institutions for encouraging, facilitating, and funding my research and writing. My greatest intellectual debts are to Trysh Travis and Robert A. Gross for their strong support of my efforts and for their own ideas that helped anchor my work. Trysh was the first person to do scholarly work on the history of the Council on Books in Wartime, the civilian sponsor of the Armed Services Editions and Overseas Editions. In a trenchant article, she identified key themes—pressures to modernize, publishers' professional ideology, the use of books to create "interpretive communities"—that resonate throughout my book.[2] As for Bob, I have taken advantage of him as a fountainhead of sparkling ideas, always generously offered, not only while I worked on this book but throughout my entire career at AAS. His early suggestion that I take a look at the refugee publishers and intellectuals who came to the United States as an important element in the internationalization of U.S. book publishing has taken root in many sections of this work.

Kenneth Carpenter has for decades been a model professional colleague and friend, filterer of ideas, fountain of knowledge on all things to do with books and libraries, and supporter of this project.

Several other scholars who, like me, study the role of books in the hot and cold wars of the twentieth century have also contributed greatly to my thinking. They include Gregory Barnhisel, Amy Flanders, Juliet Gardiner, Valerie Holman, Amanda Laugesen, Jane Potter, Erin Smith, Michele Troy, and Cathy Turner. If our ranks continue to grow as they have, can an association of historians of books in wartime be far behind?

I could not have completed my work without the support of several short- and long-term fellowships: a Friends of the Princeton University Library Fellowship (2003); a Gilder-Lehrman Fellowship (2004); an Everett Helm Visiting Fellowship at the Lilly Library, Indiana University (2005); a Marcus A. McCorison Fellowship from the Bibliographical Society of America (2005); and a Bibliographical Society (London) Fellowship (Barry Bloomfield Award) (2006). A yearlong National Endowment for the Humanities fellowship in 2006–7 provided the crucial time to write as well as complete most of the research. Having spent most of my years at AAS administering fellowships, I knew how important and stimulating these awards are. Special thanks to Ellen Dunlap and Edward Harris for facilitating my research leaves to take these fellowships. I am most grateful to other colleagues at AAS for their interest, encouragement, and research help: Megan Bocian, Paul

Erickson, Babette Gehnrich, Vincent Golden, Thomas and Lucia Knoles, Philip Lampi, Marcus A. McCorison, Jaclyn Penny, Elizabeth Pope, and Caroline Sloat.

It was especially fun to be a visiting fireman at other research libraries. I am grateful to many people for help and hospitality: at Clark University, Gwendolyn Arthur and Mott Linn; at Columbia University, Jean Ashton, Tara Craig, Bernard Crystal, and Jennifer Lee; at the Library of Congress, Daniel DeSimone; at the Lilly Library, Rebecca Cape, Erika Dowell, Breon Mitchell, Penny Ramon, and Joel Silver; at the McKeldin Library, University of Maryland, Eiko Sakaguchi and Amy Wasserstrom; at the New York Public Library, Robert Armitage and David Smith; at Princeton University, Linda Bogue, Stephen Ferguson, Charles Greene, Michael Heist, Daniel Linke, Gretchen Oberfranc, AnnaLee Pauls, Margaret Rich, Nancy Shader, and Don Skemer; at the Harry Ransom Center, University of Texas, Austin, Richard Oram; and at Reading University, England, Verity Andrews and Brian Ryder. Many people whose names I never learned were of assistance to me at the National Archives, College Park, Maryland, and The National Archives, Kew, England.

For other kindnesses, loans of material, tips, encouragement, support, and friendship, I wish to express my gratitude to the following colleagues in the United States and the United Kingdom: Blanca Hedi Arndt, John Y. Cole, Joseph Cullon, Hendrik Edelmann, William Glick, Warwick Gould, Ezra Greenspan, Terry Halliday, Leslie Herrmann, John Kerr, Willem Klooster, Christopher Lehmann-Haupt, Richard Linenthal, Emanuel Molho, Sam Nightingale, David and Martha Nord, Donald Ratcliffe, William Reese, Joel Schwartz, James Turner, David Way, and Ian Willison. Special thanks are due to Jeff Adams for taking photographs for the book.

I am most grateful to the staff of Cornell University Press for their highly professional efforts in seeing this book into print. My editor, Michael McGandy, was a pleasure to work with. He was demanding yet flexible, and always kept me in the loop. I appreciate his strong support of my work. Emily Zoss and Susan Specter ably dealt with the never-ending details involving illustrations and permissions, scheduling, and oversight of the editorial flow. My highly capable copyeditor, Marie Flaherty-Jones, made me wish I had had her skills when I performed copyediting and proofreading for many years at the American Antiquarian Society, among my other duties.

My family has supported me throughout the many years of research and writing. My daughters, Melissa and Juliann, and son-in-law Jeff, have taken considerable interest in what I've been doing. Their children—India, Charlotte, Henry, and Jack—may someday pull this book down from a shelf and actually read it, perhaps as a head start on a term paper. I think my late parents, Philip and Mary Hench, and my uncle, Atcheson Hench, would be pleased. But most of all, I want to thank my wife, Lea, for her great love and support, and for all the good times we had on my fellowship residencies in such wonderful places as Princeton, New York, Bloomington, and London.

Abbreviations and Acronyms

Abbreviations for archival sources can be found in the bibliography.

ABPC	American Book Publishers Council
AIS	Allied Information Services
ASE(s)	Armed Services Edition(s)
BNW	Bücherreihe Neue Welt
BOMC	Book-of-the-Month Club
BPB	Book Publishers Bureau
CAD	Civil Affairs Division, SCAP
CAME	Conference of Allied Ministers of Education
CBW	Council on Books in Wartime
CCD	Civil Censorship Detachment, SCAP
CIA	Central Intelligence Agency
CIAA	Office of the Coordinator of Inter-American Affairs
CIE	Civil Information and Education Section, SCAP
ECA	Economic Cooperation Administration
EMF	*Éditions de la Maison Française*
ESS	Economic and Scientific Section, SCAP
ICD	Information Control Division
JPA	Japan Publishers Association
MoI	Ministry of Information (UK)
NBC	National Book Council (UK)
OEI	Overseas Editions, Inc.
OE(s)	Overseas Edition(s)
OMGUS	Office of Military Government, United States
OPMG	Office of the Provost Marshal General, U.S. Army
OSS	Office of Strategic Services
OWI	Office of War Information
PA	Publishers Association (UK)
PID	Political Intelligence Department, Foreign Office (UK)
PMG	Provost Marshal General, U.S. Army
PW	*Publishers' Weekly*
PWB	Psychological Warfare Branch
PWD	Psychological Warfare Division
PWE	Political Warfare Executive (UK)

SCAP   Supreme Command for the Allied Powers
SHAEF   Supreme Headquarters, Allied Expeditionary Force
SPD   Special Projects Division, OPMG
TE(s)   Transatlantic Edition(s)
USIA   United States Information Agency
USIBA   United States International Book Association
USIS   United States Information Service
USO   United Services Organization
VBC(s)   Victory Book Campaign(s)
WPB   War Production Board

BOOKS ON THE NORMANDY BEACHES

On June 6, 1944—D-Day—more than one hundred fifty thousand Allied troops, transported by the largest invasion fleet ever assembled, gained a beachhead on the Normandy coast, beginning the campaign that led to the defeat of Nazi Germany and the liberation of millions of people. From these French beaches, the invading armies spread out, capturing the strategic port of Cherbourg and, in time, taking Paris. For several months after the first wave of forces had moved on, great numbers of fresh troops, along with military supplies, food, and medicine, were off-loaded at various points along the forty miles of coastline that extended from Utah to Sword beaches or in the large ports, like Cherbourg and Le Havre, after their capture by the Allies.

With the early landings came an unlikely weapon of war: crates of books. Only a few weeks after D-Day, these boxes, each weighing about eighty pounds and containing between ten and twenty-seven copies of two dozen different British and American books and pamphlets, equally divided between the two nations, were deposited on the beaches. Like the brave soldiers who had landed earlier, this odd cargo also suffered casualties. Weather and tides obliterated labels on a number of the boxes, causing damage and delays in getting them to French bookstores and news dealers. But, in good time, the books reached the outlets, where they were eagerly snapped up by customers desperately hungry for reading material from a world different from the one they had inhabited for too many dreadful years.[1]

The landing of these books on the Normandy beaches was the most dramatic episode—one rich in symbolism—in a campaign that put millions of American books in the hands of civilians throughout Europe, the Middle East, North Africa, Asia, and the Pacific. Smaller shipments had accompanied earlier invasions, in North Africa and Italy, and these served as rehearsals and experimentation just as the military landings themselves did for the big show of June 6, 1944. Like the landing of the troops on D-Day, this invasion of books was intended to effect a liberation, in this case, the unfettering of people's minds. In the full context of the long-awaited Allied invasion of Europe, the arrival of these crates of books was naturally overshadowed by the landing of troop reinforcements—more than 1 million by July 1, 1.85 million by the end of the summer—and additional war matériel, which properly took precedence in the weeks after D-Day.[2] That the landing of the books took place at all, however, where and as early as it did, signified that the civilian and military leadership had great confidence in the ability of books to free the minds of the peoples newly liberated by the Allied forces.

Why did books claim so much attention in the U.S. war effort? The answer lies in how and why the U.S. publishing industry and the government joined together to respond to challenges and problems facing the private and public players both before and during the war.

Between the two world wars, the genteel, tradition-bound book-publishing industry in the United States alternated between ignoring calls to modernize and actually grappling with the issue.[3] Most grievously, the trade had failed to solve the age-old problem of distribution, that is, how to put a book into the hands of each and every customer who needed or wanted it, at home or abroad, as efficiently as possible, as well as the related issue of finding new markets. Although U.S. publishers were blessed with a domestic market that extended from the Atlantic to the Pacific, in reality books were readily available only in areas with a bookstore, and those tended to be concentrated in the Northeast, in some of the larger cities in the Midwest and West, and in towns throughout the country that could boast of having colleges, universities, or other cultural institutions. Those bookish pockets were sufficient to ensure a decent turnover and profit to most publishers. In fact, the ease of the task often discouraged publishers from taking on the challenges inherent in expanding the domestic market, to say nothing of getting more involved in selling books and publishing rights to customers in other countries. Although American publishers had long sold their books overseas (both as exports of domestic editions and as reprints in English and foreign languages), many questioned whether the rewards were worth the considerable effort involved, particularly in the face of the historic domination of the international book trade by Britain, Germany, and, to a lesser degree, France.

A publishers' association in 1931 commissioned a thorough study of the economics of the book trade, and the final report urged the adoption of modern business practices. Most publishers, however, declined to follow through on its recommendations because the report shortchanged the notion, held by people in the trade as an article of faith, that books were something more than mere commodities, like automobiles, radios, and laundry soap.[4] The war provided a laboratory for work toward a solution to the problems of markets. Wartime was actually a boon to the industry, as it was generally throughout the U.S. economy. Increased demand for books, combined with low inventories, made the wartime publishing business in the United States unusually profitable. Accordingly, one of the biggest challenges facing the trade was to find ways to sustain and, better yet, to increase profits after the war was over. One means would be to cultivate new markets not only at home but overseas as well. That goal and the belief that books had value above the purely economic were joined together in very interesting and productive ways during the war.

The war actually sparked a cycle of profound change in the dynamics of publishing throughout the world. Virtually all countries faced shortages of paper and labor, and in Europe such shortages were particularly devastating. Military actions, blockades, and diminished shipping capacity seriously curtailed British publishers' ability to supply their huge, long-held worldwide markets throughout the empire and commonwealth—from Bermuda to South Africa, Australia, and Hong Kong. Occupied and Vichy France, moreover, could not meet the needs of its colonies or of French-language readers in other parts of the world, like Quebec and South America. The German book trade, historically the world leader in science, medicine, and technology, had been fully discredited by the racial theories of the Nazi leadership and the brutality of its armies. Britain's inventory of books suffered not only from a severe drop in the production of new titles and the reprinting of old ones but also from the Luftwaffe's destruction of an estimated 20 million books through the bombing of publishers' warehouses and institutional and private libraries. Moreover, the domination of vast territories by Germany and Japan brought with it widespread censorship and control over publishing and reading, including the censorship program masterminded by Joseph Goebbels, the Nazi minister of propaganda. Meanwhile, refugees from Hitler's Europe populated the U.S. publishing industry, bringing about significant changes.

The shrinkage of book stock available in the belligerent and occupied countries on all continents, combined with censorship of the books that remained, resulted in a deep, widely documented worldwide hunger for fresh, uncensored books that could help overcome the effects of a long intellectual blackout. Publishers in the United States closely observed this phenomenon, as did the U.S. government.

The particular issues the government faced as storm clouds gathered in Europe were of course infinitely broader and more dangerous than the marketing and identity issues that troubled the publishers. Some of the government's many challenges lay in the area of public opinion and propaganda. Even though the nation professed neutrality in the European war that began in September 1939, the government was deeply concerned about the spread of Nazi influence closer to the United

States, specifically in Latin America. With its long-standing trade ties to Germany, as well as settlements populated by ethnic Germans, the region seemed particularly receptive to the spread of Nazi propaganda. A German invasion of South America, softened up by the manipulation of public opinion, was not unthinkable.

With the bombing of Pearl Harbor, the United States found itself at war in both the Pacific and Atlantic theaters. The short-term effects of enemy propaganda on a geographic scale far greater than Latin America now became a major problem for the U.S. military and intelligence community. It was not long before the government began to worry about the long-term effects as well. Not only did Goebbels's propaganda machine spread Nazi theories of race and German invincibility, much of it was expressly designed to belittle American culture and its people for their capitalist greed and intellectual shortcomings. Among the stereotypes that field officers found rampant in overrun Europe, for example, were claims that "Americans are materialistic and their greatest ambition is the accumulation of wealth and comfort," that "immorality is prevalent" in the United States, and that "America has far-reaching imperialistic designs."[5] Ironically, the Nazi propaganda minister had drawn heavily on the stereotypes embedded in popular Hollywood films, which had reached large audiences abroad in the 1930s. These movies frequently depicted gangsters and socialites, giving foreign viewers reason to believe that most Americans were either in cahoots with Capone or whiling away their hours at the Stork Club, loosening their grip on the showgirls on both arms only to swig their manhattans. These negative clichés were not only highly effective in Germany; they also detrimentally influenced our friends, the public in Allied countries like Britain and France.[6]

These developments left government officials concerned with how to counteract the malignant effects of Nazi and other Axis propaganda in the overrun nations, from Norway to Greece, and eventually in Asia as well. How might they take advantage of the deep hunger for reading fare *not* published or censored by the enemy that gradually revealed itself during the war? These were problems that called for solutions not so much to win the war as to win the peace.

But first the war had to be won. After Pearl Harbor, the government and the private sector—indeed, the entire U.S. population—mobilized on a scale scarcely seen before. Like their counterparts in other businesses and industries, U.S. publishers were eager to "do their bit" for the war effort. Embracing a wartime "culture of planning," they established a nonprofit corporation, the Council on Books in Wartime (CBW), in the spring of 1942 to focus their collective efforts.[7] The council's programs were aimed at building and sustaining morale among the civilians at home and the troops abroad as well as increasing awareness of the issues brought on by the war—issues that books, the publishers argued, were uniquely suited to illuminate. By adopting the slogan suggested by the publisher W. W. Norton and later given wide circulation by President

Franklin D. Roosevelt, "Books are weapons in the war of ideas," the group en-sured that propaganda in some form or other was ever present in its activities.[8] It also gave publishers a cause that both drew on and reflected their professional ideals. If books were weapons, they thought, then they had the power to influ-ence events and the course of history.

The government also saw the need to focus its efforts related to morale build-ing, publicity, and propaganda. After some initial fumbling, President Roosevelt established the uninspiringly named Office of Facts and Figures in October 1941. It too stumbled, so Roosevelt replaced it with the Office of War Information in June 1942. Organized into domestic and overseas branches, OWI operated under considerable scrutiny by Congress and the press and with only mixed success throughout the war.

Officials at both CBW and OWI quickly realized how closely related their missions were and how they might better achieve their separate goals by working together on matters related to the printed word. The story of this collaboration is a rich one for understanding the interaction between private enterprise and civilian and military agencies of the government during wartime, particularly in the case of an industry, like book publishing, that would not at first blush be thought of in the same context as such heavyweight war industries as rubber and shipbuilding.

Understandably and conveniently, both entities drew heavily on the same co-hort of civilians to populate their ranks—namely, people in the publishing busi-ness. Naturally, virtually all of the volunteers and staff members in the council came from the publishing world—and a distinguished group it was. W. W. Norton (of the eponymous firm) served as first chairman. Richard L. Simon (Simon & Schuster) held the post of vice chairman. (He waited only until December 8 to offer President Roosevelt "my services in any capacity in which they may be use-ful to the country at this time."[9]) Such well-known publishers as Bennett Cerf (of Random House and, in the 1950s and '60s, a regular panelist on the popular TV show *What's My Line*) and Robert F. de Graff (Pocket Books) were members of the board of directors. It was less foreordained that publishers would hold key roles in OWI, but many did. Particularly important in solidifying relationships between OWI and the council were Chester Kerr (Atlantic Monthly Press) and Harold Guinzburg (The Viking Press).

The wartime mobilization that affected the entire nation relied largely on not only the patriotism but also the expertise, ingenuity, hard work, and sacrifice of many men and women, like these, from the book trades, through their service as civilians in government agencies like OWI and in nongovernmental organiza-tions like CBW. Examining these wartime book programs thus calls attention to the role of private, nonprofit civilian organizations in the war effort. Simi-larly, the cadre of skilled white- and pink-collar volunteers from the publishing world deserve their share of credit, along with the GI Joes, Rosie the Riveters, and Rosie's male blue-collar colleagues in the industrial workforce, for all they did in support of the nation's cause. Their contribution was not only on the domestic and civilian side of the war effort. Many of the OWI staff members, in fact, were attached to the military in combat zones as well as rear positions overseas, especially in SHAEF (Supreme Headquarters, Allied Expeditionary Force). Their work in utilizing books as propaganda and as tools for reorienting the world-views of friends and foes alike may have been a very small aspect of military activities during the Second World War, but it was far from insignificant. In fact, some key decisions in this arena had to be made by people at the highest levels of command, including President Roosevelt and Generals Dwight D. Eisenhower and Douglas MacArthur.

A close collaboration between the council and the propaganda agency on matters relating to books rapidly took root. The partnership fostered the major, and in some respects the only, long-term piece of strategy for what was called the "consolidation phase" of World War II propaganda, during which the United States set out to win the hearts and minds of the people liberated from the Axis powers.[10] That strategy called for putting millions of American books into the hands of the liberated populations as quickly as possible but only on an "emergency" basis until the publishing industries in the previously overrun nations were back on their feet and ready to fill the information vacuum themselves.[11] This was a goal U.S. book publishers naturally found entirely congenial. Justification for the program stemmed from OWI's conviction that, after several years during which scarcely anything but heavily censored printed materials and Nazi propaganda had been available to the reading public in occupied Europe, "American books can serve a very vital function as information and propaganda ... [and] are one of the most useful mediums available for helping the people of liberated areas to rehabilitate themselves."[12]

The U.S. stockpiling program was part of a larger, U.S.-British effort. The British propaganda agencies were also stockpiling publications for distribution to the liberated territories. Although Britain and the United States were clearly competing for future markets in liberated Europe, their joint efforts were deemed important enough militarily and politically to be coordinated within the Psychological Warfare Division of SHAEF, under the command of General Eisenhower.[13]

The supply of American stockpiled books came from various sources, including publishers' current stock,[14] but attendant shortcomings prompted OWI to see the need for books published specifically for the purpose. Accordingly, OWI encouraged CBW to publish Overseas Editions, a series of books in English and several foreign languages, drawn mainly from titles in the current lists and backlists of major U.S. publishers, that were "intended to reacquaint Europeans with the heritage, history, and fundamental makeup of the USA, plus a picture of our role in the war."[15] The stockpiling program included another, smaller series besides the Overseas Editions: books in French and Dutch known collectively as Transatlantic Editions, which OWI produced in England.[16]

Nearly all of the titles in the two series had been published in the United States during the war, and thus would not have been available to people in the overrun or enemy countries. All of them had to meet various defined propaganda objectives, most of which had to do with "disintoxicating" Europeans from the effects of their years of Nazi propaganda and censorship and putting the nation's best foot forward for peacetime. In short, the books were chosen for their propaganda value but were not written as propaganda. They were books that U.S. citizens had themselves been reading and thus were free of the taint of conscious propaganda. Many of them were hot literary properties for the publishers, making them exactly the kinds of books that they hoped to be able to sell around the world in far greater quantities than they ever had before.

In addition, the government, acting through a branch of the army, sponsored another series of books designed to reeducate another group of Europeans, namely, German prisoners of war in camps in the United States, who would shortly be repatriated. This program, like the OE and TE undertaking, also served the interests of commercial publishing, though in this case the publisher, Gottfried Bermann-Fischer, was a German Jewish refugee who dreamed of resuming his business in his homeland and the books were mostly modern German classics that Hitler's regime had banned or burned.

These wartime book programs often appear curiously disconnected from the events of the war itself, except in the broadest sense. They were dreamed up and advocated for by civilians, largely from the book-publishing industry, who had gone to work in CBW or OWI, mostly far away from the scenes of action. Their job was to plan, which they did assiduously. For the ultimate implementation, however, they were entirely dependent on the military, from the highest echelons of SHAEF down to the soldiers or sailors who fetched the crates of books from the Normandy beaches for transport to civilians throughout Europe. They could never be sure when, or even if, the books they assembled or published would be put to their intended use. As it happened, planning carried out by articulate, book-publishing civilians in offices left a vast paper trail; implementation in bombed-out cities in Europe and Asia, far less so. One thing that struck me in reading the correspondence of Kerr, Guinzburg, Norton, and Melcher, however, was how seldom they mentioned events of the war in their letters. Even writing letters on D-Day plus one or the day after Germany surrendered, they mostly stuck to business.

By linking up with OWI, American book publishers managed to do well by "doing good." Doing good, in their case, meant patriotically supporting their country's effort during history's greatest war by playing a significant role in the critically important consolidation phase of U.S. propaganda aimed at denazifying European thought, and, as it turned out, by providing a foil to the spread of communist propaganda during the ensuing cold war. They did well because "doing good" in this fashion gave them an opportunity to establish a beachhead for their literary properties in Europe and elsewhere around the world. The government proved to be a useful ally for the publishers by endorsing their professional ideology that books had the power to perform important cultural and political work, and by helping them establish business relations with the international community of publishers that were vital to building their franchise into the future. All of this was intentional. As a key OWI memorandum stated, "The opportunity exists as it never may again for American books to have an inside track to the world's bookshelves."[17]

As it happened, many impediments—postwar poverty abroad, the scarcity of hard currency, fluctuations in exchange rates, and the refusal of the British to cede their preeminent role in the world book trade without a fight—stood in the way of American publishers' capitalizing on the wartime effort immediately, or as fully as they wished. Many of the limiting factors were out of American publishers' control.

The World War II book programs, however, significantly influenced postwar U.S. international relations by serving as precedents for important elements in the diplomacy of the cold war, sometimes effectively, sometimes not.[18] In a sense, relationships between the government and publishers, both overt and covert (as was sometimes the case during the cold war), represent a kind of quasi-official national book policy, and, by their waxing and waning, they not only reflect the changing relationships the United States has with various foreign countries but also highlight the nation's diplomatic priorities. The relationship between the government and private enterprise, in other fields as well as in book publishing, remained an important and frequently employed means of conducting postwar cultural diplomacy.[19]

Aided and underwritten by the government, these programs represent an economically minor but culturally significant aspect in the general expansion, even domination, of U.S. culture overseas in the second half of the twentieth century. American books, whether in exported editions or republished abroad in English and scores of other languages, have penetrated widely, as the wartime publishers dreamed. With and without the government as partner, American publishers' efforts to secure and develop new markets abroad may be seen as one of a number of ways in which American culture came to predominate in the world during the last half of the twentieth century. Like U.S. political power and military might, U.S. cultural influence has been respected, envied, and reviled, leaving ambiguities, ironies, and tensions that are still with us today. Of course, what the future holds for books in general and for books as tools for explaining the United States of America to a mostly skeptical world itself remains very much a question mark and a challenge.

Part I

CULTIVATING NEW MARKETS

1

MODERNIZING U.S. BOOK PUBLISHING

Between the end of the First World War and the beginning of the Second, the book trade in the United States became distinctly American—"more rough-and-tumble" and with "a more pronounced gambling mentality"—and thus more and more unlike the other major national publishing systems, including the British. During the interwar period, many new publishing firms were founded, and the trade embraced profitable relationships with other industries in the fields of entertainment and information, including theater, radio, magazines, and films, a phenomenon that enhanced the role of the literary agent as an instrument for negotiating the complexities of the new opportunities. During those two decades, the trade pursued a series of developments that were designed to modernize the industry and cultivate new markets for books.[1]

A number of these innovations provided the general background as well as the models for the important wartime program that wedded book publishing to wartime propaganda and led to the landing of American books on Normandy beaches. These milestones include the establishment of the Modern Library, the Book-of-the-Month Club, and the early mass-market paperback publishers Pocket Books, Inc., and the U.S. branch of Penguin Books. The Roosevelt administration's policy of cultivating good relationships with the governments and peoples of Latin American countries, through Nelson Rockefeller's Office of the Coordinator of Inter-American Affairs, served as a test run of the future collaborations between publishers and government that I discuss in this book. In addition, the arrival in the United States of a number of prominent European publishers as refugees during the 1930s and early 1940s was to profoundly influence the internationalization of American book publishing during and after the war. The Great Depression of the 1930s treated the publishing industry relatively gently. Still, that experience gave publishers additional incentives not to rely on their traditional markets and business strategies for revenues and profits.

Problems of Distribution

Publishers had ample reasons to modernize operations and cultivate new markets. Although the United States had, by the end of the First World War, become one of the great book-publishing nations of the world, the vast physical size and unevenly distributed population of the country meant that access to books was highly variable and localized. The frequently unbusinesslike ways in which publishers carried on the book trade did not help matters. The stock market crash of 1929 forced a dose of introspection on the publishing world. When it became apparent that the economic downturn might be protracted, the National Association of Book Publishers commissioned a study of the economics of the trade in 1930. The resulting, exhaustive report by the primary investigator, the banker O. H. Cheney, laid out the problems that faced the U.S. book trade.

Several tables in the published Cheney report triangulated the uneven distribution of outlets for the sales of books in the country. Cheney calculated from NABP sources that there were only 4,053 places throughout the nation where books were sold, and most were small and thinly stocked. Most bookshops, of any size, were concentrated on the East and West coasts and in some of the larger cities and college towns in the hinterlands. Cheney found, in fact, that two-thirds of all the counties in the United States and nearly one-half of the cities and towns with a population between five thousand and one hundred thousand had not even one retailer where people could buy a book.[2] A dozen years later, a delegation of three prominent British publishers on an extended wartime transatlantic mission were particularly struck by the thin and uneven distribution of bookstores in the United States.[3] As a banker, Cheney found much to criticize in the business practices of American book publishers. His recommendations took up sixteen pages and included suggestions in the areas of improving distribution mechanisms, reducing waste and loss, increasing reading and book buying, improving trade relations, and increasing cash flow.[4] Members of the trade took exception to some of the findings, arguing that Cheney the businessman had missed the intangible cultural values that made making books different from making radios, wrenches, or wristwatches. In the end, the industry "decently interred" the report.[5]

Their cavalier attitude to Cheney's study notwithstanding, publishers did make some progress between the wars in finding new means to distribute books and creating new markets for them. The earliest was the launch of the Modern Library by the firm of Boni & Liveright in 1917. This was part of an effort to rehabilitate the publication of inexpensive reprints, which had gained a reputation for poor quality and became a particular medium of publishing piracy. A modest price would win customers who could not afford to buy books in their original editions. In establishing the Modern Library, Albert Boni and Horace Liveright looked to the model of low price and attractive design represented by the British reprint series Everyman's Library, distributed in the United States by Dutton. Boni and Liveright made a marketing breakthrough by inviting the public to regard the books not as individual titles but as a coherent whole, "a recognizable series with its own established reputation for excellence." Their advertising tended to feature the whole list as a collective Modern Library brand, as did many booksellers who displayed the books together, rather than shelving the titles with other editions.[6]

Boni and Liveright parted ways a year later, with Liveright winning a coin toss to determine which partner would buy out the other's interest in the firm. In 1925, Liveright sold the Modern Library, to the consternation of most of his staff—but not Bennett Cerf, a young vice president of the firm, who pooled his cash with that of a friend, Donald Klopfer, to meet Liveright's price of two hundred thousand dollars in what the publishing world called the sale of the young century. Later, Cerf and Klopfer founded Random House to provide a general publishing superstructure for the valuable reprint series. The partners ratcheted up the advertising for the series, which in time expanded beyond the avant-garde titles that Boni and Liveright had featured to encompass world classics. Cerf, Klopfer, and their editors selected the titles with advice from such outside experts as Granville Hicks, Clifford Odets, Edmund Wilson, and James T. Farrell.[7] Quickly the series gained great prestige and status. Its slogan—"the world's best books"—proclaimed the creation of a canon, one that savvy consumers would be smart to embrace.

Harry Scherman's founding of the Book-of-the-Month Club in 1926 was another attempt to compensate for the irregular distribution of booksellers in the country. A Montreal-born New York advertising man, Scherman several years earlier had gotten his feet wet in the mass-marketing of books by establishing the Little Leather Library of world classics in association with the publishers Albert and Charles Boni. Millions of copies of the small books were included as premiums in boxes of Whitman's Samplers or sold in Woolworth five-and-dimes. Later, the books were vended by mail order, cutting out the middleman and giving Scherman some useful experience in direct-mail marketing.[8] The Little Leather Library serves as a common ancestor of both the Modern Library and the BOMC by virtue of Albert Boni's involvement in both innovations.

Several innovations within the greater invention that was the BOMC provided exemplars of publishing practice that were later used in the production of books for liberated civilians in 1944–45 and, in many cases, in the making of the Armed Services Editions, which the Council on Books in Wartime began producing earlier for U.S. forces abroad. One was the use of a selection committee to choose, from among many recent books, the titles to be offered as monthly selections or alternates. The selection committee would consist of people of erudition and refined, if middlebrow, tastes, who had achieved a certain amount of celebrity through their own books, criticism, journalism, or public positions, not the least of which was in fact their service as judges for the BOMC. The selection of books for stockpiling abroad during the war, and especially those chosen purposely to be part of the Overseas or Transatlantic series, was also done by both an outside committee of experts and staff cut from the same cloth. One of them, *Saturday Review of Literature*'s Amy Loveman, for example, also served as clerk of the BOMC's selection committee. The very idea of employing a selection committee has been seen as an element of modernization.[9]

No outside committee participated in selecting the Modern Library's titles. Boni's original vision of using a book series to promote a certain kind of avant-garde, liberal cultural agenda,[10] however, was clearly echoed in the cultural work that the OEs were asked to perform, albeit without the radical titles. Like the Modern Library, the ASE series was vast, but any level of canonicity it achieved was more accidental than purposeful. By contrast, the OE series was far smaller and deliberately eschewed canonical texts in favor of current books of middlebrow appeal and topical in nature that could advance, individually and collectively, a particular propaganda objective as well as introduce strong-selling recent American books to Europeans who, it was hoped, might thereby develop a continuing taste for books from the States.

The paperback revolution in the United States of the middle third of the twentieth century, however, provided perhaps the greatest model for the ASEs and OEs, and produced some direct benefits as well. Inspired by the success of German and British paperback series, particularly Allen Lane's Penguin Books, and attempting to overcome the flaws of other recent domestic paperbound series, Robert de Graff established Pocket Books, Inc., in 1939, with Simon & Schuster owning 49 percent of the stock. His recipe for success was a familiar one in business: reduce costs and increase volume. Like the Modern Library, Pocket Books assumed iconic status. Its name in fact became generic for the mass-market paperbacks published by imitators—the Kleenex of the book world. De Graff's innovation partly overcame the spottiness of distribution that Cheney had lamented by using drugstores and dime stores throughout the country, rather than traditional bookstores, as his prime outlets.[11] This did not solve the larger problem of efficiently delivering *any* book to *any* customer, however.

One of de Graff's competitors was the U.S. branch of Penguin, which set up shop in New York City, under the direction of Ian Ballantine, around the time that Pocket Books was getting started. De Graff actually welcomed the arrival of Penguin, on the "shoe-store" theory that having several on the same block builds business for all. In any case, he need not have worried, at least for a while. The outbreak of war in Europe seriously hampered Penguin USA's development. It became nearly impossible to export British Penguins to the United States or to export the capital necessary to put the U.S. operation on a secure footing. Lane was close to shutting the U.S. branch when he arrived for a visit in 1941, but he found a way out when he met up with Kurt Enoch, an experienced German publisher who had created the distinguished line of Albatross Books—titles in English for the Continental market. Enoch had come to the United States as a Jewish refugee from Hitler's tyranny and hopeful of launching another publishing venture. Lane persuaded Enoch to take on the role of vice president. Enoch's solution to Penguin's problems was to relocate as much production as possible to the United States.[12]

The success of Pocket Books, Penguins, and other paperback series no doubt encouraged CBW and OWI to believe that paperback series would be effective in solving the problems of manufacturing costs and the difficulty of shipping books to their desired audiences—first to members of the service through the ASEs and, later, to European civilians through the OEs. The matter of gaining rights for paperback reprints had been routinized through the deals that the paperback houses made with the publishers of trade hardcovers. CBW and OWI benefited. Though offering smaller fees than commercial houses, they traded on inspiring patriotic satisfaction in the publishers who made their hardcover book available for the special wartime series. Moreover, Pocket Books had already developed experience in marketing their books to soldiers through camp PXs and even directly, while Penguin had also begun to reach the soldier market through a series of paperbacks published jointly with the *Infantry Journal*.[13]

The defining characteristic of the program of taking U.S. books to the liberated people abroad was a strong partnership between government and the industry. Here too was a precedent from the tail end of the interwar period: the Office of the Coordinator of Inter-American Affairs, an agency that grew out of President Roosevelt's Good Neighbor Policy toward Latin America. Indeed, Wilson Dizard, a veteran United States Information Agency officer, claims that CIAA was the nation's first real overseas propaganda program and that, under Nelson Rockefeller's management, it created the template for OWI and, in the 1950s, USIA.[14] CIAA was no less a wartime agency than OWI. When CIAA was established in 1940, the administration was concerned about the growing influence of Nazis in Latin America, even to the point of taking seriously the possibility that Hitler might attempt to invade somewhere south of the Rio Grande. Even without a threat of invasion, Latin America was home to many people of German blood and was rife with pro-Axis agitation and espionage.[15] CIAA's various economic and cultural programs were thus designed to neutralize Nazi influence in the region.

Among the cultural programs was one that aimed to publish U.S. books in translation in Latin America and books from Latin America in English.[16] In fact, publishers and librarians had been closely involved in discussions at the State Department that led to the agency's establishment.[17] This activity had a positive effect on the trade in American books in countries to the south. In general, Latin America dominated the overseas trade interests of American publishers during 1939–40, as the extensive coverage in *Publishers' Weekly* testifies. The public/private alliance in this case helped pave the way for the partnership that was launched with the plan to land American books in Europe.

A "Dunkirk" for European Refugees

While not exactly an innovation, the arrival of an important group of people fleeing the Nazis provided an important new context for the development of an international outlook within the U.S. book-publishing industry. Most influential were the Germans and Austrians, who formed part of an even larger group of fellow countrymen who settled in other areas of the Americas, most notably Mexico, Argentina, and Brazil. Significant numbers from other countries, especially France, also emigrated.[18] These individuals were representative of various ethnic, religious, and political groups who were considered personae non gratae in the Third Reich—Jews, socialists, communists, and others who became targets of persecution by the Nazi regime. Many of these refugees were intellectuals—academics, scientists, writers, journalists, booksellers, and publishers. Numbering somewhere between twenty-two and twenty-five thousand, they made a disproportionately high impact on the arts and sciences in their adopted United States.[19] The writers, who included Thomas Mann, Franz Werfel, and Lion Feuchtwanger, were a particularly stellar lot. With their escape, "the physical rescue of our literature has been accomplished," the exiled writer Martin Gumpert wrote. "It is a Dunkirk adventure of immeasurable cultural consequences."[20]

Nearly as distinguished a group as the writers, the publishers who began anew in the United States sought to publish material that would both serve the needs of the émigré community itself and perhaps be smuggled into Germany to support resistance to the Nazi regime. A number of refugee booksellers in New York and elsewhere had strong interests in importing anti-Nazi literature from abroad, mostly from the major German-language publishers in neutral Sweden and Switzerland. The production of German-language imprints by refugees in the United States was relatively decentralized: 353 German-language books published under eighty different imprints. The giant in this group was Frederick Ungar, an important Austrian publisher, who fled first to Switzerland in 1938 and then to the United States in 1940. Almost all of the 110 titles that Ungar published (nearly one-third of the total) were reprints of classics and reference works, the stock-in-trade of his old firm, Saturn Verlag, in Vienna. This set him apart from the other émigré publishers, who defined themselves by their "dissemination of émigré literature and opinion" and their service as spokesmen for Germans who opposed the Nazis.[21]

Friedrich Krause, an expatriate bookseller and publisher resident in the United States for a decade, understood that their rewards would be "more spiritual than financial." A shortage of cash not only limited the number of titles most publishers could issue in the United States but also hindered their ability to import books from German-language publishers in neutral European countries. They might have gained a larger market in the United States had they found any support or sympathy from the many millions of citizens of German descent. That they did not was doubtless because most German Americans remained sensitive to rampant ill will and discrimination against their group during the First World War and reluctant to identify themselves as anything less than one hundred percent Americans during the Second. In contrast, émigré French publishers in the United States could count on support and sales from Americans of French ancestry as well as from French Canadians.[22]

Some of these men and women, like Kurt and Helen Wolff, established publishing houses in the United States that lasted well beyond the end of the war. Other ventures were short-lived. Some publishers, like Gottfried Bermann-Fischer, courageously returned to Germany to reestablish their businesses. Some of the Jewish immigrants who published during the war had arrived in the 1920s, before Hitler came to power. Two of them, Isaac Molho and Vitalis Crespin, opened a French bookstore in Manhattan, Librairie de France, which became a haven for the writers and other intellectuals who arrived as refugees before or after the fall of France. Later, the two men established a publishing house expressly for the purpose of serving the refugee population and the French-reading community worldwide, for whom the war had cut off the flow of books from France.[23]

Many of the refugee publishers encountered harrowing conditions during their often-lengthy efforts to flee. Among them were Marian and Hanna Kister, owners of a prominent Polish publishing house, Roj. Two days before the Germans seized the Kisters' company, Hanna Kister managed to flee Warsaw with her younger daughter, "with a bottle of syrup and two dollars between us." Their travels took them to Denmark, Italy, and France. With the Wehrmacht nearing Paris, they fled through Spain to Lisbon, Portugal, the principal embarkation point for refugees taking Atlantic passage. They reestablished their firm in New York in 1941 as Roy Publishers and eventually opened up a sister firm in Montreal.[24] Their admission to the United States was facilitated by publisher Richard J. Walsh, head of the John Day Company, and his wife, Pearl Buck, whose books they had published in Polish. The Walshes submitted affidavits on the Kisters' behalf, attesting to their willingness to provide some financial support to the family.[25]

The refugees who established publishing firms in the United States or assumed important positions within existing businesses influenced U.S. book publishing by introducing new and different standards of literary taste, cosmopolitanism, and strong links with major players and institutions in the Old World. Both refugee publishers and many established, native-born members of the trade contributed to the industry's efforts in the 1940s to become more active participants in the international markets for books.

Depression and Rumors of War

While war clouds gathered and darkened the lands of Europe and Asia (propelling these and thousands of other refugees to the United States), the nation was weathering the Great Depression. The publishing trade was not immune to some repercussions of the severe downturn. Hard times caused a great row between publishers and booksellers over price-cutting as well as some labor unrest in the industry, even among editorial workers.[26]

On the whole, though, the publishing industry rode out the Depression relatively well. Accustomed to cyclical downturns, publishing houses followed a comparatively frugal business model that gave them the discipline to wait, if necessary, for better times. The firms cut overhead expenses to the bone and made the most of their backlists. Most lowered their profit expectations accordingly, though some publishers were pleasantly surprised to find themselves prospering more than before. Only one major firm—Horace Liveright's—failed. Some smaller firms survived through mergers or by outsourcing some back-office tasks. The great impact of the Depression on rural areas accelerated migration from small towns to cities.[27] Easy access to bookshops remained a luxury that only city dwellers could enjoy, but at least there were more urbanites than before.

The New Deal federal government also helped keep the ground under publishers' feet. The Federal Writers' Project, within the Works Progress Administration—one of the great "economic stimulus" packages in U.S. history—employed writers who produced more than three thousand eight hundred publications, including the popular American Guide Series. Many of these government-sponsored works provided good sales for the trade houses that published them.[28] The Depression years produced a considerable literary ferment—works of social realism and the flowering of the Harlem Renaissance—which, if nothing else, made those difficult times in the publishing industry exciting.[29]

The tribulations of the 1930s furnished U.S. book publishers with good training for the austerity imposed by wartime conditions in the 1940s. The Depression did not, however, entirely prepare them for the improbable boom that the industry experienced once the war began or for the kinds of wartime programs that the innovations of the interwar period had helped make possible.

WAR CHANGES
EVERYTHING—EVEN BOOKS

The total war that swept the globe during 1939–45 rained death and destruction on cities as well as battlefields, civilians as well as soldiers. Scarcely any aspect of a society or culture was left untouched, including the book trades of all countries. Publishers in the United States and neutral countries like Sweden and Switzerland were inconvenienced but they did not suffer as much as those in Great Britain, the nations overrun by the German and Japanese armies, and the Axis nations themselves. Books were among the most conspicuous victims of this vicious warfare. Millions were destroyed by air raids, ship sinkings, infantry actions, orchestrated book burnings, and civilian paper drives. These effects of war, in addition to profound shortages of paper and labor that diminished the output of new titles as well as censorship of the printed word in the areas controlled by the enemy, created a great hunger for books and much pent-up demand, which had to await the coming of peace to assuage.

In the United States (and Britain too), mundane, often improvised efforts to lobby against government restrictions on the book trade prompted publishers and their trade associations to develop broader, more nuanced arguments for the significant role they hoped books might play not only during the war but in the peace that followed. Meanwhile, a strong wartime culture of planning gave American publishers a prime opportunity to consider how to develop new, postwar markets both internationally and domestically, and thus effectively contribute to easing the worldwide hunger for the printed word.

The U.S. Book Trade in Wartime

For U.S. book publishers, the Second World War was a time of great challenge and considerable opportunity. Wartime conditions made publishers rethink almost everything they did. Publishers suffered through shortages of labor and the raw materials of books, especially paper. Many valued staff members, from top management to copy editors and office clerks, were away serving in the armed forces or in civilian jobs in Washington. Those left behind often had to perform the tasks of their missing colleagues as well as their own. Government-imposed wartime rationing cut the supply of paper available to book publishers by steps. By 1944, publishers had to make do with 75 percent of the paper they had used before the war.[1] The shortages forced a certain discipline on publishers, who found they had to project their sales more carefully and resist ordering excessive print runs.

Scarcity actually made it a fine time to be a book publisher in the United States. Put simply, demand for books grew, while the paper supply and the number of titles published decreased, so that, in a striking if temporary reversal of the usual economics of the trade, publishers were able to sell out almost anything they issued.[2] Although the number of titles decreased, there were more books in circulation, in part because of the rise of mass-produced paperbacks.[3] Even with substantial increases in the number of copies of books in the marketplace, editions regularly sold out. When the manager of the Scribner Book Store on Manhattan's Fifth Avenue was asked late in the war how he coped with the rush of customers, he said, "Oh, at 9 o'clock we just open the doors and jump out of the way."[4]

One New York publishing executive serving in the military was Donald S. Klopfer, cofounder of Random House, who maintained a steady correspondence with his civilian partner, Bennett Cerf. When Klopfer worried about going broke, Cerf told him, "You are making more money every day than you ever dreamed you would have in a lifetime."[5] Even the further cut in paper rations in 1944 (accompanied by an end to the practice by which publishers could sell or trade their unused quotas) failed to dampen Cerf's glee.[6] For him, wartime provided an excellent opportunity to plan the postwar future of the firm. He used the time and the profits to position the firm's Modern Library for an anticipated postwar boom by replacing "bad translations with good new ones" and by making new stereotype plates for dozens of the series' titles whose plates had gotten battered from frequent reprinting.[7] From his army post in California, Klopfer, realizing the great potential that the GI Bill of Rights offered to book publishers, dreamed of starting a "helluva college text book department with the gov't paying practically the whole bill and ready to really operate when the colleges go back to normal in a couple of years."[8]

Even before Pearl Harbor made the United States a belligerent, the war produced new selling opportunities for publishers by revitalizing certain genres and cultivating important new audiences. They focused particular attention on marketing their products to the growing number of GIs in training camps throughout the country, selling single copies directly to the soldiers and in quantity to the army for placement in camp libraries. Newly introduced into the hurry-up-and-wait military culture, the trainees were a captive audience, eager to read. A Random House survey of reading habits in thirty-one camps discovered that the soldiers actually had more time to read than civilians did. The survey showed that about 15 percent of the troops read an average of one book every two weeks, mostly short books or stories, and primarily light, escapist literature.[9]

Once U.S. soldiers joined the fighting, some publishers reaped a handsome financial windfall through the sale of Bibles, prayer books, and other religious materials to members of the armed services and their families. The demand continued throughout the war, and publishers and booksellers were hard-pressed to keep up with it. The trade journal *Publishers' Weekly* called the Bible boom one of the "booksellers' pain-in-the-neck stock problems since Pearl Harbor." One publisher tried to combine saving grace with physical protection by marketing steel-covered Bibles as "a Shield of Faith" against bullets, but the Federal Trade Commission charged false advertising for the books' protective qualities, and the War Production Board cited the firm for unauthorized use of thirty-one thousand pounds of steel.[10] Atlases, globes, and dictionaries also sold well and remained in short supply throughout the war.[11] All this demand drained inventories. A common response to the shortage of highly salable titles was to ration the supply to bookstores and wholesalers.[12]

Shortages of critical materials caused prices to rise, even with price controls. From 1942 to 1947, the cost of book papers increased by 37 to 45 percent, depending on the type. Cloth binding materials rose by as much as 60 percent. On top of rising costs of ink and the metals used in casting type, labor shortages also helped fuel increases in the cost of manufacturing. The cost of offset printing, for example, went up by 39–66 percent, depending on the size of the press run, while letterpress printing rose 54–58 percent.[13] Shortages of paper used to make packing and shipping materials forced some publishers to stop mailing small parcels to customers, to consolidate shipments, or to reduce the trade discount from 40 to 33⅓ percent on single-copy orders.[14] These various moves inevitably left booksellers "annoyed and handicapped, with nothing gained except that the publisher has made more money."[15] Restrictions on travel during the war also hampered what had been routine means of conducting business, from salesmen calling on bookstores and college professors to attending regional and national conventions and sales meetings.[16]

Governments tend to intervene in the lives of their citizens more in time of war than in peace, which was certainly the case in the United States from 1941 to 1945. This greater climate of regulation affected U.S. publishers in varying ways and it also differed from that in other countries, particularly Great Britain. On the whole, there was probably less regulation in the United States than in Britain. The U.S. book trade's petitions to the War Production Board and the War Manpower Commission to declare the book trades as a whole an essential industry were unavailing. This meant that employees in the book trades were more likely to be called up for service than those working in the officially "essential" occupations. The government's stand on the book-publishing industry was especially galling to publishers because the newspaper and magazine industry had been classified as essential activities because they were "devoted primarily to the dissemination of public information."[17]

The Book Publishers Bureau, the principal trade association, was especially active in efforts to gain redress. Taking a high-toned position, the BPB in March 1943 sent a circular letter to various literary organizations throughout the country, seeking support for the position that the government's paper-rationing formula limited the right of U.S. citizens to read. Signed by three prominent members of the trade, the letter argued that books are essential at all times but never so much as in wartime. The writers suggested that too much emphasis was given to "the casual and transitory mediums of radio, film, and spoken word" in conveying public information and entertainment. Books had greater value. "The quiet, solitary processes of reading, re-reading, pondering, turning back for reference and comparing one written work with another, make for clearer thought and steadier morale." While the publishers would never countenance a rationing plan that failed to provide all "the materials and manpower needed for fighting fronts," they stressed that war boards and the public needed to realize "that the use of paper for books is more important than some civilian uses of paper, and the use of manpower to print and bind books is more important than some other production operations."[18]

Later, the bureau's War Committee prepared a report that formed the core of the argument for the key public agencies to recognize the "the essentiality of books" and to grant them high priority. In the report, the committee members emphasized the export market, which, it admitted, had not particularly interested the industry before the war. But now the world was looking to the United States for leadership on many vexing questions. Books were a vital medium for communicating such ideas. The committee members pointed out that the Norwegian government in exile in London was already purchasing American books to be stored until the Nazis were routed and they could be sent to Norwegian libraries. China, Russia, and various Latin American republics were also "demanding a part of our available book supply." The importance of U.S. book exports could only grow. The publishers emphasized, however, that foreign-market demand could be met only through the production of additional books, not by cutting into the domestic supply. Since parts of the federal government—the Office of the Coordinator of Inter-American Affairs, the State Department, and the Office of War Information—were already actively promoting the use of U.S. books overseas by means that included sponsorship of publishers' trips to England, South America, and elsewhere to study conditions and potential demand, it was necessary for the government agencies that actually controlled the industry's supplies of paper and manpower to provide the wherewithal to advance this important national strategic goal.[19]

The industry's pleas fell on deaf ears where it counted most—within the WPB, which oversaw and allocated the nation's paper supplies. The situation was less serious for technical and educational publishers than for trade houses.[20] *Publishers' Weekly* editor Frederic Melcher realized the futility of pointing out that shutting down all book printing for a year would save only 1 percent of the paper supply or that one popular periodical used more paper in a year than the entire book-publishing industry.[21] The industry had only itself to blame, for it had failed to do all that it could to conserve paper supplies by shrinking trim sizes and using lighter-weight stocks to make a thinner book block, which would save a bit of binding cloth on top of the reduced paper costs, as the British had done. Three English publishers on a reciprocal mission to the United States in 1943 were appalled at such wastefulness.[22] When the members of the bureau's War Committee visited Washington twice to press its case directly with various government offices, WPB staff told them, as the committee members reported, that there was no doubt at all that "if the Industry does not voluntarily and at once begin to make real savings [in paper], it will be forced to do so by new directives from Washington." In their memo to the bureau's constituents, the committee agreed that the WPB was correct, judging from their own inspection of the shelves of newly published books in the trade association's office, on which many of the titles demonstrated that "little if any attempt had been made to save paper."[23] The BPB's campaign to achieve its goals may have had limited success—in the manpower question at least—for when the government's list of essential war activities was revised and published in February 1944, some jobs in the book trades were included.[24] Eventually publishers began, however reluctantly, to make books more compact, cutting down on "what the trade's remainder king lovingly described as 'big dick books,'" as Bennett Cerf so graphically put it.[25]

On the whole, though, the book trades had the federal government on its side, from the very top level on down—at least morally. After all, President Roosevelt adopted the Council on Books in Wartime's slogan that books were weapons in the war of ideas against the evils of fascism. He sent a message to those attending the 1942 annual banquet of the American Booksellers Association to be sure "to make them weapons for man's freedom."[26]

The War's Impact on Book Publishing in Great Britain

The worldwide Depression of the 1930s was surprisingly gentle on British publishing's domestic business, which remained strong in part because books were more affordable and available than other pastimes. But its international business was largely stagnant, leaving it more vulnerable to the disastrous effects of another world war, which came soon enough, more than two years before it did for the United States.[27] By 1938, in fact, the various "alarums, scares and crises" emanating from Hitler's Germany began to have some negative effect on publishers' bottom lines.[28] Anticipating war, British publishers had begun to organize themselves a year before the Nazi invasion of Poland, focusing mainly on air-raid preparations and planning for relocation out of London.[29]

During the war itself, British publishing experienced a similar feast-or-famine situation to that in the United States, but, at bottom, far greater problems dogged the publishing trades in Britain. In an effort to escape formal paper rationing, the publishers proposed a voluntary cutback to 80 percent of prewar consumption. They did not succeed in gaining a complete exemption from controls but did at least secure the designation of books as one of the essential purposes for which additional, extraquota paper could be used, should it become available. Rationing, which began officially in March 1940, was much more severe than in the United States.[30] Initially, each publisher was entitled to 60 percent of his paper consumption during the year that ended August 31, 1939. The total consumption in that base year was about forty-five thousand tons, enough to produce some 135 million copies of a 250-page novel. The decrease to 60 percent, therefore, would reduce the production of hypothetical 250-page novels to 81 million copies.[31]

All publishers could lament the reduced allotment, but some grumbled that the government's selection of the base year for determining it, 1938–39, was inherently unfair. For many publishers, that was not a good year to choose. As the threat, even inevitability, of war increased in 1938–39, consumers had cut back on the purchase of books and other commodities, so the base figures on which each firm's rations were calculated were smaller than normal. The major—and immensely lucky—exception was the highly successful paperback house, Penguin Books, which had had a terrific fiscal 1939. Publisher Stanley Unwin, of George Allen & Unwin, complained years later that the book trade as a whole "just didn't count with those who had the last say in the handling of paper."[32]

A year into the rationing program, the quota was reduced to 50 percent of the 1938–39 base. Later in 1941, the rate was cut further, to 42 percent. From early January 1942, when the quota was slashed to 37½ percent, the rate generally rose, to 50 percent shortly after V-E Day and to 75 percent in March 1946.[33] Not only was wartime book paper in short supply, it was also of lower quality—what, in

George Orwell's simile, toilet paper was like before wartime exigencies turned it into something akin to sheet metal.[34] Rationing did not end officially until March 1949, which some would consider a more pivotal date for British publishers than the actual end of the war in 1945.[35]

The pain of reducing quotas was offset, at least psychologically, by the creation, in late 1941, of a special pool of paper, known as the Moberly Pool after Sir Walter Moberly, the first chairman of the committee overseeing the program, to be allocated to publishers in order to issue books, mostly reprints, of national importance in wartime, what became known as "essential" books that couldn't otherwise be produced out of a publisher's normal quota.

So that the rationed paper could be stretched to make more books, the publishers negotiated with the Ministry of Supply a Book Production War Economy Agreement, which set standards for reducing the trim size, the size of type, and the weight of paper of their wartime imprints. However necessary the changes may have been, the resulting unattractive books, with their "sad, 'utility' look," produced competitive disadvantages in the export markets when compared with books from U.S. publishers, a handicap that lingered long after the end of the war.[36] It was a problem that the trade knew it must correct.[37]

Doubly frustrating, there were times when the problems of paper rationing were outweighed by the shortages of labor in the book trades. In this area, as in that of paper, the Publishers Association lobbied government agencies to rule favorably on protecting members of various occupations from call-ups. They were moderately successful, but toward the end of the war the lack of pressmen and bindery workers idled many machines that were available to turn out much-needed books.[38]

The British government's insatiable need for paper and printing was blamed for the shortages imposed upon the trade. At the height of the war effort, official publications utilized one hundred thousand tons of paper on an annual basis, while less than twenty-five thousand tons was available for books.[39] Between 1939 and 1945, the number of titles published annually in Britain dropped from 14,904 to 6,747.[40] But demand for books increased enormously because blackouts and air raids reduced Britons' access to other familiar forms of entertainment, including going to the cinema and to pubs. Like U.S. soldiers, British military personnel were reading more. Under such conditions of scarcity and increased demand, British publishers, like their U.S. counterparts, found that they could sell out almost any title they produced but still fell far short of meeting the great demand for their books at home and abroad. "They need take, practically speaking, no risks whatever," a visiting U.S. publisher wrote.[41] Pedestrian works sold as well as good literature.[42] One provincial bookseller placed an order with a London trade house for "a thousand assorted novels—*any* novel," but the publisher could let him have only 150.[43]

That was in 1942; the situation only got worse. Two years later, Klopfer, still in the army, took time on a forty-eight-hour pass in London to visit publishers. He came away with little sympathy for the British situation. "The publishers allot books over here and can sell anything put out within reason," he wrote his partner, Cerf. "No one has any books that are exciting. They're all sitting back on their asses and saying they've never imagined anything like this—all making lots of money which is then turned over to the Government and all of them selling their birthrights because inventories are getting lower and lower."[44]

The future fortunes of British publishers had become even bleaker when, during the famed Blitz of 1940–41, the Luftwaffe bombed publishers' and distributors' warehouses, destroying much of the back stock—always a major asset for the long-term financial health and reputation of publishers—of at least twenty firms.[45] Bombs also destroyed books in libraries. Unwin, whose company was one of those that lost considerable stock to enemy raids, estimated that during the war "no fewer than 20,000,000 volumes were destroyed by enemy action."[46] In one raid, more than half of Allen & Unwin's unbound stock was completely obliterated by a German bomb. "In a few minutes the work of twenty-five years went West," he wrote.[47] The worst damage occurred during the Luftwaffe raid of December 29, 1940, which was calculated to set off a second Great Fire of London in essentially the same locale near St. Paul's Cathedral as the one Samuel Pepys had witnessed. Surveying the damage, one observer noted "the glowing cavernous holes, once basements full of stock, now the crematories of the City's book world."[48] Although it is unlikely that the German air crews specifically targeted the book warehouses, a morale-boosting pamphlet produced by a U.S. book-manufacturers' trade association and promoting the industry claimed that Hitler "bombed the book section of London in order to destroy millions of books. He knew they were weapons against him."[49] Allen & Unwin also sustained significant if much smaller losses from the pilferage of books from storage in the firm's basement, which the air-raid wardens had commandeered as a neighborhood shelter.[50] The dearth of new books stimulated a brisk market for used books, at least until paper drives relegated some 50 million volumes to the shredder and pulping vat, further widening the gap between supply and demand for reading matter.[51]

Britain's travails at war gained British publishers the sympathy of most of their U.S. comrades, Klopfer aside. Frederic G. Melcher, in particular, cheered on and bucked up the London publishers from his bully pulpit as editor and publisher of *Publishers' Weekly*, the industry's trade journal.[52] Across the Atlantic, Beatrice Warde, of the Monotype Corporation, welcomed such righteous gestures as well as more tangible assistance, because the book trades of both nations must be up to their common task of defeating Hitler's tyranny.[53] Many individual publishers expressed their concerns and best wishes personally to British publishers with whom they did business. One was Richard J. Walsh, of the John Day

Company, who wrote Jonathan Cape the day after the great fire, "earnestly hop-ing that you are escaping the worst."[54] Some did more than write. Melcher led a successful drive to raise money for a mobile kitchen for bombed-out members of the London publishing trade.[55] Donald Brace, of Harcourt, Brace, took in Cape's eleven-year-old son and fifteen-year-old daughter as evacuated children and got them placed in Connecticut prep schools.[56] Later on, as American publishers' ambitions to gain international markets once dominated by British publishers became more aggressive, mere expressions of concern and sympathy began to ring hollow to the men of the London trade.

There was no question that British books faced an uncertain future in their traditional zones of influence, like Europe and, especially, the empire and com-monwealth, from which they were cut off to varying degrees owing to wartime conditions. Unwin's concern about the shortages of stock was less for his com-pany's bottom line, he claimed, than for the ability of Allen & Unwin and other publishers to have the stock necessary to keep British books circulating abroad and thus spreading the word about British culture and values and earning badly needed foreign income.[57]

Fully aware as they were of what their British colleagues were going through, U.S. publishers, not surprisingly, began to sense future growth opportunities from Britain's travail. Some voiced their thoughts very early on. The lingering effects of the Depression and the onset of the war in Europe, for example, convinced George P. Brett Jr., president of the Macmillan Company of New York, that he needed to pay more attention to his firm's export business. "We need all the business we can get in these difficult times," he wrote future prime minister Harold Macmillan, of Macmillan & Co., little more than two months after the war in Europe began. Wartime conditions in the UK also gave Brett reason to believe that the U.S. firm's expansion would come at the expense of British publishers' trade, even that of the original Macmillan enterprise.[58] John Day's Walsh had similar thoughts. During the nine months since war in Europe began, he was sorely tempted to sell rights to books directly to publishers in Australia and New Zealand rather than to British firms who would then export their editions down under, as was the normal prac-tice. At the time, however, Walsh was unwilling "to jump on England while she is down," but he believed it was inevitable that the days for continuing that practice were numbered, whether Britain lost the war or won.[59]

Later, in December 1942, the BPB sent its members a confidential memo-randum that noted how American books were already playing a greater role in the British book trade than they had prior to 1939. "At the present time," wrote the memo's author, Curtice Hitchcock, of Reynal and Hitchcock, who had been dispatched by the bureau to visit British publishers, "I am told about 27% of the current titles being published in Britain, despite paper shortages and all the rest of it, are of American origin....A further evidence of this great and friendly interest is the admirable program worked out by the British Army for its forces, which carries a very considerable emphasis on things American." It was also significant that only about 2 percent of British books were being published in the United States, on account of either changing taste or the interruption of communications, "a fact which could be viewed only with anxiety by those who were concerned with the spread of British ideas."[60]

This demand for American writing was no doubt stimulated in part by the lack of new fiction and nonfiction from British writers, too busy dodging bombs or bullets to put pen to paper. As Lord Beaverbrook, the newspaper magnate, put it, there is no room for culture in wartime.[61] The best-selling historical novelist Vaughan Wilkins, in his fifties, remained a civilian but assumed so many new responsibilities—serving as his parish's billeting officer, responsible for overseeing the placement and well-being of evacuated children, including six that he took into his own home, and later becoming a member of the Home Guard—that he found little time or psychic energy to make progress in the book he was writing.[62] Even publisher Hamish Hamilton's contest offering a magnificent prize of one thousand pounds for the best new war novel went begging for lack of a manuscript of sufficient merit.[63] Importing American books for sale in the UK by British publishers and bookstores might have helped make up the gap, but the Board of Trade severely restricted importations of books in order to conserve dollars and shipping space for more vital war matériel. After the United States became a belligerent in the European war, space was restricted on U.S. vessels as well.[64]

Hitchcock's memo was intended to alert his colleagues to British publishers' concerns about their postwar future, particularly regarding foreign markets, noting, "quite naturally British publishers are extremely tender on the subject of their overseas markets, which they believe rightly are necessary to their prosperity when the fighting is over." Such concerns, the writer added, caused some resentment in Britain over "various even rather small actions on the part of American publishers which seem designed to grab while the grabbing is good."[65] Unwin, for one, complained about U.S. publishers' aggressiveness toward the traditional markets of British firms to his authors, colleagues, and the offending U.S. publishers early, often, and loudly.[66] British suspicion of "imperialistic" tendencies on the part of U.S. publishers was a matter of concern as well to a sympathetic Yank, Richard Heindel, the able director of the American Library in London.[67]

The War's Impact on Publishing in the Overrun Nations of Europe

In comparison with the United States and Britain, however, the publishing business in the countries occupied by German troops and under the sway of Nazi propaganda and censorship was bleak—even "shot to pieces," in the words of a memorandum produced by the U.S. government's principal propaganda agency, the Office of War Information.[68] Early in the occupation, Nazi officials had been relatively lax in preventing certain types of books unfriendly to the Reich to circulate. In the Netherlands, for example, even books that were determined to be "insulting to Nazi ideals" were allowed to be sold until stocks ran out, as long as they were not displayed. Moreover, the personal liability of booksellers for the political correctness of their wares was rarely enforced at first. On the other hand, the reprints of titles burned by the Nazis in 1933 that Amsterdam publishers Querido and Allert de Lange had issued in great quantities were quickly confiscated, with no remuneration to the owners of the seized property. Control of the publishers was tightened considerably beginning in early 1942.[69] Nonetheless, many publishers took great risks to keep the flow of uncensored literature from being turned off completely.

The German military was not completely effective in blocking the flow of books and periodicals from outside either, especially those from Britain and the United States. The German occupiers of Denmark, at least early on, actually permitted local publishers to issue some American and British books as long as they also published commissioned Nazi propaganda works. The Danish houses managed to stall production and postpone distribution of Nazi titles as much as they could. In Holland, one publisher expressed amazement that the German authorities made an exception to their prohibition against the publication of any American or British works in English or Dutch by permitting the firm to issue reprints of John Steinbeck's *The Grapes of Wrath,* Sinclair Lewis's *Babbitt,* and Eric Linklater's *Juan in America* because the Nazis believed them to be anti-American. According to the publisher, the Dutch people simply "rejoiced to be able to read a good book from the other side of the ocean" and snapped them up.[70]

But in Denmark and elsewhere, British and American materials circulated more widely through partisan underground movements than out in the open. Henning Branner, one of Denmark's leading publishers and booksellers, was a focal point of this clandestine trade. Within three months of the U.S. publication of Wendell Willkie's *One World,* Branner had commissioned a translation and printed three thousand copies on a duplicating machine. Another book, *Target: Germany,* was printed in Copenhagen with a cover made to look like a timetable. As the occupation wore on, the underground trade grew more dangerous. Several publishers were arrested. Others managed to escape to Sweden. Perhaps Branner's largest and boldest undertaking was to print and distribute a nice-looking, twenty-four-page picture magazine sponsored by OWI, *Foto Revy* (*Photo Review*). His wife translated the text provided by OWI. It took Branner fourteen days to produce an issue on a small press that could print only two pages at a time using a fine, coated stock that he had laid in before the war. In the last two years of occupation, the Branners had to relocate seventeen times in order to keep the Gestapo at bay. Eventually, he had to go completely underground.[71]

Like his U.S. colleagues, Branner was planning for the future even in wartime. At considerable personal risk, he managed to travel to Sweden on business at least half a dozen times, usually taking passage on a coal barge, hidden under newspapers. There he was able to visit his father, Povl Branner, who had fled Copenhagen for Stockholm in 1944 as the Gestapo closed in. In Stockholm, the younger Branner was able to see samples of the latest U.S. and British books and make arrangements for translations and publishing rights for the future. With his father's assistance, he stockpiled substantial quantities of books along the Swedish border. Several of these were key U.S. war titles, which Povl Branner published in cooperation with OWI. They also began publishing books in English in Stockholm. The day after Denmark was liberated, May 5, 1945, the Branners shipped seven hundred crates of stockpiled books to their homeland, with another five hundred following two days later.[72]

In France, the publishing industry at the beginning of the war was "in a bad state," according to an OWI memorandum. It had declined steadily throughout the Depression and fell into an even deeper slump with the beginning of the war. Partly responsible was the devaluation of the franc, which publishers could not readily compensate for because of price resistance from the buying public. This state of affairs greatly weakened the financial base of publishers and demoralized authors.[73]

In Vichy France, the collaborationist-controlled area in the southwest, a lively underground press developed, as elsewhere, though to participate in it was "dangerous beyond words," according to Howard L. Brooks, a New York clergyman, who spent the summer of 1941 there under sponsorship of the Unitarian Service Committee. The Gestapo frequently infiltrated underground movements while the Vichy government did what it could to counter the impact of clandestine publications by preparing and circulating fakes—works that mimicked dissenting tracts in the opening pages but delivered the opposite conclusion as the clincher.[74] Brooks's memoir of his mission contains a fascinating account of a visit to Gaston Baudoin's bookstore in Montpellier, near the university, which, the proprietor boasted, "was once the intellectual center of Montpellier." But it was that no longer. "I can sell almost no good modern author," Baudoin told Brooks. "H.G. Wells, Somerset Maugham, Thomas Mann, Romain Rolland, anyone who has written against Hitler is banned. Everyone who ever said a word in favor of democracy is banned. Luckily, I still have a few books in the cellar. For my good friends."

There were hardly any new books, because the Vichy censor either rejected an application outright or accomplished the same result by failing to act on it. The only new books were those by second-rate writers who saw a chance to get into print after most of the good French writers had fled to the United States, England, or South America and who were willing to write books filled with un-critical praise of the regime. These developments, Baudoin said, were creating "an intellectual famine" in France. "People are hungry not only because they can't get any food in their bellies, but because they can't get any nourishment for their minds."[75] A local professor who invited Brooks home to view his library told him that so far the Vichy regime had left him his books to retreat into, "but I have no illusions about it, I know it won't last long....Somebody will denounce me for something....And then the *Sureté Nationale* will come and search the house. They'll take a few hundred or a few thousand books, whatever they happen to find that they don't like."[76]

In overrun countries in the east, like Poland, the war on books was even more devastating. As in other countries, the Nazis did not clamp down hard on the trade immediately. In time, however, the Gestapo searched all bookstores to identify German- and English-language books proscribed by the Nazis.[77] Not only did the Nazi conquerors exterminate a fifth of the Polish population, they also sought to systematically eradicate Polish culture by destroying museums, libraries, theaters, and schools. As the Nazi governor of Poland put it, "A nation of slaves needs no higher education. Poland has to be transformed into an intellectual desert." Having stopped the flow of new titles, the Nazis destroyed many millions of books that already existed. It was estimated that three-quarters of the holdings of Polish scientific libraries—some 16 million volumes—were destroyed, while some 80 percent of the school libraries were lost to official vandalism. The Nazis burned at least a million books of the stock of Marian and Hanna Kister's firm, Roj. A heroic but small underground trade in newspapers and books attempted to keep free information flowing, but the effort cost the lives of hundreds of par-tisans.[78] The Kisters were among the fortunate ones who escaped.

The War's Impact on Publishing in China

Wartime also had a great impact on the book trades of countries overrun by the Japanese, particularly China. Inasmuch as Japan invaded China in 1937, two years before Germany took Poland, large parts of Asia and the Pacific had been under the control of the Japanese military even longer than any European territories had been under the heel of Hitler. Japan's conquest of parts of China—and its particular brutality—evoked much sympathy in the United States for the Chinese people, with whom Americans were reasonably familiar through long-standing trading ties and the experiences of generations of American missionaries. Books by such writers as Pearl Buck and Lin Yutang were enormously popular and fur-ther seated the Chinese firmly in the U.S. consciousness. Journalists, politicians, and missionaries who formed the so-called China lobby wielded considerable power in the U.S. media and in Congress. All in all, however, in the United States, publishers and the people generally knew much less about China, Japan, and other Asian nations than they did about the nations of Europe and Latin America. Prewar links between U.S. book publishers and publishers in Asia had been tenuous at best and strained at worst compared to the well-lubricated relationships between the W. W. Nortons, Alfred A. Knopfs, and George Bretts and their counterparts in Germany, France, and, above all, Britain. Books imported from the United States were very expensive and, accordingly, piracy was rampant.[79]

China entered the war years with a healthy, if isolated, publishing trade. Chinese publishing grew while Western publishing suffered through the Great Depression. Between 1933 and 1936, the number of Chinese titles rose from four thousand annually to over nine thousand, but the Japanese invasion in 1937 reversed that trend. By 1941, the number had declined to just three thousand books. The invasion also profoundly altered the geography of publishing in China. Many entire publishing and printing businesses relocated to the interior in the wake of the Japanese invasion of the principal coastal and riverine regions. The year before, 86 percent of Chinese books had been printed in Shanghai, but, through this exodus, much production migrated westward or to the British colony of Hong Kong. The dislocations of war resulted not only in a decrease in the number of titles published annually, but also in a change in the type of books issued, with a greater emphasis during wartime on books "on timely subjects," including volumes on pure and applied sciences.[80]

Despite the special challenges, the potential of the Chinese and other Asian markets was attractive enough to both the U.S. book industry and the U.S. government to warrant the dispatch of another fact-finding publishers' mission, following earlier ones to Britain and Latin America. Under sponsorship of the BPB and OWI, William Sloane, from August 1943 to February 1944, made an arduous, zigzagging, fourteen-thousand-mile, fifty-nine-day voyage on a Liberty ship to Calcutta, from where he flew to China. He made the ten-day return trip by air.[81] The Rockefeller Foundation provided funding in the form of a five-thousand-dollar grant, of which the frugal Sloane returned an unspent $1,452.[82] This unusually well-documented mission sheds much light on American publishers' interest in expanding their influence well beyond their customary foreign markets as well as on the hardships one of the leading U.S. publishers was willing to undertake to advance the goal.

Sloane was vice president and manager of the trade department of Henry Holt & Company, a member of the board of directors of the Council on Books in Wartime, and a novelist (*The Edge of Running Water*, among others). Sloane's goals were to learn what he could about present conditions in publishing and other aspects of literary life in wartime China (that is, the portions that constituted "free" or "unoccupied" China) and to judge what opportunities and obstacles might present themselves to U.S. publishers interested in establishing reciprocal business and cultural relations with Chinese publishers. The chief impediment was without question the lack of an effective copyright treaty between the two countries, which was principally blamed for the extensive piracy of U.S. works.[83]

OWI appointed Sloane a consultant to its Book Division in order to give him some governmental status while abroad, as it had done for Hitchcock on his solo mission to Britain in 1942.[84] Nonetheless, Sloane remained very much a private citizen, with little clout, and had to wait months until his transportation to China could be arranged.[85] The uncertainty worried both Sloane and his sponsors at the BPB, who felt that a low-priority sea voyage to China rather than the higher priority of air travel would jeopardize the journey's completion and diminish the importance of the mission in the eyes of the Americans and Chinese whom he would meet.[86] In retrospect, Sloane was philosophical about having taken a slow boat to China. "A man who does not share the mass experience of his time is in danger of being separated from the great central theme of his age," he wrote in his unpublished memoir of the trip. "The Liberty Ship, not the airplane, is the basic bridge across the Pacific.... The longer the sea voyage and the slower, the better it prepares an American for the tempo of the Far East."[87]

At times Sloane must have felt he was on a fool's errand. He found little literary or scholarly production of any sort being carried on in wartime China, let alone any that might actually be worth putting before the American public, but this situation was not so different from that in wartime Britain and Europe. There was insufficient infrastructure in the Chinese government or publishing industry to facilitate international cultural exchanges. Moreover, there was little camaraderie or cooperation among Chinese publishers, meaning there were no banquets given him by the trade (and thus no photo opportunities for *Publishers' Weekly*), such as were fixtures in all of the reciprocal wartime missions among U.S., British, Canadian, and Latin American publishers. Therefore, the very act of conveying the goodwill of American publishers to the Chinese was vastly more difficult than it was in the case of non-Asian colleagues.[88]

American books were scarce in China, a situation reflecting both stark reality and great potential for growth. For example, Sloane found in Kunming, a city of half a million, no new U.S. books in any of its bookstores, and only a few in the English language.[89] It was crucial to get some actual books into the hands of influential Chinese people. But current circumstances, he claimed, made it impossible even to get pamphlets into the country to put on exhibition. But achieving limited objectives was better than doing nothing, even if it would be a considerable time before publishing relationships between the United States and China could become as natural and routine as those with other Western publishers.[90]

Sloane grew rather more optimistic as his travels progressed. Although he doubted that any real progress could be made toward marketing American books in China until the copyright situation improved, at least he found that the "substantial" Chinese publishers were just as concerned about piracy as U.S. publishers were, perhaps even more so, for the potential profits that a legitimate Chinese publisher lost to a pirate were probably greater than the royalties that an American publisher could make by selling the translation rights to one of the few legitimate Chinese publishers. Only two firms, in Sloane's judgment, were "capable of managing and building up important national-scale publishing in China after the war"—the Commercial Press and the Chung Hwa Book Company. There were perhaps a dozen and a half other entities that could possibly become useful future business partners for U.S. firms. Sloane was pleased to find that many of these companies "would like to have the first opportunity to publish American books, especially the best sellers with a Far Eastern angle."[91]

Sloane was particularly heartened by his conversations with Li Soh-Ming, the head of Chung Hwa, which was considered the best Chinese printing and publishing house. It had strong English-language interests and actively sought to publish translations of U.S. works whenever it could. That was not often, but one recent translation was of Steinbeck's book about the German occupation of Norway, *The Moon Is Down*. Sloane judged Li to be "a most vigorous and energetic man with the capacity to get things done," like taking the lead in developing closer ties between Chinese and American publishers. Li had already engaged an agent in the United States to approach American publishers about regularizing the implementation of contracts for Chinese publication rights in advance of a new copyright agreement.[92] Sloane characterized Li's plan, "in view of the conditions out here," as "nothing short of sensational" and urged the publisher and trade-association official Malcolm Johnson back home to orchestrate a response in the United States immediately.[93]

The consequences of building publishing links between the two countries in the postwar world would affect "the cultural hegemony of Asia," Sloane believed. It was imperative that China, not Japan, dominate Asia culturally. It was no less crucial that American books gain a foothold within the dominant Asian publishing system that would take shape postwar. "Our friends the Russians," Sloane noted, were fully aware of the need to influence culture through books "and are making their materials much more fully available than we are. The British are also becoming more shrewdly active in these fields," he added. "We have got to be interested in this situation and we have got to take the trouble and pains to do something about it, even if there is no cash income therefrom at this point. If we want to do any postwar business with Chinese publishers, we are going to have to keep the right ones alive and if possible flourishing right now."[94]

Sloane returned to the United States in late February 1944, with doubts about the success of his mission and the prospects for close and lasting ties between the publishers of the two allied nations.[95] But he had seen some hopeful signs in China, including bookshops crowded with customers. From his visit, Sloane observed the strength of the Chinese book culture and a belief in the sacredness of the written word. In China, he told a nationwide radio audience upon his return, "literary tradition is too deep and too old to be killed by bombs."[96] Back home, Sloane soon learned that the representative of Chung Hwa in the United States was indeed following through on the firm's plan to establish formal contractual relations with American publishers for the rights to reprint American books in English.[97] The larger problem of adequate copyright protection for American books was harder to settle and remains a problem to this day.[98]

Wartime Publishing in the Neutral Nations

The publishing industries in neutral countries generally prospered during the war, as one might have expected. An article in *Publishers' Weekly* used the word "phenomenal" to describe the book business in Sweden, which had long been, and remained, a major center for the publication of books in English and German, as well as the native tongue. A book selling twenty thousand copies was considered a best seller before the war; during it, selling thirty-five to forty thousand copies was not unusual, even though books were expensive.[99]

Indeed, Sweden's book publishers suffered very little during the war, the kingdom's publishing scene displaying an almost eerie normalcy. From mid-1941 to mid-1942, about a hundred books in English were translated into Swedish, including titles by such Americans as Ernest Hemingway, William L. Shirer, and Ambassador Joseph E. Davies. These appeared in bookshops, as they would have before the war, alongside native productions and the works of great contemporary German writers, many of whom were by then exiled in the Americas. Production standards remained high. Paper was plentiful. Its forests made Sweden a major producer of paper, and with exports curtailed by the German fleet, more was available for local use. The Swedes invented substitutes for materials that were scarce, like printer's ink and bleach to whiten book papers. Blockages to the post, however, hindered the delivery of books from the United States and Britain, making it difficult to obtain copies of the latest works for possible translation or reprint in English.

Still, a Swedish publisher's representative in New York claimed, "Now as before the book trade in Sweden offers probably the most comprehensive list of the most essential new publications in contemporary world literature of any European country."[100] Having discovered that it was almost impossible to ship

British books to Sweden (where they might be forwarded to Denmark, Norway, Finland, and elsewhere), the British Publishers Guild arranged for the publication of a series of wartime books in Sweden in cooperation with the publisher Ljus. Inasmuch as another Swedish firm, Bonniers, established the Zephyr Books series of British and American books in English for the Continental market in the tradition of Tauchnitz Books of Leipzig, and the German refugee Gottfried Bermann-Fischer brought with him the rights to many of the works banned or burned by the Nazis when he fled to Stockholm, Sweden essentially became a surrogate for German publishing, at least that part of it that was most on the side of the angels.[101]

Sweden's neutrality in the face of its democratic neighbors' dire straits caused much ill will, however. The Publishers Guild in London had fully expected that Norway and Denmark, upon liberation, would become strong customers for the Guild Books produced in Sweden, but found, on the contrary, that "the Norwegians and Danes have shown the greatest reluctance to buy anything Swedish or anything produced in Sweden. Consequently, sales have been disappointing and the idea of further production in Sweden has been abandoned."[102]

The other major (nonfascist) European neutral, Switzerland, also did not make "themselves frightfully popular with their neighbours during the war," according to the English publisher Walter G. Harrap. "I gather that they have done rather a lot [of] snaffling of rights in the German and French languages having the same big idea as some of our boys that Germany is going to accept books in German printed in Switzerland"—an outcome that Harrap considered as welcome to Germans as English-language books published in Switzerland would be in the UK.[103]

Wartime Publishing in Enemy Nations: Germany

Unlike most other countries at war or under occupation, Germany, the birthplace of printing from movable type, was able to maintain the level of its publishing activity at least through the first half of the war. As in Britain and the United States, demand was strong for almost any type of book that was published. Books virtually sold themselves. With full employment in the country, customers had plenty of money to spend on books. The famed and envied organization that lay behind the German book trade, the *Börsenverein der deutschen Buchhändler* in Leipzig, was strongly supported by the Nazi regime and functioned, as usual, like a well-oiled machine. Early on, there were few if any shortages of paper or machinery, for the Reich was able to tap raw materials and manufactured goods in the conquered areas when necessary to supply the domestic industries. Moreover, people in the overrun nations provided new markets for German books, however grudgingly. Collaborationist or Nazified publishing houses and book-sellers in the expanded Reich became members of the *Börsenverein*.

Of course, only certain publishers were permitted to prosper. Many publishers, mostly Jewish, had already fled the Third Reich to safer havens in neutral countries, Britain, and the United States. Publishers who stayed behind who were Jewish or had married a Jew, or those who held liberal political or social ideas, could find themselves subject to denunciation by employees or rival publishers. At first, they might find their paper supply drying up. Later, some pretext would be found to deny them membership in the *Reichsschrifttumskammer*, Goebbels's Chamber of Literature, which meant they could not remain in business. Worst of all, they could be sent to a concentration camp.[104]

The Nazis were fully as committed to the concept of books as weapons of war as the Americans were to become. Accordingly, the Ministry of Propaganda was the principal instrument and patron of the Reich's publishing world. Germans had long placed a high value on books and especially on the export trade, which made books the vanguard of German science and technology, culture, and trade.[105] But the kind of book culture for which Germany had been celebrated could no longer exist under the Nazis. "There is perhaps no precedent for an entire literary generation leaving its homeland almost in a body," wrote Martin Gumpert, himself a refugee writer from Germany. "Only a few writers of any stature have remained in Germany, and these have either ceased to create, or, as in the case of the aged Gerhart Hauptmann, their work has lost all force and spontaneity," he continued. "After a careful investigation, it can be said with some authority that no new talent seems to have emerged."[106] Similarly, with the removal of undesirable publishers through expatriation or arrest and the promulgation of stringent directives to the publishers that remained, the government was able to enforce a uniformity of opinion, even though censorship was not absolute in every case.[107] A visitor to Germany in the year before war began was in despair "because I could find no worthwhile books published in Germany."[108]

Conditions in the book trade eventually worsened, along with the war. Supplies of paper and machinery grew scarce. More and more workers were inducted into the military. Many bookstores closed.[109] Devastating blows occurred in December 1943 and February 1944 when the Allies bombed Leipzig, the historic center of German publishing, wiping out publishing houses, warehouses, bookshops, and libraries. German statistics revealed that as of May 1944 thirty-two of the top one hundred publishing firms had been seriously damaged by air raids and another twenty-one had suffered some damage.[110] Only the stocks of books that had been prudently moved from Leipzig to smaller communities survived. OWI field officers were able to gain a sense of the bomb damage by tracking advertisements in the *Börsenverein*'s trade paper taken out by firms reporting that their business was being carried on by others or that they were changing their address, and other means.[111] Whether the book industry was deliberately targeted or not, some might have considered the raid a fitting payback for the Luftwaffe's destruction of British back stocks during the Blitz—but not *Publishers' Weekly*'s Melcher, who editorialized that "we can feel little sense of satisfaction about it."[112]

In the end, Nazi laws necessitated by total war, which were promulgated in the fall of 1944, "almost crushed the German book trade," an official in the U.S. occupation noted later. Only two hundred publishers were allowed to continue in business, and to produce only books directly related to the war effort. Book stock held by publishers and retail booksellers was only a quarter of what it customarily had been in peacetime. The Leipzig trade organization was on life support.[113]

A hunger for books developed in Germany just as it did in areas that German forces had conquered. Party-sponsored books and pamphlets were a "drug on the market" during the last two years of the war, which left booksellers, who were obliged to carry the material, with losses. Readers fed their book hunger by buying "old and half-forgotten stock, including long series of heavy scientific works," according to a U.S. official who arrived on the scene shortly following the Nazis' defeat. Even Goebbels responded to the growing lack of interest in party publications (as well as to the bombing of the heavily Catholic Rhineland) by removing the ban on the publication of prayer books and other religious literature.[114] The enforcement of conformity to Nazi doctrine was the undoing of the German book trade for it seriously diminished the reputation of German books in the key areas of the sciences and technology throughout the world.[115]

Wartime Publishing in Enemy Nations: Japan

There is less documentation of book publishing in Japan after Pearl Harbor than on that in wartime Germany, but some clear similarities between the two enemy countries stand out, and a few differences as well. Both had historically been bookish countries, with well-organized publishing trades. Publishing was generally prosperous in both countries, at least for a time. During the war, Germany and Japan exercised strong control over publishers, censored and confiscated books unfriendly to the militarist regimes, and suffered grave damage to the infrastructure of the making and selling of books.

American books had found their way to prewar Japan in significant numbers. It was estimated that during the years 1935–1941 the Maruzen Company, a giant bookselling concern and the country's leading importer of books, obtained the second-highest percentage of its imports from the United States, at 25.5 percent, compared to 42.6 percent from Germany, 21.3 percent from Great Britain, and 3.6 percent from France.[116] The nation had long been highly regarded for the extent to which English was taught in schools, particularly for reading, so there was a built-in receptivity for books from the two major Anglophone countries in the world. But the place of English in the schools and Japanese society generally was a highly vexed topic during the war. As a product of Anglo-Saxon culture, English was seen as alien. Still, it had long been Japan's window into the larger world. A continued tolerance, if not reverence, for English won out, however, when it was seen to be a pragmatic, temporary lingua franca for its administration of the Great East Asian Co-Prosperity Sphere, until a future day when the Japanese language would assume that role.[117]

The translation of American books into Japanese had been more problematic than the importation of books in English. Under a 1906 treaty between the two countries, U.S. works were protected by copyright in Japan and Japanese works in the United States, but translations were not.[118] This meant that American (and other nations') books could be freely translated and published in Japan without permission, compensation, or implication of piracy. Sometimes there were competing translations in the marketplace at the same time. John Morris, a British writer and university lecturer resident in Japan since October 1938, found that many, but not all, of the translations were poor. Foreign books, especially best-selling novels, would often appear in translation in bookshops within two or three weeks after a copy of the original first arrived. To achieve such speed, the book was torn into sections, which were given to several translators, usually university students, to work on simultaneously. One of Morris's students earned a regular income from such work. In one instance the student "was given some thirty pages of an American novel to translate; there was no clue to its title, and his particular section started in the middle of one sentence and ended in the middle of another." Speedy, patchwork translations like this were commonly published under the name "of some comparatively well-known literary man, who allows his name to be used in return for a substantial consideration." Many translators, however, worked alone and took their task seriously, if not always completing it successfully. "There are," Morris reported, "two completely different translations of James Joyce's *Ulysses* which, I am told, bear no resemblance to each other or to the original." Importation and translation of Western books dwindled to almost nothing during the war.[119]

As in Germany, book publishers did well, at least during the first years of the war, until U.S. bombing began to take its toll on the nation's infrastructure and population. In 1942, some fifteen thousand two hundred new books were published in a wide range of fields. The house of Iwanami Shoten continued to bring out its line of low-priced, high-quality paperbacks despite paper shortages and air raids.[120]

All printing, publishing, and distribution were under tight government control. At General Hideki Tojo's direction, the Japanese Publishers Society took over propaganda, censorship, and paper rationing in 1943.[121] All books entering the country were censored before they were put in the hands of booksellers and customers, usually with offending pages torn out. Morris's copy of *Journey to a War*, by W. H. Auden and Christopher Isherwood, reached him "minus a photograph of a Japanese prisoner captured by the Chinese army, for it destroyed the legend that no Japanese soldier ever permits himself to be captured." Marxist and antiwar books were particularly prone to censorship or suppression, though, as in Germany, it was done haphazardly.[122]

Despite controls, the writing of books continued almost unabated during wartime, probably more so than in Germany, and in stark contrast to the situation in Britain and European countries. This was so largely because most intellectuals (other than Marxists and pacifists) were highly nationalistic and warm supporters of the war as a valid response to Western imperialism. There was virtually no brain drain of scholars and writers fleeing from Japan as there was from Germany and many of the lands overrun by the Nazis, and few if any underground resistance movements. The Great Japan Patriotic Writers Association was established a year after Pearl Harbor to focus support on achieving victory. Generally, however, intellectuals and other writers who chose to remain quiet were not harassed. The war itself was the most popular topic for books.[123]

The physical aspects of the Japanese book trade in time suffered great damage during the war, as did Germany's. The trade was naturally centered in the capital, Tokyo, with important secondary centers in Osaka and Kyoto. These urban areas were bombed heavily, with the exception of Kyoto. A survey showed that the number of printing establishments declined from 18,225 in 1942 to 3,833 in 1947. Perhaps half of the nation's printing equipment was destroyed, and one thousand eight hundred workers killed during the conflict.[124]

Cutting off the flow of American and other Western books created in Japan as much of a hunger for books and pent-up demand as in any other overrun or enemy country. The constant litany of observers of the book world abroad during the war that the hunger for free and uncensored books was almost as powerful as the hunger for food instilled in U.S. propaganda officers and publishers alike a sense that Europe would provide a great market for American books once those lands were free of Nazi rule. Meanwhile, some organizational developments affecting the publishing world at home helped pave the way for efforts to fill that vacuum, for both their own benefit and the nation's. The unevenly distributed destructive force of the war left the U.S. book trade uniquely situated to meet demand. Achieving the overseas goals shared by both trade and government would still require subtlety and a great deal of perseverance.

Part II

BOOKS AS "WEAPONS IN THE WAR OF IDEAS"

PUBLISHERS ORGANIZE FOR WAR AND PLAN FOR PEACE

"Don't you know there's a war on?"[1] This was a rhetorical question, of course, but most Americans would have answered in the affirmative even though they lacked the experiential clues that the British had to remind them—frequent air raids, bombed-out buildings, and the presence of a huge "occupying" force of Yanks (not Germans, thankfully).[2] The fact that sacrifices through rationing (tires, gasoline, and butter, for example) and high taxes were imposed on the people of the United States and not just on businesses—to say nothing of the loss of friends and loved ones—made it obvious to almost anyone, including even the occasional shirker, that the country was engaged in a war on the home front as well as on battlefields scattered around the world.

The U.S. penchant for volunteerism contributed to the war effort as well, though not enough to forestall a military draft. Many civilians, though, busied themselves with collecting paper, tin, or fat, working for the American Red Cross or the USO (United Services Organization), or taking up positions on rooftops as aircraft spotters on the East and West coasts. The federal government created new agencies to deal with urgent, if temporary, wartime business. Civilians within industries, including those in creative fields like motion pictures, writing, and book publishing, formed organizations to channel their own efforts in support of the war. What these entities did most and did best was to plan (and to leave a vast paper trail of their planning)—for the next week, for six months out, and for the peace that most Americans were confident would come in due course. Forming a kind of parallel universe to the country's normal economic structure, the people who went to work in government bureaucracies or voluntary associations—mostly white-collar workers and their pink-collar assistants—contributed to

FIGURE 1. An Office of War Information poster utilizing the slogan coined by Council on Books in Wartime chairman W. Warder Norton and referring to Nazi book burnings. The slogan expressed a principal propaganda theme of both CBW and OWI. Library of Congress.

the war effort in ways that have been much less appreciated than the work of their GI comrades and the blue-collar men and Rosie the Riveters who labored in the factories. Without the officials and clerks who performed civilian work for government agencies or for war-related, industry-wide private nonprofits, there would have been no D-Day for American books abroad.

The Creation of the Council on Books in Wartime

Like their counterparts in other businesses and industries, U.S. publishers were eager to "do their bit" for the war effort. To focus their collective efforts, they established a nonprofit corporation, the Council on Books in Wartime, early in 1942. Establishing the CBW provided the industry with a forum to reexamine its own professional identity, with eyes on what it could accomplish for the nation and itself not only during wartime but afterward as well. In this, the council ensured that publishers, who liked to consider themselves "bookmen," could perform important public service and harvest financial benefits at the same time.[3] Eager to develop programs that would build morale among civilians and servicemen and women and to delineate the key issues of the war, the leaders and rank-and-file of the council went forward under the banner "Books are weapons in the war of ideas," which publisher and council chairman W. W. Norton had coined and President Roosevelt had put into national circulation.[4]

The idea for such a body began percolating among a number of publishers early in February, just two months after the Japanese attack on Hawaii. An informal working committee on March 17 made the decision to form the organization, though at that point the group was still "a committee in search of a project."[5] Fairly rapidly though, the planners developed a far broader agenda than merely administering an array of programs highlighting in some fashion or other the importance of books for disseminating information and building morale, worthwhile as they were in wartime circumstances. The CBW's founders in effect decided that they should use the war crisis as "an opportunity to solve the linked, lingering problems of profitability and professional identity, and to solve them not only for the duration of the war, but for the long term, for what one observer called 'the smart man's peace' that lay beyond wartime."[6] The intellectual and strategic underpinnings attendant upon the founding of the council directly and profoundly shaped the direction that the publishers took in providing books for the intellectual liberation of millions of civilians abroad.

What could be considered the manifesto of this group of bookmen (and the occasional book woman) in forming the council consisted of Frederic G. Melcher's lead editorial in *Publishers' Weekly* for April 25, 1942, and speeches given by *New York Times* correspondent Anne O'Hare McCormick and Assistant Secretary of

State Adolf Berle at a series of discussions held before overflow crowds of five hundred people in May in the newspaper's Times Hall. All three arrived by different paths at similar conclusions concerning the basic problems of modern life that a publishing trade revitalized by wartime exigencies could help ameliorate. The central problem, they argued, was a glut of information that required mediation of a thoughtful, liberal kind—the kind that book publishers were uniquely qualified to provide.[7]

Melcher urged bookmen to turn aside from their emphasis on publishing profitable but often vacuous books of "information and diversion" and meet their professional responsibilities by being "fiercely in earnest about the selection, production, and distribution of books of ideas, not because of the delight they give the reader, but because of the direction such books will give to our own thinking on pressing problems, problems which must be answered promptly and answered right." McCormick identified the key contemporary problem as a kind of paralysis that flowed from the random onslaught of information. "The problems of modern life so baffled the intelligence and weakened the will" she said, "that millions of men just gave up the use of their minds. In their disorientation and bewilderment, they surrendered to someone else the right to think and act for them." Hitler, of course, was the primary, ghastly "someone else." His propaganda had not only saturated France, leaving "the French mind...unprepared" for his onslaught, but it also extended even to the New World, rendering South America "a continent impregnated by Nazi propaganda." Berle also concluded that too much information, especially technological information, was the bane of modernity, and urged that the modern embrace of a "literature of information" be replaced by "a literature of power," which "move[s] the spirit of men...[and] reaches to the very wellspring of the human soul."[8]

McCormick and Berle agreed that if books were to make a difference in the war effort, "they must be something more than objects of trade!" (Berle) and not "just another commodity" (McCormick). The council's skittishness about the trade's seeming to benefit from the war derived from the genteel tradition that had long characterized the trade's professional identity. The publishers also feared that the council's alliances with the federal government, which grew tighter as the war progressed, would add the taint of propaganda to that of the market. To a certain extent, the members of the council got around these twin problems by arguing that its role was to promote reading rather than books. Thus they could be seen as advancing the public good without hawking their wares directly, and as promoting democracy without adhering to any particular ideologies of the federal government.[9]

The council's adoption of the logic of Melcher, McCormick, and Berle concerning the need for serious books that cut through the clutter of modern information and for promoting reading (rather than books directly) led in time to prescriptions for *how* books should be read. The founders of the council drew for inspiration on this point from the history of the role of print in fostering the American Revolution, particularly the case of Thomas Paine's *Common Sense*—identifying a two-part process whereby, in effect, readers of a particular text shared the information in it and their impressions of it with other people individually or in a group, creating what literary scholars call an interpretive, or reading, community. Council hands were gratified that this two-stage protocol of reading did, in fact, materialize among the U.S. servicemen and women who read the Armed Services Editions, which the council provided them under contracts with the army and navy. Among the letters sent to the council by grateful GIs are many that document such communities, by noting, for example, that reading one work "caused quite a bit of discussion and argument among us" and that "the non-coms and privates at the back of the general's tent were all reading and discussing constantly." If similar "bull sessions among soldiers and sailors" continued after the war, council official William Sloane remarked, "our plan [for the ASEs] will justify itself 100 times over."[10]

In short, the elements of the working philosophy that the council developed—affirming the cultural value of serious books, promoting reading over mere commerce in books, and encouraging the creation of reading communities—underlay its efforts throughout the war, though not without tensions. The fact that Sloane foresaw profitable new audiences for publishers' wares being created by their exposure to the publicly funded ASEs indicates how difficult it was to avoid the taint of commercialism. This theoretical underpinning to the council also profoundly influenced the direction of the stockpiling-and-publishing series that the council, through its subsidiary Overseas Editions, Inc., developed late in the war in tandem with the Office of War Information. Programmatically, the council also drew upon the wartime goals of Britain's National Book Council—encouraging reading and a wider distribution of books, putting books in the service of the national war effort, and shaping a new generation of book buyers after the war was over—for its relevance to the U.S. effort.[11]

Membership in the council was institutional rather than individual. It was drawn almost entirely from the ranks of general, or trade, publishers as well as publishers of science, medicine, and technology books that either also had trade divisions or basically behaved like trade publishers. They were mostly members of the Book Publishers Bureau (BPB), the principal trade association of the general publishers. Textbook publishers had only recently established their own trade association, the American Textbook Publishers Institute, whose members had generally not chosen to join the council.[12] Early on, it was no doubt understood that the publisher part of the council's membership, which also included librarians and booksellers, was limited to trade publishers, but the council clarified the point with a tagline on its letterhead: "The Council on Books in Wartime is an

Organization of Publishers of General (Trade) Books, Librarians and Booksellers."[13] This decision on scope of membership influenced the initial exclusion of textbooks, educational books, and technical publications from the ASEs. After the success of the ASEs had become clear, however, the textbook publishers, envisioning GIs—and the veterans they would soon become—as key customers, challenged, mostly unsuccessfully, the exclusion of many of their publications from consideration.[14] The emphasis within the council on trade books, rather than technical books and textbooks, therefore deeply colored the efforts of both the government and the trade in expanding the availability of American books abroad, beginning with the implementation of the stockpiling program and the establishment of OEI.

After getting on its feet essentially as an organization staffed by volunteers, with free space in the Book Publishers Bureau's offices at 347 Fifth Avenue in Manhattan, the council decided to reorganize itself during the winter of 1942–43 in order to meet its obligations to the war effort more efficiently and thoroughly, and, above all, more pointedly. A major overhaul, which included a much larger budget and a full paid staff, was rejected, but the group did take on a full-time, paid director (initially Janet Lumb) and a small support staff. It also moved to offices of its own, at 400 Madison Avenue. The organization operated as a typical nonprofit, that is, with bylaws, an annual meeting, a board of directors, an executive committee, and a number of programmatic committees. The first chairman of the board was the publisher W. W. Norton.[15]

Importantly, the council also accepted overtures from OWI, made through Chester Kerr of the Book Section in OWI's Domestic Branch, to become more closely allied, that is, "to match the aims of the Council with those of the OWI."[16] The propaganda agency would fully share its plans with the council so that the latter body could assist in publicizing and carrying them out. The council would also take on the role of publisher, or sponsor, of war-related books that OWI had an interest in seeing published but could not produce on its own. The council would retain the right to reject books recommended by OWI, "while at the same time," in Kerr's words, "placing its facilities at the disposal of the OWI in the belief that the Government a) is best equipped to formulate war information policies and b) will not abuse its power." To facilitate this closer relationship, Kerr would spend one day a week in New York "during which his time will be entirely at the disposal of the Council's leadership and committees." Kerr assured the council members that they need feel no guilt in selling books that would contribute to winning the war. More importantly, he held before them the notion that because books were the bearers of ideas, the publishers had not only the power but also the obligation to help shape history.[17]

For his part in convincing the council to move in new directions, OWI director Elmer Davis told Norton that strengthening the level of cooperation among the practitioners of a highly competitive industry might "sound like a radical notion," but people throughout the nation were learning to work together in service to the war effort.[18] In urging adoption of the reorganization plan during the debate that took place at the council's annual meeting on February 2, 1943, Norton spoke for many in the group in believing that "if we don't do it for the Government the Government will do it for itself, and we are thereby not only neglecting an opportunity to serve our country but performing functions which we hope to keep in the post-war period."[19] At least one influential member of the council, Malcolm Johnson, then of Doubleday, Doran, and Co., came to regret the decision to ally itself so closely to the government, mainly because it limited the degree to which the council could be "commercial" by taking on all kinds of book promotion activities.[20] Nevertheless, in assuming the additional responsibilities, the council was able to enter into a remarkably close and productive partnership with the chief government propaganda agency, which aided the nation's war effort even as it advanced some of the council's own most important goals of broadening its horizons after the war ended.

On the home front, CBW carried on several kinds of promotional work—providing lists of books about the war and the war aims of the U.S. and its allies for libraries and bookstores, holding book forums and fairs, and utilizing radio and films to promote its message. Judged as its finest effort at using radio to underscore the importance of books was a May 10, 1942, national hookup on NBC of a piece by the well-known writer Stephen Vincent Benét, *They Burned the Books,* about the night, exactly nine years before, when Nazi thugs in Berlin, Munich, and elsewhere burned hundreds or thousands of books written by Jews and other "subversive" writers. It was Kerr who suggested the book-burning theme for its power as propaganda, and it proved to be a useful device throughout the existence of both OWI and the council. In fact, the books the Nazis burned or banned figured prominently among the titles provided to Germans after the war.

Other major programs of the council, unsurprisingly, employed the medium of print directly. One of these, perhaps the council's most ambitious early undertaking, was its plan to designate certain titles useful for home-front propaganda as "Imperative Books." Among these were W. L. White's *They Were Expendable* and John Hersey's *Into the Valley,* both about heroic U.S. military operations, which appeared in their publishers' editions emblazoned with the Imperative Books logo and slogan on the dust jackets. Titles in the fields of politics and diplomacy included Wendell Willkie's *One World* and Walter Lippmann's *U.S. Foreign Policy.* With publishers vying with one another to achieve designation of a favored title as an Imperative Book, the effort at times and contrary to original intent shaded into blatant commercialism. Although the Imperative Books program is considered one of the less successful council undertakings,[21] the program

FIGURE 2. W. Warder Norton (1891–1945), head of W. W. Norton & Company and first chairman of the Council on Books in Wartime, upper left, shown here with (clockwise from left) author Hervey Allen, lawyer Arthur Farmer, Frederic Melcher (*Publishers' Weekly*), Edmund S. McCawley (president of the American Booksellers' Association), and author Pearl Buck. Photograph courtesy of W. W. Norton & Company, Inc.

spotlighted the kinds of important wartime books that formed the core of titles selected for the OE series.

Kerr had proposed an even more ambitious program, in partnership with the council, of OWI-produced books to be published in paperback and sold to the U.S. public at low prices. This program was modeled on a highly successful venture by OWI's British counterpart, the Ministry of Information, of a number of books on the war that resulted in sales ranging from two hundred thousand to four million copies of such titles as *The Battle for Britain, Bomber Command,* and *Transport Goes to War.* The propaganda agency's entire domestic publications program was scotched, however, when the majority in Congress, ever wary of letting Roosevelt and his New Deal policies get too much publicity, specified that "no part of this or any other appropriation shall be expended by the Office of War Information for the preparation or publication of any pamphlet or other literature for distribution to the public within the United States."[22] It is possible that the opposition to OWI's commissioning new books for the domestic market persuaded OWI to stick with in-print books originally written and published for home consumption when it came time to select books aimed at civilians overseas. In contrast, many of the books that Britain stockpiled for use by liberated civilians were the kind of purpose-built publications mentioned above.

Armed Services Editions and Other Books for the Forces

Even if the council could no longer cooperate with OWI on domestic publications, it still had plenty do in the realm of publications to be circulated outside the United States. In fact, the council's grandest undertaking by far was just such a program, the deservedly celebrated program of Armed Services Editions, which were published by a specially incorporated subsidiary of the council to provide books for recreation and enrichment to U.S. service personnel abroad. After the failure of the so-called Victory Book Campaigns of 1942 and 1943, which were sponsored by the USO, the Red Cross, and the American Library Association and which depended on the voluntary contribution of used books by civilians at home, Editions for the Armed Services, Inc., from the fall of 1943 until the fall of 1947, issued 122,951,031 copies of 1,322 titles, which were sold to the army and navy for distribution to the U.S. military forces abroad.[23] (OWI was not involved in the ASE program.) In addition, the army responded to requests from the Canadian, Australian, and South African forces for quantities of ASEs for their troops. The council understood that making these books available to English-speaking Allied soldiers "is another way in which we can publicize American books in other sections of the world where we think we will trade after the war." This worried British publishers, who warned the Americans not to infringe on British Empire publishing rights.[24]

The genius of the ASEs, which were also known as "Council Books," was in their great diversity of titles and their uniformity in size. Despite public pleas like that expressed on an Oregon poster to "pass along the books you have enjoyed,"[25] the eighteen and a half million books that civilians on the home front contributed to the VBCs were mostly ones that the donors probably had neither enjoyed nor even read. Unwanted by their owners, these books were of questionable appeal to their beneficiaries as well. In fact, more than 40 percent of the volumes contributed during the two campaigns were deemed unsuitable for servicemen and women.[26] The cast-off books came in a variety of shapes, sizes, and bindings (mostly hardcover) and thus presented ultimately insurmountable problems in packing and distribution.[27] During the early stages of the war, the books donated to the VBCs were intended to be distributed mainly in camps and naval bases within the United States, "as near to the towns where they are collected as possible to save time and shipping costs and to give the citizens the satisfaction of helping the Armed Forces of their own neighborhood."[28] In any case, only about 10 percent of the millions of books collected during the two campaigns were shipped overseas.[29]

A special project during the campaigns bearing the slogan "Our Men Want Books," spearheaded by the trade journal *Publishers' Weekly* and organized under the auspices of the council, sought to overcome the unsuitability of the VBC donations by getting the public to purchase new books at their local bookstores and mail them to a depot for distribution to camps in the United States. Buying U.S. publishers' current titles "for the boys" thus became a patriotic gesture even as it promoted the industry. *PW*'s Melcher, for his part, wrote a check to the council for $344.49 to help fund the effort.[30] A supply of printed address labels distributed through bookshops facilitated the public's mailing of the new books they bought to various camps. The campaign early on resulted in the sale and shipment of some twenty-five thousand books, at a cost to the publishers of thirty-five hundred dollars. This turnover alone may not have produced much profit for the publishers, but Lee Barker, of Houghton Mifflin, urged patience: "In my mind the important thing is that we got the people to do it themselves and got them in the habit of sending <u>new</u> books to the boys in camp. They will keep on sending books, and this figure six months from now may well be doubled."[31]

In contrast to the widely differing sizes and formats of the Victory Campaign books, the ASEs were lightweight, mostly oblong paperbacks, printed "four-up" and then thrice guillotined to create four books with the series' characteristic, nonstandard orientation. They were printed on roll-fed rotary presses used in peacetime for magazines and catalogs, which had capacity in excess of the demands of civilian life. They appeared in two different trim sizes—6½ × 4½ inches (i.e., half the size of a magazine like *Popular Mechanics*) and 5½ × 3⅞ inches (i.e., half the size of a *Reader's Digest* and similar periodicals)—which made packing and shipping comparatively easy. The text was printed in two columns on these oblong pages, a design, it was claimed, that did not exhibit the crowded effect that vertical two-column pages displayed.[32] It also held the lines to legibly short lengths. These various design and technical innovations made the production and distribution of the ASEs feasible, even little short of miraculous. After it was decided that the books would still be needed by the troops pulling occupation duty in the Axis countries (though in smaller quantities), the format was changed to the upright version already familiar from Penguins, Pocket Books, and other mass-market paperbacks.[33]

The more than thirteen hundred titles provided material for virtually every reading taste, from classics to Westerns and mysteries and books about sports. A number of them were books that prescribed the political shape of the postwar world or helped prepare GIs for new careers following their separation from the service—one more fruit of the wartime culture of planning. These came about in part through a decision by the council to revise their selection policy to include more books of an educational or technical nature in anticipation of the requirements of the postwar occupation forces, who would have less need for and interest in "purely recreational" titles.[34] The ASEs were described, shortly after the war had ended, as "the greatest mass publishing enterprise of all history,"[35] a judgment that remains unchallenged more than sixty years later.

As dominant as the ASEs were, they were not the only books to be issued in series, bearing some appropriate collective title, and made available to servicemen and women in the theaters of combat. The most significant of these was the Fighting Forces series, which was published through a loose but inventive and effective partnership between the *Infantry Journal*, the leading professional publication for infantry officers, and the U.S. branch of Penguin Books. Penguin was already serving as *Infantry Journal*'s distributor to the book trade.[36] This unusual pairing benefited both organizations. *Infantry Journal* had been established in 1904 by the United States Infantry Association, one of several professional associations linked to the various branches of the U.S. Army. Its status was ambiguous. Organized as a private, nonprofit organization, it claimed that its contents "do not carry the stamp of official approval," though its editors were generally active-duty officers and it was under the general supervision of the army. Even so, the *Infantry Journal* generally enjoyed editorial independence, and occasionally published articles critical of the established army order. Beginning in the 1930s, editors encouraged a writing style and choice of topics that could reach beyond professional soldiers. In early 1943, the journal claimed more than one hundred thousand readers, including some civilians.[37] The partnership with Penguin Books helped it reach even larger numbers of civilians, including those who shaped public opinion.

The driving force was Lt. Col. (later Col.) Joseph I. Greene, an active-duty officer who had served as *Infantry Journal*'s editor since 1940 and was a member of a panel on the role of books in wartime at one of the Times Hall meetings that helped launch the council. Greene had arranged for Ian Ballantine, the head of Penguin's U.S. branch, to attend the conference.[38] Little known to publishing historians, the *Infantry Journal* was a significant presence on the wartime book scene, publishing or distributing, according to an observer, some ten thousand books a day bearing its own imprint or that of other publishers.[39] The *Infantry Journal* was able to rechannel some of its high-priority paper rations to Penguin USA, which, as a new venture, had only a hard-won special relief quota. In return, Penguin provided the book-publishing and marketing know-how that the military publishing firm lacked.[40] It also handled *Infantry Journal*'s distribution to the trade, as it did for another niche firm, the Military Service Publishing Company.[41] Some titles in the series bore the imprint of either the *Infantry Journal* or Penguin, while the rest carried both names. Most of the books published in the series gave soldiers useful information on various aspects of military science, about the nature of the enemy and the allies, or about far-flung places in which they served. Greene later became an important player in a number of projects relating to American books overseas, as will be seen. When Ian Ballantine left Penguin USA in May 1945 to form Bantam Books, he took with him much of the staff and the contract with the *Infantry Journal*.[42]

In setting up the ASEs, council members were confident that the series would contribute to the "mass reading of books in the world to come."[43] They were right. Historians have generally credited the ASEs with introducing books to GIs who had read little before the war, for helping fuel the paperback boom in the postwar years, and for creating a pool of new customers.[44] Of course, the other books made available to the forces also contributed to that result, but none had the scope, reach, and government imprimatur of the ASEs. Moreover, the organization of the ASE series provided a precedent for large-scale publishing projects undertaken jointly by the private sector and the government, a model that was called upon again for the conception and execution of the Overseas Editions.

Although there were conversations about maintaining the council in some form or other after the war was over, the efforts failed. The council was dissolved on January 31, 1946, the day after its fourth and final annual meeting.[45] Its subsidiary, Editions for the Armed Services, Inc., however, continued to operate until 1947 in order to complete the work of producing new titles for the use of U.S. occupation troops.[46]

The Role of the Office of War Information

Just as the council came to represent the book-publishing industry, the Office of War Information became the principal propaganda agency of the federal government during the Second World War after it replaced the Office of Facts and Figures and several other agencies following a major reorganization in June 1942. Its portfolio included both domestic and overseas programs, with branches that reflected those constituencies. OWI was frequently rent internally along lines of ideology and policy, drawn from differing views of the objectives and conduct of U.S. wartime propaganda. It was weakened by power struggles among its highest officials and by persistent congressional displeasure and public ridicule. The opposition was orchestrated primarily by Republicans and Southern Democrats, who distrusted OWI, particularly the Bureau of Publications within its domestic branch, as "propagandists for Roosevelt and his policies"—this according to Arthur M. Schlesinger Jr., who had been employed as a writer in the bureau.[47] Numerous problems and crises, mostly politically inspired, marred the agency's brief existence. Some might have been avoided had the agency taken a place at the table at which high-level decisions about the war itself were made. James P. Warburg, a high official in the agency who lost his job during a major shake-up, blamed Elmer Davis, OWI's director, for failing to assume the broad authority that President Roosevelt gave him, preferring to act as a mere publicist rather than to take a hand in the shaping of information policy.[48] Robert Bruce Lockhart, head of the secret British Political Warfare Executive (PWE), came to regard OWI's lack of input into the highest levels of war planning as lamentable.[49]

Davis was a respected journalist and popular radio commentator but no foreign-policy expert. In charge of the overseas branch was Robert E. Sherwood, the noted playwright and speechwriter for President Roosevelt, as well as his confidant. Davis's key associates on the domestic side were Archibald MacLeish, the poet and librarian of Congress, who had been the head of OWI's predecessor, the Office of Facts and Figures; Milton Eisenhower, a Washington administrator and brother of the general; and Gardiner Cowles Jr., a prominent midwestern newspaper and magazine publisher, who headed the domestic branch.

The tribulations of OWI can only be sketched briefly here. The internal divisions within OWI, which developed in the domestic branch, derived from differing views of the objectives and conduct of U.S. wartime propaganda on the home front. How best might the agency explain to the people of the United States why we were fighting the war? Many of the liberals in the agency—including MacLeish—were staunch advocates of the war because they hated fascism and wanted to root it out completely wherever it had appeared. In civilian life, many of these officials were writers, scholars, or publishers. They saw their duty as educating the American people about the fundamental issues underlying the war and, importantly, about what U.S. goals should be in the postwar future. The task also involved pointing out how much stake the United States had in the noble goal of defeating fascism as a way of justifying the war's human and economic cost.[50] Less ideologically oriented officials, like Eisenhower and Cowles, wished to concentrate their message in ways calculated to extract the greatest short-term benefits to morale and military objectives as possible rather than to cast their efforts in the broader and farther-reaching vision of those on the left.[51] In a way, the dispute was between those who believed OWI should not be afraid to disseminate *propaganda*, in the sense of trying to shape public opinion on critical matters, and others who viewed its goal as merely distributing *information*. To MacLeish, the latter was tantamount to reducing the agency to "a mere issuing mechanism [of information] for the government departments."[52]

The liberals were certainly not opposed to disseminating information but wanted it done honestly and in a way that was founded on ideas and had some depth. The dispute came to a head in April 1943, when a number of agency members (including young Schlesinger) resigned to protest not being allowed "to tell the full truth" about the war and its effects. The protesters issued a statement that the domestic program had become "dominated by high-pressure promoters who prefer slick salesmanship to honest information" as a way of minimizing bad war news and keeping silent regarding the high stakes in the conflict. The agency was no longer the Office of War Information, they said, but rather the "Office of War

Ballyhoo." A sympathetic graphic artist satirized this new direction by producing a poster of the Statue of Liberty holding four bottles of Coca-Cola in place of the torch, with the caption, "The War That Refreshes: The Four Delicious Freedoms."[53] In practice, though, the approaches of "propaganda" and "information" often shaded over into each other.

One reason for the pragmatists' victory was that the thoughtful, forward-looking arguments of those who felt Americans needed to understand that they were waging a war against fascism really didn't succeed in making their case with troops overseas or the citizens on the home front, who mainly believed we were fighting for the United States and the "American way of life." This approach was useful for people both in the U.S. and overseas. For the domestic audience, it was comfortable and reassuring; it also showed the rest of the world that the U.S. effort was noble and just. Generally these points were made by depicting ordinary Americans going about their daily lives. Its corollaries in the domestic sphere were the series of films on *Why We Fight* that Frank Capra produced for the War Department and most of the wartime advertisements that celebrated U.S. values while selling every product under the sun, including Coca-Cola.[54]

Employed internationally, this approach was meant to counter the distorted, though widely held, view of the United States as decadent and gangster-ridden, which Hollywood films and other aspects of popular culture had introduced abroad and Goebbels had hammered home. This emphasis on depicting the American way of life to foreigners was in fact not altogether uncongenial for the liberals in the Overseas Branch. After all, fascism could be depicted as being the opposite of "the American way." And the view was not entirely shortsighted, for lying behind it was the sense that the United States would of necessity become a leader in world affairs. For Davis, the message was "that we are coming, that we are going to win, and that in the long run everybody will be better off because we won."[55]

The more idealistic viewpoint, grounded in staunch opposition to fascism, thus lost out to the more pragmatic approach within the agency as a whole, but, significantly, survived within the overseas branch, especially in its Book Division. Not only were most of the key personnel in the overseas program liberal, international-minded antifascists, they, unlike the staff in the domestic branch of the OWI, actually had to contend with and counter the hard evidence of the evil consequences of fascism as part of their everyday job.

This impressionistic, upbeat depiction of the United States and its citizens came to dominate the contents of the pamphlets and magazines that the overseas branch produced for civilians abroad. It also fostered within the Overseas Book Division the major, and in some respects the only, long-term piece of strategy for what was called the "consolidation phase" of World War II propaganda, during which the United States set out to win the hearts and minds of the people liberated from the Axis powers.[56] This strategy for putting millions of American books into the hands of the liberated populations as quickly as possible was a goal that U.S. book publishers found entirely congenial in light of their desires for increased market share abroad following the establishment of peace.

That this could happen at all depended on alliances between OWI and the military. Early in the war, there was little expectation that OWI would ever get to play a role in the area of military propaganda—or that there would even be much military propaganda, because U.S. military officials were skeptical of its effectiveness. More fundamentally, there was confusion resulting from the hybrid nature of what was called psychological warfare—part military in nature, part civilian—until it became clear that its mission was simply to interpret "civilian political and propaganda policies in terms of immediate military exigencies."[57] In July 1942, MacLeish and Warburg traveled to London to set up OWI's primary base for overseas operations and to establish its relationships with the corresponding agencies in the British government.[58]

While in London, Warburg met with General Eisenhower, who had only recently arrived to take up his duties as commanding general of the army's European theater of operations, along with British and U.S. staff officers. While admitting that he knew little about psychological warfare, Eisenhower decided to give it a chance. He was then planning for the Allied invasion of North Africa (Operation Torch), and he thought that there might well be a role for psychological warfare in that campaign. But he insisted that if civilian agencies like OWI were to be involved, they must be under direct military command.[59] OWI did push to make a contribution to the military's strategic plans. Warburg is credited with proposing the integration of OWI and Britain's PWE into the U.S. Army's Psychological Warfare Branch, with each organization contributing according to its areas of strength—the provision of personnel and machinery by the Americans, and political savvy by the British.[60] Later in the war, PWB became the Psychological Warfare Division of SHAEF (Supreme Headquarters, Allied Expeditionary Force).

The Public/Private Partnership between CBW and OWI

The task of putting books into the hands of European civilians was a collaborative effort of the chief government propaganda agency and the coalition of the major publishers in the United States that was extremely tight, if not positively incestuous. That the interests of OWI and of U.S. book publishers should coincide is hardly surprising given the fact that publishers, writers, and journalists heavily populated the staff of the propaganda agency and, as a matter of course, the industry-sponsored Council on Books in Wartime. A list of individuals associated with either the CBW or OWI, or both, reads like the proverbial who's who, not just of the contemporary publishing scene, but also of the giants of the twentieth century. Among the book publishers who held key positions within OWI, mainly in its domestic and overseas book operations, were Chester Kerr of Atlantic Monthly Press, who became the head of the domestic branch's Book Bureau before moving to the overseas branch; Harold Guinzburg and Milton B. Glick of The Viking Press; Archibald G. Ogden of Bobbs-Merrill; C. Raymond Everitt of Little, Brown; Paul Brooks of Houghton Mifflin; George Stevens of Lippincott; Cass Canfield and Simon Michael Bessie of Harper & Brothers; Edward H. Dodd of Dodd, Mead; John Farrar and Philip Hodge of Farrar & Rinehart; Trevor Hill of Doubleday, Doran; and Keith Jennison of Henry Holt. Although he was not a staff member, William Sloane of Holt made an important wartime visit to China as a consultant to OWI. Armitage Watkins, a literary agent, served with the overseas branch in New York.

Other important OWI functionaries came from magazine or newspaper publishing. One of them, Victor Weybright, who had worked for both Butterick Publishing and *Readers' Digest,* performed highly valuable work based in the U.S. embassy in London as OWI's liaison with the British publishing industry. After the war he used that experience and those connections to enter the book-publishing business in the United States, first in Penguin Books' U.S. branch and later as cofounder of the New American Library.[61] Another was Herbert Agar, former editor of the Louisville *Courier-Journal,* who was serving as a lieutenant commander in the navy in London when Weybright managed to "borrow" him as his counterpart to liaise with the British press, allowing Weybright to concentrate on relationships with the British regarding such "slow media" as books. Edward Klauber, an associate director, had been a *New York Times* editor before joining CBS News. James B. "Scotty" Reston, also of the *Times,* was responsible for setting up the OWI newsroom in London as well as overseeing damage control when GIs in Britain ran amok.[62] Another *Times* man, Samuel T. Williamson, was Kerr's boss in the Overseas Bureau.[63] Norman Cousins, editor of the *Saturday Review of Literature,* was a consultant in the Bureau of Overseas Publications. George Stevens had been Cousins's predecessor at the *Saturday Review* before joining Lippincott and, later, OWI. James A. Linen returned to *Time* magazine following his OWI stint, becoming in due course the magazine's editor. Oscar Dystel, from *Coronet,* worked on OWI magazines and pamphlets. In the 1950s, he became a major player in the world of paperback publishing at Bantam Books.[64]

Kerr was not alone in retaining his close ties to the publishing industry while carrying out his governmental responsibilities at OWI. Ogden had an even closer official relationship. After Kerr resigned from the domestic branch in anticipation of entering the army, the council seriously considered asking OWI to leave the position vacant rather than settle for a less valuable and effective liaison. Instead, OWI asked Ogden to shuttle back and forth between New York and Washington as both the executive director of the civilian, nonprofit CBW and part-time member of the book division within OWI's Book and Magazine Bureau, "thus establishing a natural liaison between the Book and Magazine Bureau and the book industry."[65] In joining OWI while keeping his job at CBW, Ogden in effect was meant to replace the apparently military-bound Kerr. However, Kerr shortly took the position within the overseas branch as Williamson's assistant, mentioned above, temporarily while he awaited his induction into the service in mid-June. As it happened, he was spared induction and continued in the new OWI post to the end of the war.[66]

The coziness of the interlocking personnel within CBW and OWI troubled some within the propaganda agency. For example, in April 1944, Klauber, OWI's associate director, accused Kerr of a conflict of interest in representing the interests of commercial publishers in his role at OWI (which was kind of the point). Kerr took his case to Elmer Davis, who stood by him.[67] Most of those within OWI who had the closest ties to the industry took pains to avoid the perception of conflicts, though primarily in the sense of doing nothing to favor one publisher over another even as they created policies and programs that might benefit the book trades as a whole, while at the same time helping to win the war and secure the peace. This is not to say that some officials weren't tempted to cross the line. When Houghton Mifflin's Brooks arrived in London as an OWI official right after Germany's surrender, the firm's London representative informed David Unwin that Brooks "can't do business." Nonetheless, she said, he planned "to pay purely social calls on the publishers and told me that he is particularly anxious to pay a visit to Allen & Unwin.[68]

This group of publishers-turned-public-servants was a fairly representative subset of the cohort of leading publishers at around the middle of the twentieth century, except that it lacked much representation from the group of prominent Jewish publishers that entered the trade in the 1920s.[69] Of this group, which included Alfred A. Knopf, Horace Liveright, Albert and Charles Boni, Richard Simon, Max Schuster, Donald Friede, Pascal Covici, Bennett Cerf, Donald Klopfer, Benjamin Huebsch, and Harold Guinzburg, only Guinzburg served with OWI. A younger man, Harper's Simon Michael Bessie, served as well. Despite their religious and ethnic differences, most of the leading Jewish publishers and their gentile colleagues had similar backgrounds—Eastern-born and bred, from upper middle-class families, with college degrees, many from Ivy League or "Little Ivy" institutions.[70] The graduates of elite northeastern colleges among the book publishers who worked for OWI included Guinzburg, Stevens, Brooks, Canfield, Bessie, and Glick (Harvard); Kerr, Hill, Everitt, Farrar, and Hodge (Yale); Ogden and Jennison (Williams); and Sloane (Princeton).

This old-boy network included close relationships among the publishers in Boston and New York and involved other aspects of their lives besides OWI. Most publishers were liberal, strongly antifascist, confirmed New Dealers, with a cosmopolitan, internationalist bent. Many of them were active in various nonprofit organizations, including a number that responded to the consequences of war, whose goals matched their philosophies, such as the American Civil Liberties Union and Freedom House. Established in 1941 as a nonpartisan organization to oppose tyrannies on both the right and the left, Freedom House attracted the involvement of a number of people prominent as authors, publishers, and journalists and active in giving wartime service. Serving on the board in 1942 were the newspaper editor Agar, the columnist Dorothy Thompson, the mystery writer and Writers' War Board head Rex Stout, Book-of-the-Month Club president Harry Scherman, and publishers Farrar and Guinzburg.[71] Another beneficiary of publishers' voluntarism was the International Study Center for Democratic Reconstruction in New York City, for which both Ogden and Guinzburg served as committee members. Refugee European artists and writers were prominent among the membership and as a key program focus of the center.[72] Cerf, of Random House, chaired a committee of Russian War Relief, Inc., responsible for collecting books for Russian libraries and schools looted or destroyed by the Nazis.[73]

Two Bookmen of OWI: Chester Kerr and Harold Guinzburg

Kerr was one of two men—Guinzburg being the other—who played particularly significant roles in the book programs of OWI. A man with feet planted squarely in both worlds of trade book publishing and wartime government service, Kerr was largely responsible for linking the strategic aims of post D-Day U.S. propaganda with the long-term interests of U.S. book publishers. Born in Norwalk, Connecticut, in 1913, he graduated from Yale as a member of the impressive class of 1936, which included his roommate, John Hersey, as well as Brendan Gill, Walt W. Rostow, August Heckscher, Stewart Alsop, Jonathan Bingham, C. Dillon Ripley, and David Dellinger.[74] At Yale, Kerr majored in history and international government, perhaps with an eye toward diplomatic service. He admitted that his college record was academically "erratic, largely due to preoccupation with editorial duties on Yale News and forensic matters in Political Union; marks were good when interested in the course."[75] He began his publishing career as an editorial apprentice at Harcourt, Brace and Co., in New York, two months after his Yale graduation. Once trained, he took on increasing responsibility for dealing with authors and agents. He left Harcourt in June 1940 to become director of Atlantic Monthly Press in Boston, whose twenty or so titles a year were produced

FIGURE 3. Chester Kerr (1913–99), who served in both the domestic and overseas branches of the Office of War Information, was responsible for the production of the Overseas Editions and later briefly served as director of the United States International Book Association. *Publishers Weekly,* Feb. 9, 1946, 1016.

and distributed by Little, Brown and Co. In March 1942, at Archibald MacLeish's invitation, he joined the Office of Facts and Figures, which became OWI three months later, initially heading up the domestic branch's Book Division (later Book Bureau).

Kerr claimed credit for spurring the organization of the Council on Books in Wartime and for "godfather[ing] that group's Armed Services Editions."[76] Speaking at CBW's organizational luncheon on June 18, 1942, he expressed confidence that the group's wartime work would influence the postwar direction of the trade. "A single, representative, authoritative war council," he told his colleagues, "would be a welcome agency through which to funnel all matters of <u>general</u> cooperation between the book trade and the Government's information service." "If enough Americans are given an opportunity to learn what a book can do for them in wartime," he added, "they will have a new appreciation for its value and uses in peacetime. You can create habits today which will carry over into tomorrow."[77]

Kerr resigned from OWI in March 1944, partly in anticipation of receiving his draft notice, but also because of a downgrading of the Domestic Book

Bureau and his sense that the Overseas Book Bureau would continue to increase in importance as the war drew to a close, despite the fact that it was headed by Dr. Vincenzo Petrullo, who was, in Kerr's opinion, "no great shakes" because his personality and his lack of experience in publishing would not "impress the trade."[78] His earlier effort at obtaining a commission in naval intelligence had been scotched by poor eyesight. His draft notice never arrived, apparently because of new regulations regarding men over twenty-six.[79] He therefore rejoined OWI in April 1944, this time to work in the overseas branch, where he saw the action coming, as special assistant to Williamson, the chief of its Publications Bureau.

In this post Kerr administered OWI's part of the OE program and also served as the agency's liaison with the publishing industry and the Department of State on international book issues. He would have been a highly desirable addition to the staff of almost any U.S. publishing house (and was even courted by Geoffrey Faber, of Faber and Faber in London), but he was determined to delay his return to publishing until the war was over. "I came down here to fight the war," he told a publishing colleague, "if Congress will permit me the liberty of describing OWI activity as doing that. I want to go on fighting the war until it's over, whether from OWI or from the vantage point of the Navy...or from behind a K.P. knife."[80] During the period of transition from wartime to peacetime, Kerr collaborated with assistant secretary of state William Benton in transforming parts of OWI into the United States Information Service.

Politically, Kerr was left of center. Like most of the other publishers working for CBW or OWI, he was a solid Roosevelt New Deal Democrat. In 1943, an article in the New York *World-Telegram* charged Kerr with suppressing a book that the Communist Party had disapproved, thus painting him with a red brush. The publisher of the book, Doubleday, the editor of *Publishers' Weekly,* Melcher, and others quickly rushed to Kerr's defense.[81]

After his second separation from the government at the end of 1945, Kerr became acting director of the United States International Book Association, an organization that briefly carried on OWI's activities in facilitating the sale of American books abroad.[82] Kerr was a demanding and often cantankerous administrator and publisher, but, as one of his former colleagues at OWI told him, "You have a certain quality that inspires people to work for you and that, I know, is what kept me at it."[83] These and many other character traits, including a sharp, often cutting, wit, show up clearly in his surviving letters.[84]

The other key figure in OWI's role in the program to provide American books to liberated civilians—Harold Guinzburg, the Publication Bureau's man in London—possessed publishing credentials even more stellar than those of Kerr, thirteen years his junior. Guinzburg was born in 1899, in New York City, into a prominent Jewish family. His grandfather, a rabbi, had emigrated from Austria as a refugee from the failed revolutions of 1848. His father, Henry A. Guinzburg, was a wealthy rubber merchant and philanthropist.[85]

When he went to work for OWI in January 1942, Guinzburg was president of The Viking Press, which he and George Oppenheimer, a Harvard friend, had founded in 1925. After college, Guinzburg worked as a newspaperman and studied law at Columbia. He joined Simon and Schuster through his connection with Richard Simon, with whom he had gone to primary school, leaving that firm to set up his own shop under Rockwell Kent's elegant colophon depicting a Viking ship. Even before Guinzburg and Oppenheimer published any new titles of their own, they got a leg up in the trade by acquiring the twenty-three-year-old firm of Benjamin W. Huebsch (and the indispensable services of Huebsch himself). From this deal Viking gained a valuable backlist, including works by James Joyce, D. H. Lawrence, Gerhart Hauptmann, and Sherwood Anderson. After the demise of the firm of Covici-Friede, Pascal Covici joined Viking in 1938, bringing with him his prize author, John Steinbeck. In the prewar years, Viking's list was heavy on works from Britain and Europe, including titles by Harold Laski, Rebecca West, Graham Greene, and a group of noted authors whose works were banned or burned by the Nazis, including Arnold Zweig, Lion Feuchtwanger, Stefan Zweig, and Franz Werfel. Guinzburg founded the Literary Guild in the mid-1920s to go head-to-head with the Book-of-the-Month Club but sold it shortly to Doubleday, Doran. In the early 1940s, he established the Viking Portables, an influential and well-received series focused on the works of prominent authors. The first in the series was actually one of the various efforts to provide reading matter for the U.S. armed services abroad. It was edited by Alexander Woollcott and entitled *As You Were: A Portable Library of American Prose and Poetry.*

Like his father, Guinzburg was a philanthropist and civic activist, mostly devoted to liberal and Jewish causes. He was long active in the American Jewish Committee, in which he took particular interest in the problems of Jewish refugees. In this capacity, he worked to convince fellow Americans to regard the émigrés as "assets rather than liabilities."[86] He also was deeply involved in the affairs of Freedom House and the American Civil Liberties Union.[87] An ardent antifascist like many other publishers, both Jewish and gentile, who served in OWI or the CBW, Guinzburg was a strong advocate before Pearl Harbor for aiding Britain and intervening in the war against Germany. He may also have been an active recruiter for British intelligence services in the United States, which were headed by William Stephenson, the "man called Intrepid."[88]

Like Kerr, Guinzburg resigned from OWI (in 1943) over concern that the ideological and personnel crises within the agency would render it impossible to create a suitable publications program, only to rejoin later, as Kerr also had.[89] From his London headquarters—OWI's largest foreign outpost with some sixteen hundred employees at its peak[90]—Guinzburg supervised the stockpiling of American books

FIGURE 4.   Harold Guinzburg (1899–1961), cofounder of the Viking Press, who produced the French- and Dutch-language Transatlantic Editions from the Office of War Information's London outpost. Photograph by Carl Van Vechten. Library of Congress, Prints & Photographs Division, Carl Van Vechten Collection, LOT 12735, no. 472.

for dispatch to the Continent following D-Day. With Kerr, he was a principal in the establishment of the OE project. When delays occurred in getting OEI off the ground, which threatened to render the project useless, Guinzburg produced in England a smaller parallel series of books that bore the imprint Transatlantic Editions in the French and Dutch languages. After his death at sixty-one in 1961, a *New York Times* editorial tribute described him as being "as truly creative as the distinguished writers whose work he published" and claimed that "there is hardly any aspect of American trade publishing today which he did not help to shape."[91]

Planning for the Future

The entry of the United States into the Second World War had a great impact on the nation's book-publishing industry. The war brought the trade fully out of the doldrums of the Great Depression. During wartime, book reading assumed a greater importance among the public than it had previously. Having done so well financially during the war, publishers wished to maintain that prosperity after the conflict was over. The war fostered in many segments of U.S. society a culture of planning, which the publishers embraced.[92] The establishment of an organization through which the publishing industry could perform its war service provided an important vehicle in which planning could take place.

The industry began planning in earnest for a greater participation in world markets early in 1942, most visibly through the establishment of the Council on Books in Wartime. The process also involved a series of visits by one or more important American publishers to several key foreign countries to ascertain the wartime situation of publishing there and to judge the possible postwar markets for American books. Most of these delegations were sponsored by the BPB and OWI. The first was Curtice Hitchcock's trip to Britain in the fall of 1942, a mission that, as *Publishers' Weekly* generously put it, "made book trade history and brought to the publishers of both England and the United States a fresh sense of common understanding and common cause."[93] It was followed over the next several years by delegations to South America, China, Australia and New Zealand, and Britain again, with a reciprocal visit to the United States (and Canada) by a British delegation, and even after the war with an important postwar visit to occupied Germany in 1948.

Planning also proceeded on home shores, with the federal government a close and interested collaborator. The key event might be described as a "summit" meeting in September 1942, arranged by the Washington Committee of the Council on Books in Wartime, which included representatives of the industry and of virtually all federal government agencies that had any interest in the role of books, both domestically and overseas, or that held any responsibility for the use of books during wartime and in the subsequent peace—OWI, of course, but also the War Department, the Navy Department, the Office of the Coordinator of Inter-American Affairs, the Office of Education, the Office of Price Administration, the Office of Censorship, and the Library of Congress. Although domestic issues were a major part of the agenda—how to meet the growing requirements for books for the armed forces, for example—the needs and opportunities for

U.S. books abroad were also widely discussed at the September 17 meeting. *Publishers' Weekly* reported that the primary goal of the meeting was to enable the publishers to learn "how the industry could best serve the government in its pressing problems."[94]

What is most remarkable about these discussions is the degree to which the government agencies had already formulated ideas for publishers to implement and just how willing they were in turn to assist the publishing industry in meeting its and the nation's goals—not just domestically but internationally as well. Representatives of the State Department were particularly eager for American books to become more widely available in Latin America either through the export of physical books or in the sale of foreign editions in Spanish and Portuguese (especially books on history and science). They also wanted more Latin American books translated into English and published in the United States. The CIAA official observed that "all our efforts are headed towards the interests of commercial publishers, toward increased contacts, more correspondence, increased experience in selling literary rights."

The State Department's "four chief aims" were outlined by one member of the group as:

> 1) to get as many good United States books and periodicals as possible into foreign countries; 2) to encourage and facilitate the translation into foreign languages of outstanding United States books for sale and distribution in foreign countries; 3) to provide comprehensive information about the books and periodicals published in the United States to book review critics, editors, publishers, and other interested persons and organizations in foreign countries; [and] 4) to make the purchase of United States books and periodicals easier in foreign countries.

Another member of the group argued that the "tremendous increase of interest in the U.S. in almost every part of the world" and the spread of knowledge of the English language made it not only highly important but also feasible that inexpensive editions of American books in all fields be produced for the export market.

Even the representative from the Office of Price Administration revealed quite a sophisticated understanding of the importance of books in wartime and in the subsequent peace, one that echoed the goals set down by the founders of CBW. He told the group:

> In the last 7 or 8 years book publishing was way ahead of anybody on the war situation, on what was coming. Books laid the groundwork in people's minds of what this war would mean. Can't we again, in books,

take the long view? The Government itself cannot print what they think may happen. Book publishers have a great opportunity. There is a relationship between what we are doing this moment and the future which is the foundation for a book. The publishers can capture the field of ideas, as opposed to merely what is going on.[95]

The sense of goals and purpose shared by the private and public entities represented at this conference helped shape the course of U.S. book publishing and propaganda activities throughout the war and for some years beyond. In the meantime, this cooperative spirit promoted programs that led to finding solutions to the problems facing both the government and the publishers—the government's need to cleanse the minds of civilians under Axis control through U.S. books and the publishers' growing desire to secure postwar markets for their products abroad.

"BOOKS ARE THE MOST ENDURING PROPAGANDA OF ALL"

The idea that books could serve as weapons in the war of ideas proved to be a useful, even powerful slogan throughout the Second World War. It was applied to both domestic and international contexts and was invoked widely in Britain as well.[1] Like many slogans, and indeed like the agency of books themselves, this weapon was a two-edged sword. As every propagandist (and book historian) knows, the printed word can be used to tear down as well as to build up, to attack as well as to defend, to do the devil's work as well as God's. Print may be eagerly received or violently rejected. How ironic was it, W. W. Norton observed, that the book that most influenced the war, *Mein Kampf*, was written by a man who hated some books enough to burn and ban them and yet received perhaps the largest royalties of any living author.[2] Archibald MacLeish, the poet and librarian of Congress, challenged American writers, publishers, librarians, booksellers, academics, and the general public "to recognize the power of books as truly as the Nazi mob which dumped them on a fire."[3]

The significant role that American books were called on to play overseas during the war derived from the government's need to find solutions to a series of challenges that would arise as combat gave way to an uneasy peace. While the armed forces were battling the Axis enemy, the principal goal of propaganda was to weaken the enemy's ability to fight by confusing him, by encouraging opposition through the underground movements in the overrun nations, and by undermining the enemy combatant's will to fight on, leading, in the best possible outcome, to his surrender. As Allied forces began to succeed against the Axis enemies, first in North Africa and Italy, and later in Western Europe and the Far East, victory drew ever closer.

The propaganda effort accordingly broadened to address not just combat needs but also the project of securing the peace. Propaganda to be implemented place by place as soon as the shooting stopped was quite a different matter from combat propaganda and required alternate strategies and a different deployment of media. Books would play a far more important role in propaganda after fighting stopped than they did during the phases of combat.

The Nature of Consolidation Propaganda

Termed "consolidation propaganda," this postbattle, postliberation phase had three main objectives. The first was to pacify the civilian populations, in both the conquered and aggressor nations. This meant using instruments of propaganda to restore and maintain calm, to ensure compliance with the orders of Allied military commanders, and to inform the liberated or defeated people what they might and might not expect next. This required portraying a realistic assessment of the situation, but one that was neither too pessimistic nor too optimistic. Pacifying the civilian populations was vital in order "to reduce to a minimum the Allied troops for the maintenance of law and order," for these soldiers would need to be redeployed in still active combat zones.[4] The second was to reorient the minds of the civilian populations—or, as one propaganda planner put it, to subject them to "a process of disintoxication"—from the effects of having been, for the previous four to six years, the objects of an unrelenting onslaught of Nazi censorship and propaganda.[5] A major part of this goal was to counteract the highly negative picture of Americans and their culture that Goebbels's propaganda machine had spread widely. The third objective was to explain what the United States had been doing during the war. European civilians knew surprisingly little about the U.S. war effort, particularly about the battles that the nation was simultaneously waging on the other side of the world, against Japan. A significant military objective for these activities was "to reduce to a minimum the Allied troops for the maintenance of law and order," but all of the goals were important elements in winning the peace as well as the war. In actuality, the distinction between combat propaganda and consolidation propaganda was minor, with one sort often flowing into the other.[6] Planning for consolidation propaganda was well underway by late 1943.[7]

The Allied propaganda effort utilized many forms of media to secure a military victory over the Axis powers, including radio, films, loudspeaker trucks, and such genres of print as leaflets, pamphlets, newspapers, and magazines. All of these would also be marshaled in the postliberation phase of propaganda work but with the significant addition of books. While books had been a substantial part of the propaganda program domestically in lifting morale and informing the public about why the war was being fought, they played little if any role during the combat phase in the several theaters of operations, for understandable reasons. Radio, films, and the shorter, more ephemeral forms of print were highly useful in achieving short-range goals, such as recruiting and sustaining resistance fighters, misleading enemy troops about Allied operations, and encouraging enemy soldiers to surrender. Where books *could* play a vital role was in helping achieve *long-range* goals, including the transition from war to peace and winning the hearts and minds of the people in the conquered and aggressor countries for the future, especially elites and other opinion makers. As senior OWI officials saw it, "Books do not have their impact upon the mass mind but upon the minds of those who mould the mass mind—upon leaders of thought and formulators of public opinion. The impact of a book may last six months or several decades. Books are the most enduring propaganda of all."[8]

If books could be considered to be "paper bullets," they were projectiles that the oppressed peoples of Europe were more than willing to have aimed in their direction, as the Allies quickly discovered first hand.[9] The observation that appears over and over again in accounts from citizens of the overrun countries themselves and from government, military, and private officials on the scene, was that they felt an intense hunger for books and other reading material free of the taint of fascist propaganda. This intellectual hunger was usually likened to physical hunger.[10] For the peoples of Europe, food for the mind and soul vied with food for the body in their postliberation desires. For military officials following Allied victories in the Mediterranean theater in 1943 and 1944, there was no better evidence of the public's hunger for good reading material than the fact that civilians were willing to pay scarce money for the books that OWI brought in.[11] Publisher Victor Weybright, serving with OWI in Britain, reported home about the "growing demand for books overseas as there is no adequate reading material available."[12] Another publisher, William Sloane, learned on his trade mission to China in late 1943 that the people there too were hungry for books. On the grounds of a Confucian temple that the Japanese had bombed he found written uncertainly in English in chalk on a stone tablet, "Above all, I need books."[13] In lamenting the heavy censorship of print and speech in Vichy, a Frenchman told a visiting American, "Starvation is bad enough, but this is worse."[14] In Germany, this *Lesehunger* for non-Nazi, nonmilitaristic books was also widely felt after Hitler's demise. Some people willingly bartered food for books.[15] In Japan, devastated by conventional and atomic bombs and from an unthinkable defeat, a "craving for words that went beyond sloganeering" was as powerful a sensation as physical hunger. It even drove people to wait for hours and days outside a bookshop to buy a set of the newly published collected works of the philosopher Nishida Kitarō.[16]

Such widespread intellectual famine translated into pent-up demand—for almost any kind of reading matter that might tell the truth about what had been happening in the world the last four to six years. A publisher in Algiers reported in early April 1944 how the demand that followed the liberation of his territory had encouraged publishers to produce editions of ten thousand to twenty thousand copies, compared to usual edition sizes before the war of three to five thousand copies.[17] In Europe, though, there just weren't enough books to meet the people's clamor for them. In Paris in April 1945, about five hundred titles per month were being published, as compared with one thousand per month before the war, a local bookseller wrote. "The consequence is that many books are sold out as soon as they hit the shops."[18]

Cooperation and Competition between the United States and Britain

But how should the U.S. and Britain actually meet their long-term propaganda goals while feeding the hunger for uncensored literature—especially books—of war-weary populations newly liberated or occupied? Given the harm the indigenous book trades had suffered during the war, many months at least would be needed before printing plants and publishing offices could return to at least some degree of normalcy and be capable of meeting the enormous pent-up demand. Almost everyone concerned with these matters in the two nations agreed that the main task of denazifying the book culture of European countries should belong to each country's indigenous publishers. But, then, how could the victors both slake this thirst for print and ensure that books could accomplish their desired propaganda work in whatever time there might be between liberation and the reestablishment of the local printing and publishing trades? The matter was so critical that military and civilian propaganda officials in both countries considered that interim period of indeterminate length to be a period of emergency, requiring bold action.

Like the Americans, the British mobilized books for both domestic and overseas propaganda objectives during the war. While each nation worked independently of each other in fashioning a book program to meet their own particular national and trade objectives, they participated as partners in the overseas book programs of the consolidation propaganda phase—related first to the military campaigns in North Africa and Italy in 1943–44 and later in the invasion of Europe in 1944—under the aegis of the Psychological Warfare Division (PWD) of SHAEF (Supreme Headquarters, Allied Expeditionary Force), formed in February 1944. There were important differences as well as similarities between the two nations' approaches to the problem before, during, and after the SHAEF period. Cooperation at the highest levels of command could never completely mask the competitiveness that wartime circumstances had engendered between the two national book trades, which were represented in the alliance by the trades' surrogates in OWI and Britain's Ministry of Information. Looming largest were the competing visions each nation had for the future of its books overseas. The United States wanted to expand its international trade in books. The UK not only desired but desperately needed to retain its grip on the international markets it had been cultivating for a couple of centuries. It did not necessarily have to be a zero-sum contest, but this battle for world markets was generally fought as if it was.

The first test of the British and U.S. book programs, both individually and jointly, came through the stockpiling and eventual delivery of materials to newly liberated areas of North Africa, Sicily, and the Italian boot in 1942–43 under the aegis of the psychological warfare unit. Significantly, the involvement of propagandists in the planning of the invasion of North Africa was perhaps the first such instance in military history.[19] Magazines, booklets, and pamphlets were important parts of the consolidation-propaganda campaigns, particularly in the early stages of liberation and especially when directed to the masses of people. But the special value of books in fostering the long-range rehabilitation of liberated societies was also clearly recognized—and provided for—early on.[20]

Under the plans set up for psychological warfare activities from Operation Torch (the invasion of North Africa) to Operation Overlord (the Normandy invasion), Britain and the United States would acquire quantities of printed pamphlets and books to be stockpiled in London and elsewhere for shipment to the overrun nations as soon after liberation from the Nazis as possible. Books in English and in translation into a variety of local languages would be required. Books thus had to be either purchased from existing sources or published specially through an arrangement with some publisher or other entity in the United States or the UK, perhaps a publishing firm in exile or one in a neutral country like Sweden or Switzerland. The flow of Allied material was to cease as soon as local publishers were back on line and able to satisfy demand on their own.[21]

Several organizations and individuals on both sides of the Atlantic sowed the seeds of the stockpiling program for the postliberation period. The germ of the idea arose in Great Britain before it did in the United States, no doubt because Britain went to war earlier and was a nearer witness to the intellectual blackout that had befallen much of the Continent. Having a better developed international book trade, along with the necessary institutions to promote it, was also strong motivation.

That Britain could possibly take the early lead in these plans was to a large extent the result of encouragement and backing from a quasi-official body, the British Council. Their efforts took place in the context of grave concern about the future of British books abroad owing to wartime circumstances and uncertainties as to their competitiveness after the conflict ended. Finding in late

1939 that "British books are disappearing from many foreign markets," the British Council began to develop a strategy for reinvigorating the industry's export trade.[22] The next year it approved the Book Export Scheme, an idea proposed by publisher Stanley Unwin, who served as a member of the council's Books and Periodicals Committee. The plan encouraged foreign booksellers to buy British books "on sale or return," meaning that the retailers had the right to return unsold copies for credit, less freight charges. This imaginative scheme also provided a way to mitigate the deterrence factor that came with having to deal with various, often unstable, currencies. Under the scheme, the British Council paid for the books in sterling and, for its trouble, pocketed a portion of the sales revenue in the local currency, which it then spent to finance its work in that country.

The plan was meant to supplement the usual methods and instrumentalities for exports by making it easier for foreign sellers to obtain a more representative stock of British titles. It succeeded in bringing in orders that the nation's publishers would not otherwise have received, but only up to a point because enemy military actions rendered it inapplicable in a number of the regions for which the plan was intended.[23] Some early efforts were aimed at having significant British books published in English in Sweden for distribution to Scandinavia, Finland, the Balkans, Russia, Switzerland, and "if possible in German-occupied territories." Among the titles selected were such decidedly middlebrow titles as *How Green Was My Valley*, the Hornblower novels, and the detective fiction of Agatha Christie and Dorothy Sayers.[24] In a separate effort, the British Council arranged for good translations of English books into the various Allied languages.[25] Even a plan to produce special lightweight editions of English books for passengers on airliners in Africa and the Middle East was not too trivial to be considered.[26]

Still, the position of British books continued to worsen.[27] There were simply not enough books for the home population let alone for the British and Dominion troops fighting in North Africa or based in the British Isles, who were the British Council's main concern. Gains made in the teaching of English as a second language increased the demand for British books for both technical training and leisure reading. Following a tour of the Middle East, the British literary scholar B. Ifor Evans wrote that "this demand exists to an extent which we in Great Britain have as yet not begun to realize."[28] Books were needed for "allied Poles, Czechs, Yugoslavs, Greeks, etc., who require books not only to learn English but also in their own languages." Also unable to be met was demand from "local populations, on the bringing of whom into contact with British Culture so much effort has been spent, and who are now faced with the possibility of having one of the main links—that of literature—severed." Then there were the German and Italian prisoners of war in British custody, who would one day be repatriated. "Now is the chance to cancel out the years of fascist training and [to provide] a few new ideas to take with them; but, here again, books are needed."

Book shortages were such that the British had to rely for their needs more and more on outside sources, particularly the United States, whose shipments of fifty thousand pulp magazines at a time were popular with the British troops, as were titles in Random House's Modern Library with the general population.[29] But none of these outside sources provided an answer to the acute problem of defending and promoting British culture. On the contrary, the Books and Periodicals Committee strongly recommended that the British Council should refrain from purchasing American books "save in very exceptional circumstances."[30]

The British Council began during the summer of 1942 to develop a more comprehensive, forward-looking plan to supply books in English and in translation for distribution, in the case of the books in English, and for publication, in the case of translations, throughout Europe immediately after the war.[31] Europeans would provide a great demand for British books "as soon as the countries concerned have passed beyond the immediate danger of anarchy, famine and plague." The plan involved the reservation, acquisition, or commissioning of British Council publications in English and other languages, titles from other publishers, and microfilms, together with microfilm readers, of key learned journals, which, however important, would be consulted by only a few specialists.[32]

Unwin was one of the strongest advocates of stockpiling. In early 1943, at an international conference of P.E.N., the writers' group, Unwin argued (as paraphrased by a journalist) "that one of the most pressing tasks for intellectuals on the cessation of hostilities would be to satisfy the hunger of writers and the intelligent public as a whole in occupied countries, to know what had been going on in free countries while they had been cut off from them." Representatives of the overrun nations were to be asked for suggestions as to what sorts of books would be needed for the people of their countries. One of those in attendance who spoke in support of the plan was particularly anxious that subventions be found to guarantee that important books on politics, philosophy, science, and economics would be translated and not just financially valuable bestsellers. A delegate from India urged that such a program be extended to Asian countries.[33]

Previously, in November 1942, the British Council had turned to the Conference of Allied Ministers of Education, which had just been organized, for help both in selecting the most needed titles and in building a list of foreign libraries to benefit from the distributions.[34] CAME's membership at first consisted of representatives of the governments in exile in London (the Netherlands, Luxembourg, Norway, Czechoslovakia, Greece, Poland, and Yugoslavia, and the French National Committee of Liberation) and Great Britain. Observers from China, the Soviet Union, and the United States (in the person of a foreign service officer at the London embassy) were present at some of the meetings.[35] Other nations joined in time. The purpose of the organization was to address the problems facing educational institutions in countries conquered by Germany and Japan and to propose solutions for remedying them in the postwar world. Within this mandate, considerable attention was given to the problems of books and librarries and such potential solutions as gathering up publications to restock the devastated libraries through one of its subgroups, the Commission on Books and Periodicals, headed by Britain's Sir Ernest Barker.[36] The United States upgraded the seniority of its observer when Ralph E. Turner, of the State Department, was dispatched to London to attend CAME's meeting in October 1943.[37] The first official U.S. delegation attended meetings toward establishing the organization on a permanent basis in April 1944. It was a distinguished group, including Congressman J. William Fulbright, librarian of Congress Archibald MacLeish, and Nobel Prize–winning physicist Arthur Compton. The group chose Fulbright to chair the meeting.[38] The planning resulted in CAME's transformation into UNESCO during the organization of the United Nations.[39] During the war, CAME was a very useful body for examining postwar book needs, particularly since it brought together both the nations starved for books as well as those that might be able to supply them. Its plans, however, were not expected to be implemented until well after the PWD/SHAEF period had ended and thus would not be particularly relevant to the immediate, postinvasion need for books.[40]

Another center of activity regarding the supply of British books abroad was the Ministry of Information, working closely with the Political Warfare Executive, one of the nine secret services within the government.[41] In due course, MoI and PWE represented Britain among the civilian agencies within the PWB/SHAEF, which was under the overall command of General Eisenhower. The British PWE-MoI tandem began preparing books for France and other areas in the spring of 1943. There was some debate on how best to go about it, particularly to what extent the British would control the early stages of providing books for the French reading public and how much would be left to reestablished French publishers. There was general agreement that the process needed to be started as quickly as possible and not get bogged down by intellectuals serving on committees. For the Normandy operation, the British publishing program preferred the commissioning of works specifically as propaganda. This was especially true of pamphlets and other small works, though to a large extent also for books.[42]

The first step was to prepare three books, on a fast track, that could be "fairly described as basic PWE documents of the sort that will be badly needed from the earliest moment of contact with the population in France." One was a military history of the war, which was to be cobbled together from existing articles reedited and brought up to date by two journalists. The second book, to be written by an Oxford don, would focus on Great Britain and the war. Running to about ninety thousand words, the book was "designed to present to the people of France a picture of the war as it has appeared to the British, with the propaganda object of counterbalancing the systematic misrepresentation by the Axis and the Vichy government of Britain and her motives and the part which she has played in the war." The third was a survey of Franco-British relations since June 1940, to be written by a man who had access to intelligence information and the Foreign Office archives. PWE would finance these titles up to the point of the production of the final manuscript. MoI would undertake to have the books published commercially.[43] Presumably, the French versions would be issued in France by local publishers once they had reestablished themselves. These first three books might lead to a total of sixty such productions, "a neat pile of books to be sent over as soon as the enemy is kicked out."[44]

In late 1943 the well-known British feminist, journalist, novelist, and critic Rebecca West publicized the need for an Anglo-American book program for the overrun nations under Britain's leadership. Her proposal appeared as an article entitled "Books for Liberated Europe" in the English-Speaking Union's magazine for December-January 1943–44. It apparently originated as the text of an address West made before the Society of Authors in her country. The *English-Speaking World* was a highly appropriate, if low-circulation, journal in which to publish such a proposal. Probably more people learned of it from accounts published elsewhere. *Publishers' Weekly,* for example, ran an article on West's piece, ensuring that it would be read by most of the top officials of both the Council on Books in Wartime and the domestic and overseas publishing bureaus of OWI.

"People who have been enslaved hunger and thirst for books," West declared. When the captives of the Nazis are at last freed, she added, "they will call for books," books to educate the young, books to retrain doctors, books for architects and engineers that tell of wartime technological advances in the West that they will need to know about in order to rebuild their nations. The demand for books will necessarily be addressed to the two great English-speaking countries but mainly to Britain, "because, on the whole, the Continental public would rather take their reading from us than from America." In the end, of course, she noted, "the only culture which confers a lasting benefit on a country is its own. But we have the opportunity of providing the ferment which will start their artistic process working again." It was vital that British books, both in English and in foreign languages, be delivered to the occupied countries as soon as possible. In stating that "the books that first get to the liberated countries will have the advantage of stamping the deepest impression on the virgin minds of the young readers who have never read before, the war-stunned minds of their elders who have forgotten what they used to read," West implied a race with the United States and, perhaps, with other nations as well. Only the government, she concluded, could tackle this work, with the complex necessities of commissioning translations, of exporting the books, and of coping with the inevitable currency difficulties.[45]

West herself was in a position to work directly toward her goal through her service on the Books and Periodicals Committee of the British Council.[46]

Americans Take the Upper Hand

Not long after West's call for the Allies to provide books for liberated Europe was reported in *Publishers' Weekly,* the American publisher Stanley M. Rinehart Jr. decided that the United States must challenge West's call for British leadership of the program. He suggested to Chester Kerr and CBW that OWI prepare a number of translations of "worthwhile" American books for publication by European publishing houses as soon as their countries were freed. He proposed that American publishers as well as foreign writers currently exiled in the United States be called on to help pick the titles. He hoped that regular hardbound trade books would be collected for donation to overseas libraries and that CBW, with OWI's cooperation, would begin to sell translation rights through established agencies in order to prepare for an increased presence of American books abroad after the war.[47]

In the first stage of the U.S. program, items chosen for stockpiling were acquired from a variety of sources, such as American publishers' existing stocks (including those of refugee, foreign-language publishing houses in New York), plus remainders and some reprints; OWI's own published pamphlets and books; and other books for which OWI specially arranged translation and publication, by American as well as foreign publishing houses and European governments in exile in London. In April 1943, OWI was busy obtaining some sixty thousand copies allocated among ninety titles to be sent to North Africa. PWB officers were pleased to find that civilians in North Africa and the Mediterranean were willing to pay for the publications. The officers believed that printed propaganda played an important role in lessening tensions between the French and natives in North Africa, in securing their assistance in ousting the Nazis and their sympathizers, and in encouraging Italian civilians and POWs "to aid the war effort in their daily work and to build a democratic Italy." All in all, they judged the books to be very effective, but there were simply not enough of them. What's more, they complained that "British material overshadows us."[48]

At first, the impetus for the selection and dispatch of American titles came from field officers, United States Information Service librarians in the freshly liberated territories, and various regional editors. To a large extent, information officers were simply servicing the requests, large and small, that came from OWI's various foreign outposts.[49] All such recommendations and requests were submitted to the Book Section, which bore responsibility for adding additional titles from their study of the publications lists of foreign-language publishers in the Western hemisphere as well as acquiring any necessary copyright clearances and ultimate approval of the specific titles from OWI and other pertinent government agencies.

The Book Section's personnel also handled all matters involving reprint and translation rights for books and periodicals. This meant dealing directly with authors, agents, and publishers—in effect acting like "international literary agents." They believed they could frequently perform these functions "with better results than commercial agents...since American authors and publishers invariably give heed when their government appeals to them." The staff took care to protect the interests of U.S. copyright holders abroad. They also assumed a responsibility to exercise some judgment, when necessary, to authorize the publication abroad only of literature that reflected the U.S. and Allied viewpoints and objectives. For example, officials discouraged certain deals, like requests from Spanish publishers for translation rights to Richard A. Wright's *Native Son* and Erskine Caldwell's *Tobacco Road*,[50] which could well have given enemy propagandists grounds for spotlighting the darker sides of life in the United States. Denying such rights to the Spanish publishers had to be done "with the greatest tact," which might have meant simply telling publishers that the Spanish rights to the titles were not available.

Toward the end of 1943, the process was tightened up and centralized in the interest of reducing inefficiencies and, particularly, of obtaining books, in single copies for review or in quantity for dispatch to overseas libraries and for stockpiling for future use by civilians. Speed was increasingly important, for whatever propaganda value the materials possessed could be entirely forfeited through delays.[51] The need to arrange for translations into several foreign languages was another major challenge. Since the U.S. book program was aimed at a narrower, more elite segment of the liberated populations, a few foreign languages—basically, French, Italian, Dutch, and German—would suffice, and books in English could serve well in areas where English was widely understood, especially the Low Countries, Scandinavia, and even certain areas in Asia.

Though not without value, the practice of allowing the needs and wishes of officers in the outposts to drive the stockpiling program was too random and inefficient. The military success of the North African and Italian campaigns opened the door for the long-awaited invasion of France to strike a direct blow to German forces occupying the heart of Europe. The stakes for both British and U.S. consolidation propaganda through printed materials rose considerably as plans for this operation—code-named Overlord—developed. Moreover, the Mediterranean campaigns had confirmed the usefulness of books and other printed materials among the civilian populations in areas newly liberated from the Axis. For example, some members of the PWD in Bari, Italy, said they had, as an experiment, "chiseled" a number of Armed Services Editions and dropped them by parachute on an island off the coast of Yugoslavia. Those who found the books took them to someone who could read English, and soon people gathered around to hear the book "translated aloud on the spot." The creation of this instant reading community was credited in part with the warm feelings those islanders had toward the liberating GIs.[52]

In the months leading up to the big invasion (then planned for May 1944), the book programs of the two major Allies had to be more closely integrated so as to facilitate the stockpiling and distribution of books into Europe. But to respond adequately to its half of the challenge, the U.S. program had to be strengthened.

The first change occurred in December 1943, when Joseph Barnes, a deputy director of OWI, recentered the book program within the Overseas Book Section. Although it would still be important to work closely with the outposts, the change reflected a need to develop a more centralized and coherent strategy. To that end, OWI set up several advisory committees, involving both staff and outside experts. Included among these were representatives of publishing and printing companies, which strengthened the "business angle to our program which cannot be ignored," according to Vincenzo Petrullo, head of the Overseas Book Bureau.[53] By early 1944, OWI was actively acquiring books for use after D-Day in various parts of Europe.[54]

The highest priority was to secure books to be used in France and Belgium, nearest the planned invasion landings. OWI asked the French-language publishers that had established operations in New York before or after the fall of France to recommend titles "they feel valuable in the way of showing democracy in action and as an example of American thought and writing." Once OWI had approved certain titles, the agency would contract with the publisher to purchase a quantity of the title, to be published in French. The publisher would be responsible for contracting for the rights, commissioning the translation, and arranging for the typesetting and printing. OWI would have the responsibility "to make certain of a proper and adequate translation and format." The first such title aimed at the French public was Secretary of State Edward Stettinius's book *Lend-Lease,* which the firm Les Éditions de la Maison Française in New York agreed to take on. OWI placed an order for five thousand copies on January 20, 1944, with delivery promised for April 30. The type was to be left standing for possible reprinting. OWI expected that several other translated books would be ready for distribution by midsummer, including selections from American books already in print, some still in manuscript or proof stage, and possibly a few others that OWI might wish to commission. In addition, OWI arranged to purchase suitable French titles published in the province of Quebec, which wartime exigencies had made an international center for printing and publishing in French following the fall of France.[55]

Plans were in far more preliminary stages for other areas to be liberated. Nothing had yet been developed for Dutch- and Flemish-speaking people in the Low Countries, but a committee would be set up soon. A committee had been appointed to plan for the selection and translation of books for the Balkans. This region presented a special problem: translations would almost certainly have to be done abroad because it was proving almost impossible to find competent translators in the United States. Book digests, instead of full book texts, were therefore being considered for the Balkans. Nothing was astir for Czechoslovakia and Hungary yet either. A U.S. firm was actively buying Polish translation rights for a number of titles chosen with an OWI committee, with *Lend-Lease* being the likely first one to be ready. As for Germany, OWI had made a preliminary study of the quite different problem of supplying books for the citizens of the chief aggressor nation once it had been defeated. A committee would be chosen shortly. It was quite likely that books in German suitable for the program could be obtained in Switzerland and Sweden. Some planning had taken place regarding books for those two neutral countries, and examination copies of a number of American books had been sent there (occasionally on microfilm) to allow local publishers to consider taking them on. The other European neutrals—Spain and Portugal—were being treated gingerly because of their fascist regimes. So far, only a Portuguese edition of *Lend-Lease* was in the works. Although the main focus of the stockpiling program was on Europe, some early consideration was being given to Asia. China was the principal objective, so no planning had yet been done for a defeated Japan. The Book Section had already obtained Chinese rights to a few American books that officials at the Chungking outpost had requested and had forwarded microfilm of the books so that the texts could be translated over there. The goal was to have local publishing firms produce the books.[56]

The inadequacies of these various efforts to acquire sufficient quantities of books for liberated civilians from existing sources, or to contract for them with U.S. and foreign publishers, became apparent by March 1944. Petrullo was told "to speed the selection and publication of books in foreign languages for use in liberated areas." Additional staff, particularly "specialists in various book publication operations," were being recruited.[57] The greater sense of urgency stemmed not only from the realization that the invasion was less than two months away and the books would be needed soon afterwards but also from growing concerns that the U.S. program, as it had developed thus far, was no match for either the German use of books as propaganda in occupied as well as neutral countries or the magnitude of the British postliberation book program.

Creating Allied propaganda that could effectively counteract years of Nazi propaganda would not be easy. The Nazis had developed a highly effective program of introducing their own books and other printed materials into both overrun and neutral countries, a program that won the grudging envy of U.S. propagandists.[58] Reports from field officers overseas provided direct testimony as to how extensive the German program had become. For example, the Germans provided great quantities of books, both in German and in translation, in areas from neutral Turkey to occupied France. The selections, according to an OWI report, tended to emphasize "technical and scientific works which reach officers, doctors, engineers, and other professional people...being part of the propaganda line designed to impress foreign peoples with the invincible superiority of the Germans."[59] It would take a great effort to counteract these influences with American and British books. And inasmuch as competition between the United States and Great Britain for market share following the war was increasing, OWI officials were greatly concerned that the U.S. program was still "very modest in comparison with that of the British."[60]

These ideas formed the basis of a proposal for a revised and expanded program of stockpiling that was formally offered on April 12, 1944. The plan observed that "a book program is our only long range program. Because its effects will persist into the future, American publishers are vitally interested over and above their desire to cooperate in the war effort. This cooperation is assured, and is...an important prerequisite in planning our operation at reasonable cost and maximum efficiency."

The new operations plan acceded to the staff members' calls for a larger program, including the matching of Britain's plan to publish translations of a select list of forty titles in a variety of languages, in edition sizes of forty thousand copies. But it would go further, to include the reprinting of ten thousand copies of one hundred fifty titles in the ASE series for distribution in areas where English was widely read by the opinion makers, as well as the purchase of additional titles from Pocket Books and the *Infantry Journal*. Books, some in hardcover, would be directed to OWI and other libraries abroad, but most would be sold to civilians. The plan assumed that most of the books needed would be published by domestic or foreign publishers, but it provided no clear-cut blueprint for how and by whom the necessary translations would be supplied nor did it propose any specific strategy for gaining the cooperation of publishers to issue the translated titles.[61] The difficulties in stockpiling books in London had become so urgent as to constitute its own emergency.[62] Even the revised and expanded program, useful as it might be, provided no guarantee of working. But almost immediately would come a complete reconceptualization of the program, which would ultimately bring hard-won success.

SEEKING "AN INSIDE TRACK TO THE WORLD'S BOOKSHELVES"

No one had become more frustrated by the slow pace of the D-Day stockpiling effort than Harold Guinzburg, and it fell to him to sound the loudest alarm with his stateside colleagues. As head of the Office of War Information's book program in London and working as he did with British counterparts in the Psychological Warfare Bureau, Guinzburg knew how far ahead the British were in the stockpiling race. The delays jeopardized the overall goal of providing desperately needed books for European civilians as soon after D-Day as possible, since under wartime conditions Britain alone could not supply all of the books that were needed. They also threatened to diminish the potential for American books to gain headway in world markets after the war. Since the project was designed to be an emergency measure to fill a critical need in what would become an informational and ideological vacuum following the ouster of the Nazis, Guinzburg worried that the books would arrive so late that indigenous printers and publishers would already have gotten back to business and be able to fill the void themselves. The extent and effectiveness of German propaganda in France and elsewhere continued to be laid bare, underscoring the gravity of the problem of counteracting years of Nazi censorship.[1] To be sure, OWI's stated objective for the operation was deliberately self-limiting—to prime the pump—but having to abort the project before actually delivering any of the American books overseas would have been an enormous disappointment to both the publishers and the government and a serious blow to plans for the postwar future of American books abroad.

This fear is what had prompted Guinzburg to keep urging stateside officials to beef up their efforts, both procedurally and quantitatively. Meanwhile, it appeared that, if nothing changed on the OWI end of PWD/SHAEF, the British would be in a better position to reeducate the liberated populations than the Americans. The OWI people in London had learned that about half of the British books earmarked for shipment to the Continent—hundreds of thousands of books at least—would be ready by June 30. In contrast, the London office of OWI reported in early May that it held in England only twenty-three thousand copies of French books published in the United States from 1940 to 1943, with a second shipment of twenty-one thousand four hundred books dues to be shipped shortly, and a request placed for a third batch. These would certainly not suffice. For Guinzburg, therefore, it was urgent that he receive a much larger stock of French books in London by the middle of the summer at the latest.[2]

Establishing Overseas Editions, Inc.

Chester Kerr had recently rejoined OWI, this time in its overseas branch, headquartered at 224 West Fifty-seventh Street in Manhattan, not far from the Council on Books in Wartime's own quarters at 400 Madison Avenue.[3] As Samuel T. Williamson's special assistant, Kerr was assigned to oversee from the New York end the pre-invasion stockpiling of American books in London and elsewhere.[4] It would therefore be his responsibility to provide the books Guinzburg so desperately wanted. Under present conditions, this would be difficult if not impossible. Operating primarily in response to the specific needs of individual officers abroad had proven to be too scattershot. Relying mainly on acquiring in-stock books was too limiting both in terms of selection of titles and the number of copies of each title. What, then, *should* be done? Guinzburg returned to the United States briefly in early April, during which he and Kerr discussed the defects of the current procedures. They decided that the time had come to view the project "as an entirely new problem," for which they were ready with a solution.[5]

The new idea was to publish a number of existing American books in special paperback editions expressly for the stockpiling program. The titles would be carefully selected for their ability to meet the goals of consolidation propaganda and translated as necessary. The new direction had been a matter of discussion between Kerr and influential members of the Council on Books in Wartime since mid-March. The concept drew upon at least two models. One was the work of the Office of the Coordinator of Inter-American Affairs, which produced translations of American books into Spanish and Portuguese with Rockefeller Foundation financing. In March, publisher Stanley Rinehart, of Farrar & Rinehart, specifically cited the CIAA precedent in asking Kerr about the possibility of getting OWI help to underwrite translations of American books for postliberation purposes and about the feasibility of printing such books in the United States.[6]

At a meeting of CBW's Executive Committee, Rinehart later expanded on the notion, suggesting, according to the minutes, that "OWI with the advice of book-men and foreign writers now living in this country…pick out and arrange for translating certain books which would be ready, in translation, for publication in foreign countries as soon as the presses were freed of Nazi control."[7] Rinehart's statements left unclear whether the books should be printed in the United States or overseas. Production in the United States meant that the books would require a lengthy Atlantic voyage to reach their destinations. Production on newly restored presses in the occupied countries, on the other hand, would require waiting until the infrastructure of printing and publishing were restored. In either case, Executive Committee member Richard Simon, of Simon and Schuster, argued that such a plan would require the full support of the government for it to succeed.[8]

The other model was the Armed Services Editions project. When the acquisition of a wide variety of donated books for soldiers' reading proved to be both inefficient and ineffective, CBW had partnered with the army and navy to undertake a comprehensive, tailor-made series. ASEs themselves might even be used for OWI's purposes, especially if the required paper stock did not have to come out of the publishers' own paper quotas.[9] In any event, perhaps another private/public partnership—this time between OWI and CBW—might accomplish OWI's mission to provide American books for liberated civilians abroad.

Kerr discussed the matter of an alliance between OWI and CBW at the latter's Executive Committee meeting on April 19, 1944.[10] He judged the group's response to be "generally favorable."[11] On April 26, he presented the proposal formally in a letter to council chairman Norton, outlining the government's situation relating to the Allied book program during the consolidation propaganda phase, shortly to be launched.[12] Kerr was at liberty to inform him that the book project was to be conducted at the very highest level of the Allied military command. OWI's operations, he explained, were "to merge with U.S. Army psychological warfare units and their British civilian and military counterparts into something called the PWB [Psychological Warfare Branch; later PWD, Psychological Warfare Division] which is a recognized feature of the coming Allied military operation in Europe and will be under the direct jurisdiction of the Allied commander, General Eisenhower," that is, part of the operations of SHAEF. The ultimate goal was to assist in rehabilitating local publishing facilities, which had for years been under Nazi control, but it seemed necessary, for an estimated three to twelve months, he said, "to prime the pump with Allied publications, prepared in advance for this purpose in New York and London." Kerr assured Norton that OWI had "no wish to set up its own publishing house to supply this need." Rather, the government's interests, and those of the trade, could best be served if the publishers acted "in concert" through CBW.[13]

What Kerr outlined went beyond anything that had previously been considered. He recommended that "another wholly-owned subsidiary to be known as Overseas Editions, Inc." (OEI) and under the same management as Editions for the Armed Services, Inc., be established for the task. To undertake the smaller project without separate incorporation, Norton argued, would be "not only excessively costly and inefficient," but it would also lay CBW open to charges that it was using facilities that had been built up under contracts with the War and Navy departments for the ASEs "in an unauthorized way."[14]

Kerr assured the industry that OEI's books would be kept out of the domestic book market and that there would be "no dumping on the American or any other market of surplus stocks should the war progress so rapidly as to invalidate any part of this program before it can be put into operation." OWI would choose the titles in consultation with CBW, working through established boards and committees already serving the ASE effort, as well as OWI. "The OWI's general aim," he continued, "will be to provide books intended to reacquaint Europeans with the heritage, history, and fundamental makeup of the USA, plus a picture of our role in the war to date."

Kerr reported OWI's "considered opinion" that the oblong ASE format was not appropriate for the OEs, instead favoring an upright format, standard for Penguins and Pocket Books and, more pointedly, for French paperbacks, which would make the American books seem more familiar to Europeans. He explained that PWB would be in charge of distributing the books through lending libraries, propaganda shops, and information centers. All books, except for "a fair number of judiciously placed 'review' copies," were to be sold or rented, not to make a profit "but to avoid handouts and avoid devaluing book markets for rehabilitated local publishers who will follow with their own products." "If I were still a publisher," he disingenuously told Norton in conclusion, he would likely subscribe to such a program out of a desire to continue to put the publishing industry at the wartime government's service and from the knowledge that setting up a central organization to carry out the task "and placing it in [ASE manager Philip van Doren Stern's] able and experienced hands," would mean that "my own printing and paper requirements would not be interfered with nor would those of ASE."[15]

CBW officials were generally supportive of OWI's request. Kerr already had Elmer Davis's approval to commit OWI resources. Gen. Robert McClure, the commanding officer of PWB, endorsed the project as well.[16] One particularly nagging issue was OWI's insistence that the council guarantee delivery of the books at an agreed-upon unit cost of ten cents. The council challenged this point, saying that they would be willing to sell the books at cost (as they were doing for the ASEs) even as they insisted that they were not in a position to put the organization itself or its members at risk of financial loss. They eventually won this point. In any case, they maintained that the lowest unit costs could be achieved only if the total number of copies printed was no less than two million and the edition size of any given title no less than forty to fifty thousand.[17]

The committee established to review and supervise the project from the council's side, which consisted of three prominent publishers—Rinehart, Marshall Best (Viking), and William Sloane (Henry Holt)—judged the suggested program a marked improvement over the way the British were carrying out their program of books for liberated civilians "since the OWI's proposal leaves the operation of its plan in the hands of American private publishing enterprise, while the British system seems to depend on His Majesty's Stationery Office and The Ministry of Information."[18]

OWI's blueprint for the program underscored the collaborative, mutually beneficial relationship between the government and the publishing industry in bridging the gap until local publishing industries got back in business. Shortage and the well-documented hunger for books resulted in "an unmatched opportunity to secure readership for the books we deem most important for implementing our long range propaganda objectives," the policy stated. This important objective for OWI was matched by one embraced by the publishers. During implementation of the program, efforts should be made "to keep channels open for worldwide distribution of American books," the plan continued. "The opportunity exists as it never may again for American books to have an inside track to the world's bookshelves."[19]

In effect, OEI was to serve as a vendor of services for OWI, assuming responsibility for securing the publishing rights to the selected titles, commissioning translations into several foreign languages, and producing the titles ordered by OWI in editions of no fewer than fifty thousand copies. A separate contract between OWI and OEI provided funds for translations, with the government agency also pledging to cover the indeterminate cost of rejected or unneeded translations. The propaganda agency held ultimate responsibility for the selection of titles, although OEI, via the Council on Books in Wartime, would have substantial input. Initial production was keyed to the highest-priority needs of the military and thus would focus on books in French (to meet the most immediate post-Overlord requirements) and in Italian (to meet the needs of the growing number of Italians liberated prior to the time that Italian publishing houses were expected to reemerge). The imprint to appear on the title pages of the books, "Overseas Editions, Inc.," was in accord with OWI's policy against the use of its name in the imprint statement for books destined for the European market, which was based on the agency's belief that it would be "poor propaganda" for the books to bear a government imprint.[20] The OE imprint thus provided cover for the agency. The council's sponsorship, however, was acknowledged in all but German-language editions.

Delays in Getting Under Way

Kerr made his proposal less than six weeks before D-Day, June 6, the beginning of the Allied military invasion of Europe. Back in the British capital, Guinzburg was pleased with the developments at home and hopeful "that we will be able to make up some of the deficiencies in the book field,"[21] but he knew it would still be a daunting task. He confessed to Kerr: "We find ourselves presumably on the eve of the big show with so little printed material on hand that we blush for America's vaunted ability at salesmanship." In fact, the publishers' D-Day, the anticipated flood of American (and British) books onto the European Continent, remained vexingly, frustratingly more distant than Kerr, Guinzburg, and their OWI colleagues expected at the time. Although the new plan for a separate corporation to administer the program held great promise, it brought along some problems of its own, which took time to solve. These difficulties included the definition of exactly what OEs were to be, decisions on where to print the books, the convoluted and protracted process by which titles for the series were selected, financial problems, impediments in the way of obtaining translations, production bottlenecks, and larger, political controversies involving OWI as a whole, especially roadblocks to gaining necessary congressional appropriations.

Once it was determined that the books should not carry a government imprint, issues of an identity for OEs had to be resolved. Robert de Graff, chairman of Pocket Books, Inc., offered to publish the books on behalf of OEI. The firm would make existing plates for titles available for the series, in order "to get a sufficient number of titles ready quickly" and with less expense. He suggested that Pocket Books' "imitators" might also lend their existing plates for suitable titles.[22] All the titles under de Graff's scheme would have been in English, but it no doubt would have launched the project on a fast track. However, this proved to be impossible because the War Production Board would not grant the project a special quota of paper if the Pocket Books imprint were used. De Graff agreed to drop the logo.[23] In the end, Pocket Books enabled OEI to begin operating while awaiting funds from the government by paying for OEI's paper and manufacturing costs, giving it, in effect, an interest-free loan, but only after being assured that the paper would not be charged against the paperback giant's own quota.[24] Although OWI had investigated the possibility of printing consolidation propaganda books in Scandinavian countries, Britain, and, perhaps, the Netherlands in order to avoid the long transit time across the Atlantic, the OE scheme called for production in the United States. Stern was already out scouting possible vendors.[25]

A final decision on the format took time as well, even though Kerr had clearly favored a vertical format that Europeans would find familiar.[26] Although

Guinzburg earlier had recommended using reprinted ASEs for European civilians, he came to agree that the upright format was preferable but not worth adopting if it entailed further delays.[27] As it happened, the service editions played their own small role in introducing American books in Europe, where GIs gave them to civilians or randomly left them behind. Troops also left copies of the books behind in Japan, where they found their way into used bookstores, an unauthorized market that military government apparently did not squelch.[28]

There were also debates about the criteria for selecting the titles for the series. There was never any question that the books must have significant propaganda value by projecting American values and culture to foreigners in the best possible light, but, in doing so, how much emphasis should be given to fiction versus nonfiction? To works of high literary merit as compared with other, perhaps more utilitarian, fare that might get the message across more pointedly if less elegantly?[29] Since books in the series were to appear in several languages in addition to English, finding reliable translators to work quickly, accurately, and with flair was a task that proved troublesome from the start. Since the responsibility for approving translations was OWI's, the chore produced many nightmares for Kerr and his associates over the course of the program.[30]

But it was finances, which were linked to the overall appropriations for OWI, that presented the greatest barrier to launching the project expeditiously. Given the strained relationship between the agency and Congress, a stiff fight was predicted, especially in the House of Representatives.[31] There turned out to be more opposition in the Senate instead. When Davis and other top officials of OWI testified before a subcommittee of the Senate Appropriations Committee (only days before the Normandy invasion), they received an unexpectedly hostile response, particularly from Democratic Senator Kenneth D. McKellar, of Tennessee. In remarking early in the hearing that "we are in a war, you know, and I don't seem to see very much use for books," McKellar put the OWI officials on the defensive throughout their appearance. He particularly questioned "the efficiency of publishing books in foreign languages during a war, especially in a place like France,...which is near as much at war with us as she can be. She has given every aid on earth to Germany; she surrendered for the purpose of giving aid to Germany." The French people were angry with the United States, McKellar added, and so were the Polish, Austrian, Hungarian, and Italian people. "It just seems to me that this wholesale attempt to create a kindly feeling for America during a war is too far-fetched....I do not see what good books will do at all. I think your program of books ought to be stopped." The OWI officials did their best to make it clear to McKellar and his colleagues that the books were going to go into Europe only after the fighting was over and that they would be sold rather than given away. Senator Carl Hayden, Democrat of

Arizona, understood these points and was supportive, but McKellar never got the message. "I would not make war in this way," he told Edward Klauber, OWI's associate director. "I think killing a dozen men in battle would be worth all the books you could send them, because these people are angry with us, and there is no use denying it or bothering about it. We shall have to lick them physically."[32]

Senate opposition delayed the agency's offer of a contract to the Council on Books in Wartime for the OE program until June 22. The value of this contract was one hundred thousand dollars, which came out of the fiscal 1944 budget. The budget for FY 1945 made an additional two hundred fifty thousand dollars available for the program after July 1, for a total of three hundred fifty thousand dollars. These appropriations did not end the project's cash-flow problems, however, because OWI was not legally able to advance money to the council to begin the work. For their part, CBW and its constituent members were unwilling to take on any financial risk for the OE work. Efforts to break the logjam through the government's V-Loan program and the Reconstruction Finance Corporation were unavailing. When, months later, de Graff agreed to allow use of his Pocket Books credit minus the joint imprint and to gain no profit from the program, the last financial hurdle was cleared.[33]

Until funding was assured, the train of discouraging news from the home office left Harold Guinzburg, in London, as fretful as ever about the lack of progress on Overseas Editions. Of course, the earlier stockpiled U.S. publications commingled in crates with British works and deposited on Normandy beaches had begun to circulate in France by early July, but Guinzburg knew these would not suffice. In August, he sent a strongly worded cable to New York, reiterating his fear that the books would arrive too late to do any good. Although the French had been "enthusiastically" receptive to the OEs as long as they represented nothing more than a temporary, emergency response to the need for books, Guinzburg reported that they, along with other Europeans, were concerned about the overall motives of the British and U.S. publication plans, which exhibited "imperialist tendencies." Of course, the French desired to protect their own domestic publishing industry as well as their own interpretation of events. If the books did not arrive soon—that is, before the publishers were back in business—the French and other Europeans would most likely want unprinted paper from the United States rather than finished books, which would deny OWI and the U.S. publishers full control over the program of postliberation propaganda, to say nothing of lost opportunities for publicizing American books abroad.[34]

Guinzburg was not alone in worrying. Williamson, head of the Bureau of Overseas Publications, argued there was "neither the time nor the money to develop the perfect program." Directives should assist the progress of the program, he emphasized, rather than hinder it. "We are late in plans for every area and the swiftness of events is widening the gap," Williamson added, particularly in Italy, where domestic publishing was reestablishing itself faster than expected.[35] Although they were worried that proceeding with the Italian program would create ill will, OWI officials at home decided to forge ahead but reduced the number of Italian titles in the series from fifteen to five. The press run was still to be fifty thousand copies, in anticipation that the impending liberation of northern Italy would supply larger markets for the books.[36]

Launching Transatlantic Editions

By October 1944, it seemed that the delays might indeed force the abandonment of the program. OWI persevered with the OEs but hedged its bets by implementing two other plans. One was to "purchase approximately three hundred thousand low cost books in English from American publishers, mainly for distribution in Western Europe."[37] More importantly and more in keeping with the new strategy, Guinzburg was permitted to publish a smaller, parallel series from the agency's London office, known unofficially as Transatlantic Editions (TEs). London OWI issued ten books translated into French under the imprint "New York: Les Éditions Transatlantique" and an additional ten titles in the Dutch language under the imprint "New York: Uitgave 'Transatlantic.'" These books were produced in England.

The concept of the TEs seems to have been developed around the same time that OWI proposed the OE scheme to the Council on Books in Wartime,[38] and they provided an opportunity for Guinzburg to do something constructive while seething over the painfully slow progress of the OEs back home. Inasmuch as Guinzburg worried that the "emergency period," in which books for Europe were to be supplied from abroad, would end before the books reached their intended customers,[39] the London scheme to produce Transatlantic Editions was an emergency program within an emergency program.

TEs also provided more flexibility than the OEs. While the OEs had to be published in editions of no fewer than fifty thousand copies each if the unit cost were to be within the limit set in the government's contract with OEI, the TEs could be printed in England economically in smaller editions. This made it more appropriate for certain titles to be published in French and, especially, in Dutch.[40] The minimum edition size for the French TEs was twenty thousand copies, which could be increased to forty thousand if demand warranted. For the Dutch books, ten thousand copies were planned for each title.[41] Some ten thousand copies of the French titles were earmarked for Belgian Francophones, and five thousand copies of the Dutch-language titles were reserved for the Flemish population in Belgium.[42] Books manufactured in Britain, of course, could be rushed to their intended markets, while American-made books had to find scarce space on ships for a slow and still-treacherous voyage across the Atlantic.

OWI arranged for production of the TEs in England through the auspices of His Majesty's Stationery Office, the government printer. The British agreed to this reluctantly, naturally concerned about the great shortages of labor, printing facilities, and paper in the country. The provision of text and cover stock for the books specially imported from the United States at least mooted the paper question. In the end, though, carrying out this project for the Yanks was one way in which Britain could help fulfill its obligations to repay U.S. loans through what was called "Reverse Lend-Lease." Still, British discomfort about their cooperation forced OWI to limit the project beyond what it might otherwise have become, canceling plans to add five thousand copies to the agreed-upon press runs for distribution to the Far East out of fear that requesting any changes in the agreement with HMSO would scotch the whole deal.[43]

The London products did not necessarily have to bear a different imprint from those published in New York, but the distinction made sense inasmuch as the Council on Books in Wartime and its subsidiary, OEI, had no direct, official role in the production of the London series because it was not covered by OWI's contract with OEI.[44] In terms of production, the TEs were entirely an OWI enterprise. From the standpoint of the propaganda agency, however, there is no question but that the two series were part of the same grand effort. A note to readers carried on the half title even credited them with having been produced under the auspices not only of CBW but also, as it was worded in French, of "les services d'Information Américains" ("Américains" was replaced by "États-Unis" in some titles). This translates to United States Information Service (USIS), the alias by which OWI operated in the public arena abroad, where the name Office of War Information would make little sense.[45]

Why the London books were called what they were is not clear, but the two imprints clearly conveyed contrasting attitudes towards their presumed audiences. The name Overseas Editions betrayed an imperialist stance, made even more obvious through the presence of a Statue-of-Liberty logo on the covers and the fact that the imprint was rendered in English even in the foreign-language editions.[46] The term *overseas* itself assumed a center-periphery relationship between publisher and audience, between the United States of America and the rest of the world. In contrast, the Transatlantic Editions bore imprints in the French and Dutch languages, not English, and carried no recognizably American graphic symbol on the front cover. Here the relationship is more reciprocal, with the United States and Europe as equals in an Atlantic world. It is not unlikely that Guinzburg, whose sympathies, interests, and activities were highly cosmopolitan, coined the name, since he had suggested that the New York books might also bear the imprint Les Éditions Transatlantique.[47]

The two series differ also in the geopolitical definition of their audiences, a distinction signaled both by their names and a brief note within the front matter. Although the bulk of the OEs were destined for Europe and the Middle East, a number went to the Pacific theater as well. Transatlantic Editions were intended only for Europe. The word *overseas* denotes a broader geographic scope than *transatlantic*. The note on the half title of the OEs declares that these books appeared as an emergency measure until the local book trades could recuperate after the defeat of Axis aggression, while the note in the TEs specifies the resumption of "normal publishing activities" in *Europe*.

Shipping the Books

By early September the various logjams at home had been effectively cleared and the OE project could at last proceed as planned.[48] The London TEs, which began to ship in early 1945, did in fact beat the New York OEs to market.[49] Extant records show that ten thousand copies each of two of the ten French-language Éditions Transatlantique were dispatched by sea for Paris on January 18, 1945, and ten thousand each of a third and fourth title on February 1. A shipment of five hundred copies each of eight French-language books in the series was airlifted to one S. Goldstein for distribution in the Balkan countries on April 24.[50] Sales in Belgium began March 12, and within ten days 10,843 copies had been sold.[51]

In contrast, the first OE titles were not even shipped from the printer in Chicago to OWI's New York warehouse until the middle of February 1945, with the others expected to come off the press over the following three months. Plans called for thirty thousand copies of each of the French-language titles to be distributed in metropolitan France, five thousand for Belgium, and the remaining fifteen thousand to be divided among North Africa, the Balkans, the Near East, and the Far East. Of the English-language OEs, three thousand were to go to France, one thousand to Belgium, three thousand to Holland, one thousand to Norway, one thousand to Denmark, fifteen hundred to Germany, some twelve thousand split among Italy, the Balkans, and the Near East, and about twenty-one thousand to the Far East (nine thousand for China, eight thousand for the Philippines, thirty-five hundred for Japan, and eight hundred for Korea), with the remainder held in reserve.[52] The Italian- and German-language editions were not meant for worldwide distribution, as the French- and English-language titles were. France's allotment for the first six titles were put on sale July 24, following which additional titles reached Europe and fanned out over the Continent.[53]

Getting to that point had required great effort on the part of both OEI and OWI and utilized much of the skill and experience that the civilians in both organizations had brought with them from the publishing world. Still to be described are the formidable challenges of selecting the titles and producing the physical books (most of them in languages other than English), to say nothing of the arduous job PWD/SHAEF and its successors faced of distributing the books to intellectually hungry readers. Some of the tribulations involved were difficult and frustrating enough "to make even Job weep," in Kerr's vivid phrase. But the work done to establish OEI and to select, produce, and distribute the books was fully necessary to achieve the goals that both the government and the industry desired—that American books would help "disintoxicate" the victims of Axis hegemony, win friends for the United States, and put some of the best products of American writers and publishing houses on a track to the bookshelves of the world.

"EVERYONE BUT THE JANITOR" SELECTED THE BOOKS

The Office of War Information had been in the business of selecting books for shipment to civilians abroad ever since Gen. Dwight D. Eisenhower authorized the deployment of consolidation propaganda in advance of the North African and Mediterranean campaigns in 1942–43. The decision made in April 1944 to publish the customized series of Overseas Editions and Transatlantic Editions represented a significant advance over the earlier plan in which the majority of the selected books had to come from existing stocks. Now OWI and its partner, the Council on Books in Wartime, could select titles to meet the government's propaganda needs and the publishers' overseas ambitions head-on and produce the chosen books in sufficient quantities. The new, more elaborate process of selecting books greatly expanded the pool of titles from which to accept. It also complicated and slowed down the process, since, as OWI's Chester Kerr quipped, "everyone but the janitor" had a hand in it.[1]

Because the OEs and the TEs were tailored to fit the needs and capabilities of the Office of War Information and the Council on Books in Wartime, the selection of titles provides a window into both the nature of the propaganda goals of the program and the hopes and expectations of the U.S. publishing industry. During 1944–45, seventy-two editions of forty-one titles were published in the Overseas Editions series, meaning that some titles were published in more than one language. A total of 3,636,074 copies were shipped. OEs ultimately appeared in four languages. Listed in the order in which the decisions to publish in those languages were made, they are French, Italian, English, and German. Series in the Balkan languages, Polish, Chinese, and Japanese were considered but abandoned for various reasons.[2] Books in Chinese and Japanese were still part of the plan as late as March 1945.[3] Since the books were aimed at people in Europe, the Middle East, and Asia, publishing in English was not a given and in fact had been ruled out at one time, but, as Kerr convincingly argued, runs of the titles in English could find audiences in the Low Countries, Scandinavia, eastern Europe, the Balkans, Italy, Arab countries, and the Pacific, reducing, if not eliminating, the need for translations into a greater number of languages.[4]

The TEs appeared in another twenty editions, in two languages, of sixteen different titles. Ten of these were the so-called Éditions Transatlantique, in French; ten were Uitgave "Transatlantic," in Dutch.[5] The press runs of these French- and Dutch-language Transatlantic Editions totaled approximately five hundred thousand copies, making the total number of copies in both series about 4.1 million.

The Strategic Context

Selection was carried out in a broad strategic context. The books chosen had to advance the propaganda goals for the book program, which were in turn derived from the overall goals of the consolidation propaganda effort, both for the United States and Britain separately and, ultimately, under the overall direction of SHAEF's Psychological Warfare Division. Guidance usually took the form of "directives" and "working plans," issued and revised at intervals and conveying either theater-wide strategic goals or aims for a specific country. How the titles would affect intended audiences was another important question demanding consideration. Although OWI continued to produce some leaflets and pamphlets for the consolidation propaganda phase, it privileged books as "the most enduring propaganda of all" and as being particularly suited to reach the elite audiences of civilian European opinion makers who were the primary targets of the operation. The more ephemeral leaflets and magazines may have appealed to the masses, who were assumed to possess only a brief attention span, but books were most appropriate for the long-term reconsideration of whole worldviews.[6] Books were also important in efforts to reeducate Italian and German prisoners of war incarcerated in camps throughout the United States.[7] Having had firsthand experiences with Americans, these men would be expected to take what they learned back to their vanquished communities.

The selection process was both centralized and decentralized. While there was a core of objectives that the United States wanted to accomplish throughout this propaganda effort, the specifics of the message were to be tailored to what one OWI official called "the differing interests, intellects, economics, politics and cultures of our many target areas."[8] Reports and analyses from OWI field officers provided evidence of a number of negative images of the United States that the agency wanted to counteract through the book program. The stereotypes that the operatives reported depicted Americans as being, among other things, "without culture or taste"; "barbarian destroyers of ancient civilizations"; "boastful, rash and superficial"; prone to "terrorism and gangsterism"; and possessors of "far-reaching imperialistic designs."[9]

Similar stereotypes were prevalent in Britain as well. According to opinion research conducted by the Ministry of Information, 30 percent of those questioned found American braggadocio, conceit, and cocksureness their ally's least likable traits. About half that percentage said they were most repelled by the gangsterism, graft, and corruption they believed existed or by Americans' obsession with money.[10] Of course, in return, many GIs training for D-Day in England held negative stereotypes of their hosts as snobs, citizens of a waning power, and not up to the task of fighting the enemy.[11] Even after V-E Day, Wallace Carroll, a senior OWI official, declared that "there is not a European today who has not been influenced" over the previous five years by the Nazi propaganda message that "the United States is a reactionary, capitalist nation dominated by Wall Street and fighting this war for profit in dollars and territory."[12]

Many within and without OWI placed at least part of the blame for the inculcation of many of these negative images on foreigners' access to American popular culture, particularly the movies. It was the Hollywood pictures of stars like Fred Astaire and Ginger Rogers, George Raft and Edward G. Robinson that gave Europeans the impression that most Americans were either well-to-do, fancy-free socialites or craven gangsters cavorting with Capone.[13] But the Nazi propaganda machinery had stated and restated these stereotypes relentlessly in the areas the Third Reich had conquered as well as at home. It is ironic that the great success that U.S. motion-picture producers had in achieving widespread distribution abroad before the war—overseas venues having provided about one-third of the industry's revenues in 1940[14]—contributed to an epic propaganda problem for the United States, and that American book publishers, who had downplayed foreign markets before the war, were called to the rescue. The selection process was thus largely designed to identify books, which were *not* a mass medium, that would counter negative impressions communicated *by* a mass medium, by projecting positive images of Americans and their culture.[15]

Realizing that a more favorable opinion of the United States would be crucial when the time came to make a peace settlement and other postwar arrangements, and fully aware that OWI would be dismantled after the war, the policymakers of the agency elected "to give top priority to topics bearing directly on the attitudes foreigners will have toward our international policies for the immediate postwar period" and "to relate our handling of those topics to a few simple and easily transmittable themes, namely that Americans are well-informed, well-intentioned, progressive, and not standardized." Within each of these themes, OWI directives provided summaries of "desired impressions," treatments, and useful topical themes.[16] The publishers of the OEs and TEs cleverly utilized the books' back-cover blurbs to telegraph these themes to their purchasers and readers in Europe. Thus, Bernard Jaffe's *Men of Science in America* demonstrated that Americans could make great contributions in pure and theoretical science, not just in technology and invention. David A. Lilienthal's *TVA: Democracy on the March* alerted European readers, some of whom were still attracted to the idea of state planning, to the notion that a decentralized, democratic nation like the United States could successfully undertake planning.

Running the Gauntlet of Committees and Boards

The sheer number of committees, advisory boards, and individuals that had to approve titles for use in the stockpiling program, including the OEs and TEs, helps account for some of the delays. For the OEs, Samuel Williamson proposed a screening plan encompassing at least four levels of scrutiny within OWI, including staff in outposts abroad, with advice from the outside committee that advised on the ASEs. OWI's Book Section initiated the selection of titles (accepting suggestions proposed from anyone anywhere within the chain). Then it submitted the list to the New York Review Board for clearance. Those works approved in New York went to a special subcommittee of the Washington Review Board.

If a proposed title survived the Washington subcommittee's scrutiny, it went to the full Washington Review Board. Approval there meant acceptance by OWI as a whole, but the process was not finished. The list then was to go to an "outside independent advisory committee (the same one that served the ASEs)."[17] This group consisted of a number of respected and well-connected members of the U.S. book world: Mark Van Doren (author and critic), Harry Hansen (book reviewer, New York *World-Telegram*), Rosemary Benét (writer and wife of poet Stephen Vincent Benét), Edward Aswell (Harper and Brothers), William Sloane (Henry Holt and Co.), Amy Loveman (*Saturday Review of Literature* and secretary of the Book-of-the-Month Club's selection committee), Joseph Margolies (Brentano's bookstore and American Booksellers Association), and Jennie Flexner (New York Public Library). Benét and Flexner later left the committee, while Louis Untermeyer (poet, critic, and anthologist) joined it.[18] This was the same sort of middlebrow selection committee that defined the Book-of-the-Month Club.[19] The Washington Review Board approved Williamson's plan but recommended, successfully, that the outside advisory board be brought into the process earlier.[20]

Selection was even more complicated in practice. Books that had gone all the way through the committee and advisory-board structure and were approved for the program in general were also vetted by regional advisory committees (with considerable input from personnel in OWI/USIS outposts abroad), which had responsibilities for administering consolidation propaganda activities in, say, Italy, the Balkans, or Germany. A title with OWI's general imprimatur might be judged suitable for the civilian populace in Germany but for some reason not for the Austrian public. Finally, the list of approved titles would "be submitted to all OWI officials concerned with the decision as to which titles should be translated into which languages."[21]

OWI's archives contain dozens of typed and handwritten lists of books, dated and undated, revealing the slow and painstaking workings of this bureaucratic gauntlet. Long lists of nominated books were presented to a committee, where titles were whittled away. Lists of approved titles at one level were circulated to the next higher one. Titles that seem to have been approved on one list appear crossed off on later tabulations. OWI's working goal was to wind up with a list of at least sixty books that had made it all the way up the chain of decision, "out of which the necessary number will be selected for each month's production schedule on the basis of (1) the priorities determined by the Washington Review Board (2) on the basis of an effort to produce a balanced list, and (3) the problem of securing rights, editing, translations, etc."[22] The expectation was to publish forty different titles in the series, a number that deliberately matched the target of the British program.[23]

To complicate the process further, because distribution of the books was a joint U.S. and British responsibility under SHAEF, the titles also had to be cleared with the command's PWD.[24] Moreover, books destined for France, at least, were to be approved by French authorities in Algiers or London.[25] At one time, the Washington office of OWI had eliminated most of the titles still on the list, so Chester Kerr had to plead with colleagues to make additional suggestions. Even if "everyone but the janitor" had a say in the "painful process," he believed the system was capable of producing "a reasonably good list." All in all, Kerr wrote, "these books should remind the Germans that we know how to fight too, that civilization can flourish in Brooklyn, and that it is possible to achieve Strength through Sloppiness."[26] Samuel T. Williamson, Kerr's boss, also complained about the deleterious effects of the disagreements between the various reviewing bodies, noting "that such a condition is bad for morale of the staff of this Bureau....Furthermore, this condition breeds frayed tempers, mistrust, petty quibbling, and feudin' between perfectly decent people in Washington, New York, and abroad who should be getting along together." His judgment was even harsher than Kerr's, grimly comparing the chances of acceptance of a title to "the life expectancy of a Marine on Tarawa."[27]

Propaganda in Disguise

Nearly all of the books approved for OEs were taken—quite deliberately—straight from publishers' current lists or backlists, most of them having been published since the war in Europe began. As an OWI field officer in Europe observed, the books had been "chosen with a canny eye to the 'five-year gap,'" meaning that they were books that Europeans would have had almost no chance to read.[28] The preference for current books had a precedent, having apparently been part of the initial concept of the ASEs, although many older books, including classics, ultimately were included in that enormous series.[29]

Selecting in-print books for OEs had even more to recommend it. "It is the opinion of practically everybody, regardless of class or group, that the best Allied propaganda is No propaganda," wrote one official. By choosing already-published books rather than commissioned works written specifically as propaganda, the agency could vouch that the books were the same ones that Americans were reading at home.[30] Richard Simon, Robert de Graff, and others argued that the best way to avoid overt propaganda was simply to publish "the best American literature," but that goal gave way to the need to choose books, mostly nonfiction and often of slender literary merit, that would more pointedly address specific propaganda objectives.[31] The decision to reissue in-print American titles was certainly an attraction for the publishers who were backing the series, especially those whose books would make it through all the hoops of the selection process. The British preference for commissioning books to meet propaganda objectives directly, rather than to select in-print books that bore the required messages, may well have been more an act of necessity than design inasmuch as there would have been far fewer appropriate British wartime books to consider owing to the decline in authorial output.[32]

Only a few of the American titles were not, strictly speaking, right off the shelves. As Kerr noted, Stephen Vincent Benét's *America* "was especially written for the Office of War Information" but had been published domestically by Farrar. *Prefaces to Peace* was a "dividend of Book Clubs taken from four different books." *U.S. Foreign Policy and U.S. War Aims* was a combination of two books by Walter Lippmann, one old, one new. J. C. Furnas's *How America Lives* originated as a series of articles in the *Ladies' Home Journal* and was published as a book in 1941 but was issued in the OE series with several new, wartime articles added. Kerr asked Furnas to draft a new preface to provide an updated context for the pieces, which would help explain and justify its publication in three languages (actually two in the end) and its distribution in Europe, the Balkans, China, and the Philippines.[33] Furnas complied, noting for the readers of the one hundred fifty thousand copies slated to be printed that the "real, living people and actual places" written about bore no resemblance to the distorted views of Americans that foreigners might possess, stemming in part from the actions of U.S. tourists abroad and the portrayal of Americans in Hollywood films.[34]

For budgetary reasons, a few books, including Carl Van Doren's *Benjamin Franklin*, Alfred Kazin's *On Native Grounds*, and Gilbert Chinard's *Thomas Jefferson*, needed to be abridged by their authors. Ever the hands-on operative, Kerr pro-vided OEI with the exact wording, in English, French, and German, of the note on the verso of the title page, explaining that the book was "abridged by the author to make possible production in this edition."[35] Further editorial changes might occur in the translation process, for the Washington Review Board permitted OWI's edi-tors to make, with the author's permission, "minor changes and condensations" unaffecting "the general tenor of the book," and to permit the author voluntarily to make any changes that he wished.[36]

Even if regular, in-print books were chosen to avoid the taint of propaganda, the books were nevertheless meant to *serve* as propaganda. The lengthy selection process that ensued was designed to identify those titles that would maximize the propaganda benefits, while avoiding as many potential propaganda gaffes as possible. The Washington Review Board directed that its subcommittee on books "present their recommendations and reactions of other committees to the Washington Board in written form, including a brief summary of [the] nature of [the] book, why it was recommended, and [its] propaganda value."[37] Still, the archives are not as complete in documenting the decisions made as one might like. A list that survives from a meeting on July 5, 1944, noted that four titles—Hamilton Basso's *Mainstream,* Constance Rourke's *American Humor,* Robert Trumbull's *The Raft,* and George R. Stewart's *Storm*—had been "que-ried" by the council's Advisory Committee.[38] *Mainstream* and *The Raft* eventu-ally made it into the series, but the other two (*American Humor* and *Storm*) did not. Why did CBW's committee raise special questions about these four books, and how were those questions resolved?

Documentation exists to provide answers about some but not all. What seems clear from the records is that decisions about which titles to approve were based not only on how well the book in question achieved the required positive projection of the United States but also whether anything in the text might of-fend the intended audience and thus be counterproductive. For example, the unnamed official on OWI's French desk who vetted a sample translation of Wil-liam Saroyan's *The Human Comedy* urged that approval of the translation be held up until there could be assurances that the title would be changed. "Mr. Saroyan's conceit in selecting for this little by-product of his brain the very title of Balzac's monumental masterpiece is in itself well-nigh incredible. To call it La Comédie Humaine, would be nothing short of a sacrilege and a sure way to infuriate any thinking Frenchman."[39] The warning apparently was effective. Perhaps Saroyan refused to allow the title change in translation, or OWI never bothered to ask him about it, but in the end the book was omitted from the list of French OEs.

The Raft was one of the books on the agenda for the Washington Review Board's meeting of July 13, 1944. It came with the recommendations of the New

York Review Board and the Washington subcommittee before it. The New York committee called it "a straight narrative of universal appeal, well told and relatively easy to translate into any language." It also used the conversations of the three characters (one of whom was, helpfully, of Polish descent) to project the United States favorably. As a story of survival, "it shouts loudly that man can master almost any fate."

Another title reviewed at that meeting was Donald Hough's *Captain Retread*, which the New York committee "recommended as an excellent and amusing account of the life and character of the American soldier as seen through the eyes of an officer of the first World War. The elimination of references to Americana and to World War II would improve [the] book for foreign audiences." The Washington subcommittee concurred in its suitability, particularly for France and Italy, praising its depiction of the "democratic nature of our Army and our nation." The group, however, urged a change in a passage implying that all Italians supported Mussolini, which was by then no longer the U.S. propaganda line. *Captain Retread* also made it into the series, in English, French, and German, but, interestingly, not in Italian.[40]

A "list of books rejected by the Washington Review Board and considered unsuitable for translation in any language" offers an interesting comparison with the books that were approved and published in the series.[41] One should probably not interpret the use of the word "unsuitable" as necessarily pejorative. It is unlikely that the reviewers found major faults with most of the titles but rather judged that certain intrinsic factors precluded their inclusion in the series, at least in translation. Anna Sewell's *Black Beauty* was probably rejected because it was a nineteenth-century English novel. Or it and the otherwise more suitable, contemporary, American-authored and published animal books—Mary O'Hara's *My Friend Flicka* and Marjorie Kinnan Rawlings's *The Yearling*—failed to make the cut because the series, which was aimed at elite opinion makers, deliberately excluded books for children. Perhaps President Roosevelt's *War Papers*, which almost certainly would have run afoul of the Soldier's Voting Act (which prohibited political materials to circulate to the troops) as an ASE, but not as an OE, was left out because there was little interest in having it translated into foreign languages. Other titles were likely omitted because their genre was already represented in the series. For example, with Rackham Holt's *George Washington Carver* and Jaffe's *Men of Science in America* already accepted, such other books on science as George Gray's *Science at War* and Hans Zinsser's *As I Remember Him* were redundant. Similarly, Gordon Seagrave's *Burma Surgeon* was perhaps not necessary with so many other books about the war in the Pacific already approved.

Other, more challenging titles, such as Charles Beard's *The Republic*, Merle Curti's *The Growth of American Thought*, Vernon L. Parrington's *Main Currents in American Thought*, Erich Fromm's *Escape from Freedom*, *The Education of*

Henry Adams, and Walt Whitman's *Leaves of Grass* had also been rejected.[42] The emphasis on nonfiction may have precluded OWI from tapping into the works of several of the most popular modernist U.S. novelists abroad—Jack London, Upton Sinclair, Sinclair Lewis, and Theodore Dreiser. Of course, many books by these authors exhibited, as British public-opinion surveyors noted, "a sociological and usually a 'debunking' theme," which might have been reason enough to steer clear of them during the emergency period.[43] Sinclair actively lobbied for the inclusion of his works in postliberation translation and publishing programs abroad. He kept in touch with OWI officials from Davis on down, emphasizing the usefulness of his books in the postliberation book programs. He even wrote both President Harry S. Truman and General MacArthur to encourage the translation of his books into Japanese.[44] Actually, the army unit in charge of libraries in U.S. prisoner-of-war camps for German soldiers had ordered Sinclair's book *Presidential Agent* to be kept off the list of approved titles but to "use greatest diplomacy in doing so."[45] Many edgier, more challenging titles did find their way overseas once American and overseas publishers were able to resume the trade in foreign rights, and a few of them—Jack London's *The Call of the Wild* and Mark Twain's *Huckleberry Finn,* for example—were shipped even earlier, alongside but not part of the OE series.[46]

OWI staff in outposts abroad provided considerable input into the selection of titles to be translated into foreign languages and circulated in particular regions. Their knowledge of their territories provided nuanced rationales for choosing or rejecting certain titles. For example, *Victory at Midway,* which the New York Review Board had cleared for Dutch translation as being "excellently written and present[ing] a vivid picture of the War in the Pacific," was criticized by a regional specialist, who cautioned that its depiction of warfare "as a sporting, thrilling and glamorous adventure, just as in the good old days," would not go down well with readers in the Low Countries "who have slowly and very painfully plodded through years of the most ugly and unglamorous warfare" imposed on them by "a pathological, sadistic oppressor."[47]

OWI directives required that the TEs be chosen through the same rigorous process as OEs.[48] The distance between New York and London, however, made communications more difficult and prone to misunderstandings. Guinzburg jumped the gun on at least one occasion by going through with plans to publish Herbert Agar's *A Time for Greatness* even though OWI at one point had turned it down as dated.[49] The London branch was not very successful in recommending titles for the TE series on its own. The war-related books—best sellers at home—on a list of twelve proposed titles might have been rejected as essentially unnecessary since others approved already by Washington met the propaganda aims as well or better. The choice of a basic history of the United States by Allan Nevins and Henry Steele Commager probably doomed London's recommendation of Samuel Eliot Morison and Commager's *The Growth of the American Republic* and, perhaps, Merle Curti's *The Growth of American Thought* as well. A few of the other titles, however, might be thought of as somewhat bolder and more challenging selections than the largely middlebrow works approved for OEs. *American Harvest,* for example, was an anthology of excerpts and shorter works from some of the best U.S. writers between the wars, including Ernest Hemingway, Stephen Vincent Benét, Willa Cather, Erskine Caldwell, T. S. Eliot, Edmund Wilson, Carl Sandburg, and John Steinbeck. A whole Steinbeck anthology was on the list as well. A general disinclination to deal with race questions may have doomed Edwin R. Embree's *Brown Americans.* Joseph C. Grew's *Report from Tokyo* was the only one of the dozen books actually chosen to appear as a TE.

A glimpse at how titles for books in Dutch were chosen illustrates how the TE series both differed from and resembled the OEs. When the latter series was planned, it was expected that the English-language titles could serve effectively in Holland and in other western and northern European countries where English was widely read and spoken, especially by opinion leaders. There was no plan to translate any OEs into Dutch. But it became expedient for the London office of OWI to proceed with the parallel series of the French-language Éditions Transatlantique and the Dutch-language Uitgave "Transatlantic" when the OE project was slow to get off the ground.

The TEs had the same goals as the OEs. They were intended, first, to be an emergency measure, to feed the hunger of Europeans for non-Nazi books only until such time as the domestic publishing trade could get back in business.[50] But supplying solid American books for this interim period was also meant to instill a taste in Europeans for American books even after the local publishers were back in business. The choice of titles for the Netherlands was made in the context of OWI's and SHAEF's overall propaganda strategy for that country.

OWI chose ten titles to translate into Dutch and to take in for sale in Holland.[51] All the titles stemmed from a United States at war, and half of them had the war against Japan as their subject. None of this was accidental. The five books on the war in the Pacific, in particular, were chosen with reference to one of the principal objectives of SHAEF/PWD's Working Plan for the Netherlands: "To interest the Dutch people in the war against Japan and to prepare them for the task of participating in that war which will include the liberation of the Netherlands East Indies."[52] The importance of convincing Europeans that they needed to take an interest in the Pacific war had concerned OWI chief Elmer Davis since early 1943.[53] With the approval of the Dutch Ministry of Education, OWI London made plans to publish these ten books in runs of up to ten thousand copies, at a unit cost, including paper, translation, and rights, of thirty cents, with the expenses being borne by Reverse Lend-Lease funds. The first title to be approved for the list was *The Story of Dr. Wassell,* or, in Dutch, *De Geschiedenis van Dr. Wassell,* by James Hilton.[54] Since the book dealt with the heroic trek across the Dutch East Indian island of Java, following the Japanese invasion, by a dozen wounded U.S. troops under the leadership of a military physician, this first selection was totally on message.

Meanwhile, both OWI and Dutch publishers in exile were looking toward the resumption of free publishing in Holland. The information service's contacts in the Dutch government were confident that domestic publishing would be back in business not long after the cessation of hostilities. Exiled publishers, like Querido, in New York, and the Netherlands Publishing Co., in London, were actively planning their repatriation. Accordingly, OWI decided, in the words of an official, to leave "to these firms the publication of American books of general interest, and that we include in our own programme only books of official status or which obviously describe the American war effort." OWI asked the Netherlands Information Bureau in New York "to recommend titles, from suggestions made by us, of books they believe will be of interest in Holland.[55]

Stockpiling Books for the Pacific Theater

Any preliberation stockpiling of books, pamphlets, and other consolidation-propaganda media for China and other Asian countries presented greater logistical problems for OWI and the military than did similar preparations aimed at the populations in the European theater. Distances to the Pacific theater were formidable, the Philippines at some point would have to substitute for Britain as the nearest stockpiling location, and the questions of which languages to use were particularly perplexing. Finding enough people fluent in Japanese and Chinese to staff the Pacific programs was difficult enough, even without attempts by the Office of Strategic Services to poach some of OWI's best Asian linguists.[56]

But stockpiling for the Pacific theater proceeded nonetheless. Planning for books for the Pacific was able to draw upon preparations already underway for Europe, particularly since OWI strategy had come to rely on a central directive for consolidation propaganda to cover both Europe and the Far East rather than separate directives for each country. The best approach was to work within the lists of titles approved for Europe.[57] With no plan then in train for Japan, China was the principal Asian client for which books were selected.

Even armed with William Sloane's findings from his mission to China in 1942–43,[58] planning for the introduction of American books into the comparatively terra incognita of China presented OWI with greater challenges than planning for Europe did. But consolidation-propaganda objectives for Europe were valid in China as well. They included describing the United States' reasons for and actions in pursuing the war, providing a primer on U.S. history and culture and the contemporary scene, conveying U.S. thinking about the eventual peace and the postwar world.

The conditions to be remedied in China were also similar to those that lay behind the European program. Since 1931 in Manchuria, and 1937 in occupied China, there had been an information vacuum created by the stoppage of the flow of Western books and magazines as well as of books in Chinese "of an informational or controversial nature." In their place were publications carefully produced or controlled by the Japanese occupiers. These included novels as well as schoolbooks written to cast the "new order" in the most favorable light. In areas not under Japanese occupation (mostly in the interior, well away from the coast and major rivers), the situation was little better. Far from the historic lines of communication, the unoccupied areas in the interior were in general not very bookish to begin with. There were few libraries and few Western books to circulate. Paper was scarce, hampering localized production.[59]

OWI's book plan covered both free and occupied China, including Manchuria (called Manchuoko by the Japanese). Beginnings could be made fairly quickly in the free sections and in the unfree regions as they were gradually liberated from the enemy. Given the vastness of the country, anything OWI could do would be "merely a scratch on the surface"—nothing like the much broader coverage envisioned for Europe. Instead the strategy was to make at least an impression by placing distribution points in some thirty urban centers rather than to saturate the whole country. Despite China's widespread illiteracy, OWI believed that many millions of educated Chinese "read serious literature and writings translated from foreign languages" and would be "eager for literature of all kinds." OWI also perceived "considerable demand for English books by an English-reading public of perhaps one million persons." American books in English about the U.S. war effort, postwar plans, and developments in science, technology, and industry during the years China was in an intellectual blackout would particularly appeal to elites, as such titles did in Europe. Books that had been published originally for the home markets in the United States (as OEs had been) "will arouse less suspicion than will material prepared especially for use in China." By supplying American books in English, OWI believed, "we can make a definite impression on the educated and influential individuals whose attitude toward America in the future can be an important force."[60]

OWI's plan for English-language books for China was to produce cheap editions of most of the titles approved for France (including those to be designated as OEs). It is not clear whether these would be drawn from the press runs of the English-language OEs or whether they would be produced separately. At any rate, the plan called for books to be sold, as in Europe, through regular, indigenous bookstores. For China, the price was to be the equivalent of ten cents U.S., that is, 60 percent less than the quarter charged for paperbacks in the States. It was expected that additions to the list would be made from time to time—perhaps some twenty to thirty titles already available commercially in the United States from such paperback publishers as Pocket Books and Penguin Books. A thousand copies each were to be purchased for the China stockpile.[61]

For China, books in the vernacular were almost entirely to be published locally by Chinese firms such as the Commercial Press and the Chung Hwa Book Company, without the pump-priming books introduced into Europe in French, Italian, German, and Dutch through OEs and TEs. Translations might be supplied by OWI or commissioned locally by the publishers. OWI would need to subsidize translations as necessary, likely meaning books that lacked strong sales potential. In the plan as drafted, no specification was made of which Chinese dialects were to be used. The agency would also have to subsidize Chinese publishers to sell at as low a price as possible. To encourage and enable the printing of substantial press runs, the United States would also probably need to supply paper from abroad and, for the long run, to encourage the building of new paper mills in China. The first three titles proposed for publication in Chinese were *Burma Surgeon,* by Gordon Seagrave, *The Story of Dr. Wassell,* by James Hilton, and *America,* by Stephen Vincent Benét.[62]

Selecting titles of value for consolidation propaganda in China was relatively easy; providing instrumentalities that would perform both the nation's propaganda work and the trade's market aspirations was less so. Sloane had returned from his trip to China convinced that the Chinese needed to gain a fuller understanding of the United States to counter the widespread tendency to believe that Western civilization "is rotten at the core" (a prejudice that he was obviously not alone in believing was in part self-inflicted by the Hollywood films that were widely exhibited in Asia). It was imperative, he felt, that "we set up a permanent method, and an official one, of representing the United States to China as truthfully as we can. An American Ministry of Information, or its equivalent, is an absolutely indispensable tool or our postwar Far Eastern policy, and nothing will do more to damp down anti-foreignism and promote mutual understanding than this."[63] Sloane, in short, was among the strongest advocates of the close, mutually beneficial collaboration between the public and private sectors that the war itself had initiated.

How the Books Met Their Goals

How well did the ninety-two editions of OEs and TEs selected through such a convoluted, multifaceted vetting process meet the goals of the Office of War Information and the Council on Books in Wartime? Appendix A records the numbers and detailed characteristics of the two series and provides some documentation for the observations that follow. The selection process itself demonstrates both adherence to broad strategic goals along with a fair amount of improvisation. On the whole, the list shows how well the public and private partners in the enterprise came up with a list of books that would provide useful propaganda to readers without having been written as propaganda and would appeal to the target audience of educated, though not necessarily intellectual, adult opinion makers. They would come from a variety of American publishing houses, allowing a broad cross section of trade publishers to showcase some of their most valuable and timely literary properties before people hungry for new books to read.

That the books in the two series were recent titles and for the most part still present on the publishers' lists of books in print responded directly to the special interests of the publishers in finding customers abroad who would have had, before this, almost no chance of reading them. So, too, the facts that seven of the OE and TE titles had been on best-seller lists in the States[64] and that several had been selections of the Book-of-the-Month Club[65] emphasized the popular appeal and sales potential abroad of OE and TE titles. These same characteristics of the series also advanced the desires of OWI for books that could serve effectively as propaganda without having been written as such and for books that might appeal to a broad cross section of intelligent and educated shapers of opinion. Since the largest category of books had to do with the origins, course, and projected aftermath of the war itself, OWI could feel good about accomplishing the important goal of acquainting foreign civilians with U.S. contributions in the European and Pacific theaters. Since U.S. publishers were uncertain whether the popularity of war books at home would survive into peacetime, they hoped that the deployment of these titles as part of the series might give them a new life overseas.

The selection process clearly favored propaganda value over the literary quality of the books. They were works of topical interest—mostly middlebrow nonfiction books. Alfred Kazin's critique of modern American literature, *On Native Grounds,* perhaps attained the highest "brow level" of all the titles in the combined OEs and TEs. Since the books chosen for the postliberation series were representative of the kinds of topical, bread-and-butter products that had served the publishers well during the war, they had no reason to complain.

Most of the books had been reviewed favorably in the *New York Times.* Several of the reviewers were impressed with the importance of the books' messages for the people of the United States. Thus both supporters and opponents of the Tennessee Valley Authority needed to understand how broadly the project benefited people throughout the country and demonstrated how government could perform social planning democratically and in a businesslike fashion, according to the *Times* reviewer of David Lilienthal's book on the subject.[66] What Alfred Kazin provided his fellow citizens in *On Native Grounds* was a nuanced critique of the theorists Thorstein Veblen and Vernon Parrington along with strong criticism of the extremes of both communist fellow travelers and Southern apologists like

Allen Tate and John Crowe Ransom.[67] Hamilton Basso's book *Mainstream,* which located the legacies of U.S. forebears as diverse as John Smith, Cotton Mather, Thomas Jefferson, P. T. Barnum, and Andrew Carnegie in a fictional "Everyman" named John Applegate, "affirms and renders articulate what most Americans want to believe about their past and their prospects," wrote the reviewer. "In so doing it will help to make the Americans of tomorrow worthy of the promise of the many yesterdays which are here so well realized."[68] None of these reviews suggested that the books might also have important messages for Europeans and other peoples abroad, nor was there any reason that they should have. In selecting these titles for the program, however, OWI understood that American books aimed at provoking audiences in the United States to think could also make good propaganda without being obvious about it.

Among the books receiving unfavorable notices were Saroyan's *The Human Comedy,* which Wallace Stegner characterized as hopelessly naive and sentimental, and Van Doren's biography of Franklin, which Henry Steele Commager found confused and two-dimensional.[69] Another was John Steinbeck's *Bombs Away: The Story of a Bomber Team,* which the U.S. Army Air Forces had commissioned to make a favorable impression on U.S. audiences at home. The *Times* reviewer called Steinbeck's writing "excellent, distinctive prose," but the substance, he said, seemed to have come from "War Department training schedules and recruiting pamphlets." The reviewer was Samuel T. Williamson, who later became the head of OWI's overseas publication program and, as such, Chester Kerr's boss.[70]

OWI's decision to view the program to provide American books to liberated Europeans as "an entirely new problem" led to the ultimately successful twin series of Overseas and Transatlantic Editions. With its partner, the Council on Books in Wartime, OWI published an array of books, in English and in translation, that would meet U.S. propaganda objectives head-on as well as showcase some of American book publishers' hottest properties overseas. The selection of titles for the program—with "everyone but the janitor" taking part—was time consuming, but at least it resulted in a shrewdly chosen series. Unfortunately but understandably, the remaining task of actually producing the volumes also took more time than anticipated. This too became a race to ensure that the books could fulfill their intended propaganda and promotional roles before the book trades of France, Italy, the Netherlands, and many other newly freed countries were able to resume their own publishing, which would be done on their own, rather than on American, terms. But while work proceeded on the OEs and TEs for Europe, OWI also had to consider what sort of a book program to implement for the civilians in the two enemy powers still in the war, Germany and Japan. This turned out to be an even more complex challenge, in which the Overseas Editions could supply only a partial solution.

BOOKS TO PACIFY AND REEDUCATE THE ENEMY

Any book program for the defeated enemy nations of Germany and Japan had to conform to the overall plan for governing the vanquished people during the period of occupation. The U.S. Joint Chiefs of Staff's directive issued to Gen. Dwight D. Eisenhower in September 1944 made the matter clear regarding the former Third Reich: "Germany will not be occupied for the purpose of liberation but as a defeated enemy nation....Your aim is not oppression, but to prevent Germany from ever again becoming a threat to the peace of the world." Eisenhower was given almost absolute power in the governing of the people within the U.S. zone of occupation.[1] Similar attitudes and conditions underlay Gen. Douglas MacArthur's more flamboyant military governorship of Japan.[2]

The earliest planning of programs for stockpiling books had focused on meeting consolidation-propaganda goals for the victimized nations, primarily those in Europe. Only later, after the decision was made to publish the Overseas and Transatlantic Editions, did the military and civilian officials behind the programs begin to contemplate the potential usefulness of good American books in pacifying and reeducating the citizens of the vanquished aggressor nations. This was so in part because the implementation of book programs abroad tracked the flow of military operations in the theaters. It also followed from the political and military decision to demand unconditional surrender from the enemy belligerents, which dictated a quite different tone for the propaganda aimed at their citizens than that intended for civilians in lands that the Axis armies had conquered. In any case, the question of just what to do about books for the enemy nations, in contrast to the liberated territories, did not admit of easy answers. What resulted took much trial and error and turned out to be more problematic than the work undertaken for the overrun countries. Many of the procedures and the criteria affecting the selection of books for friendly countries were found not to be fully applicable to the Axis nations.[3]

For Germany, but not Japan, a second government agency developed a significant book program that ran on a separate track from the Office of War Information's OE and TE series and was aimed at German prisoners of war in camps in the United States, who would soon return to civilian life. Like OWI's books, these volumes were also meant to perform propaganda work as well as to develop markets abroad. This time, however, the POWs would hand-carry the books home, and the publishers hoping for postwar markets were Germans who had taken refuge in the United States. One thing was certain: U.S. presence in Germany would be far more comprehensive and longer lasting than in other countries, necessitating both new approaches to reaching the German people and a different posture toward the rehabilitation of indigenous book publishing.

A Rudimentary Plan for the Japanese

In contrast to Germany, there is little to be said about the rudimentary planning that took place for the use of books in reorienting Japanese civilians away from their militaristic moorings. The surprise atomic bombings of Hiroshima and Nagasaki on August 6 and 9, 1945, followed by Japan's unconditional surrender on August 15, left U.S. officials unprepared to administer the kind of book-based consolidation-propaganda program being implemented in territories liberated from the Third Reich or even in Germany itself. The program's timetable had depended extensively on the calculation that defeating Japan would take another year or so, and only after a costly invasion of the Japanese homeland. To be sure, OWI had done some planning and title selection for the information needs of a liberated Asia and a vanquished Japan. Some publications (probably more ephemeral material than books) were being assembled for shipment to Japan,[4] but this stockpiling scheme was very much unlike the one that OWI put into play for Europe.

OWI had planned for series of OEs translated into Japanese and Chinese to serve the needs of the populations in both the aggressor and overrun nations of Asia, but no work had been done before the new weapons were unleashed. The very contents of the OEs were also predicated on the belief that a long and bloody road lay ahead before Japan would surrender. All the titles that dealt with the U.S. war effort in the Pacific theater were aimed at both counseling Europeans not to expect the United States to spearhead the reconstruction of their countries any time soon and gaining the support of such liberated Allies as France and the Netherlands in helping wrest their own Asian colonies from the Japanese.[5]

But the early and sudden end of the Pacific war trashed those calculations. Not only that, OWI itself went out of business shortly after V-J Day, with many of its duties transferred to the Department of State. The Council on Books in Wartime, OWI's partner on the OE project, was dissolved a few months later. Other plans for a Japanese book program could not be made and implemented until after the U.S. military government for Japan (and its own cadre of publications officers) was in place, but even then the program took several years to develop.[6]

Selecting Books for German Civilians

Planning a book program for a defeated and devastated Germany was particularly tricky because the top echelons of the government and the military were slow to define U.S. policy in general toward Germany, let alone make it known to OWI. Any draft of a German plan therefore had to be flexible. A German translation and publication program could encompass four possibilities—the extension of the OEs into the German language, a program of selling rights for publication of American books by publishers in Germany, the importation of German-language books from Switzerland or Sweden, and the financing of the manufacture of other American books in German printing plants.[7] These were not necessarily mutually exclusive alternatives, just as they had not been in planning for programs for other regions.

OWI had begun to contemplate providing books for German civilians in the spring of 1944, around the same time planning for the overall OE program began. A decision on whether or not the OE project would be extended to Germany, however, was put on hold. For a time, it looked like the Allies might play virtually no direct role in providing books to the former Reich. As late as August, Gen. Robert McClure, the commander of the Psychological Warfare Division of SHAEF, headquartered in London, recommended that Britain and the United States, both jointly and individually, not undertake the publication and exportation of books for German civilians but rather work toward the reestablishment of an indigenous book trade as soon as possible to supply the domestic needs. The importation of books by the British and Americans, officials argued, would both divert scarce Allied resources—labor, paper, and shipping—and produce "a psychological effect contrary to what we desire," which was basically to stimulate the Germans to take ownership of their own rehabilitation toward democratic ways rather than to force their ideas on them, resulting in stiffened opposition.[8]

The possibility of obtaining books from German-language publishers in the neutral countries of Switzerland and Sweden had much to recommend it, including proximity and a good supply in those countries of German-language titles fully capable of doing effective denazification work.[9] But the approach was problematic. U.S. economic and political policy toward the neutrals in general flowed from the popular perception in all the Allied countries that the neutral nations were either enemy sympathizers or amoral vendors of gold and vital war-related supplies to ruthless enemies. In general, the Allies were reluctant to spend limited dollars or sterling on books from the two neutrals, which could well compete with U.S. and British interests.[10] OWI officials eventually did work with publishers in these neutral countries but on a small-enough scale so as to avoid running afoul of Allied policy against stimulating the Swiss and Swedish book trades.[11]

In order to be ready in case PWD/SHAEF ultimately decided in favor of importing Allied books into Germany—a likely scenario, OWI figured—it was necessary at least to begin to approve titles for the program and perhaps to secure rights and translations as well. Even if German-language OEs were not in the end going to be used for Germany itself, they could still be employed effectively in such places as Austria and Czechoslovakia and among German prisoners of war in the United States.[12]

The matter was in fact resolved in favor of importation. The decision was made at the highest levels, that is, with both General Eisenhower and President Roosevelt involved. The president favored a free flow of publications but left the decision to the supreme commander. Eisenhower agreed with the policy as well, at least in principle. In any case, Roosevelt announced, there would be limits on what would be published: "We are not going to lose the peace by giving license to racialists, pan-Germans, Nazis, and militarists so that they can misuse democratic rights in order to attack democracy as Hitler did."[13] The president's statement effectively gave the production of OEs in German the green light.[14] This was a welcome development. The general policy of turning as much production over to the Germans as soon as possible still stood. But, as GIs made their way into the country kilometer by kilometer, the necessity of importing books became increasingly clear. The German publishing trade was not likely to be rehabilitated anytime soon.[15]

Needed in the process of reorienting Germans, in the words of Maj. Douglas Waples, chief of the Publications Section of SHAEF/PWD, were "solid publications...to quiet, inform, and guide the civilian population."[16] The overall objective of the book program—to reach primarily audiences of elites and opinion makers—was reemphasized in the planning for Germany.[17] Whereas the selectors and editors were inclined to accommodate the national and ethnic sensitivities of the overrun regions, including Italy, into their choices, so as not to offend, they took a harder line with respect to the Germans. Consideration of books for inclusion in the entire publications program (not just the OEs) often turned on how well the titles would bring home to the German people not only a favorable projection of U.S. culture and values but also information about German aggression, their conduct of the war, and their war crimes (including the Nazi death camps).[18]

Such a stance was in keeping with the government's strategy of accepting nothing less than unconditional surrender from the Germans, and indeed this political decision informed the selection process. It shaped OWI's policy, as enunciated by the director, Elmer Davis, that it must present to Germans the "hard facts" of their own monstrous behavior during the war.[19] Great care had to be taken, however, "so that no material should be used which has any chance of being discredited in the light of further information."[20] In publicizing the completion of the series, an OWI spokesman characterized the selection of titles in German as being part of "one of the biggest demolition projects of our time. The thing to be demolished is the myth of Germany as an innocent and misunderstood nation, surrounded by envious inferiors and brought to bay only by a stab in the back." The publications "may not be palatable reading matter" for the Germans who buy them, but they may give their audiences "the basis on which to mount their own attack against Nazi attitudes." The messages conveyed were for the long term: "This material, in other words, may not have the immediate effect of a mass barrage, but it will supply the ammunition."[21]

The selectors for Germany agreed on a number of points concerning the proper message to be delivered under this general policy, which at times involved elements of self-censorship. For example, the subject of what was to happen to Germany after the peace was to be avoided. And no books should be approved that "have passages relating to anti-Semitism in the United States."[22] Written evaluations of books up for consideration by selection committees reveal their mind-set on how to regard and to treat their imagined future German audience. An army major argued against Hamilton Basso's *Mainstream* on the grounds that "countless passages afford excellent American documentation for the Goebbels line," including what he regarded as "much too much emphasis upon America as a money-grubbing community." Back in New York, however, Kerr successfully argued just the opposite, that *Mainstream,* along with *How America Lives,* countered the Goebbels take on the American character, much as *The Road to Teheran* thwarted the Nazi propaganda chief's efforts to divide the United States and the Soviet Union "against the national interest of both countries."[23] Another selector, a civilian, contended that *Apartment in Athens,* by Glenway Westcott, ought to be rejected because it gives the impression that "Germans should never be trusted"—not, however, because this might offend Germans, but rather out of a fear that German readers might instead "be very proud of the subtlety and culture of the German protagonist, rather than ashamed of his cruelty."[24]

That German readers were not to be mollycoddled is nowhere clearer than in a memo, inspired by Davis's dictum that "hard facts" needed to be told to the Germans, that Norman Cousins, the influential editor in chief of the *Saturday*

Review of Literature then serving as chairman of OWI's editorial committee for Germany, sent to Harold Guinzburg shortly before Germany's collapse. "Since we continue to be at war with Nazism in a propaganda sense," Cousins wrote, "we must recognize the hard fact that we are not now trying to please, seduce, court, wheedle, flatter, cajole, or pamper the German people. Our job is to eradicate whatever remains of Nazism or the spirit of German militarism. We can do this effectively only by hitting as hard as we can where hitting is to be done."[25]

"In the long run," an "Operational Plan for Germany" stated, "it must be the Germans who must re-educate themselves....Such re-education presupposes the full realization of what the Nazis have done to other nations."[26] These were the hard facts that Davis and Cousins insisted had to be told to the Germans. As it happened, though, most of the hard-hitting was done by means of the more ephemeral pamphlet and magazine literature. None of the German OEs, for example, dealt with the extermination of Jews or other Nazi war crimes. To do so would have required a book commissioned for the purpose, which would have run counter to the overall plan of using books previously published and read by Americans.

By November, OWI was ready to choose books for Germany. Among the many committees and other bodies to participate in the decision was the German desk of OWI London, headed by Hellmut Lehmann-Haupt. The task was to make recommendations from the basic list of forty titles cleared for OEs in any language. The German desk went beyond this mandate and suggested other titles to be considered as well. Lehmann-Haupt grouped the suggestions under three heads, providing rationales for the choices. For the section on "American History," books by James Truslow Adams, Charles Beard, Robert Birley, D. W. Brogan, Samuel Eliot Morison and Henry S. Commager, Allan Nevins and Commager, Carl Sandburg, and Arthur Schlesinger Sr. would counter Nazi distortion of the United States by emphasizing "the gradual development of present-day American institutions by a process of trial and error" and by explaining "the less creditable events rather than gloss them over, thus showing that the growth of the USA was no easy and painless process but was only achieved by the constant exertions of her citizens." Only by being presented with "an honest and properly balanced interpretation of American history" would the Germans be disposed to accept the arguments. Under the rubric of U.S. problems, books by Merle Curti, John Dos Passos, Edwin Embree, and Frank H. Knight would "serve our ultimate purpose better than over idealized or limited pictures of men and conditions. Such reasonable and honest accounts may also be of practical value to the Germans in their difficult task of reorientation."[27] No titles on this challenging list were adopted for the OE series, though many if not all of the books likely entered Germany in post-SHAEF programs. Interestingly, it was recommended that explication of the war against Japan be an integral part of the German program, as it was for the overrun nations, in part to underscore the fact that the United States was powerful enough to help defeat Germany with, in effect, one hand tied behind its back.[28]

PWD/SHAEF had no doubts as to the potential effectiveness of a book program for Germany, "traditionally a book reading country, where the printed word in book form enjoys the greatest prestige and can be of very great and lasting influence." In fact, OWI reasoned, for Germany, "books can perhaps be employed more effectively in carrying out our Long Range objectives than any other use of the printed word." A British army officer, Capt. Curtis Brown, a member of the family that owned one of the largest literary agencies in London, with an important branch in New York, was assigned the duty of liaising between PWD and the civilian agencies.[29] An early task would be to take firm control of the German book trade, before it could be allowed to operate and flourish on its own. Before the goal of restoring "publishing on a free basis and the encouragement of non-Nazi authors who can themselves speak to the German people in their own idiom," could be attained, it was "essential to eliminate certain classes of books and the firms and personalities responsible for their publication."[30] This led to a system of purging the bad apples—Nazi party members and sympathizers—from participation in the book trades and the licensing of a cadre of new and presumably clean practitioners, a system that applied throughout German society. Under these circumstances, the German OEs, unlike those in English, French, and even Italian, carried no notice on their covers that they were being published and distributed as an emergency measure, that is, only until a free German publishing industry could arise (and only with the permission of the Allies).[31]

Using Books in the Reeducation of Prisoners of War

While the OWI and the Council on Books and Wartime were busy developing the OEs and TEs, quite different elements of the government and the publishing industry also began work on projects to challenge the hegemony of Axis thought. The players were, on the private side, an eclectic mix of German publishers exiled in the United States, an ambitious professional publication for soldiers called the *Infantry Journal*, and the U.S. branch of Penguin Books. The governmental entity was the army's Office of the Provost Marshal General, the unit responsible for German, Italian, and Japanese prisoners of war housed in camps throughout the United States. The three hundred seventy-nine thousand German POWs in the United States were the intended audience for these publications rather than the civilian populations targeted by the OEs and TEs, but the objectives were similar, that is, to calm the people who read them, to win their hearts and minds, and to cleanse them of Nazi, fascist, and militaristic thinking. As was the case with the native trade publishers and the OWI, the POW publishing programs mutually advanced the goals of the publishers involved and the government, in this case, OPMG.

The decision to ship Axis prisoners to the United States was made in early 1942, when the government realized how difficult it would be to hold the expected magnitude of detainees within the theaters of combat. Moreover, in August, the United States agreed to Britain's request to relieve it of some of its burden of interning enemy POWs, who already numbered as many as a quarter million, in the small island nation that was rapidly filling up with hundreds of thousands of GIs. The United States began to do this within several months. Later, the German prisoners would be brought to the States directly from the battlefields of North Africa, Italy, France, and other western European countries in the aftermath of the Normandy invasion.[32] In contrast, nearly two-thirds of the captured Italian soldiers remained in Italy and North Africa.[33] Only 5,435 Japanese prisoners were held in the United States.[34]

For much of the war, U.S. politicians and military officials were content to demand nothing of the hundreds of thousands of prisoners in U.S. camps other than to provide crucial labor on farms and in forests.[35] Along with a relatively small number of organizations and individuals, German émigrés in the United States were eager for the government to make an effort to denazify, or reeducate, the captured German soldiers on their soil but were unhappy with government officials' reluctance to utilize their talents and skills in a reeducation process. The British, in contrast, made more use of their German refugee intellectuals in various efforts to change their captives' worldview.[36] The Roosevelt administration had little interest or hope that reeducation efforts aimed at such a brutal and bitter enemy could ever prove effective. Rather, it employed heavy strategic bombing and a policy of requiring unconditional surrender to destroy the Reich's infrastructure so thoroughly that neither Nazism nor any other form of fascism could ever again take root.[37]

There were other reasons to reject reeducation programs. Some derived from concerns, importantly held by Maj. Gen. Allen W. Gullion, the PMG, that doing so would violate the Geneva Convention and risk retaliatory indoctrination efforts on captured American soldiers. Others grew out of fear that any such efforts would produce a dangerous ideological counter reaction among the targeted audience. Using propaganda to reeducate German POWs, the sociologist Talcott Parsons argued, could just as easily result in a tilt toward Communism as to democracy.[38]

By mid-1944, however, attitudes about reeducating Axis prisoners of war began to shift, thanks in part to public opinion and Eleanor Roosevelt's intercession with her husband.[39] As the government's thinking about the problem of POW reeducation evolved, making no effort to reeducate Germans at all, it seemed, could by default lead them to embrace other unpalatable ideologies, like communism. At the very least, a reeducation program could, as Secretary of War Henry L. Stimson argued, remake Germans in the image of Americans, so as to become dependable allies in future international conflicts. Since it would be impossible to begin to indoctrinate German civilians in their homeland until victory was secured, making the effort to reeducate German POWs could serve as basic training for the larger task ahead, a strategy that the British had adopted earlier. Still, the Geneva convention remained an obstacle. It had been decided from the beginning of OPMG's study (and initial rejection) of a POW reeducation program that even its contemplation had to be considered as secret. As the War Department parsed the language of the Geneva convention after President and Mrs. Roosevelt applied pressure, it looked for and found a loophole, in Article 17, which stated that, "So far as possible, belligerents shall encourage intellectual diversions and sports organized by prisoners of war." To officials at both War and State, this provision meant "that if selected media for intellectual diversion were made available in the camps, the curiosity of the prisoners concerning the United States and its institutions would provide the means for their reeducation."[40] There does not seem to have been any similar concerted program to reeducate the Italian POWs, who nevertheless had access to magazines, newspapers, and books, including the Italian-language titles in the Overseas Editions.[41]

Once it got under way, the effort to reeducate German prisoners in the United States took several forms, all overseen by the new Special Projects Division of the OPMG.[42] Most of these included providing POWs with ideologically safe material to read while interned, including material to be read in the growing camp libraries or supplied to the inmates individually. Some program materials, like the official national POW newspaper, *Der Ruf* (*The Call*), were edited by SPD officers. Other reading matter came from outside sources—U.S. magazines and newspapers in English as well as newspapers and books in German, published in both Germany and the United States, from the War Prisoners' Aid Committee of the International YMCA and the International Red Cross and other aid organizations, from émigré booksellers in the United States, such as Friedrich Krause and Wieland Herzfelde's Seven Seas Bookshop in New York, from fellow émigrés as far away as Chile, and even from the German government itself, in the form of some textbooks.

Krause and Herzfelde's firm each week filled large orders for titles printed in German outside Germany for prisoners in the camps.[43] Some of the books donated to the pre-ASE Victory Book Campaigns for U.S. troops were "carefully selected" and sent to libraries for German and Italian POWs in the States.[44] The North American representative of International Student Services, another provider of books for POWs, personally went to great lengths to locate a rare or out-of-print book specially needed by a prisoner to facilitate his study of a particular field.[45] This was not easy, since copies of German-language books were in short supply in the United States even when demand had been slack. In time, enterprising secondhand book dealers saw a potential market in this, and began to send their catalogs to all of the POW camps. Since most of the titles listed in any given catalog were naturally represented by a single copy, the orders for these single copies coming from many camp librarians inadvertently stimulated a sellers' market. Soon the dealers were commanding upwards of ten dollars per copy, an unexpected version of war profiteering. Camp libraries in time grew fairly large. At Camp Hearne, Texas, in 1945, some seven thousand books in German and five hundred in English were available in the library for the camp's four thousand inmates.[46]

It was inevitable that a number of the books deposited in camp libraries bore traces of Nazi ideology. The authorities adopted a policy of screening books delivered to the camps as well as weeding undesirable titles already there, but the work did not really get under way until after V-E Day when the prospect of hundreds of thousands of war prisoners returning home sooner rather than later put real urgency into the matter.[47] The SPD prepared guidelines for camp personnel to use in judging whether or not to reject a book. "All books which misinterpret...the significance of the contribution of all races" were to be banned, mostly, no doubt, as a way to keep anti-Semitic writings out of the camps. Also proscribed were books that were filled with "contempt for America as a country without its own 'culture,' without a 'soul,' a country which is only interested in making money," precisely the stereotypes that the OWI's OEs and TEs were meant to counteract. Any books characterizing the armistice ending World War I as a "stab in the back" were to be avoided, as were books unsympathetic to U.S. allies, including the Soviet Union. Interestingly, the policy statement cautioned camp officers to be more careful in selecting books than films precisely because incendiary books could have a longer-lasting effect, and not necessarily a good one. "While the impression a film might make wears off after a certain period of time, the impression of a book does not," according to the guidelines. "The book actually remains in the possession of the prisoners. It can be re-read and made the basis for subversive Nazi activities."[48]

Ferreting out Nazi propaganda necessarily involved an elaborate procedure for examining both English- and German-language books. In this effort, SPD officers enlisted the assistance of trusted, anti-Nazi German POWs. For every proposed title, the trusties were to fill out a standard response form, giving a brief synopsis of the work, making a recommendation as to the book's "suitability" for distribution to all prisoners or only "safe" segments, and suggesting whether it might be sold in camp canteens or restricted to use in libraries. The task of the officers in charge of the camp libraries was later eased by the preparation of a long list of approved and unapproved titles under the guidelines.[49]

Making a more exacting, though still formulaic, deselection of a large, heterogeneous assortment of library material could do only so much, however, so the OPMG took the important further step of obtaining books and pamphlets published specifically for the German POWs, just as OWI had seen the need for a custom-built publications program, namely, the OEs. The OPMG had begun, in the fall of 1944, to plan ways in which new books, both in English and in German translation, could be acquired in sufficient quantities to be sold to German captives in the canteens of the prison camps throughout the United States. Among the various sources of such books were the twenty-three German-language titles published as OEs; books published by the War Prisoners' Aid agency of the International YMCA, which had considerable experience with POW matters both in the United States and abroad plus the benefits of neutrality; the textbooks published by the United States Armed Forces Institute for courses given to U.S. military and naval personnel; and the Fighting Forces series of paperback books published by the *Infantry Journal,* some in association with Penguin and some on its own.

German émigré publishers were also keenly interested in the problem of supplying books to the POWs. For them, the war offered up potential markets on both sides of the Atlantic—the sizable prisoner-of-war contingent in the United States and, across the water, the benumbed citizens of the vanquished Third Reich, whom the repatriated POWs would soon join. Two refugee firms were particularly attentive. One was the house of Bermann-Fischer, and the other was the Aurora Verlag, which had been founded at least in part with the goal of providing prisoners with German books untainted by Nazi ideology.

Creation of the Bücherreihe Neue Welt Series

It fell to Bermann-Fischer Verlag of New York to make the greatest contribution toward reeducating German POWs in the United States through books via the series Bücherreihe Neue Welt, or "New World Bookshelf." Produced in association with the OPMG, the series consisted of twenty-two titles, in twenty-four volumes, in the German language to be sold at twenty-five cents apiece in the canteens of U.S. POW camps.[50] First printing was to be ten thousand copies of each title. The *Infantry Journal,* which had already undertaken a significant program of book publications for army personnel, served as a silent partner in the program.[51] Penguin Books, whose U.S. branch had extensive ties to the *Infantry Journal,* was even more invisible. Like the reeducation effort in general, this project was carried out in great secrecy until V-E Day. The program merits extended attention for the interesting comparisons and contrasts it bears on the larger governmental book-publishing program aimed at denazifying European thought, the OEs and TEs.

Charging a quarter for the books rather than giving them away made sense since the books were the products of a commercial publisher, Bermann-Fischer Verlag, but it had the greater advantage of demonstrating that buying the books was an act of free will, that prisoners who purchased the books had not been coerced into reading them, which might have been illegal under the Geneva convention. Selling the books was feasible because the POWs had discretionary cash to spend from work performed in and around the camps, in accordance with Geneva rules. Enlisted men were paid a maximum of eighty cents for a day's work. Interned officers were paid a salary of twenty to forty dollars per month, depending on rank, whether they worked or not.[52]

Gottfried Bermann-Fischer had been put in touch with the SPD by the Office of Strategic Services as being "an expert on German books and especially on the importance of the German book market."[53] What he also had going for him was his ownership of the copyright on many of the books in German by leading antifascist authors, several of them themselves exiles, and held stocks of these in Sweden, Holland, and Switzerland. Also, he had already published in Stockholm a German translation of one of the titles by a U.S. author ultimately chosen, John Scott's *Jenseits des Ural.*

Lt. Col. Edward Davison, the head of the SPD, made an inspired choice when he plucked Lt. (later Capt.) Walter Schoenstedt from the army's Morale Division to serve as point man for this undertaking. The staff of OPMG lamentably included few people with a requisite knowledge of German culture and language, and Davison was not one of them. Most of the highly talented Germanists in the military had already been recruited by the more glamorous branches focused on intelligence and psychological warfare. Schoenstedt, on the other hand, was a German native, recently naturalized as a U.S. citizen, a former associate editor of a liberal Berlin newspaper, and a moderately well-known novelist. What's more, he had been an ardent communist in his youth but later exchanged that ideology for American-style liberalism.[54] An exiled German intellectual himself, he would have been thoroughly familiar with Bermann-Fischer, at least by reputation.

Negotiations proceeded toward an agreement between SPD and Bermann-Fischer. His ownership of the U.S. German-language rights to publish such an impressive group of books was key since it promised savings not only of money but also of the time that otherwise would have been spent clearing rights, a difficult-enough task in the best of times but almost impossible in the particular wartime circumstances.[55] *Infantry Journal* would oversee production, with a high-level staff member of Penguin USA serving as an intermediary.

That man was Kurt Enoch, who himself cast a wide shadow in both European and U.S. publishing circles in the first half of the twentieth century. A Hamburg-born Jew, Enoch took over the family book and magazine business. He was in time drawn into a partnership with two other publishers to form Albatross Modern Continental Library to compete directly with the venerable but increasingly ossified Tauchnitz Edition series of books in English for the European market. In 1934 Albatross bought out Tauchnitz. Two years later, Enoch left Germany to work for Albatross in Paris. After the fall of France, Enoch—"now stateless, having been expatriated by Hitler"—made his own harrowing journey to New York, where he inserted himself in the community of fellow refugee publishers. He quickly observed how the U.S. book world differed from the European. Bookstores were in short supply, literary agents had great influence, comparatively vast sums were spent on advertising and promotion, and backlists and the classics were neglected. In his long career in paperback publishing, he sought to profit by overcoming those conditions. Soon, Allen Lane, the founder of Penguin Books, made him a vice president of Penguin's new U.S. branch, to take charge of design and production, while the firm's head, Ian Ballantine, concentrated on sales and distribution.[56]

The United States' entry into World War II saved Penguin USA. Ballantine and Colonel Greene of the *Infantry Journal* struck a deal to publish a series of paperbacks on war-related topics for inclusion, at government expense, in basic kits for service members, with surplus copies to be sold to civilians. Greene was under instructions from his own superiors not to incur any business risks.[57] *Infantry Journal*'s substantial paper quota could be tapped for Penguin's use in joint ventures, most of which were issued under the rubric the Fighting Forces Series.[58]

Since Bermann-Fischer was not only fiercely anti-Nazi but also unencumbered by the leftist leanings of Aurora Verlag's Wieland Herzfelde, who characterized his competitor as the "right-wing of exiled publishing houses,"[59] his firm was a politically and ideologically safe partner for the government. Ironically, most of the titles he offered to OPMG were written by left-leaning authors, but given the fact that they were mostly books that the Nazis had banned or burned, their usefulness for the purposes at hand was undeniable.

Since Bermann-Fischer's eye was, from the beginning, on the postwar market in Germany, he was particularly anxious that selling the BNW books in the POW market would in no way compromise his marketing them later in Germany and other liberated parts of Europe. This meant keeping the books out of hands of the civilian population in the United States or abroad, in occupied or nonoccupied territories, and ensuring that his contract with OPMG could not be transferred to some other army unit for use in the occupation of Germany.[60]

Selecting the BNWs

Choosing the BNW titles was considerably easier than the task that Chester Kerr and his colleagues at OWI faced for the OEs. In a sense, the selections or, more accurately, the relatively small pool of titles from which the choices were made, were predestined once Bermann-Fischer joined the project. The German titles under his control, all but one by liberal, fervently anti-Nazi refugee German intellectuals, provided the core, to be supplemented by several works by U.S. and other authors and a single earlier German classic, by Heinrich Heine. All, however, had to meet the general criteria already established for books to be introduced under any circumstances into the camps, which was no problem for Bermann-Fischer's titles. Most of them—all of the works of German authorship and all but one of the books by Americans—were virtually ready to go, thanks to Bermann-Fischer's control of the rights for German-language publication in the United States. The exception was Benét's *Amerika,* which had been commissioned by OWI.

This is not to say that there was no selection process at all. Other Bermann-Fischer titles were considered and rejected by OPMG officials.[61] As was the case with OEs, names appear in one list in the records of OPMG only to disappear in a subsequent tally. For example, what he judged as unfavorable reports soured Davison on *Wie war das möglich,* by Kurt Stechert. He expected he would receive the same kind of negative reports on another title already on the current list, *Friede ohne Sicherheit,* by Fritz Rück. Both were dropped from the list (as numbers twenty-three and twenty-four), but probably as much because the books were not available in the United States and might be difficult to procure from Bermann-Fischer's warehouse in Stockholm as on account of negative reports.[62] Other books deleted from a list were *Pelle der Eroberer,* by Martin Andersen-Nexö, and *Marie Antoinette,* by Stefan Zweig, which had appeared as first choice and alternate, respectively, for title number sixteen.[63] It seems unlikely that many books other than those to which Bermann-Fischer held rights were seriously considered. Given the secrecy of the project, the partners in the POW publishing program could hardly cast a wide, public net for nominations. After V-E Day and subsequent publicity about the series, suggestions for additions of titles not controlled by Bermann-Fischer were made. But a contemplated second series was not undertaken, and so it was too late.[64]

In early April 1945, the OPMG issued a memorandum headed "Justification of the Selection for the First Series of the Buecherreihe Neue Welt." That first word seems an honest one, for the memo really is a justification, even an after-the-fact rationalization, of choices made largely from few options, that is, from within the small pool of books under Bermann-Fischer's control. Elements of the justification include assertions that the series was undertaken "at the request of prisoners of war and because of a scarcity of reading material in the German language," that under the circumstances the books had to be both inexpensive and produced with as little consumption of critical war materials as possible, and that, since the series was "a useful experiment," it was "necessary to select for the first series books the copyrights for which were available without difficulties or costs."[65]

The memo further stated that "the selection of the various titles can be justified" by the general criteria mentioned above and then by what it termed "detailed considerations" regarding each title. These were brief, hardly "detailed" descriptions of the books in terms of desired propaganda goals, which followed. The author of the memo arranged the titles in two main groups. The first was headed "Six books of translations into the German language, five of which are books by American authors[, which] is to be explained by the fact that German translations of such books are not easily available in this country." Here are sample descriptions (in their entirety) from this category:

Amerika by Stephen Vincent Benét.
This volume has been explicitly written with the aim of making the foreigner familiar with the main features of American history and American life. A special translation and edition was provided to fit the needs of the prisoners of war.

Wem die Stunde schlägt by Ernest Hemingway.
A representative novel by an American writer.

Jenseits des Ural by John Scott.
This book was included because of the need to counter-attack Dr. Goebbels's propaganda on Soviet Russia by an objective account of conditions in that country. This book also is apt to provide a healthy respect for the Russian achievements in this war.

The second group, "Books by German authors," was intended, "on the one hand to present to the prisoners of war truly great German culture in examples which were, before these reprints, no longer available in this country, and on the other hand, to make the prisoners of war familiar with some of the important works which had been banned by the Nazis." Descriptions of books in this category include:

Die schoensten Erzaelungen deutscher romantiker.
This volume illustrates peaceful German romantic writing at its best and shows unmartial values in German civilization.

Der Zauberberg I and *Der Zauberberg II* by Thomas Mann.
The most important novel by the greatest living German author, who exiled himself because of his disliking of the Nazis. This particular work recommends itself by the famous long-drawn conversations between a defendant and a critic on the values of western civilization.

Der Hauptmann von Köpenick by Carl Zuckmayer.
Very amusing satire on the stupidity of the German adoration of uniforms and officialdom.

Radetzky March by Joseph Roth.
A historical novel with an Austrian background with special appeal to Austrian prisoners of war.

Im Westen nichts neues by Erich Maria Remarque.
A novel which became known all over the world because of its objective account of the horrors of war. The novel was extremely popular in Germany but was viciously attacked by the Nazis ever since its publication.

The descriptions of the twenty-two titles in the series are hardly rigorous or even highly explanatory of their possible uses in the reeducation of German prisoners of war. They are little more than blurbs, though not as carefully written as most dust-jacket endorsements. They were no doubt primarily intended to give politicians, the press, and the public some information about the contents of the series, but not too much. In fact, the report's basic concept, if not the exact language, was emulated in a pair of documents prepared several weeks later—one that was in effect the draft of a press release about the program, to be ready when necessary, and the other essentially a repeat of the brief descriptions rationalizing the title selections, to be available "should questions be made by official agencies that are aware of the program." If and when the program was declassified, this paper could also be released to the public.[66]

The papers reiterated the basic context and criteria for the project, as defined in the early memorandum, but with important amplifications here and there. For example, the statement went beyond the earlier version by cleverly recasting the "intellectual diversion" clause of the Geneva convention as mandating the reeducation program rather than merely furnishing a loophole for it. It also made clear that the internees would purchase the books, leaving the U.S. taxpayer off the hook for the bill. The new version made even more of the necessity of working easily and inexpensively around the issues of copyrights. The release revealed that the *Infantry Journal* had been engaged "to arrange all details for the actual publication." Moreover, it acknowledged that, by means of the cooperation of Bermann-Fischer, "a list of books meeting the above specifications was obtained." What was more, the titles were "of high literary merit."

The document postulates an overall scheme for the series that also seems largely to be a retroactive formulation rather than an original mission statement: "It was decided that the selection of books should contain as nearly as possible equal selections of German and American literature." OPMG admitted, however, that parity was unachievable under the circumstances. As the release put it, "Obviously it would be possible to reflect upon the history of American literature and select at random titles of books which might better further the program than the selections listed," but the stipulations regarding easy and economical access to rights holders and to translations from English into German "had to be referred to constantly." Nevertheless, OPMG believed, "the selection fortunately represents American literature which will decidedly benefit the program despite the necessary limitation of choice." In this version, the original blurb for Hemingway's *Wem die Stunde schlägt*, probably the lamest of all of them, had nine words added to it so that it read, "A representative novel by an American writer describing the fight of the common people against totalitarianism."[67]

Comparing the titles selected for the Bücherreihe Neue Welt series with the choices made for the Overseas and Transatlantic Editions is like comparing apples and oranges, though more interesting. First, of the twenty-two titles in the series, only five were American books, while the OEs and TEs were, by design, virtually all American. Except for the books by the Frenchwoman Eve Curie and the Polish-born British writer Joseph Conrad, the remaining authors were German or Austrian. Of the five American books, three appeared as OEs or TEs— Benét's *Amerika* (in English, German, Italian, and French, as a TE); Hemingway's *For Whom the Bell Tolls* (in English); and Saroyan's *The Human Comedy* (in English and Italian). Probably only one of the two American works not selected for the OWI-produced series *could* have been. The exception is John Scott's *Jenseits des Ural* [*Behind the Urals: An American Worker in Russia's City of Steel*], whose sympathetic view of the Soviet Union might have been too left of center to prevail over the much more complex set of hurdles built into OWI's selection process. On the other hand, both series featured modern works. Of the German and Austrian literary works chosen for BNW, only one—Heinrich Heine's *Meisterwerke in Vers und Prosa*—dated from before the twentieth century. The rest were works of the twentieth century. The OE and TE titles were more contemporary, mostly published from 1941 to 1945, to showcase representative American books that would not have been available to their prospective audiences while the war was going on. Unlike the OWI-produced series, which were mostly middlebrow works, the BNWs were more challenging. Several had already achieved the status of literary classics or would subsequently gain it.

Just as most of the OEs and TEs were valuable literary properties to their original American publishers, most of the books chosen for the POWs held considerable value as well—not so much to American publishers, but to Bermann-Fischer, who aspired to reintroduce them, under the distinguished imprint of S. Fischer Verlag, later in his native Germany after the BNW editions had paved the way. Their authors were among the intelligentsia who had fled Nazi Germany in the 1930s to various places, primarily the United States.[68] All of the German or Austrian authors were Jewish except for Mann, Zuckmayer, and Remarque. Most if not all of the German books on the list were by authors whose works were burned or banned by Goebbels and his thugs as "un-German."[69] Perhaps the most interesting comparison between the OPMG and OWI series is that the

OE and TE titles were selected mainly to give the lie to Goebbels's propaganda about U.S. shallowness and corruption, while the BNW selections were meant to contradict Goebbels about Germany's historic mission and its invincibility. In this sense, the BNWs better fulfilled OWI's desire, as voiced by Norman Cousins, to hit the Germans hard, than its own series did.

Finally, the BNW series also suffered from delays but none as serious as those that faced OEs. The involvement of Bermann-Fischer obviated almost all of the problems that slowed OWI's venture. The only major problems the BNW team faced were for *Im Westen nichts neues* by Remarque, who for a while balked at the assignment of rights, and *Amerika* by Benét, over the translation. OPMG had planned to use the German translation provided by OWI, but BNW rejected it on the advice of experts, who judged it as ranging from "adequate" to "bad in many spots," and had to obtain a better one.[70] Although it was listed as number one in the series, *Amerika* apparently came out last, probably because of the translation delays and a small bit of censorship.[71]

OPMG's reliance on the clause permitting "intellectual diversion" to cover the activities allayed any concerns about the legality of the reeducation program under the Geneva convention. Still, it was crucial that the reeducation effort be kept secret from the U.S. public as well as the Nazis lest the enemy retaliate against U.S. prisoners in German custody, ardent Nazis sabotage the program, or, at the very least, even the non-Nazis take them less seriously.[72] Orders were given to all involved in the project—in the OPMG headquarters and in the camps—"that no publicity be given this matter."[73] The War Department ruled that an "independent" body should appear on the imprint as the publisher of record, specifying the ad hoc "Bücherreihe Neue Welt," which served to mask the true governmental, propagandistic origins of the books.[74]

Public knowledge of Bermann-Fischer's role in the operation was limited to crediting him for licensing the titles he controlled. On these he was permitted to claim copyright and to have his firm's name attached to the "reprinted by permission" statement on the verso of the title page, along with the firm's handsome colophon. It was also considered vital that the POWs themselves, including those who worked in the canteens, be unaware that the War Department, the OPMG, or an entity with an official-sounding name like the *Infantry Journal* was behind the book program. This required that the packages of BNWs carry no label connecting them with *Infantry Journal*. Accordingly, a New York City post office box was given as the address for inquiries and orders for BNWs from the prison camps.[75] Every day a courier from the SPD picked up the mail at PO Box 20 and immediately forwarded it to the *Infantry Journal*. "Since you will not be in a position to sign letters as 'Buecherreihe Neue Welt,'" Davison told Greene, "any answers required by letters will have to be made by us, after you give us the pertinent facts, in a form like this: 'The publishers of Buecherreihe Neue Welt have informed this office....'"[76] The POW camps would pay the invoices to the custodian, Central Prisoner of War Fund, further masking the origin of the books.

Books in the Repatriation of German POWs

V-E Day put an end to any further need for secrecy concerning the BNW project. The press had begun to get wind of it in March,[77] prompting the drafting of the statements to be made available, on short notice, to politicians and the press. The program was declassified by June 12, 1945, whereupon the PMG released the statement to the press. Now canteen officers in the camps were permitted to order BNW and other titles directly from *Infantry Journal*.[78]

With Germany defeated and plans in train for the repatriation of the inmates, the BNW titles began to reach the camps in early May 1945, right around V-E Day—later than optimal, but not irredeemably so. All twenty-four editions were produced and distributed by the middle of September. At a quarter a copy, the BNW books sold like *pfannkuchen* following their introduction into the camp canteens. To help ensure that every prisoner who wanted to read a book had purchased it, senior OPMG officials ordered that the books were not to be put into the camp libraries at least "until their sale had been actively promoted."[79] Even so, some remained unsold even as the prisoners were returning home, but it is possible that these were overruns.

In any case, the books sold very well. An officer at a POW camp in Tennessee reported that his entire shipment of 420 copies was gone in less than a day. He noted that all groups of prisoners there seemed particularly interested in Willkie's *Unteilbare Welt* and Mann's *Achtung, Europa!* Staff at a camp in Texas asked for at least 250 more books "in addition to the regular quota." Officials in Arkansas noted that the response at two branch camps "was beyond our fondest expectations," with the supply selling out within an hour. The books "are being read widely and passed around.... These books have certainly filled one of our greatest needs, since the German book market is so limited." The officials requested a total of one thousand more copies for the two facilities. Trusted prisoners cooperatively provided puffs. One Wehrmacht officer in Kansas testified that the availability of the series "was the cause here of general rejoicing and gratitude." It was "a ray of light," bringing "comfort and strength to all who do not close their hearts and minds to the signs of the coming new world (Neue Welt)."[80]

Greene and the *Infantry Journal* were also deeply involved—now openly—in another book-related undertaking of the SPD. Greene was in effect to act as a "jobber" to provide an additional reliable supply of good books in both English and German for sale to the prisoners in the camp canteens.[81] Davison assured him that "the prisoner market is very large and involves thousands of books every month."[82] Here, if anywhere, was a real "captive market." Even if these customers' level of disposable income was not large, at least books did not have to compete against a full range of consumer products for the POWs' nickels, dimes, and quarters, and books had the advantage of occupying a lot of the prisoners' time, one might hope productively. In trying to find a better way to procure German-language books than the rather haphazard methods that had been the rule, Greene would consolidate all such searches and purchases through the *Infantry Journal*, utilizing his connections with Kurt Enoch at Penguin and with Stechert and Company, a long-established New York dealer specializing in German books.[83] He promised efficiency and economies of scale in a market in which prices for ever-scarcer German books had skyrocketed to meet the increased demand. Easier to find, books in English would be particularly useful in connection with the English-language lessons that many prisoners were receiving.

The encouragement to learn English became even more important around V-E Day, for it certainly seemed to be in the long-term interests of the United States for at least some of the people rebuilding the shattered Reich into a liberal democracy friendly to United States to be able to read and speak English.[84] Greene prepared lists of English books available from the *Infantry Journal* to be sent to each camp commander, assistant executive officer, and camp canteen officer from addresses supplied by the unit. The books he sought to offer included some of his own "Fighting Forces" books, selected Pocket Books, and some of the books in the Illustrated Modern Library series. A number of the books were on military subjects, which, it was thought, would "have an obvious interest for the prisoners of war and will serve to increase respect for American achievements and purposes." The army even offered to help gain access to Central Prisoner of War funds in order "to underwrite [Greene's] financial risk."[85]

As camps began to close, unsold books were returned for distribution to the remaining camps, at which some POWs were consolidated pending their departure from the United States.[86] SPD officers had noticed a falloff in prisoners' purchases of books and believed that this stemmed from the inmates' concern that they would not be able to take the books home with them. In fact, proposed restrictions on the weight of baggage that the POWs could take home with them worried SPD as well. After all, as one OPMG officer noted, "prisoners of war have continuously purchased, legitimately and in good faith, literature, particularly books in anticipation or obvious expectancy of permanent personal ownership."[87] Bermann-Fischer's contract precluded the books from entering "the regular or secondhand book market."[88] So that as few books as possible would go to waste, books that remained unsold—at least eight thousand copies as of April 1946, out of at least two hundred forty thousand printed—would be distributed free to departing POWs.[89] Later, provision was made for the surplus to be shipped to Europe for use by civilians in Germany and Austria and

FIGURE 5.   Covers of three books in the Bücherreihe Neue Welt series of paperbacks published for German prisoners of war interned in camps in the United States. Collection of the author. Photograph by Jeff Adams.

distribution to libraries elsewhere in Europe by the American Friends Service Committee.[90]

The books published in the Bücherreihe Neue Welt series are quite hand-some. Responsible for this was Bermann-Fischer, from whose "beautifully printed" Stockholm editions most of the volumes were reprinted, using pho-tographic plates slightly reduced from original size.[91] This eliminated most of the cost of setting new type. The trim size is the same as Pocket Books and other paperback series available in the United States, namely 4¼ × 6⅜ inches. Their orientation is upright—like those standard U.S. paperbacks—and thus resembled them and the OEs and TEs more than the oblong ASEs. The blue or yellow paper covers are mostly typographic, except for a small vignette or printer's ornament appropriate to the subject of the book on the front covers. On Benét's *Amerika*, for example, is a device depicting what apparently is an American eagle (although the vertical upsweep of the wings makes it look like a phoenix, an equally plausible symbol) and a motto in German—*Wie es wuchs— was es ist—an was es glaubt*, or, "How it grew, what it is, what it believes." The *es*, or "it," presumably refers to the United States. On the title page of book num-ber twenty-two, Zuckmayer's *Ein Bauer aus dem Taunus*, is the phrase "Verbil-ligter Sonderdruck für deutsche Kriegsgefangene"—"Special cheap edition for German prisoners of war." Both roman and old German typefaces were used, no doubt depending on which had been used for the Stockholm editions that served as the typographical basis for the BNW productions.[92] Prisoners' names may be found inscribed in copies.

The solid sales of the BNWs, of course, did not necessarily mean that the messages contained in them actually got through. The PMG admitted that "there is no absolute measure of the influence upon the minds of the Prisoners of War of the good books made available to them," even as he maintained that "surely these books have exerted some influence, and perhaps a great one."[93] Given the boredom that prisoners anywhere suffer, the books may have merely provided the inmates with something to do. POWs might have read the books with derision as easily as with admiration. In some camps that harbored the most hard-core Nazis, the introduction of the BNWs met with resistance and sabotage, as OPMG officials had feared. The prisoners' own internal command structure sometimes operated to block access to the books. An investigation at a camp in Tennessee found that trusty prisoners who worked in the library blacklisted books that their officers deemed subversive to the Reich. As one testified, "If books are not allowed to be read in Germany, they should not be read here. After all, they are Germans even if they are prisoners of war, and they are still held responsible for their actions as prisoners of war. They swore allegiance to their fatherland."[94]

Finally, the relatively highbrow character of most of the books in the BNW series (especially the several works of Mann) may have rendered them inaccessible to the average Wehrmacht private or corporal, who entered the military at increasingly younger ages as the conflict wore on. The administrators of the series seem to have recognized this problem, for some of the later additions to the series, like Werfel's *The Song of Bernadette* and Saroyan's *The Human Comedy,* responded to more popular tastes. At a minimum, the BNW paperbacks provided the repatriated German soldiers with a nice souvenir of their time spent somewhere in the United States, and might have been more effective than that for some returnees.[95] In my collection is a copy of the BNW edition of Mann's *Lotte in Weimar,* which the owner's inscription identifies as being just such a souvenir of his time spent at Camp Princeton, Texas. The fact that he had the book rebound in hard covers, with family bookplate affixed, shows that it held real significance for him.

MAKING THE "NICE LITTLE BOOKS"

After the lengthy and complex process of selecting the Overseas Editions titles came the exacting and tedious nuts-and-bolts work of putting them into print—making what Blanche Knopf, a fierce champion of good book design, called those "nice little books."[1] At least making books was a process that all publishers—including those working for the Council on Books in Wartime or the Office of War Information—knew how to do, in time of peace as well as war. Rights to publish the books in English and in the selected foreign languages had to be secured. For the books selected for publication in one or more foreign languages, suitable translators had to be located, contracted for, and hounded to meet their deadlines. Translations had to be vetted by a number of responsible officials. All books in foreign languages had to be copyedited. Once the decision was made that OEs were to be upright paperbacks resembling the books familiar to French and other European readers, a general design scheme had to be established for the series and particular specifications written for each title. Compositors (including firms that would be capable of accurately setting type in French, Italian, and German) had to be sought out and engaged. So, too, makers of mats and shells, suppliers of paper, proofreaders, printers, and bookbinders had to be found and put to work. Although both of the partners in the enterprise played roles in the production work, the staff of CBW's subsidiary, Overseas Editions, Inc., assumed far more of the burden than OWI did. The most troublesome part of production was securing and vetting the translations, tasks in which the publishers were least experienced. Most critically, all of this work had to be done fast, or the window of time in which the books could be put to their purpose would close on them.

Securing Rights

As the official publisher of the series, OEI was to hold the rights to republish the titles, but OWI's Chester Kerr had to secure rights early on until the new entity was, at long last, incorporated, funded, and fully operational.[2] The underlying principles and procedures behind the securing of rights to the titles in OEs were largely borrowed from those developed for the Armed Services Editions, that is, to obtain the rights from many publishers on the basis of a standard contract for nonexclusive rights for a limited period (in the case of the OEs, one year, renewable from year to year, but cancelable on ninety days' notice). A fee of one dollar was payable to the owner on signing, along with payment of a royalty of one cent per copy published (based on the quantity attested to in the binder's affidavit), with the original publisher splitting the royalty equally with the author.[3] The publisher, or other lawful seller of the rights, was assured that the books would not be put into circulation domestically, an important point since most of the books selected were titles still in print with considerable commercial value. The publishers were free to sell the nonexclusive rights to any foreign publisher as well.

Although the seventy-two separate editions selected for the OEs represented only about one-twentieth the number of the 1,322 ASEs, securing rights for the OEs was not twenty times easier. For one thing, the overseas project involved the far more demanding task of negotiating foreign translation rights in several languages. For another, OWI had to negotiate rights not just for the titles that wound up in the OE series but also for all titles that had successfully negotiated the pyramid of approval bodies for publication or distribution abroad, whether by OEI, foreign governments in exile, or domestic publishers in Britain and any of the liberated or vanquished countries. Although OWI claimed it had no intention itself to "acquire rights wholesale," as long as they were at it, they would buy from the publisher of a particular work translation rights in a dozen or more languages to cover all possible eventualities.[4] Contracts, however, would be issued only when a decision had been made to publish a specific title in a particular language. When a few of the planned editions could not be published, for various reasons, the contracts were voided. Delays in the securing of rights for a single title could hold up production of additional books as well, for the OEs went through the production process in groups of eight titles.[5]

OEI received nearly universal cooperation from the publishers of the selected works in the purchase of rights, no doubt from the precedent set in the ASE operation. Blanche Knopf, of Alfred A. Knopf, was perhaps the publisher most in need of persuasion, at least in certain cases. Knopf at first declined to turn over any Italian-language rights to OEI but ultimately relented.[6] The most serious rights problem involved the French-language publishing firm Éditions de la

Maison Française (EMF), which had been established by the bookstore Librairie de France, located in La Maison Française, one of the buildings comprising New York's Rockefeller Center, to provide "artistic refuge" for exiled French writers in the United States.[7] OWI wanted to package two books by Walter Lippman— *U.S. Foreign Policy* and *U.S. War Aims*—into a single volume for English- and French-language OEs. EMF owned the French rights to *U.S. Foreign Policy.* OWI offered a half-cent royalty to EMF and the same royalty to Little, Brown, which controlled the French rights to *U.S. War Aims.* It offered to pay EMF an additional $250 for its existing translation. The firm's Vitalis Crespin would cooperate only if OWI agreed to purchase at least four thousand copies of his edition of the foreign-policy book at seventy-five cents each, out of fear that he would be unable to dispose of that stock in France, as intended, if SHAEF got a double-titled edition there first. This OWI refused to do, directing OEI to publish *U.S. War Aims* alone as a French OE.[8]

Securing Translations

Next to coping with lengthy delays in funding and launching OEs in the first place, the translation program was the most troublesome phase in the history of the series. In the publishing trade on both sides of the Atlantic, the responsibility for commissioning a translation traditionally belonged to the purchaser of the foreign-language rights rather than to the seller. If Knopf, for example, bought the translation rights to a book published in France, Knopf would arrange for someone, most likely in the United States, to translate the French text into English. If, however, Knopf sold translation rights to one of its own titles to a French publisher, the foreign firm would arrange for the translation into French, no doubt in France. In the case of Overseas Editions, OEI, Inc., as the publisher and purchaser of translation rights, properly bore the responsibility of commissioning the translations. But the situation was otherwise opposite of what normally faced an American publisher in that OEI's task was to arrange for translations from English into several foreign languages—not from a foreign language into English—and to find skilled and willing translators in the United States to do them. Since it is generally best for the translator of a book to be a native speaker of the language of the translation, finding people in the United States to perform the latter task successfully was far from simple.

If this problem had a solution, it was the presence in the country of as many as three hundred thousand refugees from Hitler's Europe, a significant number of whom were writers, artists, scientists, and academics.[9] It was to this source of translating talent that Archibald Ogden, who had taken over as executive director of the Council on Books in Wartime in September 1943, and his colleagues at OEI and OWI turned most frequently. Many from this cohort—including those who were considered or recommended as translators, but not engaged—were distinguished professionals of one kind or another before the war, or became so afterwards. A number of them had some professional experience in translating.[10] Since the texts chosen for OEs were fixed and, with a few exceptions, no longer negotiable, the project was really just a reprint series. The publishing professionals within OEI and OWI therefore had neither the pleasures nor the travails that come from close dealings with authors. Instead, they had translators, who brought a highly individual, human dimension to their work and their relationships with the OEI and OWI staffs, resulting inevitably in both warm satisfaction and deep aggravation. Unfortunately, there was more pain than delight.

In the end, fifty acceptable translations had to be acquired for the foreign-language OEs—twenty-two in French, twenty-three in German, and five in Italian.[11] OEI was responsible for engaging the translators and for carrying on the necessary communications with them. OWI had final approval of the completed translations, a responsibility it exercised mainly through the agency's French, Italian, and German desks. The first set of translation contracts was authorized on October 31, 1944.[12]

Translators were paid four hundred to eight hundred dollars, depending on the length of the book. These fees, for what was a short-term project, seem reasonably generous. In comparison, an OWI clerk earned about eighteen hundred dollars per year, while the head of the Bureau of Overseas Publications was paid eight thousand dollars, the same amount Kerr made as Williamson's assistant.[13] The rate of compensation was substantially higher for shorter books than for longer. A two-hundred-ten-thousand-word manuscript, for example, earned the translator $3.57 per thousand words, but a translator would be paid at almost twice that rate, $6.67 per thousand words, for translating a seventy-five-thousand-word manuscript for a fee of five hundred dollars and three times as much, ten dollars per thousand words, for forty thousand words.

OWI was not without experience translating texts into foreign languages before the OE program began. Most of this work, however, had to do with producing various forms of white, black, and gray propaganda that were both shorter and more ephemeral than books—the leaflets, pamphlets, and magazines that were directed toward German soldiers and civilians as well as resistance fighters and ordinary citizens in the overrun nations. These materials were translated into a multitude of languages, including many less familiar ones as the needs beyond Western Europe became apparent.[14]

In finding available qualified translators for the OEs, where the texts were much lengthier and needed to aspire to higher literary quality, Ogden and his colleagues quickly learned that they could not depend on sources inside the

government for translating talent. Even though there were plenty of people employed by OWI and other federal agencies, like the Office of Strategic Services
and the State Department, who possessed the necessary skills, if not the experience or flair, for the task, it was difficult to pay such individuals on top of
their government salaries. Requiring federal employees to perform translations
as part of their regular duties was often impractical, since most were already
overburdened with their own important war work. The publicity given to the
program in newspapers and in *Publishers' Weekly* helped recruit some people
who applied for commissions,[15] but mainly Ogden and his staff sought suggestions from various contacts. Among the more fruitful sources were people connected with agencies performing relief work for war refugees, particularly artists
and writers.[16]

Who, then, were the translators of Overseas Editions, both collectively and
individually? The Council on Books in Wartime's records abound in correspondence between OEI and council officials and prospective and actual translators.
Under the circumstances, it is not at all surprising that many, if not most of
them, were European-born immigrants to the United States.[17] Many of these
men and women were refugees from Nazi Europe, but one cannot always know
for sure when a particular foreign-born individual arrived in the United States or
whether or not he or she was Jewish.

The majority of the translators resided in New York City—no surprise since
New York was the literary and publishing center of the country and immigrants'
principal port of entry. Most of the New Yorkers lived in Manhattan, with a significant number of them domiciled on the Upper West Side and Morningside
Heights, near Columbia University. Several of the translators apparently lived
as transients in Manhattan hotels. A few lived in the outer boroughs. At least
five translators—Jacqueline Levi, Julius Elbau, Ernst Behrendt, Ilse Behrendt,
and Vera Eliasberg—resided in Queens, specifically Kew Gardens, Forest Hills,
an area known for its significant Jewish refugee community.[18]

Of the translators with addresses outside New York City, most were academics at such institutions as Princeton, Yale, Dartmouth, Penn, Brown, Illinois,
Michigan, Vanderbilt, Duke, North Carolina, Haverford, and Wheaton (Massachusetts). Judging from their names and other clues, most of the academically
employed were also foreign born, perhaps refugees. Whether resident in or outside New York, the academics were connected with the same kind of elite educational institutions that had produced Kerr, Ogden, and many other publishers
performing wartime service as employees of OWI or volunteers in CBW.

Several of the translators cited reasons why they were eager to participate in
the translation program, including patriotism, loyalty to their adopted country,
a desire to aid in the war effort, or, as in the case of C. A. Rochedieu, a wish to
assist France in "establishing new foundations, resting on purely democratic

principles."[19] A few others made it clear that they needed the work and the money. Simone David, for example, poignantly indicated that she really had nothing else to occupy herself at all, telling OEI's able manager, Irene Rakosky, that "I am quite free of my time and have long hours to give to that kind of work."[20] Having gotten OEI to agree to pay him in installments, Hans Sahl "insisted that he and his family will starve if he doesn't get his [final] check next week," according to Rakosky.[21] This represented a great decline in fortune for Sahl, who had been born into a wealthy and assimilated Jewish family in Berlin. A poet and novelist, he left Germany in 1933, spending time first in Czechoslovakia and Switzerland before getting to France, where the Nazis interned him along with Walter Benjamin. He managed to flee to Marseille, where he assisted Varian Fry, a young American classicist known as "the artists' Schindler," in rescuing many other intellectuals, before he was himself able to flee to the United States. In Sahl's case at least, OWI proved to be a keen judge of talent, for he later had a brilliant career as a translator of the plays of Arthur Miller, Eugene O'Neill, Thornton Wilder, and Tennessee Williams.[22]

Having some translation experience and great incentive to participate in the program was, alas, not always a predictor of success in translating an American book into French, Italian, or German for such a politically and militarily important project and under the pressure of very tight deadlines. Many of the problems that occurred in the translation program stemmed from the failure of both OWI and OEI to establish and follow a coherent policy. Whatever rules and procedures the program had, it would seem, were made up on the fly. This led to some inconsistency in how the overseers (principally Ogden and Kerr) applied the vague rules. Perhaps, in the emergency circumstances facing the agencies, it could not have been otherwise.

The program's managers had no clear notion even of what kind of translation was called for: literal, word-for-word translations versus looser ones that might better catch, in English, the tone and style of the original.[23] Some translators were criticized for adhering too closely to the text, while others caught heat for straying too far away from it. Either of these types of translation might have been perfectly suited to the particular text, but it would have helped if the translators had been given firmer guidance. Absent that, some of the better translators made their own rules—deciding how to punctuate, where and when to deviate from the exact text, when to add explanatory text to make American ideas or references understandable to foreigners, and so on.[24]

Matching a translator to a text was burdensome. The archives document numerous fruitless quests to place one of OE's titles in the hands of someone likely to succeed in translating the English text into one of the three languages. But the troubles were only beginning. From the standpoint of OEI and OWI, most of the problems the translators created fell into two, not unrelated, categories—delays in meeting the agreed-upon deadlines and inferior-quality translations. In the translators' view, it was better to be late than to produce a flawed translation. The publishers demanded both speed and quality.

There were nearly infinite variations on the kinds of problems and disagreements that arose. Delays were probably the most frustrating problem for the OEI and OWI staffs, mainly because the program was necessarily on a very tight schedule. Going through the printing process in groups of eight, as the OEs did, meant that delays on any one translation would set back seven other titles as well. Since there was only a brief period of time when the OEs could be effective in performing the propaganda work for which they were designed, OWI understandably worried that the books would not become available until after the domestic publishing trades in France, Italy, and elsewhere were able to produce their own books. Disheartened by Jean Boorsch's delay in producing his translation of *Tarawa*, Ogden stressed how important it was to the government that the program should proceed rapidly, inasmuch as "the military is now racing through France."[25] A distinguished French professor at Middlebury and Yale since his entry into the United States in 1929, Boorsch successfully completed his assignment.[26]

Kurt Pinthus had thought it would take him and a collaborator four weeks to translate *The Navy's War*, by Fletcher Pratt, into German. Instead, it took them three months to produce the 420-page translation. "It was the hardest job I ever did in my whole life," he claimed. "The book is simply not translatable, or, at least not simply translatable" because of the high degree of technical terminology in the original. Pinthus told Ogden that the only way to make Pratt's text understandable to Germans was to abstain from delivering a literal translation. He also claimed that working on his translation every night until 2 a.m. for weeks damaged his eyesight enough that he had to undergo an operation. Even after struggling with such a difficult text, to the impairment of his health, Pinthus felt obliged to give most of his five-hundred-dollar fee to his collaborator, who had spent much more time on the job than anticipated.[27] Under great pressure themselves to meet their deadlines and budget for a wartime project of such high military and political importance, neither Ogden nor Kerr could afford to sympathize with him.[28]

Ironically, Pinthus was himself victimized by delays in being paid. On returning home from his eye operation, he learned that OEI's check, which was supposed to have been mailed two weeks earlier, had not arrived. He had to wire Ogden to ask to have payment expedited.[29] In the end, OEI and OWI were highly pleased with the work of Pinthus, who was among the most glittering of the cadre of translators for OEI. A novelist, journalist, and critic in Germany, his works had been banned by the Nazis. He served as an advisor and manuscript reader to two major German publishing firms, Rowohlt and Kurt Wolff Verlag, before immigrating to the United States in 1937. He was a sometime contributor to *Books Abroad,* a journal published at the University of Oklahoma that reviewed foreign literature for American publishers and librarians. He taught at the New School for Social Research from 1941 to 1947 and at Columbia University from 1947 until 1961.[30]

Ogden and Kerr had to reject a number of translations for poor quality— most after sample translations of a chapter had been found wanting by people on OWI's foreign desks, but some that were further along, even finished. Kerr usually conveyed the reviewers' judgment to Ogden, who would pass the bad news on to the translators, sometimes after softening Kerr's more hard-nosed language. Translators saw only brief summaries of the written critiques. Some were so general they could not have been very helpful to the translators. Others provided more significant details, but none could be described as painstaking reports. Although translators were paid a "kill fee" if their translations were not used because of poor quality or because the title was dropped from the series at the last minute,[31] they could not have been pleased to hear the judgment of the reviewers, particularly when the objections were expressed so tersely. Of the sample sent in by the translator assigned *Prefaces to Peace,* Paul Jacob, it was said that "the French text follows awkwardly and unimaginatively its English model." In conveying OWI's criticism to Jacob, Ogden softened the language to "your French text follows too literally its English model," a kindness he repeated to others.[32] *Prefaces to Peace* was, in the end, not among the books published. Domenico Vittorini, in contrast, was one of those criticized for "taking rather more liberties than a good translator should" in rendering his Italian version of John Hersey's *Into the Valley.*[33]

As to how much the general style of an English text should be followed in the translation, the OEI and OWI officials could be capricious. In his "top-notch" translation of E. B. White's *One Man's Meat,* Walter Mehring successfully captured "the same kind of humor as the original" by his ability to find "equivalent German expressions for American farm life."[34] Mehring had been a major literary figure in Weimar Germany, known for what the *New York Times* called "his caustic, Expressionist style reflected in songs, poems and plays." His sarcasm greatly annoyed the Nazis, who, on taking power, burned his books. He fled the country, and two years later the authorities stripped him of his citizenship for being a "Jewish subversionist." In France, he was caught up in the Wehrmacht's web and imprisoned for a year, before escaping to the United States with the help of American contacts, including Varian Fry. During the war he managed a warehouse in Long Island when not translating E. B. White.[35] On the other hand, Stefan Possony was told "that your style is dry but correct, but so is the style of the English original [*Der Bericht des Amerikanischen Oberkommandos* or *Report of the American High Command*]." Ogden's advice was to change the tone, that is, to "bring a little more warmth ... into the translation to make it more readable."[36] A Jewish refugee who also had a harrowing escape to the United States after the fall of France, Possony had perhaps the most unexpected postwar career of all the translators. First at Georgetown University and later at Stanford's Hoover Institution, he was a highly influential cold war military strategist and political scientist, who is credited with being the intellectual godfather of the "Star Wars" antimissle defense.[37]

On the whole, reviewers found more to fault than to praise, although they did pronounce Marian Chinard's translation of her husband's biography of Jefferson "excellent," Elbau's German work on Jaffe's *Men of Science in America* a "model" translation, and Pinthus's rendering of Pratt's *The Navy's War* into German "an excellent translation of a very difficult book."[38] The German desk rated Eliasberg's translation of David Lilienthal's *TVA* as one that "could not be improved upon."[39]

Almost alone among the translators whose work had been faulted, Jacob told Ogden that he considered the reasons for the rejection of his translation of Walter Lippman's *U.S. Foreign Policy and U.S. War Aims* to be "fair," although he felt his work could not be accurately judged because of the need to hurry.[40] Domenico Vittorini, a U.S. resident since 1917 and a professor of Romance languages and literature at the University of Pennsylvania, on the other hand, "needed to reacquire a certain sense of composure" before responding to Ogden's letter. He took particular issue with criticisms made "by some pompous nothing" on the Italian desk. His work was not abandoned but was edited by OWI before publication. Having undertaken the work "out of patriotic duty," Vittorini was embittered by his treatment by OWI—not by Ogden, who, he claimed, always was "most kind," but by the rest of those with whom he dealt. Echoing some of the other translators, Vittorini claimed that the work "almost ruined my health."[41]

A few translators voiced other criticisms as well, mostly over the fees offered for their work. Rochedieu, for one, questioned why a fee of four hundred dollars should apply for both a work of forty thousand words and one twice as long.[42] When Roger Picard told Ogden that for-profit publishers paid more for translations, Ogden reminded him that OEI was a nonprofit organization "established only to perform a service for the government," and that the budget for translations was established by contract with OWI. He added that many other translators had willingly accepted the $750 honorarium for translating books of similar length "in order to help us bring to a rapid conclusion a service which many of us hold to be extremely important at this time."[43] Picard declined to translate Kazin over his dissatisfaction with the fee, but Rochedieu soldiered on with a text that was twice as long for the same fee.

Finally, Marc Denkinger expressed disappointment that his name did "not appear anywhere, even in the most microscopic characters," on the copy of *Le citoyen*

Tom Paine, by Howard Fast, that Ogden had just sent him. He urged Ogden to credit the translators in future editions, such a change in policy being of no direct benefit to him. "Personally," Denkinger confessed to Ogden, "I find a compensation in my anonymity, because the defects of my translation glare in my face."[44] The suggestion was rejected, and no translators' names appear in the books.

Putting the accepted translations into production presented problems that texts in English simply did not. OEs in English could easily be typeset from existing editions of the books, in rare cases with some text marked for deletion (for example, where a book was abridged, or where certain front or back matter was not to be set), or in the few situations where there was some new text to be added. Since the translations used for OEs were newly commissioned, type could be set only from the typescript. A few translators had their manuscripts professionally typed, but most probably did the work themselves, however ineptly, since typing was a skill that few educated Europeans possessed in the 1940s. However messy the typescripts were when they left the hands of the translators, they then went to copy editors, who added handwritten emendations of their own.[45]

With the entirely French and Dutch TE series of twenty titles being produced in the OWI post in London, parallel translation operations were being carried out under OWI auspices on both sides of the Atlantic. The work of the London office, and therefore of TEs, is far less documented than that of the stateside operations. It is clear, however, that under Harold Guinzburg's direction, the London program arranged for all of the translations into Dutch to be done locally, primarily from among the refugee Dutch citizens who had accompanied their government-in-exile to the British capital. For the French series, London typeset several translations commissioned by the New York publications branch as well as some produced in Britain.[46] The division of labor appears to have worked well enough, but there was at least one snafu—a "grievous confusion" in which French translations of E. B. White's *One Man's Meat* were underway simultaneously in the United States and in England.[47] On the whole, the process of securing and approving translations in London seems to have gone more smoothly than in New York. Kerr noted with envy that London staff member Ronald Freelander "had the privilege of handing a manuscript to the printer immediately after the translator delivered it." Back home, in contrast, "it often takes as long to get a manuscript approved by OWI as it does to translate it in the first place."[48]

Although OEI and OWI managed to commission, vet, and put into production fifty translations into French, Italian, and German in the space of about six to eight months—no mean feat—the operation was problematic from the outset. Much of the trouble lay in the failure of Kerr, Ogden, and their subordinates to create a set of useful guidelines for the program, which may have stemmed from their own lack of knowledge and experience in the field of literary translations. The cumbersome bureaucracy of OWI, which required multiple layers of officials to sign off on virtually any decision, was enough, in Kerr's words, to "cause Job himself to burst into tears."[49] But there was nothing to do but persevere. The necessity of publishing most of the OEs in foreign languages was absolutely key to the success of the program both as a propaganda campaign and as a means of priming the pump for American publishers to capitalize on the anticipated demand for foreign-language editions of American books after the war. All in all, however, the translation program for Overseas Editions was not the finest hour for either OEI or OWI.

Manufacturing the Overseas Editions

The personnel of OEI and OWI no doubt were more comfortable transforming manuscripts into printed books than they were commissioning and overseeing the foreign-language translations. These tasks—drawing up specifications, securing paper, and engaging typesetters, plate makers, printers, and binders—were thoroughly familiar to them, although the fact that about two-thirds of the titles were in languages other than English made the task of finding skilled foreign-language compositors more than routine. Wartime shortages of paper, printing materials, and labor also added a certain degree of difficulty, but the key staff members would have been dealing with the same problems if they had remained with their peacetime employers rather than going to work for OEI or OWI.

Philip Van Doren Stern, who had taken charge of the OEs on top of his duties with the ASEs, wasted no time in beginning to scout out available vendors of composition, printing, and other services in April 1944, shortly after the Council on Books in Wartime agreed in principle to take on the task. Various delays had already set back the beginning of production by several months. The first major tasks were to seek a paper quota for the project from the War Production Board and to iron out arrangements with Pocket Books, Inc., whose line of credit OEI would tap.[50] The first contract between OEI and OWI to produce the books was finalized on June 22.[51] Locating the necessary paper from among several vendors as well as Pocket Books went fairly smoothly, though contracts issued by OWI had lower priority than those let by the departments of War and the Navy in the production of ASEs.[52]

A man from OEI and another from OWI shared the tasks of overseeing production of the books. W. Kenward Zucker joined the staff of OEI on November 20, 1944, from the publishing house of F. S. Crofts, with "unqualified recommendations."[53] Shortly before, OWI had engaged the services of Milton Glick, who headed production at Harold Guinzburg's Viking Press, as a consultant on the production of the OEs in conformity with the OWI-OEI contract that required, in the words of an OWI official, "that OWI provide a representative 'to assist and advise' the contractor [OEI] in the performance of the work required under the contract and to insure that the interests of the government are fully protected."[54] While Glick would serve as a check on the cost-benefit ratios of various design and production decisions and procedures (and their budgetary and propaganda implications), the corporation's own man, Zucker, would be in charge of production.[55]

The English-language titles were the first to be typeset. It was relatively easy to find compositors able to take on such straightforward work, although no single firm could meet OEI's needs and schedule. Far from it: OEI had to work with sixteen different companies to set the books in type. The English-language texts were essentially ready to go, although the depletion of stock in publishers' warehouses and at out-of-print booksellers sometimes made it a challenge to locate a copy of the book from which to set type.[56] There were far fewer firms that could be tapped for the foreign-language work.[57] Many compositors did not possess the necessary fonts with special characters. Of those that did, some already had all the work they could handle.[58]

Having to do business with so many different composition houses removed the possibility of gaining significant volume discounts. It also precluded any one-size-fits-all approach to the task of drafting typesetting specifications. The fact that all of the firms did not possess the same fonts, together with variations in the length of the books and other considerations, made it necessary to have almost as many typographical approaches as titles. This situation put compositors in the driver's seat.[59] Stern even investigated whether French work could be obtained from compositors in the province of Quebec. Although under normal circumstances the typesetters there would have considered such work "manna from heaven," as their agent put it, the Quebec book trade already had more than enough business between their regular domestic work and the substantial additional work of supplying books to French-language readers throughout the world after the flow of books from occupied and Vichy France was cut off.[60]

All questions of manufacturing specifications, especially the design of the page, had to be answered within the context of two constants—the fixed tonnage of paper allocated to the project and the total budget from congressional appropriations. The books had to be readable, but they could scarcely be luxurious. Most of the texts were set in 10-point type, "solid," that is, without "leading," or extra space, between the lines. Because some of the foreign-language books were quite lengthy, it was necessary to set them in 9-point type, but with one or two points of leading to make them more readable.

The printing specifications for the OEs derived also from the constraints of the budget appropriations. It was imperative under the contract to keep unit costs at between ten and thirteen cents, and the only way this was possible was if the edition size of each title was no fewer than fifty thousand copies. This, then, dictated that the books be printed on large web-fed, rotary presses. The publishers were fortunate that one company would be able to meet all (or nearly all) of their printing order—the W. F. Hall Printing Company, of Chicago, which boasted that it was "the world's greatest printing plant of catalogues and magazines."[61] The books were printed mostly from stereotype plates. In order to make the paper quota go as far as possible, "lean" typefaces were chosen over "fatter" ones. Also, efforts were made to have the text fill as much of the final signature as possible, without forcing a short additional gathering. OEI officials urged the printers to guard against "unders," that is, delivering fewer copies than the specifications required, usually because of errors or spoilage, and to keep "overs" to a minimum.[62] Most of the titles came out of the bindery in quantities just under or over fifty-one thousand. Costs ranged from three thousand to sixty-five hundred dollars each for the English-language books, from under three thousand to about seven thousand dollars for the French books, from under twenty-five hundred to about four thousand dollars for the Italian, and from just over three thousand to nearly nine thousand dollars for the German books.[63]

Plenty of mishaps occurred throughout the phases of production, most of them attributable to the difficulties inherent in publishing foreign-language texts domestically. Finding capable non-OWI copy editors and proofreaders for the French, Italian, and German texts was a challenge similar to that of locating skilled translators.[64] The proofreading of foreign-language page proofs done by the compositors was supplemented by a final reading by OWI staff on the appropriate foreign desk.[65] This was necessarily always a rush job—three days was the usual time allowed, except for some of the longer texts.[66]

Even though the managers overseeing design and manufacturing matters had to economize at every turn and to deal with overworked and underachieving colleagues and vendors, they took considerable pains to make the books look as good as possible—not just to meet their own professional standards, but to make the final products appear attractive and, above all, familiar to the liberated civilians who would read them. These small books were to be ambassadors of American culture, which many in their intended audiences were predisposed to belittle. As OWI's "Operational Plan for Germany" put it, the best editorial and technical efforts should be made in the preparation of the OEs so as "to demonstrate that we can use <u>well</u> instruments which our enemies assert we use <u>vulgarly</u>."[67]

The process had begun with the design of the cover. The OEs were vertically oriented paperbacks, with a trim size designed to be $4\frac{3}{4} \times 6\frac{3}{8}$ inches, although surviving exemplars are closer to $4\frac{7}{8}$ inches on the horizontal dimension.[68] Although proponents of the upright format compared them with the standard appearance of Penguin Books in Britain and of Pocket Books in the United States, the OEs were actually slightly bigger and squatter. Made of light-colored, "Indian

JOHN STEINBECK

LÂCHEZ
LES BOMBES!

OVERSEAS EDITIONS, INC.

L'édition américaine de cet ouvrage n'est mise en circulation
dans certains pays que jusqu'au jour où les publications libres,
suspendues par l'agression des pays de l'Axe, pourront rep-
rendre leur cours normal.

FIGURE 6.   The cover of the French-language Overseas Edition of John Steinbeck's
Bombs Away! Collection of the author. Photograph by Jeff Adams.

Tuscan" stock, the covers of the OEs were, in the French style, almost entirely
typographical, with no graphic devices except for the publisher's colophon, a
rendering of the Statue of Liberty (along with the author's name and a box rule)
in red.[69] A Frenchman would have felt comfortable holding one of these in his
hands because its spare design looked like the paperback books—as published,
for example, by Librairie Gallimard—that he might have read in a café while

drinking an aperitif and smoking a Gauloise cigarette. The resemblance was entirely intentional.

Paper used for the OEs was basis 25×38–31#/500 white ground wood English finish, graded "A-1 Printing" by the Office of Price Administration, delivered in fifty-four-inch-wide rolls.[70] This was the same grade of paper used for the ASEs.[71] The paper, as judged by a complete set of the OEs in my collection, has not aged particularly gracefully, but the books were not designed to last. The designers tried not to skimp on such standard, if wasteful, features of books as half titles, unless space limits absolutely required deletions.[72] The necessity of conserving paper forced the designers to specify new chapters to start on the next new page rather than the next recto page, which is publishing convention, and, on some occasions, to begin a new chapter on the same page the previous one ended. They followed the advice of translators to ensure that the standard French, Italian, and German practice of punctuation and word division would be followed for any of the foreign-language books.[73]

The TEs resembled the OEs in their upright format and even more purely typographical covers (there was no graphic device at all), though the trim size of 4¾ × 7 inches made them a bit taller. They were even more elegant than the OEs, which prompted Kerr to ask Glick for his professional comparison of the designs of the two series. Glick noted "a number of points in which the English books are superior to ours according to our present specifications."[74] The covers boasted printed colored panels, which he said would show less dirt that the lighter covers of the OEs. The books displayed lovely borders and rules, and the title pages were also more handsome than those of the OEs. The bindings were Smyth sewn in signatures like a regular hardbound book and apparently like most European paperbacks, rather than wire stitched and perfect bound, as were most American paperbacks, and would thus be more durable. A wider typeface, Baskerville, was used rather than the OEs' more "pinched" Granjon. This, plus the fact that the lines were always leaded, rather than set solid as were many OEs, made for a much better-looking and more legible page. What's more, the paper (120 tons of which OWI shipped from the United States) was a finer stock than the U.S. paper specified for OEs. Glick observed that it contained no ground wood and was "even much whiter than the average currently being used in the English trade editions."

How ironic it was that the books printed in war-torn Britain on U.S. paper outshone those made in the United States, where the printing infrastructure had been far less compromised by the conflict. The irony was not lost on OWI officials, who, while admiring of them, were concerned that the books were not in keeping with the requirements of wartime austerity. Guinzburg was forced to defend the design, assuring New York that the books had been produced within

FIGURE 7. The cover of the Dutch-language Transatlantic Edition of Julian Huxley's *TVA: Adventure in Planning*. Collection of the author. Photograph by Jeff Adams.

the British wartime restrictions and that the costs were not excessive. In any case, he added, the home office furnished the higher-grade paper.[75]

Given the many impediments to speedy and trouble-free production that existed in the United States during the war, it was a minor miracle that the men and women of OEI and OWI, along with their many vendors, were able to turn out these bullets-that-were-books as rapidly as they did. For a typical English-language OE title, the time from the order for composition to finished books was about four to five months. For a typical foreign-language title, actual production time was perhaps a bit longer, but the translation, of course, added months at the front end of the whole process of putting a selected title into print. It is all the more a pity that the many delays in getting up and running resulted in OEs becoming available to their intended audiences many more months beyond D-Day than people like Norton, Kerr, and Guinzburg had expected and wanted.

Between late November 1944 and the third week of January 1945, the thirty-five manuscripts released by OWI had been placed with compositors, even if the contractors were not yet able to provide a firm production schedule. Proofs of only nine English titles, three French, and one Italian had been received, although the proofs of six to eight more foreign titles and additional titles in English were expected by the end of February.[76]

The first OEs shipped in mid-February. By mid-April, sixty-five manuscripts—all but seven of the total—had at least been placed with compositors. Twenty-three books had been delivered, with the twenty-fourth in transit, accounting for the first three groups of eight titles. The fourth group of eight was due off the press, at the rate of one a day, by the first week of May. The fifth was seven-eighths in foreign languages, and thus somewhat delayed, with the first title not expected until mid-May. The sixth group was still in some disarray.[77] By mid-June, however, the end was in sight. Typesetting for seventy-one manuscripts was either finished or under way. All but eight titles had been shipped by September 12, with the rest to follow in early October.[78]

On leaving OEI in August 1945 to become London representative for Twentieth Century Fox, Ogden heaped lavish praise on Zucker's stewardship of the production effort. "Coming to us only nine months ago," Ogden wrote, "you started from absolute scratch to produce over three and a half million books at the lowest possible cost consistent with readability. This you have accomplished in record time and at an overall cost of $89,000 less than OWI appropriated for the operation."[79]

In addressing the third annual meeting of the Council on Books in Wartime in early February 1945, Kerr likened the OEs to a new baby in a large basket left on the council's doorstep and remarked that "housebreaking this baby proved to be a long and difficult and complex business." That was probably an understatement. But at least the job of getting the books overseas was well under way. The task of getting them into the hands of their intended audience, the newly liberated civilians, lay ahead. It too was a complex undertaking, which required the resources of the vast military apparatus that was SHAEF.

Part III
U.S. CULTURAL POWER ABROAD

LIBERATING EUROPE WITH BOOKS

A combat photographer who swam from a landing craft to a Normandy beach four hours after the initial wave of troops went ashore on D-Day was the first Office of War Information man attached to the Psychological Warfare Division of SHAEF to reach France. Accompanying him were a liaison officer to two army units and an intelligence officer.[1] Many others followed shortly, as did personnel from the British Ministry of Information. The landing of the first crates of British and American books for the consolidation-propaganda program took place several weeks later. Given the shifting, dangerous conditions that accompanied the efforts of the Allies to make a treacherous landing and to extend their Normandy beachhead right up to Hitler's bunker in Berlin, the hard job of distributing the American and British books prepared for the consolidation-propaganda phase could be assigned to no other entity than PWD/SHAEF. An official history of the unit described the task of distributing its publications in the liberated territories of Europe as being "probably even more difficult and ramified than the job of producing those publications."[2] While the author of the account probably knew little about the vexed history of the Overseas and Transatlantic editions, the statement is likely accurate.

Before the Allied landings took place, no one knew how the French people would greet the liberators. With flowers and kisses or with contempt for the Allied forces, who, lamentably if necessarily, visited great damage to civilian lives and property during the Normandy campaign? Would a general uprising occur throughout the country? Would the populace follow Allied military orders or wait for the establishment of a French government? How those questions were answered would determine the success or failure of consolidation propaganda, including the book program. There was some resistance to the program from both the French military and French publishers.[3] Fortunately, the French mostly welcomed the Allied troops, and the ultimate legitimization of the provisional government under Gen. Charles de Gaulle helped maintain order, thus smoothing the way for the books.[4]

Getting the First Books to France

At least the publishers at Overseas Editions, Inc., and the New York and London offices of OWI knew how to perform their assigned tasks. On the other hand, the experience that PWD/SHAEF, as a military unit, had gained from distributing propaganda in the North African and Italian campaigns did not fully prepare the division's personnel to solve the problems of transporting large quantities of heavy, bulky printed matter from the PWD base in Britain across the English Channel to the Continent, and from there by inland transport to all regions liberated by GIs. Probably few of the British and U.S. soldiers and civilians from the Ministry of Information, the Political Intelligence Department of the Foreign Office, and OWI had themselves been involved in the earlier operations.[5]

Deciding whether to sell or give the materials away was one of the first issues to be addressed. On this, the North African and Italian experiences provided valuable guidance. PWD/SHAEF's predecessor, the Psychological Warfare Branch of the Allied Forces Headquarters (PWB/AFHQ), also under General Eisenhower's command, had been tasked with distributing publications in North Africa. There, the field officers gave the materials away, free of charge, through outlets noneuphemistically called propaganda shops that had been opened in the main cities. Children and even some adults would occasionally grab the complimentary copies as souvenirs. By setting no price on the materials, PWB could not prevent people with little real interest in the contents from taking whatever they felt like.[6]

For the Italian campaign, PWB wished to charge for the materials. The proposed policy was unconventional and had to be approved by the treasuries of both governments, even though the advantages were striking. If retail prices were placed on the materials, the existing web of news dealers could be tapped to make distribution much more effective and measurable, with the merchants able to buy the printed goods at a discount and thus have an incentive to push sales and make a profit for their troubles. Most importantly, pricing the publications made it far more likely that the purchasers would be among the elites of a community who would actually read the pamphlets and books and be in a position to provide secondary transmission of their contents to family, friends, employees, and others.[7] But setting a price that was appropriate for both the publishers' return and the realities of the French market was difficult. It even produced an unexplained "three-day crisis" for Chester Kerr and Harold Guinzburg.[8]

PWD/SHAEF's staff wound up following the Italian campaign precedent by charging for the post D-Day consolidation-propaganda materials. France would provide the first—and perhaps the most important—market for the publications that had been stockpiled in London. Given the Allied mandate to sell the books in the liberated territories only until the local book trades could get back on their feet, it was logical that PWD would distribute its publications through existing channels, wherever possible, as well. In France, PWD had no choice but to do business with Messageries Hachette, which enjoyed a monopoly of the distribution business. Having continued to function during the war years, Messageries Hachette should have been in a strong position to begin the task immediately, but it took some time before it was able to service the entire country. Unhappy about the necessity of dealing with a monopoly (especially one whose relationship with the Nazis was clouded and controversial), PWD officials drew up agreements with the firm that gave the division the right to deal with any competitors that might be established later on.[9]

The capture of Cherbourg on June 26 (and the German surrender the next day) greatly strengthened Allied control of the coastline and made it possible for distribution to begin.[10] On July 6, the first team responsible for publication distribution arrived in the port city on a truck carrying a ton of publications, most likely a mixture of books—including a few of the one hundred fifty thousand volumes in French purchased in the United States for the D-Day stockpile—and more ephemeral matter like booklets and magazines.[11] This group was part of the Allied Information Services (AIS), under which name the OWI and MoI elements within PWD collectively operated on the Continent.[12] The inventory of printed goods went on sale four days later.

As AIS teams accompanied the army's advance through France, a member would inform the highest local French authority in each new locality of AIS's purpose and seek his cooperation in identifying a local dealer "of clean political record who was equipped to handle the material."[13] If the chosen dealer's shop had been damaged or destroyed, the Allied official did what he could to have the shop repaired or relocated. He also requisitioned sufficient gasoline for the agent to distribute the publications successfully.[14]

The first inventory that news agents in France had to sell were the items contained in "formula" (sample) packages. These were most likely the eighty-pound crates that had been filled in London with equal numbers of British and American titles and landed on the Normandy beaches a few weeks after D-Day. The eclectic assortment provided variety for customers to choose from, but inevitably some of the items sold more slowly than others. This made the dealers wary of taking on new sample assortments. When additional supplies from the stockpile in London and some new publications became available, the dealers felt less constrained, and in due course the sample packages were discontinued. With greater variety and larger quantities available, both the dealers and the AIS field officers were better able to judge the sales potential of individual items.[15]

An AIS publications team member was also present when the forces liberated Paris on August 25. His first item of business was to draw up commercial agreements with the French Ministry of Information and top officials at Hachette's headquarters. On September 2, a truck bearing three tons of Allied printed material arrived in Paris, which was quickly put on sale in various outlets in the city. Gradually, additional personnel arrived in the capital and set up a headquarters from which to coordinate activities elsewhere in France.[16] With Hachette not yet able to service areas beyond Paris, AIS personnel for the time being distributed materials directly to agents in towns and cities from Nancy to Lyon and Grenoble to Marseille throughout the fall of 1944.[17] As rail transport improved, Hachette was able to secure priority status for Allied publications. The firm took over distribution to some of the provinces by February 1945 and to all of them by April 1.[18] In order to serve the whole of France, AIS publications officers had to resist meeting the full demand in areas, like the Normandy peninsula, that were liberated early. They needed, in the words of a contemporary military historian of the operation, to ration "their supplies of intellectual food with almost Nazi-like coldness of eye."[19]

To achieve the desired saturation, AIS had to overcome some difficult logistical problems. Wretched weather conditions obliterated some of the label markings on the crates of books scattered throughout the four hundred square miles of Normandy beaches. Where this happened it was necessary to open crates just to identify the contents, which in some cases were left at least partially exposed. After the closing of the beach operations near the end of November, PWD's Shipping and Transport Section made a concerted effort to gather in and effectively distribute the remaining publications. Damage or loss of material had exceeded 10 percent of some shipments, but the overall total of losses of material shipped from London up to April 16, 1945, was only about a quarter of that.[20]

The fact that the publications were in effect a commercial product required certain kinds of controls, which were slow to take hold. Enlisted men in the warehouse in Cherbourg were assigned the task of logging the publications in and out of their custody. With little if any experience or training in warehousing or business practices, let alone the handling of books, they had to cope with keeping track of scores of separate publications, all with titles in French. Shortages of personnel, trucks, and fuel during the rapid liberation of France following the fall of Paris dogged the efforts. Distribution was easier in areas where the U.S. Army had established posts near the delivery points. Where these were absent, the crews had to carry enough food and fuel for the entire journey. Trucks on

FIGURE 8. The damaged display window of Brentano's bookstore in Paris, showing Overseas Editions (mostly in the lower part of photo) and Transatlantic Editions (mostly in the center) on sale with other books. National Archives, College Park, Md.

the Paris-to-Bordeaux run, for instance, had to haul forty jerricans of gasoline, which reduced the space available to carry the publications.[21]

Distribution, Sales, and Reception

In Paris, copies of the American books were put on display in bookstore windows still showing the effects of wartime, as depicted in photographs of the display window of Brentano's with a long crack in it, partially patched by a piece of wood.[22] Demand for the OEs and TEs was generally strong. The first six OE titles went on sale in France on July 24, 1945, and were sold out within a few hours.[23] OWI's Paris office reported that a Hachette official told him on August 24 that there would be "practically no unsold copies either of Editions Transatlantique or Overseas Editions."[24] This prediction was a bit overoptimistic, as later titles moved more slowly. Paul Brooks, Houghton Mifflin's editor in chief serving as head of OWI's book program in London, suspected that some OEs went begging "largely because they arrived too late to be palatable, but most of them disappeared with gratifying speed and are doubtless worn and dog-eared by now [late 1945]."[25]

Getting books to readers in the Netherlands took much longer. Liberation of the country proceeded piecemeal and slowly, culminating only in early May 1945. Although some of the English-language OEs, along with other, nonseries books in English and Dutch, would find their way into the country, the Uitgave "Transatlantic" paperbacks published by OWI in London were to be the primary tool for denazifying the country's book culture. Since the Netherlands was not fully liberated until nearly a year after France, both the Uitgave "Transatlantic" and the OEs were actually more "on schedule" there than the books were in France.

Books were sold to the general public through local booksellers whenever possible. Prices were set from a calculation that took into account both the pre-war price of such items and a sense of what postwar prices might prevail.[26] All ten Dutch TEs were sent to a reviewer at *Vrij Nederland* (*Free Netherlands Weekly*), a resistance newspaper. The reviewer noted (in OWI's translation) that these were "ordinary books," meaning that they were not written specifically as pro-paganda, but were merely books that might "be bought by any educated person, who wants to remain abreast of world conditions, just as well as in normal times when there is no dearth of good books in the Netherlands." That they were being perceived as "ordinary" American books must have greatly pleased the god-fathers of the series within OWI and the Council on Books in Wartime, for this was exactly the intent. The unnamed journalist predicted that the Dutch people, who were "starving for literature of this nature," would buy the books so fast "that the bookdealers will not be in a position to immediately satisfy the de-mands of those wishing to purchase them."[27]

As in France, transportation in Holland was the first hurdle. As one of the first OWI officials on the scene, Sidney Sulkin reported that the trains and street-cars were still not running two months after liberation. Without coal to power the engines of canal boats, horses or men had to pull them with ropes. Although the army provided some motor vehicles, Sulkin and his colleagues had to round up local means of transportation as well. In an effort to make trucks available to a particular Dutch book distributor, Sulkin visited the transport minister, who told him that first food, then clothing, medicines, and coal were the highest pri-orities for shipment. "Books, he was afraid, would be far down the list of priori-ties. Nevertheless I argued with this official for some minutes on the theory that talking would do no harm. Strangely enough he suddenly turned to me and asked: 'How soon would a copy of the Lend-Lease book be here?' I told him that that would depend in some measure upon his decision." Sulkin's response did the trick.[28] Because SHAEF worked with local booksellers for distribution, bookshops, according to Sulkin, "were among the first stores to reopen their doors as the Germans left." He commended Dutch booksellers for their efforts to equalize distribution of the American books throughout the nation, citing the heroic efforts of one book dealer who carried the books into the countryside on a decrepit bicycle.[29]

PWD spent some one hundred fifty thousand dollars, exclusive of the cost of salaries of U.S. and British civilians and of the substantial quantities of supplies and equipment requisitioned from the army, on the distribution of Allied publications, which must have included the OEs and TEs along with various booklets and magazines. This sum was contributed in equal measures by the United States and Britain. PWD/SHAEF earned far more than this amount from the sale of the publications in the various liberated countries of Europe—a total of $2,061,188. France accounted for more than half the revenues, with Belgium and the Netherlands contributing most of the other half. Government-produced films took in far less—only about four hundred thousand dollars—from screenings in the same liberated countries.[30]

One of the millions of copies of OEs reached the hands of an elderly Greek by the name of Sophocles Theodotos, who stopped into the American Library in Athens for a Gideon Bible. There was none, so the librarian steered him to the OEs. The next day he wrote to thank the librarian for the opportunity to read *The Pocket History of the United States,* which "fascinated [him] from the first pages." He confessed that he entered the library expecting blatant propaganda, even though he didn't believe that the Americans needed to propagandize in order to gain Greece's sympathies. His visit convinced him "that in reading American books the new Greek generation will little by little gain and obtain some of the precious characters that are the privilege of the practical American, and will learn to be serious and educated."[31] He also wrote directly to OEI in New York to acknowledge the Athens librarian's kindness in pointing him to the series. He purchased all of the titles in English except one that was unavailable. He expressed hope that the New York office could supply it. He also volunteered to translate three titles for a Greek-language series. These, he believed, "would greatly interest the Greek readers, owing to the attachment we feel specially to your country, where true freedom, liberty, and all virtues are duly cultivated and practiced."[32] The publishers could hardly have received a better validation of their labors.

But Theodotos's testimonial is the only fan letter in the archives of the Council on Books in Wartime, although there are scores of such tributes to the ASEs from GIs.[33] The records of OWI contain only a few glimpses to add to Theodotos's statement into how European civilians used the books and to what extent they valued them. An OWI press release quoted an unnamed Norwegian bookseller on the excitement of the moment: "There has been a shortage—a starvation for intellectual food for, in the last years, we have not had any books at all. The books were received with great enthusiasm by the public and especially, of course, the books in which Norway is mentioned."[34] Determining the effectiveness of wartime propaganda is difficult.[35] Although audience research might have been conducted for response to the postliberation book program, the incentive of military emergency was lacking, as, to a large extent, was a cadre of people to carry it out owing to the dissolution of the wartime propaganda machinery and the reduction of military forces.

A Feeding Frenzy Begins

Even if useful documentation of the propaganda value of the OEs, TEs, and other stockpiled books is largely absent, their effectiveness as ambassadors for American books abroad is nevertheless clear. As Allied armies moved through Europe, liberating area after area, the freedom to read was regenerated. A 1940s newsreel might have depicted this awakening with a black-and-white map of Europe, with lights marking key cities going on, one after another, like an electric grid recovering from a massive blackout. At last, book publishers and book dealers, only just released from the Nazi boot, were free to reestablish contact with the outside world, to learn what had gone on during the last five or six years, and to resume their trades. As soon as they were able, publishers wrote to firms in the United States (and in Britain) to ask for lists of books published during the war, from which to choose what they might publish in translation in their own countries. As the traffic in rights heated up, there was increased optimism among the Americans that the quest for new markets abroad, as well as at home, might well pay off, and that at least part of the reason would be the government's program of putting American books in the hands of Europeans as the Nazis were defeated.[36]

Many of the letters overseas publishers wrote to firms in the United States contained emotional accounts of the travails through which their writers had passed and noted how hungry they and their customers were for uncensored books. A Danish publisher wrote Blanche Knopf, "I dare say that as an American you can hardly appreciate the pleasure it means to an inhabitant of an ex-occupied country again to be able to communicate with friends abroad. We have all been through hard times, and we realize but slowly that we live in a free world....The feeling of gratitude to all Americans is strong everywhere."[37]

When transport improved, some British and European publishers journeyed to the United States to renew old ties and make new connections. The chairman of the Heinemann firm in London made his first visit to New York following the five-year "cultural dimout." Face-to-face contacts were more important than ever, he claimed, for they constitute the forum out of which "publishing ideas grow." He found in U.S. publishing "an atmosphere of vitality and vigor in spite of production problems which seem minuscule to a British visitor."[38]

In reality, the intense need that publishers in the overrun countries felt to get back into business could only be met through the republication of American and, to a lesser extent, British books, since there had been too little domestic literary output to jump-start their new lists. Because writers' productivity in the UK had also seriously diminished during the war, British publishers turned mostly to U.S. firms. British publishers thus occupied a kind of middle position in strength and vitality between the Europeans and the Americans. The collective quest to nail down rights to publish foreign books was like a vast feeding frenzy. Some publishers sought out almost anything, indiscriminately. One newly established firm, which clearly had not thought through the question of what kind of books it should publish, wrote for "practically every American book they see announced or advertised," according to a London agent.[39] Brimming with optimism, the proprietor of a Swiss publishing house told Scribner's that he was "anxious to resume import from U.S. as soon as possible and on a much larger scale than before."[40] Some foreign publishers seemed intent on locking up rights to as many American titles as they could even if there was little likelihood that they could publish the works any time soon. American publishers naturally frowned on this practice and grew cautious about granting such blanket rights since it would remove the opportunity for publishers that could move quickly to secure the necessary rights.

Rather than wait for letters or visits from overseas firms, the John Day Company, among other firms, prepared and mailed publishers abroad a catalog listing all its books published since 1939 on which the company controlled foreign rights, complete with notes regarding the availability of translation rights.[41] The Association of American University Presses prepared and distributed six thousand copies of a catalog of its members' books related to Latin America. The AAUP deemed this so successful that it planned to publish a catalog of books for the world market, with the English-speaking countries and Europe particularly in mind.[42]

Some U.S. firms sought to engage the new publics on their own turf by establishing offices abroad. Houghton Mifflin opened one in Paris in September 1945, to supplement the branch already in operation in London. Paul Brooks returned to the firm's Boston headquarters with a brief to take charge of its foreign business, having gained much useful experience in his work of distributing American books as a field officer with OWI.[43] Another old OWI hand, Ronald Freelander, joined the London sales office of McGraw-Hill.[44] New organizations sprang up to deal with overseas opportunities, including Far East Service, Inc., which Kay K. Nishamura, who also had gained useful experience in OWI as well as in the State Department, established.[45] Many firms formalized, or beefed up, their foreign marketing operations, including Prentice-Hall, whose manager of the foreign business looked on overseas markets as being of almost equal importance to domestic markets.[46]

Remnants of the U.S. government's mechanisms for facilitating the exchange of publishing rights with European firms, vested in OWI and its transitional successors, were ready to be of service. Later, so was the United States International Book Association, which took over many of these functions from the government after its incorporation in January 1945. These agencies acted as middlemen in facilitating contact between U.S. firms and both old and new publishers abroad.[47] Both OWI and USIBA published book lists for the information of foreign publishers. Government- or USIBA-sponsored exhibitions of recent American books held in several large cities also provided a way for would-be purchasers of rights to view the wares.[48] Often, a foreign publisher would seek an option on a book for a period of three months or so to allow time to obtain a copy of the U.S. edition to read and discuss with colleagues before making a firm offer. OWI, USIBA, publishers' agents, and the U.S. publishers themselves were all involved in the task of locating and shipping reading copies to publishers overseas.[49]

The trade journal *Publishers' Weekly* worked particularly hard to publicize U.S. overseas trade. It carried much news of international transactions and provided advice and encouragement to publishers with little prior experience in marketing abroad. The magazine began a regular department about the industry's growing export business, called "All Over the Map."[50] In collaboration with USIBA, *PW* even experimented throughout 1946 with the publication of a spin-off magazine, *U.S.A. Book News*, which was focused entirely on stimulating interest abroad, especially in Latin America.

One way to understand the expanding contacts and business relationships between American and foreign publishers that Allied liberating armies made possible is to focus on a number of representative firms. This makes it possible to gauge the level of involvement of U.S. companies in foreign trade; what instrumentalities, both private and governmental, facilitated the commerce; and under what financial terms and other understandings deals were made. From the myriad details involved in exporting books and selling foreign rights, one may gain a sense of how much trouble the enterprise entailed. But American publishers had finally come to view overseas business as worth the effort. The flurry of activity that occurred between the liberation of France and the defeat of Japan thus prepared the way for each firm's participation in postwar book exporting and the sale and purchase of foreign publishing rights.

The John Day Company

The John Day Company, a comparatively small firm based in New York City, became one of the most internationally focused American publishers during the late stages of the war.[51] What set John Day apart from most other export-minded U.S. firms was its special focus on Asian rather than European or Latin American markets. This stemmed from the nature of its backlist, which in itself was a product of the interests of the firm's four principals, including Richard J. Walsh, who founded it in 1926. Walsh was the survivor and led the house until 1959, the year before he died.

The firm twice ran into serious financial difficulties during the Depression, but managed to recover each time. No supplier or customer, Walsh boasted, "lost a cent on us." The economic hard times would doubtless have been worse for the firm had it not published, in 1931, Pearl Buck's *The Good Earth*, the number-one fiction best seller during 1931 and 1932 and the anchor of the company's backlist for years to come.[52] It also set the pattern for the imprint's emphasis on fiction and nonfiction with Asian themes, as was evident through the acquisition of several other strong-selling books by Buck as well as Dagny Carter's *China Magnificent* (1935). Buck's friendship with Lin Yutang, a Chinese writer, translator, and philosopher, brought him under the John Day umbrella with the publication in 1935 of *My Country and My People*, which proved highly lucrative for the firm in years to come, as did many other works by him. The company's publication of Margaret Landon's best seller, *Anna and the King of Siam*, in 1944 solidified its reputation in the niche.

The event that clinched this specialty had been the 1935 marriage of Buck and Walsh. In early 1945, the company established a subsidiary, Asia Press, Inc., as a means of increasing its attention to books about the Far East without submerging the purely American books on the John Day list. Walsh named his wife to direct it, giving her the right to select the books and to exercise full editorial control. Asia Press would become "Pearl Buck's own publishing business," according to *Publishers' Weekly*.[53]

Although China provided much of the subject matter of John Day and Asia Press books, the firm was more interested in finding markets in India than in China, because it was thought that India would be far easier to enter than China. The head of the U.S. Information Library in Bombay reported after the war that India held the promise of "a very considerable market" for American books. "Many Indians," she wrote, "have such an aversion to the 'British Raj' that they would buy an American book at a high price rather than an equally good British publication at a bargain."[54] But John Day's interest in the great potential of the Indian market was threatened by British publishers' efforts to protect their traditional overseas markets in the British Empire and Commonwealth.[55]

With the prospects of increased foreign trade beckoning so brightly as the world was liberated from Axis tyranny, John Day, like many other publishers, modernized, strengthened, and institutionalized its management of foreign rights. Its small staff was top-heavy with members of Walsh's family, including his son, Richard Jr., who was involved with editorial matters, and his brother, Albert, who served as treasurer. The firm had to improvise, with Albert adding coordination of international business to his other financial duties.[56] The accounting and contract departments were short staffed, owing to the continuing labor shortage, so the considerable increase in foreign-rights sales made for a "terrific whirl of work."[57]

With China's visibility on the world scene growing in the 1930s, the broad popular appeal of the works of both Buck and Lin, in many foreign languages as well as English, made them literary celebrities. Buck's 1938 Nobel Prize guaranteed strong sales in perpetuity. During the 1930s, eight different translations of *The Good Earth* were available in China alone.[58] Next to Buck's works, the books of Lin Yutang and his daughters, Tan Yun (the pen name of Lin Adet) and Lin Taiyi, were the hottest properties that John Day had to offer both its readers in the United States and, through the sale of reprint and translation rights, new audiences in Asia, Europe, and elsewhere.[59]

Little known now, Lin Yutang was in his day a best-selling author and cultural phenomenon. Lin was born in China in 1895, the son of a Christian minister. He failed to finish a PhD at Harvard but later earned one in Germany. He returned to the United States following the warm reception accorded *My Country and My People* (1935). Like *The Good Earth,* Lin's book greatly influenced the development in the West of a friendly and positive attitude toward the Chinese people. Lin followed up with another highly popular work for John Day, *The Importance of Living* (1937), a work of middlebrow philosophy reminiscent of books today by Mitch Albom, Wayne Dyer, and others. The war produced three other popular books—*The Wisdom of China and India* (1942), which dealt with Asian humanism; *Between Tears and Laughter* (1943), which urged westerners to broaden their perspective on the world; and *Vigil of a Nation* (1944), which was an account of Lin's time spent in wartime China.

As free publishing resumed throughout the world, Lin's books were in great demand, keeping the Walshes busy fielding requests for foreign rights in English and for translation into many other languages. A major Italian firm, the house of Valentino Bompiani, authorized an Italian naval officer attached to the U.S. submarine base in New London, Connecticut, to act as its agent for dealings with American publishers. Because of errors made during wartime, the Italian rights to several of Lin's books were confused and took time to sort out.[60] Established agents, like Franz Horch in New York and Curtis Brown Ltd. in London, were involved in many of the transactions. Deals were made in short order for books by Lin and his daughters to be reprinted in English in the UK and translated into Swedish, Danish, Norwegian, Finnish, German, Hebrew, Dutch, Spanish, and Italian, among other languages.[61] Buck's *The Good Earth* was the subject of rights sales in less familiar languages as well, including Bulgarian, Czech, and Ibo.[62]

John Day carried on its international business far more through the sale of publication and translation rights to foreign publishers than by the export of physical books.[63] Whether or not the company controlled foreign rights on a title depended on the terms of the original contract between the author and the company. Buck, for example, retained her foreign rights and engaged an agent, David Lloyd, to represent her. In late 1944, however, she renegotiated the agreement to exclude Lloyd from being a party to further contracts with John Day, for the reason that her husband's firm could represent her just as well.[64]

In cases where the firm was the proprietor, the contractual details followed a general pattern. Under John Day's agreement with the Bompiani firm in Rome for Italian translation rights to Landon's *Anna and the King of Siam,* for example, Bompiani was obligated to publish the work within twelve months of the date of the contract. If it failed to do so or if the translated edition went out of print, John Day could reclaim the Italian rights on three months' notice. The Italian publisher was responsible for commissioning the translation. Standard agreements involved an advance against royalties, payable on signing. The royalty was normally a tiered percentage of the retail price of the foreign edition, with the percentage rising with sales. In the case of the Landon book, the advance was $250 against royalties of 10 percent of sales of the first four thousand copies, 12½ percent on copies from 4,001 through seven thousand, and 15 percent on copies beyond seven thousand. Three gratis copies of Bompiani's edition were to be sent to John Day.[65] In other contracts, the advance generally ranged from one hundred to eight hundred dollars. The royalty almost always began at 7½ or 8 percent and rose to 12 or 12½ percent, with the threshold of each increase and even the number of tiers being highly variable. For contracts made with publishers in poorer countries, mostly in Latin America and the Middle East, the advance might be nominal. For example, John Day agreed to sell Hebrew rights to Lin Yutang's *Leaf in the Storm* for a fee of £10.[66] The royalty was shared with the author at the percentage specified in the author's contract, usually 50–50.

Alfred A. Knopf, Inc.

Alfred A. Knopf, Inc., was without doubt one of the most prestigious U.S. publishing companies. Its graceful colophon, depicting a borzoi (a breed of dog), was among the most recognizable of publishers' devices, and its books in general were widely admired for their fine design. Alfred Knopf prided himself on not hesitating to publish a book of quality with slim commercial prospects. Like most of his peers, he was convinced that a good publisher was an important force in a culture—no exaggeration in his case. Knopf's backlist contained works by some of the most stellar twentieth-century authors. Many were properties that were very much in demand by publishers in postwar Europe and elsewhere, and Knopf aggressively marketed these abroad. But what especially characterized the firm, both before and after the war, were its great efforts to find some of the best works by foreign authors and to buy rights for their own list. Blanche Knopf, Alfred's wife, was a formidable publishing figure in her own right, and it was she who was most responsible for the distinction of Knopf's titles of foreign works in English translation.[67] Both Knopfs knew that a publishing house could make money, gain prestige, and do important cultural work by buying books abroad as well as by selling them there.

The firm's internationalist bent was evident from its founding in 1915. The first eleven books included none of American authorship. Ten were translations from French, Polish, and Russian, while the eleventh was a British novel. Among the British and European writers who adorned the Knopf lists were Robert Graves, Katherine Mansfield, Mikhail Sholokhov, Knut Hamsun, Oswald Spengler, and Thomas Mann. Blanche Knopf was particularly effective in acquiring notable French titles for translation, including works by Albert Camus, Simone de Beauvoir, André Gide, Jean-Paul Sartre, and Jean Giraudoux. Her services in introducing modern French literature to Americans earned her induction into the French Legion of Honor.[68]

During the war, she set her sights on doing the same for Latin American literature, a goal very much in tune with the aims of President Roosevelt's Good Neighbor Policy and Nelson Rockefeller's Office of the Coordinator of Inter-American Affairs. The government had been urging publishers to engage in two-way literary and publishing exchanges with Latin America since 1939.[69] Toward that goal, Blanche embarked on a trip by air to and through South America in 1942, the first of several adventurous and risky journeys abroad she made during wartime and the early postwar years. Her accounts of these trips are fascinating. Nazi influence in South America was strong, and the continent was rife with espionage and intrigue. In Latin America, she attended numerous dinners, luncheons, and receptions at U.S. embassies, and was everywhere met by authors pressing manuscripts into her hands. The trip, however, was full of inconveniences, discomforts, and even a hint of danger. She could not shake the presence of an individual she described as a "Peruvian Indian" of "shady character," who made veiled threats based on his allegations that the

Germans knew about all the anti-Nazi books that the firm had published and might retaliate.[70]

It took two years for her to develop a publishing plan for the books she had discovered on the South American trip. She sought and received advice on books to select from Sumner Welles, a Latin American specialist and a former under-secretary of state. She also persuaded Welles to write a preface to a brochure listing the books, which, according to Knopf's Herbert Weinstock, would note that the firm had "embarked on a policy of building up a really first-rate, distinguished list of Latin American books, both non-fiction and fiction....Knopf intends to do for Latin American writings what we have for so long been doing for important European writing."[71]

A trip to England followed in 1943. While there, she calmly had her hair done during a German bombing raid but developed nighttime headaches from the noise of the antiaircraft guns near her Hyde Park hotel. She returned from London with a number of British titles for the Knopf list.[72]

She also made postwar trips. In 1946, she managed to gain accreditation as a correspondent, having been asked by the army air force "to obtain material for a book on air war."[73] During the trip, she apparently conducted some Knopf business, which brought the ire of fellow publishers down on her because at the time all publishers' contacts with Germany were to be carried out through the occupation force's information control officers.[74] She traveled to Germany again in early 1949, at the invitation of Gen. Lucius D. Clay, the U.S. military governor, whom she had approached about writing his memoirs. Fitted out with a parachute, she flew to Berlin on a C-54 carrying a load of Kansas wheat during a mission of the celebrated airlift. Clay told her that he could not sign a contract until he had resigned his post, but did dictate and sign a letter agreeing to give Knopf his book. Something must have happened to void that agreement, for Doubleday rather than Knopf published his memoir, *Decision in Germany,* in 1950. On the 1949 trip, Blanche also managed to telephone or visit a number of German publishers, who testified to the continuing hardship of life in the former Reich.[75]

Although Blanche Knopf's trips to England and the Continent during and just after the war may have been advantageous to the firm, her ventures did not win universal approbation and, according to some, may have even been counter-productive. Houghton Mifflin's representative in London, for one, believed that she had "done a good deal to sour British publishers toward us."[76]

The Knopfs' dedication to finding great foreign literature to publish in the United States did not lessen their interest in selling their books to publishers in Britain and Europe. The firm's eastbound traffic in books was highly active. No less than other publishers, Albert and Blanche were aware of the great hunger that Europeans felt for books from the liberating countries, and how much helping to fill that need could advance the position of the United States abroad. As Blanche put it in regard to the foreign country that held her greatest affection, "France is alive and interested in reading, but is hungry for books from England and America, particularly America. There is a terrific cry for books for translation and in the English language. We here cannot conceive how a country like France with no free literature, no free reading for five years, what it means for them to get books again. The most important thing is to make it possible for the French to get our point of view both politically and culturally."[77]

Charles Scribner's Sons

The venerable firm of Charles Scribner's Sons was making preparations to celebrate its centennial as the Second World War concluded in the radioactive infernos of Hiroshima and Nagasaki. Founded in 1846, the blue-chip company remained firmly in the hands of generations of Princeton-educated Scribners. During the first half of the twentieth century, the firm was best noted for its outstanding list of American fiction, which included Edith Wharton, Ring Lardner, Ernest Hemingway, Erskine Caldwell, Thomas Wolfe, Marjorie Kinnan Rawlings, Zora Neale Hurston, and, preeminently, a fellow Princetonian, F. Scott Fitzgerald.[78] All were valuable literary properties in world markets.

Scribner's was also one of the last American publishers to retain a prewar branch in London. A brief account of the firm thus provides a view of an alternate method by which an American publisher operated in international markets. The continued existence of the London office meant that the firm would endeavor to balance its international business between selling its American books overseas and acquiring British and other books for the United States.

Scribner's international operations were nearly as old as the company itself. In 1857 the firm established a subsidiary in New York to import books from Britain. The unit was transferred to London seven years later. The London subsidiary was fully merged into the New York company in 1891. The firm also conducted an important rare book business there. Over time, Scribner's also engaged in retail bookselling as well as in importing and exporting books bound or in sheets and dealing with the trade in rights.

The years of World War II were, to say the least, difficult for the London office, but the staff persevered with stiff upper lips. When war was declared in 1939, Britain severely limited imports of noncritical materials, including books, in order to conserve its dollar resources. The head of the London branch, the American Charles Kingsley, worked with the Publishers Association to warn the government that a reduction in imports would also reduce exports, which could cripple the economy. Scribner's own exports back to the United States were also threatened, because British books had become less attractive to readers in the United States.[79] Even when the import restrictions for books were later relaxed, fiction and juvenile literature were still proscribed (owing to the sense that such material did not contribute to the war effort), but "it should be possible," Kingsley thought, "to bring in at least a fairly representative list of books."[80]

By late winter 1940, the difficulties had persuaded both Charles Scribner (the one known as CS III) and Kingsley that much of the London branch's business should be put on hold for the duration. After Kingsley returned to the United States with his wife, John Carter, a British citizen who headed the London branch's rare book department and who had a long, distinguished career as a bibliographer and antiquarian bookman, was put in charge of the office and a staff that had been pared down to two.[81] The firm remained as a "shadow organization" to be brought fully back to life after the war.[82] The office continued to carry on some export and import business and retailing but did very little publishing. In contrast, the antiquarian book business flourished during the war. Carter himself performed his duties essentially part-time, having joined the Ministry of Information within days of the outbreak of war, working from four in the afternoon to midnight reading and digesting news reports.[83] Fortunately, MoI's headquarters in Bloomsbury was just around the corner from the Scribner's office. Carter's going to work part-time for MoI was "a God sent solution" for the London office, and not only because it minimized Carter's commute.[84] It made it possible for him to continue with Scribner's and underscored the patriotic position of a British subject employed in London by a U.S. firm. After three bombs fell nearby in 1940, the head of the office defiantly had "the Stars and Stripes and the Union Jack put up over the front door."[85] From the fall of 1943 until 1946, he spent extended periods away from London on assignment to MoI's British Information Services in New York.[86]

Although the longtime London office manager, Arthur Dust, had feared "that Jerry will cause no end of trouble, and loss of life, before he finally goes down," by May 1945, he could happily inform New York that "the house survived the final temper of Hitler, except for several broken windows in the rear of the building, the result of one of the last rockets." If anything, the fact that the London office was a branch of a U.S. firm—and "the only American [publishing] concern to carry on throughout hostilities"—gave the staff in New York all the more reason to empathize over the travails of their English colleagues.

The opportunities that Scribner's, like many other U.S. firms, envisioned for expanding world market share postwar prompted reconsideration of the

FIGURE 9. Staff members of the London office of Charles Scribner's Sons in 1941, with the Stars and Stripes and Union Jack over the front entrance. *Publishers Weekly,* Dec. 27, 1941, 2291.

functions of the London branch. Through his service on the Book Publishers Bureau committee on Anglo-American relations, Scribner clearly saw "that we have a chance that we cannot afford to lose" in strengthening the role of London. With "interests in both countries," however, Scribner's, more than most other U.S. publishers, was "anxious to see that there is no conflict between the American and English publishers in the export of books to the Continent, the Colonies, and for that matter, the rest of the world."[87] But serious disagreements developed between publishers in the two nations nevertheless.[88]

A reorganization of the London operation gave a higher priority to the export and import of new books than before. In addition to continuing to regard the rare book business as "my special preoccupation," Carter assumed responsibility for acquiring U.S. rights to English books, for managing the wholesale exports of books from London to New York, and for overseeing the publishing functions of Charles Scribner's Sons, Ltd., in Britain. He was to split day-to-day duties on these aspects of the business with office manager Dust. To assist him in scouting British books that New York might import or acquire rights to, Carter had the part-time services of two travelers.[89]

Scribner's carried out its reciprocal Anglo-American trade both by shipping physical stock—ranging from flat printed sheets through folded and sewn gatherings, all the way to bound books—from one country to the other or by having the books set in type, printed, and bound in the receiving country. Scribner's was not obligated to publish its American books through Scribner's London. New York could, and frequently did, contract with other British houses to publish their books in Britain (which, as was customary, would also gain them access to the empire and commonwealth markets). Only infrequently, on the other hand, was a book published by Scribner's London brought out in the United States by anyone but Scribner's, although not all London productions necessarily made the westbound passage over the Atlantic.

In order to hold down foreign debt, the British government continued to impose stringent quotas on books imported from the States. Theoretically, this situation made the import of physical books (from sheets to bound volumes) to Britain less appealing than having the American book printed in the UK.[90] This was because the only physical item that had to be shipped across the sea—and potentially subjected to import quotas and duties—was a manuscript or a single copy of the book to be set in type rather than several heavy crates of printed matter. In practice, though, many other factors were involved in a decision whether to import books or have them printed in Britain, including not only the continued paper shortage in Great Britain but also crippling bottlenecks at the printers and binders.[91] Usually, decisions on how best to proceed were made on a case-by-case basis, with many variables taken into account. Scribner's took part in the postwar flurry of rights deals in the same ways that other American publishers did. They worked through the London office, using literary agents in the United States and abroad and taking advantage of the matchmaking services of OWI and, later, USIBA. Scribner's certainly had as much success as any domestic rival in placing their better books with publishers abroad.

McGraw-Hill Book Company

The McGraw-Hill Book Company was established in 1909 out of the merger of the book departments of the McGraw Publishing Company and the Hill Publishing Company. James H. McGraw, a schoolteacher in upstate New York, founded McGraw in 1899. John Alexander Hill, an engineer-turned-editor from Colorado, established Hill three years later. The original professions of the two men—teaching and engineering—provided the connecting link for the merged company's historic specialty, textbooks and technical publications. It was not until 1930 that the firm entered the trade-publishing business by setting up a department with its own imprint, Whittlesey House, so that the text-and-technology and trade sides of the business would maintain their own strong identities, free of confusion between the two.[92]

McGraw-Hill was representative of American textbook and technology publishing. This important and profitable corner of the book-publishing industry was not the principal focus of the joint efforts of publishers and government directed toward international markets during the war; trade books were the main thing. But the technology and textbook markets were very important on the home front. James S. Thompson, who became McGraw-Hill's president in 1944, said in 1942 that the whole nation had been turned into a "university of war."[93] The textbook and technical-book operations, however, did become a major part of the effort of American publishers to expand their markets abroad after the war was over. The government was interested in part because of the belief that "trade follows the book": exports of a book on the latest treatments for tropical diseases, for example, could lead to increased exportation of U.S. medical equipment and pharmaceuticals. For textbooks and technical publications, the export of physical books (or sheets) in English was a much more viable option than it was for most trade publishers, because English was more readily understood in books about science and technology than it was for novels and general nonfiction, where translation was generally called for. Despite its nontrade focus, McGraw-Hill was very much a part of the establishment dominated by trade publishers.

The possibilities of a strong international market for its books became apparent to McGraw-Hill when Thompson joined four other publishing-company executives on a government-endorsed mission to several Latin American countries, in 1943.[94] The travelers could not fail to notice the historic dominance of British and German textbooks and technical publications in the region, nor could they miss seeing the extent to which the flow of such books from Europe was being cut off by the war. Thompson's report to headquarters led to the establishment of a Book Export Department, to focus on developing new markets for books in Latin America even as it was beginning to set its sights on potential new buyers elsewhere in the world. After a year of operation, the foreign department's sales to Latin America had "increased tremendously," with revenues in Mexico up 90 percent from the previous year. Its principal business method was selling translation rights to its technical and trade books to foreign publishers, though it did not neglect exports. To publicize its wares to publishers, book dealers, and universities abroad, it began publishing a newsletter, *McGraw-Hill Overseas Book News*.[95] By the end of the war, it was obvious how much market share McGraw-Hill and other technical publishers had wrested from the weakened German and British publishers. A month after V-J Day, Thompson reported large orders from booksellers in India, which could threaten British interests.[96] Still, it was not certain how long the United States could retain that advantage if resurgent British and German publishers tried to reclaim their former dominance in their customary markets.

Accordingly, in 1946 the firm dispatched one of its college travelers on a round-the-world tour to visit publishers, educators, engineers, scientists, and librarians in twenty-five countries. The chief finding of the trip was that American textbook and technical publishers would have to promote and market their products as aggressively as possible if they were to maintain their advantage. McGraw-Hill thereupon enlarged its export department, placing increased emphasis on cultivating close relations between its salesmen and foreign university faculty members by mail, just as they did in the United States by paying personal calls on faculty on their campuses. They also stepped up communications with scientific and technical journals to encourage reviews of the company's new books. The company also created its own translations program for books that might sell well in the European languages, as well as in languages or dialects in the Middle East and Asia. During the U.S. occupation of Japan, special government funds made it feasible for the company to sell technical books and magazines to that country, which, an interested local observer believed, was twenty years behind in industrial techniques.[97]

German and French Émigré and Refugee Publishing Houses

The flight of refugees from Europe to the United States in the decade or two before the war brought with it a cadre of publishers, writers, and other artists and intellectuals with broad, cosmopolitan interests and experiences. These individuals, a number of whom established publishing houses in the United States, provided a new focal point for the internationalization of U.S. publishing during and after the war. Most arrived as refugees from Hitler's Germany. Some stayed in the United States after the war, others returned to Germany or elsewhere in Europe, but all helped increase ties and trade between American and European publishers. Some of the German publishers who remained were Kurt and Helen Wolff, who established Pantheon Books, and Frederick Ungar, who set up shop under his own name. Among the firms that returned home were Bermann-Fischer Verlag and Aurora Press.

German was not the only language of publication in the United States by and for refugees. There were, for example, at least three series of books published in French by firms in New York City, beginning in 1941. The targeted audiences for these were French émigrés throughout the Americas as well as Francophones in North and South America, Africa, and Asia, whose normal supply of books in French and access to publication in French in Paris and elsewhere in Europe the war had cut off.

The proprietor of Bermann-Fischer Verlag was Gottfried Bermann-Fischer, a Jew and the son-in-law and heir to Samuel Fischer's S. Fischer Verlag in Berlin, one of Germany's most distinguished publishing houses. Under pressure from the Nazis, S. Fischer Verlag was reorganized, with an Aryan publisher, Peter Suhrkamp, assuming control of a portion of the firm. Nevertheless, the Nazi government in 1935, following difficult negotiations, permitted Bermann-Fischer to leave Germany and to take with him and his family the rights to and stocks of titles by "the authors prohibited or 'undesired'" by the regime. These names constituted an "A-list" of German (and other) writers, including Hugo von Hofmannsthal, Arthur Schnitzler, Jakob Wassermann, Thomas Mann, Franz Werfel, Carl Zuckmayer, Alfred Döblin, André Maurois, and George Bernard Shaw.[98]

Having relocated to Vienna, Bermann-Fischer, his wife, Brigitte, and their three daughters were forced to uproot again in 1938, ahead of the Anschluss, leaving behind some four hundred thousand volumes in the warehouse to be confiscated by the Nazis. This time, he set up shop in Stockholm, long a center of both German- and English-language publishing, where he received financial support from the important Swedish house of Alfred Bonniers, which was also run by a Jewish family. Some of his associates in Vienna were able to join him in Stockholm. He had a couple of productive years there before the toleration of many Swedes for all things German, including Nazism, convinced him that he must take his family to the United States.[99] He had been reluctant to move and reestablish his business yet another time, he told a friend in the United States, the Dutch American writer Hendrik Willem Van Loon. Van Loon agreed with Bermann-Fischer's judgment then, but within months he acknowledged how conditions had changed in that ostensibly neutral nation: "The Swedes have lost everything they had ever gained by way of Good will.... They have been about as materialistically selfish as any race could be and to hell with them says America."[100]

With help from Van Loon, the Bermann-Fischers obtained U.S. visas. Before Gottfried and his family could depart, however, his anti-Nazi sympathies and activities, apparently an actionable offense in neutral Sweden, were reported to the Stockholm police, who arrested and imprisoned him. His arrest not only jeopardized their trip to the United States but also endangered their lives because there remained a strong possibility that the Germans would soon take over Sweden, as they had Norway. The authorities released him on June 24, 1940, after several months in jail, and ordered his deportation. Under the circumstances, this was an easy sentence to accept.

The family left Stockholm the next day by plane for Moscow, merely the first leg of a mostly harrowing, opposite-way journey to New York from Sweden via Moscow, Vladivostok, Yokohama, and San Francisco, necessitated by the closing of the normal westbound sea and air routes to the United States.[101] Van Loon's long-distance intercession with U.S. consular officials at various points along the way facilitated their journey.[102] A welcoming letter from the generous Van Loon greeted them on their arrival in San Francisco. The Bermann-Fischers spent two weeks with Thomas Mann at his home in Santa Monica before heading to New York. Van Loon helped them locate in the New York suburb Old Greenwich, Connecticut, where he lived. Shortly, Alfred Harcourt, of Harcourt, Brace, invited Bermann-Fischer to his Madison Avenue office and gave him a desk with a telephone and typewriter, from which he might establish himself in an unfamiliar publishing world.[103]

It did not take Bermann-Fischer long to make his move. In 1941, he and a partner established the L. B. Fischer Publishing Corporation in New York, with backing from Harcourt. The "B." in the company name stood for Bermann, the "L." for Fritz Landshoff, also a distinguished Jewish refugee publisher from Berlin, who was at the time the head of a German-language affiliate of the noted Dutch publisher Querido.[104] Although Landshoff, like Bermann-Fischer, had managed to flee Europe, Emanuel Querido and his wife were gassed at Auschwitz. The L. B. Fischer Publishing Corporation (also known as the Fischer-Landshoff Company) was strictly an English-language house, with most of its list consisting of English translations of important German works to which Bermann-Fischer held the rights. The firm also issued antifascist books, including a series published in collaboration with the Free World Movement.[105] Before setting up L. B. Fischer, Bermann-Fischer had decided that it would be impractical to establish a German-language publishing house in the United States, at least for the time being. Instead, he made arrangements with other firms, including Harcourt, Brace, to import his Stockholm-published German-language books and distribute them in the States. But U.S. entry into the war against Germany made further shipments of his books from Sweden impossible.[106]

Cut off from his remaining Stockholm inventory, Bermann-Fischer had no choice but to revisit his original plan and "to print in the United States the German texts of important books."[107] The publisher issued only a few such titles, but those were of high literary merit and popular appeal, mainly works by his star authors, Mann and Werfel. Bermann-Fischer continued to direct the affairs of his Stockholm office, despite the inhospitality that the Swedish authorities had shown him by imprisoning and deporting him.

Most but not all of the titles were printed in Sweden. At least one Stockholm imprint bore a note that it was printed in Switzerland. This operation was very complex in that the publisher and many of his authors were in the United States and the printers in Sweden or Switzerland. To make such an arrangement possible, Bermann-Fischer took advantage of a commercial treaty between Sweden and Germany that enabled him to send printed materials between Sweden and Switzerland through Germany in sealed boxcars—an ironic use of a procedure that Bermann-Fischer surely would have denounced when the Nazis shipped weapons and other war matériel through Sweden to occupied Norway. Manuscripts prepared in New York were flown to Stockholm for typesetting, but it was not practicable to have proofs sent back for checking. Inevitably, a number of editions in the Free German books series contained corrupt texts. Some of the books were also published in the United States, where more care could be taken. One of Mann's titles was affected by paper shortages. Because in 1944 allotments were based on 1942 consumption, which for Bermann-Fischer was scant, he tried to purchase additional paper from the unused quotas of other publishers, but the War Production Board had recently disallowed that practice. The book eventually appeared in an edition of eighteen hundred copies. Mann found "more joy in the 1800 German copies in America than in the 200,000 English."[108] In 1945, Bermann-Fischer was actively involved in the production of the Bücherreihe Neue Welt books for German POWs in U.S. camps.[109]

Despite his activities publishing in Stockholm and New York, Bermann-Fischer kept his eye on an eventual return to Germany. To enable him to reintroduce into Germany his German-language publications, untainted by both fascist and socialist ideologies, he took care to build up stocks printed in Sweden. These, he believed, could be used to reeducate the Germans struggling to find their way in the ruins of the Reich.[110] He sold L. B. Fischer, his English-language imprint, in early 1946 in order to concentrate on his German-language publishing as Bermann-Fischer Verlag. He returned to Europe in February of that year. He spent time in Stockholm, overseeing his business there in person for the first time since he took flight in 1940, and made the first steps toward converting it from a wartime footing to a peacetime operation. He soon discovered how much demand there was for German books in Europe and was gratified to learn of the interest of British and even Soviet officials in using his publications in their zones of occupation. He also visited Amsterdam, where "the hunger for German books that was displayed there," his wife wrote in her memoirs, "was a first confirmation of our future hopes after the long drought of the war years."[111]

Shortly after the war ended, he reestablished contact with Suhrkamp, the former associate who had held on to a portion of the S. Fischer Verlag interests under his own name. The next year he assigned Suhrkamp the rights to some of the most important of his Free German books. He still had to negotiate the complexities of receiving the approval of the information-control authorities in the U.S., British, and French zones. A second postwar trip to Stockholm, in April 1947, gave him a closer vantage point from which to obtain visas to the three Western zones in order to press on toward his goals. He received clearance, and was able to return to his homeland in May. He wrote his wife that the U.S. military government treated him like a VIP, and the papers he received from them "have made me a superman able to bring a bit of happiness to the poor figures crawling in the dirt." While in Germany, he arranged with Suhrkamp to publish inexpensive editions of émigré literature in substantial quantities—up to one hundred fifty thousand copies per title.[112]

The next step was the removal in 1948 of Bermann-Fischer Verlag from Stockholm to Amsterdam and the merger there between his firm and Querido. This was but a prelude, however, to his primary goal, the reuniting of his exile firm with the remnant of the old S. Fischer Verlag that Suhrkamp had been caretaking in Berlin. "The path to this goal was to be long and thorny," his wife wrote. Success was finally achieved in 1950, when he reclaimed full title to the name and assets of S. Fischer Verlag. He and his family moved themselves and the resurrected firm to Frankfurt. His wife joined him in full-time work for the firm, including a great deal of responsibility for the firm's international trading. With the return of S. Fischer Verlag to Germany, the Bermann-Fischers' odyssey had come full circle.[113] Bermann-Fischer once wrote that the problem of re-educating the German people "is essentially a publishing problem."[114] He made considerable contributions to solving that problem through his publication of the BNWs and his Free German books, but probably no more than he did by his decision to return to his homeland to reconstitute his distinguished publishing business.

Another German refugee publisher, the Aurora Press, had powerhouse credentials like Bermann-Fischer's but was less successful, largely because of its leftist orientation. Aurora was established in New York in 1945 as a cooperative by the radical refugee publisher and bookseller Wieland Herzfelde and ten of the most significant émigré German literati in the United States—Ernst Bloch, Bertolt Brecht, Ferdinand Bruckner, Alfred Döblin, Lion Feuchtwanger, Oskar Maria Graf, Heinrich Mann, Berthold Viertel, Ernst Waldinger, and Franz Carl Weiskopf. Aurora Press's ideological focus could not have been more different from Bermann-Fischer's, but Herzfelde's press shared the goals of participating in "the cultural rebuilding" of Germany by helping alleviate the country's intellectual famine.[115] Like Bermann-Fischer, Aurora also hoped to respond to the need to provide German prisoners of war incarcerated in the United States with German-language books void of the Nazi taint, and, ultimately, to play a role in the postwar German market.[116]

Herzfelde established Malik Verlag after returning from the western front in World War I. After Hitler assumed power in 1933, Herzfelde relocated the firm to Prague, and then immigrated to New York in 1939, where his Seven Seas Bookshop became a focal point in the community of refugee German intellectuals. Aurora published twelve books in 1945 and 1946. Distributed by Schoenhof Foreign Books in Cambridge, Massachusetts, they were issued in editions of from fifteen hundred to four thousand copies. Another dozen or so books were announced but never published in the United States.[117]

Herzfelde was eager to have his books bought in quantity for the use of German prisoners of war on U.S. soil. Aurora Verlag's left-wing principles (and principals) attracted suspicion from the military authorities responsible for the POWs. Some form of censorship may well have been responsible for the fact that the planned first offering by Aurora aimed at the POWs—a reader called *Morgenröte*—failed to appear until 1947, well after it could have been read by its principal intended audience.[118] Bermann-Fischer set off no such red flags ideologically.

After Germany's defeat, Herzfelde tried unsuccessfully to export books or sell translation rights in the U.S. zone, though he had some luck in the French zone. Herzfelde moved his press back to Germany (the Soviets' quadrant in Berlin) in 1947, renamed it Aurora Bücherei, and achieved strong sales. Two of his colleagues in the Aurora Press venture in New York, Brecht and Bloch, returned with him to East Berlin.[119]

The most notable of the French-language publishers was Éditions de la Maison Française. The publishers, Isaac Molho and Vitalis Crespin, were immigrants of Sephardic Jewish ancestry from Greece and Turkey respectively, who came to the United States in the 1920s and set up a French-language bookstore in Manhattan. The shop—the Librairie de France—survived as the oldest continuing retail tenant in Rockefeller Center, across Fifth Avenue from St. Patrick's Cathedral, until it closed its doors in the fall of 2009. (It plans to continue selling on the Internet.) Given the wartime circumstances in occupied and Vichy France, French publishers provided short-term, limited rights to EMF to publish French-language editions in New York to serve worldwide communities of Francophone readers. André Maurois, himself in exile in New York, was the chief patron of this enterprise, which included a number of his books on its list. Ultimately, EMF published 120 titles by seventy-seven authors. Mainly, the titles attempted to meet the exiles' most basic needs for information about the course of the war and to help them grasp the magnitude—and causes—of France's humiliation. Print runs (executed by Molho's brother-in-law) ranged from ten thousand to

fifty thousand copies per title. That these edition sizes tended to be overly optimistic is vouched for by the fact that one could still purchase pristine copies
of many of these wartime titles from the tables and shelves in the Rockefeller
Center shop's basement until it closed.[120] In any case, Crespin lost no time in
traveling to Paris to reconnect with publishers and booksellers in the French
capital.[121]

The other French series were similar in purpose and content to the EMF
books. One was published under the name Éditions Didier and the other by the
New York and Paris bookseller Brentano's. Brentano's issued nearly a hundred
titles, Didier far fewer. All three series were issued in what *Publishers' Weekly*
characterized as the "traditional French format," that is, upright paperbacks, a
bit squatter than American paperbacks of the day, with black-and-red typog-
raphy on a cream-colored stock and little ornamentation. Like Crespin, Arthur
Brentano hurried back to reopen his Paris bookstore, the first U.S. retail establishment to return to business after liberation. Apparently, it was also the
only bookstore in the capital with any stock left—some twelve thousand books
that the German occupiers had for some reason left untouched.[122] Substantial
and important as it was, the New York French-language publishing scene was
dwarfed by that of the province of Quebec, which catered to exiles as well as
native Quebecois.[123]

As U.S. and Allied soldiers made their way through Europe following D-Day,
liberating and pacifying the civilian populations, millions of books followed,
thanks to the work of personnel from OWI and other agencies in getting the
volumes distributed. These books primed the pump, filling the emergency need
for non-Nazi books. Gradually, publishing houses throughout Europe began to
awaken. With little if any domestic literature to publish, the firms turned mostly
to the United States for their supply of titles. The U.S. government actively facilitated what became a highly charged market for translation rights to many of
the American titles published during the war, much in demand by book-hungry
European civilians. Many American publishing houses—both long-standing
firms and newcomers established by European refugees—retooled their operations to meet increased international demand. But peacetime produced its own
set of obstacles as well as the opportunities for new international markets that
had revealed themselves not long after Hitler invaded Poland. Among the many
challenges facing the publishers and the government was finding how to carry
on the internationalization of their trade once the main public and private players in the wartime partnership had been disbanded, namely, the Office of War
Information and the Council on Books in Wartime. Would a new partnership
emerge, or would it not?

THE RISE AND FALL OF THE UNITED STATES INTERNATIONAL BOOK ASSOCIATION

In the summer of 1944, well before the Overseas and Transatlantic editions were shipped abroad, senior officials in both the government and the publishing industry were already planning for the postwar future of American books abroad and the institutional structure that might facilitate increased international trade. The Office of War Information was still very much alive, and more involved in propaganda efforts overseas at that point in the war than at home. The Council on Books in Wartime was fully occupied overseeing the massive Armed Services Editions program as well as the production of OEs. While the council's partnership with OWI in international book programs had yet to bear fruit, the project was at last moving ahead and held great promise. In the spirit of the wartime culture of planning, the public and private parties to the undertaking took time to contemplate what the future would look like when the chief players would more than likely no longer be OWI and CBW. The legislation creating OWI authorized it to operate no more than six months after the cessation of hostilities. Although there was no sunset provision for CBW, the organization would clearly have to remake itself for peacetime, if it carried on at all.

It was not too early to think seriously about what would happen after the shooting stopped. Would the publishers still be interested in building up their international business? What would be the federal government's attitude toward maintaining an international information program after the war, and what role, if any, might books play in it? Would it still be desirable for government and publishers to cooperate as they had done during the war?

Planning in fact resulted in the establishment, at the turn of the year 1944–45, of a private, nonprofit creature of the industry, the United States International

FIGURE 10. One of the offices (possibly Chester Kerr's) in OWI's quarters at 224 West Fifty-seventh Street in Manhattan, being cleared out after the propaganda agency's dissolution shortly after V-J Day. The Vendome apartment building is visible through the window. After mobilizing for its extensive domestic and overseas duties, the agency quickly demobilized as the country returned to a peacetime footing. Courtesy of the Princeton University Library

Book Association, which held promise of maintaining a strong public/private partnership to advance American books abroad. It existed for only a year, but was succeeded by a variety of instrumentalities that linked interests of the publishers and the government, however tenuously, for a number of years thereafter.

A Second "Summit" on American Books Abroad

During August and September 1944, representatives of OWI and other government agencies, as well as officials of the Council on Books in Wartime and other private-sector book organizations, busied themselves preparing reports in advance of a second "summit" meeting on how the government and the trade could advance their mutual agendas.[1] Chester Kerr and his associates in the wartime book programs believed maintaining the collaboration in peacetime to be of the utmost importance. They intended to press the issue with both Elmer Davis, the director of OWI, and with Secretary of State Edward Stettinius as well, because it was almost certain that the department would take on an increased role in book matters following the dissolution of OWI. Before approaching Davis or Stettinius, however, it was necessary that all parties to the collaboration sketch out and agree upon their positions.

Accordingly, Kerr prepared several drafts of OWI's report, with input from senior colleagues. Meanwhile, the position of the trade was being laid out by Malcolm Johnson, the chairman of the Book Publishers' Bureau, and that of the State Department by Harry Warfel, chief of the Book and Publication Section, Division of Cultural Cooperation. These position papers were to be the topic of discussion at a conference, which Kerr had proposed, to take place at OWI's Manhattan offices on October 3.[2]

The document that Kerr wrote served two purposes: to codify and rationalize all of the rather ad hoc, experimental, and emergency practices that had accrued in various parts of OWI in response to the exigencies of the war and were later centralized within the Overseas Book Bureau; and to reenergize the close public/private partnership to promote and market American books abroad well after the war had ended and OWI had ceased to exist.

While Kerr's memorandum was still under internal review, his boss, Samuel Williamson, briefed Edward Barrett, the director of OWI's overseas branch in New York on the context of the report. He pointed out that OWI was, for all intents and purposes, in the book-export business. Given OWI's status as "a war agency doing emergency work," however, it could not remain in the business for long. The State Department was also in the book-export business, had been in it longer, and would remain in it well after OWI's demise, Williamson added. State's involvement, however, was on a smaller scale than OWI's, and more closely focused on what in peacetime would be considered educational and cultural affairs. The war had in fact stimulated the U.S. book trade's efforts to overcome its traditional diffidence toward overseas business, and all signs pointed to the industry's concentrating on solving this problem after the conflict ended. Most American publishers hoped and expected that the United States would assume a greater role in world affairs in general. They also believed that the United States' increased influence would not only facilitate but positively mandate publishers' efforts abroad. All this underscored how interrelated were the interests of the government and private enterprise. As arms of the government, neither OWI nor State wished to remain in the publishing business permanently, as some foreign governments had done. In the United States, government's interests in books were better met through a fruitful voluntary partnership with the industry, which Williamson, Kerr, and others felt needed reconfirmation. The planned conference was intended "to create a closer working relationship" between the governmental and private entities.[3]

Kerr's lengthy report thoroughly and efficiently outlined OWI's book program. For background, he enumerated all of the various book-related activities that the agency was then carrying on; described how the tasks had developed and where they were coordinated; reiterated the fundamental concepts and operating policies of the program (emphasizing the unique place of books in long-term propaganda aimed at indigenous opinion makers); showed how books implemented the Long Range Directive for propaganda of June 14, 1944, by linking specific titles to the several propaganda objectives; recounted the effect that the war had had on the publishing industries of the United States, its chief allies, and the Axis countries; and described the principal means by which both Allies and enemies had used books for purposes of propaganda.

Next Kerr addressed the present and future of OWI's book operations. Grounding this section was a discussion of the procedures and diplomacy of putting books into the hands of foreign civilians up until the time that domestic production was reestablished, together with lists of books proposed and cleared for the two custom series (OEs and TEs) as well as other books purchased or produced for specific countries. The report concluded with budget figures for all of the various OWI-sponsored book programs.[4]

For the participants in the October conference, Kerr produced a six-page redaction of his longer, internal memorandum, mainly by omitting the lists and the budget figures. It alerted its readers to the fact that the memo necessarily dealt only with OWI's book program for Europe, because no program for Asia had yet been worked out and Latin America remained the preserve of the Coordinator of Inter-American Affairs (Nelson Rockefeller), not OWI.[5]

Warfel's brief contribution on behalf of the State Department was primarily a recitation of existing book-related programs carried out under its auspices. These included the maintenance of three libraries in Latin America, which had been established in 1942–43 by Rockefeller's Office of the Coordinator of Inter-American Affairs, then independent of the State Department, as well as other library-related programs. The department also facilitated the republication abroad of American textbooks in English, underwrote translations of a limited number of books, prepared bibliographies of American books, and assisted publishers in clearing permissions. The paper also listed ways in which the department provided assistance to the book trade, including the preparation of bibliographies and the forwarding of requests from foreign publishers to translate or reprint American titles. Warfel also noted that the department sponsored several publications, including a handbook for Chinese students in the United States and a history of the United States in Arabic.[6]

The position paper that Johnson wrote on behalf of the Book Publishers' Bureau deftly compared the industry's business interests to the national interest. What the U.S. publishing industry wanted, the report began, was "to be able to sell its wares abroad on as nearly an equal basis with other nationalities as possible. It would like to see the U.S. book as freely available in other countries as those of any other foreign supplier. The industry believes that by thus giving other peoples an opportunity, at least, to become familiar with the purposes, ideals and consequences of our culture it is doing a public service as well as furthering its own particular interests. Minus the commercial aspect, it is believed that the State Department shares this view." These points clearly targeted British claims to its traditional marketing territories, free of U.S. encroachment. The American publisher, Johnson continued, has "three things to sell: third party rights in the English language; rights of translation into foreign languages; and his own books." A number of factors complicated the proper development of those transactions. A principal roadblock was of the country's own making—its nonadherence to the Berne convention on international copyright, which left U.S. literary properties insecure throughout the world except in the British Empire. Removing this obstacle by reforming U.S. copyright policy was of the highest importance.

Another important factor, less susceptible to amelioration domestically, was the operation of "government subsidised cartels in Europe, particularly those operating out of France for books of the French language and from Spain for books in the Spanish language both of Spanish and German origin or inspiration, and out of Great Britain for books in the English language." These arrangements limited U.S. penetration into many areas of the world, either through agreements (such as foreign-rights contracts, especially with British publishers) or the realities of distributing American books, often at considerable geographical distance from the markets and in competition with foreign publishers in countries with strong governmental support for exports.

While acknowledging the commonality of interest with the U.S. government in increasing American book exports, the BPB paper sought to strike a favorable balance between its interests and those of the government. The industry, in other words, desired to limit the government's side of the partnership to a service function. While the publishers were in theory more than willing to contribute to the government's objectives for postwar propaganda and, especially, cultural diplomacy, they were no more agreeable to spending their own money on these ventures during the peace than they had been during wartime. This made them leery of schemes in which American books in English were to be sold at below-market prices, except in certain cases of critically important, outright propaganda. Even in such cases, the criterion "for publication of any book especially prepared for government use abroad [should be] whether it would be acceptable on the domestic market." If not, its effectiveness overseas would be questionable. This point echoed OWI's policy in choosing in-print American books for distribution abroad as OEs or TEs.

U.S. publishers, no less than their British colleagues, had an interest in the promotion of English as the principal second language of the world, according to Johnson. But, until that goal could be achieved, English would have to compete around the world with other important international languages such as French, Spanish, and German. It would therefore be wise, "in peacetime, to keep a proportion of important works, particularly in the informational field, untranslated," so as not to discourage the trend toward the wider understanding of English. Recognizing how important it was that the domestic publishing businesses in the liberated nations recover from the blows of war and occupation, the bureau nevertheless urged the government to exercise caution in this regard. "The line marking the wise limits to which we should go in helping the Germans, French and Spaniards, without damaging our own future interests must be a matter for informed study. It is well enough to load Hatchette [sic] with favors, assuming its present control is acceptable to us," Johnson continued, "but Hatchette is a bitter competitor of ours in Latin America, and these favors may mean the continuation of French medical books in the Argentine where ours might have displaced them."[7]

The most important recommendation of the BPB was to encourage the successful development of "an instrumentality to serve as a common meeting ground for industry and government," specifically "the export corporation now in process of formation by the industry." Such an entity should promote American books abroad, "and through them, the interests of this country. It should serve as a vehicle "to supply the government with a means for doing certain things abroad involving books which could not properly be done either by government directly or by government through an individual publisher." It could best do this by emphasizing the delivery of information about American books overseas, through the preparation and distribution of lists of new U.S. titles and the establishment of book centers in important foreign cities, where the books themselves could be examined by publishers and potential readers. The government's role as an intermediary between American publishers having foreign rights to sell and foreign publishers anxious to buy them should, after communication improves, be limited to the supplying of information.[8]

The October meeting took place at the West Fifty-seventh Street offices of OWI. Attendees from OWI, the CBW, and the BPB provided additional information not covered in the reports, but the main discussion was on continuing the government/industry partnership into peacetime, specifically through the proposed export corporation that was being developed by the BPB's Foreign Trade Committee with the blessing of the State Department. There was general consensus that the rising tide of nationalism among book publishers abroad, among such other factors as currency problems, made continued cooperation between the trade and the government at home necessary, because, with so much international diplomacy involved, private industry could not achieve the desired results without government aid.[9]

Origins and Goals of the USIBA

The idea for a postwar export corporation, which came to life several months later with the establishment of the United States International Book Association, originated in a trade mission that the BPB and the American Textbook Publishers' Institute, with the support of the State Department and the CIAA, sent to Latin America during June and July 1943. Five prominent publishers, representing trade, paperback, textbook, and technical publishing, traveled from Mexico City to Buenos Aires, with many intermediate stops along the way. The delegates—George P. Brett (Macmillan), Burr L. Chase (Silver Burdett), Robert F. de Graff (Pocket Books), Malcolm Johnson (Doubleday Doran), and James S. Thompson (McGraw-Hill)—returned full of enthusiasm for the prospects of American books in the region.[10] That the U.S. government "should entrust the task of opening up fresh business—and also fresh political—contacts in South America to a mission composed solely of book-publishers" astounded three former presidents of the Publishers' Association in London when they heard of it on their own mission to the United States not long afterwards.[11]

For a year, a committee of publishing executives planned the program for a postwar export agency in conjunction with officials of the State Department and, especially, CIAA. OWI was not involved. In fact, Kerr claimed that the agency knew nothing about the publishers' plans before the October "summit," when the BPB's report sketched out the corporation in considerable detail.[12] That OWI was in the dark was an astonishing admission, considering the close ties that Kerr and many OWI colleagues had with the BPB and top officials of its member firms.

This may not have been a deliberate slight to OWI. Inasmuch as fostering trade with Latin America was the purpose of the mission, OWI's participation might simply have been deemed irrelevant, since Latin America was the responsibility—some said the fiefdom—of Rockefeller's office. What became the CIAA had been established in 1940 with extensive mandates in the areas of economics, trade, and culture, but its main purpose was to offset the strong influence of Nazism and fascism in the region, including German espionage. It was independent of the State Department but was expected to maintain close communication with it. Rockefeller waged legendary turf battles with two other agencies, OWI and Col. William Donovan's Office of Strategic Services, for the right to run U.S. propaganda programs in Latin America. He succeeded in preventing OWI from playing any role in the region.[13] There was some logic to this, inasmuch as OWI's portfolio was essentially limited to the United States and the regions in which U.S. forces were fighting.

The strongest support for a postwar public/private partnership seems to have come from the State Department, which made it clear that it would welcome

such an arrangement as a means by which the government could continue to influence public opinion abroad by assisting publishers in increasing international
trade in American books beyond the wartime emergency.[14] By the time USIBA
was formally proposed, CIAA, like OWI, was being phased out as an independent agency, with most of its activities to be assumed by the State Department
directly; it was still, however, to be administered by Rockefeller as the newly appointed assistant secretary of state for inter-American affairs.[15] With propaganda
and cultural diplomacy with Latin America now completely under its jurisdiction, the State Department could attempt a more coherent, worldwide information strategy. Any doubters may themselves have become more optimistic as
discussions throughout the trade and the government neared completion, for
there was much to recommend USIBA.

Despite being shut out of the early planning, Kerr and key OWI colleagues
became strong advocates of the corporation.[16] After performing due diligence
regarding OWI's participation, Kerr could report in November to Edward M.
Crane, the chairman of the BPB's Joint Committee on Foreign Trade, that OWI
had agreed in principle to cooperate with the proposed export corporation,
with certain conditions attached. Essentially, OWI agreed that it would (1) purchase books through the corporation and forward purchase orders from foreign sources; (2) direct inquiries from foreign publishers about the purchase of
American books and the clearing of foreign rights; and (3) advise the corporation on publishing conditions abroad and supply information to it about specific foreign publishing firms. OWI's cooperation was contingent upon receiving
evidence that the corporation was "truly representative of the trade, text and
technical books publishers of this country" and that it was adequately staffed to
meet its goals.[17] At its annual meeting on November 21, the BPB unanimously
approved the recommendation of its foreign-trade committee to proceed with
the establishment of an export corporation.[18] USIBA was formally incorporated
as a nonprofit in January 1945.[19] The publishers had been urged to give the new
export body a trial of at least two years "as an investment to expand their business."[20] CIAA provided seed money through a twenty-five thousand dollar grant-
in-aid.[21] Assistant Secretary of State Spruille Braden told the members at its first
meeting that he welcomed "the invasion of Latin America with our literatures,"
invoking another, somewhat different D-Day for American books abroad.[22]

The constant lament—and battle cry for action—of people like Melcher,
Harold Guinzburg, and Kerr, that American publishers "have been behind all
other great publishing nations in recognizing the importance of export business,
and in providing means for its development" was cited in the prospectus for
USIBA as one of two prime motives for setting up an export corporation. "We
have had no medium through which government and industry could cooperate
in forcefully employing books as ambassadors of good will and information, as

instruments to the introduction of United States technology and science, and as interpreters of our life and culture." The association "would supplement, but not displace, the efforts of the export agents already in the field, and would bring to bear on foreign problems the whole strength of the book industry," the prospectus continued. USIBA was obviously modeled on the British Council, with its highly developed mechanisms for supporting Britain's worldwide trade in books and its quasi-governmental status.[23] As Melcher, of *Publishers' Weekly,* maintained, USIBA "is in no way government-controlled, yet it could not have been organized without government encouragement."[24] Melcher also pointed out that "USIBA provides United States publishers with the instrumentality to compete on favorable terms with other nations; particularly those nations having subsidized export sales."[25]

As the second incentive, the founders wrote, "many branches of the Government, using our books abroad in their work, could profit by the existence of such an entity and...the advantages would be mutual."[26] It thus also somewhat resembled the Council on Books in Wartime, also a private, nonprofit corporation, in its ability to provide certain agreed-upon services for government. As was the case of the working partnership between CBW and OWI, the publishers proposed to do well by doing good. The legality of the organization was vouchsafed under the Webb-Pomerene Act of 1918, which granted partial exemption from U.S. antitrust laws to associations "engaged in exporting that handle the products of similar producers for overseas sales."[27]

Membership in USIBA was open to all U.S. book publishers for annual dues of one hundred dollars. Dues were set low in order to attract as many members as possible and thus meet OWI's requirement of broad representativeness. Each firm, regardless of size, was entitled to one vote. Members were not required to deal exclusively with the association in carrying on their export business and could quit at any time. The board of directors was a blue-ribbon group of prominent industry executives, most of whom had been active in CBW. The group was drawn from various types of publishers, including trade houses, textbook publishers, and firms producing science, medical, and technical books. USIBA was thus more representative of the industry as a whole than CBW, whose members were trade houses.

Crane, of D. Van Nostrand, who had not participated in the publishers' mission to Latin America but had played a significant role in the BPB committee that developed USIBA, was elected chairman of the board. All of the travelers on the Latin American trip were on the governing body except De Graff, of Pocket Books.[28] Other directors had taken part in trade missions to other spots on the globe. As managing director, the group chose Eugene Reynal, a partner in the firm of Reynal & Hitchcock and a major in the army air force during the previous two years. Operating funds were to come from income derived from membership dues and handling orders, from fees for services provided to government agencies, and from other sources yet to be developed. "For some operations of a specialized and non-commercial nature," said the prospectus, "it will apply for grants-in-aid to the government." The directors believed that there were sufficient funds in hand, or promised, to begin operations immediately.[29]

The proposed operations of the association were broad, if vaguely defined. It should be remembered that, as USIBA was being established (late 1944–early 1945), the war was still raging in Europe as well as Asia, OWI and CIAA were still very much in business, and the OE series remained a work in progress. Thus USIBA had to focus on the wartime present as well as the postwar future. It also had to overcome many preexisting attitudes and prejudices, held both by American publishers and their hoped-for clientele, if it were to succeed. As Reynal noted, U.S. publishers had not completely altered their prewar mind-set that looked upon foreign business as simply a nuisance. No more putting orders from abroad in a "hold" basket and hoping never to hear from the customer again. USIBA also had to reverse the image of U.S. business methods widely held abroad that "we are in this as in any business enterprise—purely for what we can get out of it—as a hit and run proposition in which we take while the taking is good."[30] The latter statement in effect sought to remedy the impression Curtice Hitchcock had reported on more than three years earlier that the British resented "various even rather small actions on the part of American publishers which seem designed to grab while the grabbing is good."[31]

The first task was to establish the necessary central machinery to handle large orders of books for export originating with various governmental and nongovernmental organizations, including OWI, CIAA, foreign governments in exile, and the American Library Association. For the duration of the war there was likely to be plenty of such business, and even greater volume in peacetime. Next, the corporation would work with existing exporting entities in territories that they currently covered, as well as developing means of servicing areas in which there was as yet little if any exposure to American books. Among the tactics would be setting up a chain of permanent sites for the display of current American books and undertaking a variety of other promotional activities. USIBA would also attempt to solve the problems of widespread piracy of U.S. books in China and to open up the Soviet Union as a market. Third, the association would provide other services to branches of the government on a fee basis, including assistance in translation programs and consulting on the uses of books in government programs abroad. In addition, USIBA proposed to rectify a major stumbling block to exports, the comparative lack of reliable statistics. Working with the State and Commerce departments and with statisticians in other industries, the group would at the least compile basic figures on the number and classes of books exported and eventually perhaps compile lists of

"the advertising rates and circulations of newspapers in Bogota and Chungking."
Fifth and finally, USIBA would offer a variety of additional services to members,
also on a fee basis, such as taking charge of publishers' promotional activities in
foreign countries. It would also offer to serve industries outside the book world
in related promotions, taking a page from British publishers' mantra that trade
follows the book. For example, the plastics industry might engage USIBA to promote the sale of books on plastics in order to advance the export of U.S.-made
plastics and plastic products.[32]

In the optimistic language of the prospectus, USIBA was "designed to combine the commercial skill of the pre-war German Borsenverein with the broader
activities of the book development work of the British Council and similar organizations in other countries." With both Britain and Germany hobbled by the
war's devastation, this time the U.S. industry might have a competitive edge. But
cooperation was part of USIBA's game plan as well—not just competition. This
was particularly so in the association's pledge to work closely with the similar association in the UK, Book Export Service, Ltd., "in promoting the use of English
as the second language in non-English speaking areas of the world."[33]

Left off the list of five main activities because the work could not be "clearly
defined" was the endeavor that already lay at the heart of OWI's book efforts,
what the USIBA prospectus called "cultural relations in general and the improvement of our relations with various countries through the medium of books."
Nevertheless, the organization considered this to be of great importance. Participating in such work "pre-supposes the closest possible contact with the Government in all matters concerning book export problems, so that USIBA becomes
the official agency of the industry for such co-operation," as the Council on
Books in Wartime was during the war. A key aspect of this would be to supply
information on American books to publishers abroad as well as help to facilitate
the exchange of rights. As it solicited the firms that would constitute its membership and its clients, the directors were hopeful "that USIBA will for the first time
in our history put our export operations on a widely expanding basis, and will
supply the increasingly urgent need for one focal point, one common meeting
ground, through which the interests and the ambitions of this publishing industry, of our Government, and of booksellers and publishers abroad, can meet."[34]

Despite coming late to the party, OWI expected to play a major role among
the governmental agencies that would be associated with USIBA. USIBA chairman Crane, no doubt with some encouragement from Kerr, agreed to seek the
opinion of Raymond Everitt, who was about to become OWI's chief of book
operations in the European theater, on the main problems that would face the
new export corporation. Writing in February 1945, Crane had lots of questions
to ask Everitt, and a few favors as well. Wartime conditions and, especially, the
rivalry between the United States and Britain for international book markets
colored most of them.

Crane was mainly interested to learn what OWI knew about the activities of the British Council and the Book Export Scheme (a plan to overcome currency exchange problems), so as to ascertain the nature of the competition USIBA would face. What relationships existed between what the British Council and the export scheme were engaged in and the steps that individual publishers were taking both on their own and collectively to advance their foreign sales? What was Britain doing about trade on the European continent? Had they already started to sell on the Continent or were they waiting for V-E Day? What about British activities elsewhere? With an eye toward wresting market share away from Britain in the volatile Australian and South African markets, Crane asked how much money the British were spending there on promoting exports. Crane asked also for statistics and other data: about the proportion of the costs of export activities in the UK between the government and the trade, on the volume and geographical distribution of British exports, and on the creditworthiness and political record of as many foreign booksellers and publishers as possible. He also inquired about British publishers' attitudes toward USIBA, assuming they were aware of it. Were they antagonistic, or "do they accept our sincere statement that this entity should cooperate rather than be hostile to British publishers?" The USIBA chairman also sought advice on whether OWI or the U.S. embassy in London could help USIBA make contacts with officials of the various governments-in-exile there and how important translations and the sale of translation rights abroad were to the success of the program both culturally and commercially.[35]

The Launch and Brief Career of USIBA

USIBA established its home office in Manhattan, at 24 East Sixty-seventh Street. At the end of the summer of 1945, OWI signed contracts to purchase various services from the new corporation, even as it prepared to go out of business. The government of France had agreed to channel its purchases of American books through the export association. More than sixty publishers had signed on as members. The organization had announced plans to set up branch offices in Mexico City, Buenos Aires, and Rio de Janeiro (to honor its commitment to CIAA) and in Paris, Stockholm, and, possibly, Rome (to carry on the work begun by OWI). These foreign branches were to include facilities where American books could be enticingly displayed for publishers, booksellers, and the general public. No outpost materialized in Rome, but the Stockholm and Paris display centers opened in March 1946, each with an exhibition and gala reception. In Paris, Ronald Freelander had supervised a display of thirty-five hundred American books under the theme "Read American books, for they will show you the true face of the United States." In Stockholm, Sidney Sulkin and his staff exhibited three thousand American books to guests, including the crown prince and crown princess, who, uncharacteristically, lingered for an hour and purchased a number of books before taking their leave.[36]

The new corporation recruited personnel being phased out of OWI, CIAA, and other wartime government agencies, which instantly provided USIBA with continuity, experience in publishing and the export trade, and a historical memory of wartime book programs. Robert L. Wood, formerly of CIAA, was named manager of the sales and promotion division, while E. Trevor Hill, ex-OWI, was chosen to head up library services and translations, with two other former OWI staff members under him as department heads. Sulkin, who was put in charge of USIBA'a northern European activities, was one of the former OWI (and PWD/SHAEF) officers who remained in Europe to work for the new association. Freelander, another former OWI official, became the central European representative. When Eugene Reynal had to step down as managing director in the spring of 1946 to return to his firm following the death of his partner, Curtice Hitchcock, the board named Kerr—the OWI veteran most involved in the propaganda agency's overseas book programs—as interim director.[37] Wallace Carroll, a former OWI colleague and one of the chief architects of the government's psychological warfare planning, wrote Kerr that he was pleased that he was going to USIBA, which, he thought, "promises to be one of the most fruitful enterprises growing out of the activities in which we have been engaged."[38]

Building on his work in delivering wartime stockpiled books in the Netherlands as an OWI staff member attached to PWD/SHAEF, Sulkin brought to USIBA his knowledge of the territory and his enthusiasm for pitching American books abroad. His experiences in the Netherlands and elsewhere as the north European director of USIBA nonetheless demonstrate the obstacles that the organization faced in doing its job in an impoverished and disorganized Europe. Despite his energetic efforts to promote the organization's goals by meeting with members of the Ministry of Education, the Dutch publishers' association, and booksellers, by arranging exhibits of American books, by holding press conferences and giving lectures, and by being interviewed on the influential Hilversum Radio, progress toward opening up a traffic in books between the two countries was slow.

As was the case elsewhere in Europe, a shortage of hard currency and official restrictions on the number of dollars that could be spent on particular commodities were the principal trouble spots. Sulkin judged the situation in Holland to be more difficult than elsewhere, which he considered a shame given Holland's reputation as "a great book-buying country before the war." He noted that Holland restricted American book and periodical purchases to one hundred sixty thousand dollars, in contrast to Norway, which set the limit at three hundred thousand dollars, and to Denmark, which had no restriction on how many dollars could be spent. Moreover, Holland required that 80 percent of its dollar pool had to be expended on scientific books and periodicals, an unwelcome restriction for the major trade publishers in USIBA. Norway made no such requirement. Sulkin strenuously and successfully lobbied key officials within the education and finance ministries to raise the limit to three hundred thousand dollars, with a separate allotment to purchase translation rights. Both Sulkin and Freelander considered the securing of dollar allotments for the purchase of American books in European countries USIBA's most important achievement.

Enthusiastic customers for American books were reported everywhere, raising optimism. A Dutch schoolteacher rode her bicycle the fifty miles from Utrecht to The Hague, where American books were being exhibited, in hopes of obtaining some for her school. In Warsaw, Edith Sulkin, Sidney Sulkin's wife and assistant, found people greeting the arrival of American books as if they were loaves of bread. As the USIBA officers noted, Europeans were eager to buy books because there was as yet little else to buy with whatever money they had.[39]

USIBA had set its sights—cultural as well as commercial—high. Reynal asserted that USIBA had the chance to fulfill the publishing industry's wartime goals of doing well by doing good. "We are still basking in the sun of the wartime conditions," he told the membership. "Competition is at a very low ebb. If we use this opportunity and use it well to build the right kind of structure for presenting American ideas throughout the world, we will have something which will not only mean profits for years to come but something in which America can well be proud."[40]

In spite of such lofty goals and a hopeful start, USIBA was soon dogged by problems, and its prospects for success quickly faded. Although Reynal found during a two-month trip to postwar Europe much encouraging interest among government officials and publishers, he also learned that "Europeans are still primarily distrustful of American culture and American business methods. They tend to think that we are in this as in any business enterprise—purely for what we can get out of it—as a hit and run proposition in which we take while the taking is good." In providing another echo of Curtice Hitchcock's findings on his mission to Britain in 1942, Reynal admitted that neither the American publishers nor governmental cultural diplomats had yet succeeded in their goals, but he was not ready to give up the effort. While assuring Europeans that their impressions were incorrect, Reynal realized that "it is up to us to prove it."[41]

By the middle of 1946, USIBA's condition had turned grave, in considerable part from faults in the business plan. Funding and earned income were less than expected, and disagreements about the proper direction of the organization divided the membership. In time, current income kept pace with expenses, but the deficits rung up early in USIBA's existence were hard to erase. Short-term fundraising efforts fell short. Some of the publisher members, grown in number to about 150 by late 1946, were becoming restless, both with the undercapitalization of the association and with the tactics it employed in trying to increase the nation's book trade abroad.

The main point of dispute was the value of the efforts that the association's staff had been putting into general publicity for American books and the USIBA itself as well as planning and mounting major exhibitions of American books in various European cities. Even though the organization worked hard to broker foreign rights and arrange for translations, the unhappy members complained that glamorous exhibits and other publicity programs caused the organization to emphasize the cultural-propaganda goals desired by the government, while skimping on what the dissidents felt was USIBA's main task—selling books abroad. USIBA had in fact undertaken a policy in Europe of generating continuous publicity, leaving scarcely a day in which American books were not the subject of some newspaper article or radio program.[42] Many defenders of the activities claimed that the early publicity efforts, however time consuming and expensive they were, had prepared the way for increased sales, but those pushing for a renewed emphasis on sales forced a retrenchment and reorganization upon the association.[43]

Changes were decided on at a special meeting of the membership on October 30, 1946, which called for an increased emphasis on sales in the New York and foreign offices even on a reduced budget. Within Europe, the more robust sales efforts would have to be carried out with the consolidation of the European offices into a single branch in Amsterdam. Reductions in staff, which then numbered sixty people in New York and twenty-five in the foreign posts, naturally were to accompany the contractions. With the closing of their branches, both Freelander and Sulkin resigned. Ben Russak, who had been a field representative for USIBA in Europe, was to set up the consolidated office in Amsterdam and supervise a sales force that would be responsible for essentially the whole continent. The publicity and translation-rights efforts were to continue, but also under reduced funding. With the de-emphasis of these efforts, Hill also resigned. Latin American operations, on the other hand, were not affected by the changes. The display center established in Mexico City was set to open within a couple of weeks and plans for centers in Buenos Aires and Rio de Janeiro remained in effect.[44]

But the biggest personnel change had been decided upon a month and a half before the reorganization was approved, when Kerr, the acting director, informed Chairman Crane that he wished to step down on November 1 in order to assume a position with Reynal & Hitchcock.[45] He planned to take two months off before joining the company, which bore the names of two of the strongest supporters of expanding U.S. publishers' market share abroad. He had had, he said, "no appreciable break since 1941 and if I'm to do any good to R&H, it seems wiser to take a couple of months to restore my tissues, physical and mental such as they are, and my sense of proportion, which is badly out of whack due to that final hellish year at OWI and these past months at USIBA."[46] Kerr told Crane he was leaving for professional reasons, but also because he was on the "losing side" in the debate between "the two schools of thought as to USIBA's functions and future which emerged during the Board's recent consideration of USIBA's financial problems."[47]

In short, Kerr, the quintessential publisher cum public servant and model liberal internationalist, chose to privilege the view of USIBA as a force for the nation's good in international affairs over the mere selling of books. One of the leaders of the opposition was James S. Thompson, of McGraw-Hill, one of the travelers to Latin America in 1943 and founding fathers of USIBA. Thompson's stance was governed by the logic of his own firm's business plan.[48] He and his company were by no means uninterested in expanding their sales abroad. Far from it. The company had been assiduous during the war in formulating strategies for new business opportunities that could be implemented immediately upon the dawn of peace. McGraw-Hill considered Latin America its main future overseas market. Between 1943 and 1945, the company arranged for translation into Spanish of thirty of its books on industry, science, and business, as well as translation into Portuguese of seventeen titles. It also had in readiness a table converting English weights and measures into metric units and a technical English–Spanish dictionary containing a half million words used in industry and business.[49] For Thompson and his firm, going it alone made better sense than continuing in USIBA. Mainly a technical and textbook publisher, McGraw-Hill perhaps had less interest in the softer forms of cultural diplomacy that Kerr and the likeminded in the association and in the government believed in. Moreover, the significant attention USIBA paid to Europe was probably for McGraw-Hill only a distraction from its own business strategies.

Macmillan's George Brett warned Kerr that resigning might make him a scapegoat if USIBA were to fail. Kerr agreed that might happen. If so, he felt that "the blame should be pretty evenly distributed; that a number of others have been pushing out bricks lately and will continue to do so." For one thing, John Wiley and Sons (like McGraw-Hill, mainly a technical/scientific publisher) had served notice that it wished to terminate its exclusive sales agreement with USIBA as soon as possible. For another, there was a growing sense that some members' minds were made up and they were already blueprinting the termination of the association.[50]

Momentum to disband USIBA continued to grow even after the vote to reorganize and to redirect the association's mission toward sales and away from cultural diplomacy. Kerr may well have been correct in thinking that a number of members had already made up their minds to close the organization down. Perhaps, too, he and Brett were right to think that his resignation would hasten the demise, though there seems to be no direct evidence that that was the case. Even his opponents admired Kerr's talents and dedication in trying to keep USIBA afloat.[51] Perhaps it just seemed better to pull the plug sooner rather than later. Kerr told a colleague on his last day at USIBA, "I think we've been swimming against the tide of history."[52]

In the end, there were still more members in favor of keeping the organization alive through the reorganization plan than those opposed. But the minority was large and powerful enough that going forward with an organization that was no longer fully representative of the industry—an attribute that was considered at its founding to be the indispensable key to its viability—was impossible.

The decision to dissolve USIBA was made at a special meeting of the membership, held on December 12, 1946. The official termination date was December 31.[53] Some of USIBA's champions expressed the hope that the committee overseeing the liquidation would find a way to transfer some of USIBA's activities in publicity and cultural diplomacy over to other organizations. Some said the dissolution was a "'sign of the times,' reflecting a cooling of the wartime ardor for idealistic projects," the *New York Times* reported.[54] A Paris correspondent for the *New York Herald Tribune* called USIBA "an experiment that had the blessings of the State Department, which considered the export of American books an important adjunct of the success of American foreign policy." French booksellers were reported to be upset with the decision. A Parisian dealer who had stocked his shop with many English-language titles lamented, "It took U.S.I.B.A. six months before it really functioned well, and now at the time it has really become useful to us, it has dissolved." The *Herald Tribune* reporter also contrasted the U.S. situation with that of Britain, which, she said, had greatly expanded their export operations for France.[55]

In an editorial that showed keen understanding of the issues that led to USIBA's creation, the Paris edition of the *Herald Tribune* scolded the dissident publishers, "who should very definitely know better," for sabotaging the organization:

> There was every indication...that American publishers had fully appreciated the great hunger that existed in Europe for the best of American writing, for the technical knowledge that can be passed on by the printed word, for the contributions to human culture and political progress that can be compressed between the covers of a book. British publishers, to be sure, energetically backed by their government, had been in the field months ahead of the American publishers, but the setting into motion of the U.S.I.B.A. program was welcomed on all sides as logical and sensible. Not only might the publishers themselves hope in the long run to benefit financially, but the program was deemed likely to serve the United States and international understanding in a major way.

Now the British and the Russians would have the upper hand in influencing the minds of peoples around the world.[56]

The Republican-leaning parent paper in New York reprinted the Paris editorial as a sidebar to its own story about the liquidation. It also published an editorial dissenting from some of the viewpoints expressed in the European edition. The goals of USIBA remained important, the editorial asserted, and perhaps "could just as well be assumed by the State Department, a different publishers' cooperative, or merely by the publishing houses themselves, operating individually," who might thereby "give to foreign distribution of their product an attention and a skill which competitive enterprise in this country can still match, when it wishes to, against any techniques of mass public education yet developed anywhere in the world."

The dissolution of USIBA in accord with the wishes of a minority of member publishers deeply embittered those who had fought to save it as well as key government officials, who believed the demise of USIBA compromised their ability to convey the U.S. message abroad. For Melcher, of *Publishers' Weekly*, the end of USIBA was "lamentable, not so much because of the loss of trade—this will be picked up—but even more because of the loss of face with the book trade overseas and with our own Government agencies which had come to rely upon USIBA."[57] Crane, the former chairman, blamed USIBA's demise on "an isolationistic trend on the part of some individuals and a loss of interest in overseas affairs."[58] Macmillan's Brett believed that the opposition of some publishers "prevented a wholesome world-wide distribution of the books containing the ideologies of this government."[59] In exiting the stage, USIBA officials urged that the successors keep fully in mind the continuing interest of government agencies in extending the flow of American books overseas, and to cooperate fully with them toward their mutual goals.[60] Now it was up to the publishers to find solutions to carrying on the grunt work of actually selling books abroad in the absence of USIBA.

Carrying On after USIBA

That the quest for increased foreign trade remained a high priority for American book publishers is attested to by the fact that the trade association and most publishers wasted little time in finding their own best ways forward after the demise of USIBA. The American Book Publishers Council (successor to the Book Publishers Bureau) formed a Foreign Trade Committee to promote U.S. books abroad in cooperation with the State Department's cultural programs. The constitution of the committee's membership, however, rankled Kerr, confirming his darkest thoughts about the motives of the opponents of USIBA.[61] Although some firms chose to go it alone, others formed new alliances and mechanisms, great and small, for marketing their books overseas in the absence of an industry-wide instrumentality like USIBA. The government's blessing, if not its active partnership with the publishers, remained a desideratum nonetheless, as evidenced by the publication by the ABPC in 1948 of a pamphlet, entitled *Books in World Rehabilitation*. The textbook publishers and university presses, through their associations, joined in the preparation of the booklet, which was intended to convince members of Congress, the State and Commerce departments, and the army of the importance of books in the rehabilitation of war-damaged countries and, consequently, of providing a positive image of the United States and attracting other trade as a result.[62]

Although it was far from the largest, the most important group symbolically was the association consisting of several of USIBA's loyalists.[63] The group began with seven members—Harcourt, Brace; Harper's; Reynal & Hitchcock; Silver, Burdett; Viking; Van Nostrand; and World Publishing. Duell, Sloan & Pearce joined the group later.[64] These firms, personified by Kerr (by then at Reynal & Hitchcock) and many others who had believed in the cultural diplomacy efforts of USIBA and OWI before it, remained convinced of the need for publishers to serve the national good in this way, but they had to be content to concentrate, through this partnership, on marketing and sales alone.

The members engaged Russak as their agent, headquartered in Stockholm, so the group came to be known informally as the Russak Group. Russak had already spent three years in Europe, first with the American Red Cross, then with OWI in charge of book and magazine distribution on the Continent as part of PWD/ SHAEF. He later joined USIBA, which chose him to consolidate its operations in Europe in the attempt to remain viable.[65] Russak was thus a thoroughly known quantity, a man with great contacts and knowledge of the territory. His willing-ness to do general publicity and other services, including mounting exhibitions, that USIBA had undertaken no doubt was another point in his favor with the seven firms. Russak was optimistic that the enterprise would succeed, even if it would "not be smooth sailing at all."[66] Having to reinvent all of the logistics and procedures for a new enterprise, however, proved to be a huge chore for the seven partners, especially after their strenuous efforts to establish and save USIBA.[67]

Publishers also formed various other alliances. Faustina Orner International, Inc., managed by Lyle Fowler, took on the European representation of at least fourteen publishing houses. This was a very eclectic group of mostly small firms, including highly specialized technical publishers like Chemical Publishing Co. and Coyne Electrical School; the refugee publisher Querido; and the paperback giant Penguin Books (USA). A much larger group of publishers—more than sev-enty of all types—agreed to engage the services of William S. Hall & Co. to repre-sent them in Europe. Hall had previously been associated with the major export firm of H. M. Snyder & Co., which was leaving the European market to con-centrate on other parts of the world.[68] Clients included Bobbs-Merrill; Crowell; Duell, Sloan & Pearce; Dutton; Henry Holt; *Infantry Journal;* John Day; Norton; Pantheon; Random House and its Modern Library line; Scribner's; Simon & Schuster; William Sloane Associates; Watson-Guptill; and Ziff-Davis. In addi-tion, nine leading university presses joined the Hall group, including California, Columbia, Minnesota, North Carolina, and Yale.

Other publishers found various ways to go it alone. McGraw-Hill established a new International Division "to promote sales of books and translation rights throughout the world." The firm recruited Freelander for his wide experience with OWI and USIBA, assigning him to McGraw-Hill's London office to oversee business in France, Belgium, the Netherlands, and Switzerland. Another company, Macmillan, also decided against a cooperative approach to European marketing despite its strong support of USIBA under Brett, its president. Macmillan would rely upon the channels it had employed before the war. The Macmillan Company in London represented the U.S. company's sales in Europe. A U.S. staff member was stationed in the London office with special responsibility for developing his own marketing program, but also worked through the UK firm's travelers. The New York entity also utilized Macmillan's branches in Melbourne, Sydney, Madras, and Calcutta in similar ways. Prior to USIBA, Macmillan had its own representatives in Latin America, and would reinstitute coverage there.[69]

One of the most significant stopgap successors to USIBA was the one the U.S. government turned to for the kinds of services to its overseas book programs that OWI, PWD/SHAEF, and other agencies had performed and that USIBA would have handled had it survived. This was the *Infantry Journal,* under the management and editorship of Col. Joseph I. Greene. This publisher had already become a major player in war-related publishing ventures, including the Fighting Forces series of paperbacks (with the U.S. branch of Penguin Books).[70] The demise of USIBA was a blow to the book programs in the occupied enemy territories of Germany and Japan. Although stockpiled American books, including the custom-made OEs, might provide emergency reading while indigenous publishing enterprises came back to life, the government's goal was not only to hand over book publishing to the Germans and the Japanese as soon as possible but also to develop the mechanisms by which American publishers could contract with the new publishing houses for the rights to translations of American books. Because these were still occupied enemy countries under military government, the publishers had no other means to conduct business there except through the instrumentalities the government authorized. USIBA was to have been the agency to broker these deals. Without it, the government turned to the *Infantry Journal* to take on this role in both Germany and Japan, with decidedly mixed results.

A major reason for some to lament the failure of USIBA was that it dashed hopes that the United States would at last have an organization with enough clout from both the government and the trade to serve as a counter to the overseas book programs of the British Council. With peace came the end of the forced cooperation of Britain and the United States in the book programs of PWD/SHAEF and the Allied Information Services. American publishers had high hopes that the lingering problems facing the British book trade at home and abroad would provide them the opening to gain market share from their ally. For their part, British publishers did what they could to counter the Yankee threat.

THE EMPIRE STRIKES BACK

The imprint statement of the title page of books published in the United Kingdom around the time of the Second World War, especially by the university presses of Oxford and Cambridge, spoke volumes about the global reach of British books. In the literal sense, the words "Oxford New York Bombay Karachi etc.," merely indicated the locations of the branches of the press, but they symbolically affirmed the reach of British ideas and trade throughout the world. Such imperialistic imprint statements testified that British publishers' ability to sell their products worldwide was not only the key to their own success or failure financially, it also deeply colored their professional identity. Exporting books, in other words, was of the greatest importance for British publishers both economically and psychologically. Moreover, when the war transformed the UK from the world's greatest creditor nation to one of the biggest debtor nations, exports of all commodities assumed an importance not seen before.

During the war, British publishers grew ever more fretful that their American cousins would succeed in gaining world market share at their expense by taking advantage of the weakened state of the trade caused by the war. Representing American publishers, Curtice Hitchcock had taken clear note of this discomfiture when he visited Britain in late 1942. The concern only continued to grow. In time, influential members of the British book trade came to feel that the aggressiveness of American publishers was only part of a broadly national, "deliberate, collective drive toward the economic hegemony of the world," which, in time, "may take on a definitely political and imperialistic character."[1] Impelled by these fears, which had ramifications for the economic well-being not only of their trade but of the nation as a whole, and led by perhaps the most distinguished among them, Stanley Unwin, British publishers struck back.

Britain and the Necessity of Exports

British publishers' dependency on book exports for their survival followed from the nation's demographic realities. At the onset of the Second World War, the population of the United Kingdom stood at about 46 million people (compared with about 131 million in the United States). Although the trade itself was sophisticated and highly developed, its domestic market was insufficiently large to achieve the optimum balance between volume of sales and selling price in order to ensure profits.[2] Precisely how vital export business was to the industry did not really become apparent until the Publishers Association, in an effort to justify having book publishing exempted from wartime rationing, asked the publishers to provide statistics, something that the firms had previously resisted reporting. The principal measure of the importance of overseas business is the ratio of export sales to overall turnover, which, the PA discovered, ranged just before the war from no less than 15 percent for any publishing firm to as much as 60 percent for particularly export-minded houses. The average was around one-third of annual turnover. The percentages for the trade as a whole dropped significantly during the war, reaching the low 20s.[3] Because export sales were so vital to Britain, their reduction produced high anxiety at home, as U.S. publishing executives well knew.[4] That the figures did not fall further is a testimony to the importance of exports to the British book trade and its determination to do what it could to keep their foreign business as robust as possible, even during a global conflict.

Export volume dropped during the war for several reasons. First, there were simply fewer books to send abroad, owing to rationing, labor shortages, and the Luftwaffe's destruction of millions of books of publishers' stock along with much printing and bookbinding machinery. Second, Axis military actions globally cut British publishers off from many of their customary foreign markets, making it difficult if not impossible to export books, assuming there had been books to ship. Third, the arrival of Lend-Lease funds from the United States made exporting goods to pay for war supplies temporarily less critical. Finally, it became politically expedient to give a higher priority to the needs of Britain's own citizens, including the forces abroad, for scarce books for education and entertainment during the war.[5] This adjustment of priorities toward the home market forced publishers to ration their wares, often shipping fewer copies than a foreign purchaser ordered, sometimes even none.[6] Weighing domestic versus export needs became a delicate balancing act.

Once communications were restored after liberation, European and other foreign customers abroad were eager to buy British books (and American books too). Unwin noted that "callers from the Continent continue to pour in" to his office in such numbers that he could not give them adequate time. Even more frustrating, his firm was "flooded with orders we can't cope with."[7] Meanwhile, U.S. firms were stepping in to fill the gaps. Portugal was reportedly "inundated with American books."[8] American publishers were making inroads in Spain, partly as a way of supplying South America as well. If the spread of American books were not countered by larger supplies of British books, it would be much more difficult for British books to compete and the UK would be in danger of losing the Spanish market.[9]

The wartime emergency was accompanied by pervasive governmental regulation of the book trades along with every other facet of the British economy. Among the more troubling items was the licensing of exports and imports of all manufactured goods, including books.[10] Another was the proposed imposition of a "purchase [sales] tax" on a wide variety of products, including books. Advocacy by a coalition of trade associations, together with appeals to public opinion and the substantial moral support of the archbishop of Canterbury and the author J. B. Priestley, succeeded in keeping books off the list of taxable commodities despite the chancellor of the exchequer's protestation that there were plenty of books in the country and "if I exempt books why not boots?"[11] In the end, the chancellor reversed himself. The exemption from the purchase tax, along with the diminished opportunities for social life in an overstressed, blacked-out society, was credited with bringing about a great increase in book sales domestically. Just as importantly, the exemption established the precedent that "books are different," "something more than a commodity of trade," a mantra that the publishers invoked with varying degrees of success to the end of the war and beyond. Since food, drink, children's clothing, and—ironically, in light of the chancellor of the exchequer's statement—even boots were exempted from the tax, the advocates for the exemption of books could persuasively argue that, in the government's eyes, books were among the necessities of life and that it was just as important to assuage the British people's intellectual and spiritual hunger as it was to feed their bellies and shod their feet.[12]

The Board of Trade served as the publishing industry's liaison with the government, sealing the relationship with a mission statement that "book production itself will henceforth be treated as production of national importance, and it will be the responsibility of the Government to ensure that labour and materials are available for the quantities and kinds of books which it is deemed in the national interest to produce." But actions did not always live up to words. The unwillingness of some figures in government to relax paper regulations particularly to support the export of books, which other officials urged, was shortsighted at best. The Earl of Huntington warned his peers in the House of Lords that "if we do not do something to encourage [the export trade] we shall lose both our colonial export of books and our export to America, and once those export markets have been lost it is extremely difficult to get them back."[13] The publisher Geoffrey Faber told a BBC radio audience, "We are about to miss a chance we have never had before and shall never have again—the world crying out to us for our books, and no books left to send!" a phrase that closely echoed the statement in the OWI book plan that American publishers might never have the chance again to have "an inside track to the world's bookshelves."[14] Strenuous efforts by Unwin and others "to secure official encouragement of books at Cabinet level" failed.[15] That this sort of shortsighted, bureaucratic mentality prevailed more often than not in the crucial matter of paper rationing was evidenced when an official was unable to make any distinction between the relative importance to the war effort of paper for books and paper to wrap the slim pickings at the local butcher shop.[16]

The book trade set up an Export Group in response to the creation of the government's Export Council. Most firms joined the group, in large part because those that did not had to settle for a smaller quota (40 percent) of regular and potentially additional paper. A critical assumption behind the Export Group was that the supply of British books to foreign shores would have to stem from the domestic trade itself, that no purpose-built program for export books was feasible.[17] But hopes for as much as an additional 20 percent allotment for books were dashed when the Nazi invasion of Norway halted paper imports from Scandinavia, while France's capitulation stopped the supply from North Africa of esparto grass, the key ingredient in two-thirds of the book paper used by UK publishers.[18]

Even in the postwar shift of workers out of war industries, the book trades remained critically short of the workers needed to produce the estimated fifty-two thousand books (new and reprint titles) that were already in the publishers' production queues, or about the same number of books that the trade would have published in three and a half years at the prewar average. Thus the continued shortages of both paper and labor hampered the trade's efforts to regain ground lost during the war in the export markets. The restoration of "normal" conditions of publishing production was likely to take years rather than months.[19]

That books were not run-of-the-mill commodities but rather possessed intrinsic cultural and political significance in addition to economic value was a theme that British publishers used constantly in their various battles with government regulatory agencies during the war, especially when discussing exports.[20] "Books are ambassadors of British culture," the president of the Publishers Association told members of both houses of parliament.[21] In *Britain Needs Books,* a small volume intended to stimulate support for the publishers' side in a "war on books," John Brophy derided certain government regulations that the trade construed as excessive and counterproductive, like ever-deeper cuts in paper rationing and taxation. Despite the small economic contribution books made, "their importance in the personal and public lives of the English-speaking world is enormous." Books, he said, "are the principal means, often the solitary means, by which we are known to millions of our fellow human beings. They are our most lasting and most comprehensive form of propaganda. Unless we continue to export new books…we shall be isolated, misunderstood, misrepresented, and our enemies will be left a clear field in which to caricature us in the eyes of our allies and the neutral countries."[22] Books had almost a mystical power in Britain, as Victor Weybright, who had served with OWI in London before becoming head of Penguin USA, astutely noted. There was a strong psychological link between publishing and culture in Britain, he wrote, where "the literary profession…is more deeply integrated into the political, commercial, social and cultural life…than we can aspire to in this fleeting twentieth century in the United States."[23]

Britain's need to export books was even greater after the war. In purely economic terms, the country had to ramp up its exports if it were to earn the funds to pay for all the imports that it needed. As Unwin, who boasted of a keen understanding of economics, noted, Britain had for a century or more been "the world's biggest creditor nation "because we always took the precaution of importing rather more than we exported, thereby…always enabling our debtors to pay their debts in goods and leaving them free to buy yet more from us with the certain knowledge that our imports would enable them to pay us." But two world wars had dissipated Britain's foreign investments and gold reserves. "There is now no way for us to get out of debt other than by exporting more than we import."[24]

Books could contribute to that goal well beyond the relatively small cash value of book exports themselves. As Unwin argued, the exposure that foreigners had to British ideas and aspirations through books could actually create stronger markets for other British products as well. Because "trade follows the book," in Unwin's formulation, the export of British books was vastly more important than the mere export turnover would indicate. In *Britain Needs Books,* Brophy emphasized this theme, providing examples beyond the more obvious ways in which scientific and technical books "have again and again produced orders for British machinery, apparatus, and other products. Even novels (so often despised by those who pride themselves on possessing a serious outlook), by inspiring citizens of other countries with curiosity about and admiration for the British way of life, have been known to stimulate trade in articles of clothing, tobacco pipes, watches, fountain pens, and china. Books are excellent unsalaried trade representatives."[25]

But book exports were vital in the geopolitical arena as well. The war left in its wake some serious political problems affecting the relationship between Britain and its dominions, to say nothing of the rest of the world. These included

FIGURE 11.   Sir Stanley Unwin (1884–1968), head of the London publishing firm George Allen & Unwin, Ltd., and staunch advocate for the role of British books overseas. Photograph by John Gay. © National Portrait Gallery (London).

postwar expectations in many parts of the empire and commonwealth for greater self-rule, if not outright independence. Such considerations, along with ideological competition with the Soviet bloc during the early stages of the cold war, made it imperative that British books continue to make their way around the world, just as they had during the previous three centuries.

Unwin's assertion that "trade follows the book" was a clever variant on a key tenet of colonialism, that "trade follows the flag." He was prescient in understanding that British books might someday have to substitute for the British flag in a postcolonial world. Thus when American publishers continued to take the "small actions" into new publishing territories that worried their British colleagues as early as 1942,[26] the latter, led by Unwin, pushed back as best they could, given the government's unwillingness to bolster the trade's efforts by allocating sufficient stocks of paper to supply the demand for British books abroad after the war. His activities in this arena were representative of what British publishers could—and could not—do to counter the incursions of Yankee publishers at their expense.

Stanley Unwin and the "Battle for Britain"

Stanley Unwin was as well suited as anyone in the United Kingdom to lead the counteroffensive, for he had spent his entire publishing career trying to understand foreign markets and to sell to them. He had to fight not only U.S. poachers but also his own government, whose bureaucrats and their misguided regulations hampered his ability to wage what he called the "Battle for Britain."[27]

Born in 1884 into a family that owned a printing business, Unwin, at the age of eighteen, accepted an offer from his father's younger step-brother, T. Fisher Unwin, to join his publishing firm, but not before he embarked on a nine-month trip to Europe.[28] As an unpaid intern in a book-selling and publishing firm in Leipzig, the center of the German book trade, he learned the rudiments of his craft, including the importance of knowing the customer's needs and thoroughly reading the daily trade paper, the *Börsenblatt*. Following additional travels, he joined the firm of T. Fisher Unwin in September 1904 and did very well for it until he resigned in April 1912 after numerous rows with his uncle.

He had no other job lined up. Instead of searching for one immediately, he tapped his savings to fund a twenty-month-long round-the-world tour "to fill the most important gap left in my publishing experience"—understanding potential customers for British books through direct contact in countries far and wide. The trip took him to South Africa, Australia and New Zealand, various Pacific islands, Hong Kong, China, Japan, Ceylon, Egypt, and Morocco. It was the first of four world tours Unwin undertook during his career. These journeys left him knowing that "there are now very few parts of the world in which I have failed to call in person upon any bookseller who was selling, or could be persuaded to sell, British books. . . . The study of foreign markets fascinates me and the fact that 55 percent of my firm's turnover is represented by export sales demonstrates, I think, that my traveling has not been altogether in vain."[29]

After returning home, he purchased the firm of George Allen & Co., Ltd., which had just gone into receivership, rather than start one from scratch. The new firm of George Allen & Unwin, Ltd., took time to grow, but by 1930 one close observer of the British publishing scene could comment that, "in proportion to its size, the firm…has probably done more than any other to add to the stock of human knowledge."[30] Among Unwin's star authors were Bertrand Russell, Mohandas Gandhi, J. M. Synge, and Harold Laski. Adolf Hitler might have been another one, had the firm not turned down the opportunity to publish *Mein Kampf* in Britain. The phenomenal popularity of Lancelot Hogben's *Mathematics for the Million* helped raise the firm out of the Depression of the 1930s.[31]

It took time for Unwin to gain acceptance in the trade.[32] But by the onset of the Second World War, he had become a distinguished citizen of the profession. He owed his new status largely to the publication of a book he wrote in 1926, *The Truth about Publishing*. This detailed examination of virtually every aspect of the publisher's trade was intended to demystify the subject for authors. It quickly became "accepted as a kind of 'Publishers' Bible'" and textbook for novices.[33] It went through numerous editions in Britain and was translated into several languages.

The book presented clear evidence to his detractors that Unwin was a master of all the details of his trade. His son David recalled how pleased his father was to discover that the New York publishers who entertained him at the Publishers Lunch Club shortly after the book was published there "had all read my book! and were most excited about it." Praise and appreciation, David noted, went to his father's head "like strong drink."[34] The book's publication earned him a spot on the council of the Publishers Association, which had blocked his membership after he took over the Allen firm.[35] This was the beginning of what an American colleague, Edward M. Crane, termed Unwin's "book diplomacy" and his nephew and Allen & Unwin associate, Philip Unwin, called his participation in "book trade politics." From 1930 on, Philip wrote, "fully half his time, and I think much of his creative thought, was absorbed by it." He became "a sort of Uncle to the Trade; and everyone in need of advice, be it competing publisher, failing bookseller or hopeful seeker after a job, tended sooner or later to be told to 'go and see Stanley Unwin.'" This work in the public arena, Philip lamented, may have come at the expense of the firm.[36] Nevertheless, it was largely through such trade organizations—that and a penchant for sending letters to the editor of *The Times* whenever something irritated him—that Unwin became such a staunch defender of British publishing and British books abroad against both the mindless bureaucrats who hobbled them at home and the aggressive yet often naive Americans who threatened British trade zones abroad during and just after a catastrophic war.[37]

When Unwin began his deep involvement in trade affairs, there was no shortage of organizations serving the interests of the British book trades, but little coordination among them. The PA was founded in 1895 as an organization to negotiate with the Associated Booksellers of Great Britain and Ireland, which had been formed earlier that year. Finding that neither of these groups was particularly interested in jointly promoting reading and the purchase of books, Unwin led an effort that resulted in the establishment of the National Book Council in 1925. In effect, the NBC was to serve as an unofficial bridge between the book trade and the public, but the PA for years ignored it. Unwin worked hard to bring the various trade organizations into more cooperative relationships. With the Oxford bookseller Basil Blackwell he connived successfully to have them elected president of each other's association, which led in 1934 to closer cooperation.[38]

Yet another organization came into the mix around the same time, one with a broader mandate than publishing or bookselling alone. That was the British Council for Relations with Other Countries, which came to be known simply as the British Council. However unwieldy, the full name was perfectly descriptive, for the organization's mission was to promote an understanding of British life and thought and the English language throughout the world. The British Council had, and still has, a quasi-governmental character to it. It was established as a public charity, but it developed close relationships with the Ministry of Information during the war and today is accountable to both the Foreign and Commonwealth offices.[39] When Unwin was nominated by the PA for a seat on the governing board of the British Council and a special position as consultant on book-trade matters, he was disappointed to find that "books were not then regarded as being of the first importance in connection with British Council work."[40]

Unwin changed that. He played a role in the creation in 1939–40, under the aegis of the British Council, of the Book Export Scheme in order to solve the problem of making books available to countries that had no British currency with which to purchase them. Under the plan, the British Council paid for the books in pounds sterling while plowing back the local currency in which residents paid for the books in order to advance local projects in that country. This risk-sharing plan emphasized the importance of making British books visible, if not always profitable, in bookshops abroad, particularly in southeastern Europe, the Near East, Spain, Portugal, and Latin America—all places the Foreign Office and the Ministry of Information deemed important.[41] Unwin's long service to the cause of his nation's books abroad earned him a knighthood, given under the Labour government in the New Year Honours for 1946.[42]

Britain's Traditional Markets and U.S. Encroachments

The export-related issue most crucial to Unwin and the book-trade groups centered on an informal understanding that identified Britain's traditional markets abroad and defined the trade's response to the encroachments of American books into those territories during and after the war. What British publishers deemed their traditional markets were mostly the ones they had developed as literary handmaidens to British imperialism, and, to a lesser extent, as publishers of books in English for export to the European market. British publishers had for a long time diligently guarded their prerogatives throughout the empire and commonwealth and in Europe. Like the British constitution, the concept of a traditional market for British books was largely the accretion of custom, precedent, and willing compliance.

The United States, of course, had been a major market for British books when the future states were members of the British Empire and for many years after. Some publishers established branch offices in the United States—Macmillan in 1869, Ward Lock in 1882, Oxford University Press in 1896. Not nearly as export-minded as the British, U.S. publishers had posed no real threat. However, the Great Depression and, even more, the Second World War led to increased interest on the part of U.S. firms in finding new markets abroad and to a corresponding nervous response from the British. In 1931, the council of the PA agreed that, "with regard to books of English origin, the English publishers should unite to resist any further encroachment by the American publishers on their market," by aiming to obtain "in their contracts all rights in the English language outside the United States of America," except possibly Canada, and also to reserve "the exclusive market in Europe" for "books of American origin."[43]

The general understanding of territorial rights that British publishers had gained by the 1940s was as follows: British rights and territories were principally defined as against those of the other major publishing nation, the United States. The home markets of each were the British Empire and Commonwealth on the one hand and the United States and its territories and possessions on the other. In selling edition rights for a British book to an American publisher or in buying rights to an American book, British publishers would draft contracts that included exclusive rights to sell the books in the traditional British market. American publishers in similar circumstances would include the domestic market and U.S. territories (including the Philippines). American publishers would frequently ask for, and British publishers would often grant, the rights to Canada. The rest of the world was, to varying degrees, an "open market," in which editions from both the United States and Britain could freely compete. Europe was considered a special case for British publishers, like Unwin, who insisted that his firm had the sole right to sell on the Continent books in the English language that it had published, or in the case of American books, to which it had purchased the rights for the UK.[44]

The problem was that most American publishers—and even a few in the British houses as well—neither fully understood nor cared to observe these divisions of world markets. When, during the war, American publishers made various inroads, both calculated and accidental, against British interests, Britain's publishers and trade groups, often led by Unwin, improvised tactical defenses. Later, they dealt with the problems more strategically, primarily through negotiations with their U.S. counterparts.

The main crux of the dispute was relatively simple, though not entirely easy to explain. Through mutual agreement of the members of the PA, a British publisher would not buy rights for an English-language edition for the British Empire from an American publisher that had sold the rights separately to, say, an Australian, New Zealand, South African, or Indian publisher. If no British publisher wished to buy rights to a particular book, however, the U.S. firm was free to contract with a publisher in India or in one of the other countries. In addition, a U.S. publisher could freely enter into a contract for a translation into a language other than English.[45] In short, an American publisher could not put his competing editions into the same market as the British editions.

But U.S. editions frequently did manage to enter a British market and compete with the UK editions of the same title. Wartime conditions encouraged—and even excused—these incursions. British books were in short supply everywhere, especially in the farthermost reaches of the empire, like Australia and the Union of South Africa. The lack of books to sell in these and other parts of the empire prompted even Unwin, the most consistent defender of British territorial rights, to make a "gentleman's agreement" with W. W. Norton, the least likely of U.S. publishers to encroach on a British colleague's turf, that Norton could fill "the occasional order" coming from booksellers in the empire, as Norton put it, "mainly because of the nuisance value of having to refer it to you and also, of course, because of the obvious fact that your stocks were apt to be depleted or even in some cases, non-existent."[46] Some of the transgressions were clearly inadvertent, but even these Unwin and other British publishers took to be a threat to their interests. In several of the contested countries, local demand for American books either with or in preference to British books was a significant factor in the resulting trade war. With British books in such limited supply, where else but from eager American publishers with plenty of books could booksellers in the dominions obtain the supplies needed to survive in the business?[47]

Publishers and booksellers in the traditional British markets were themselves not uniformly supportive of the restrictions imposed by the publishers thousands of miles away, in London. Australia was highly attracted to the lure of American books, and thus a principal market for British publishers to defend. Demand was brisk in the smaller New Zealand market as well.[48] The increased demand for American books originated with Australian booksellers, who chafed at British publishers' enforcement of their territorial rights, at the higher cost of

British books, and at the import restrictions their government placed on products from the United States.[49] This was one of the hottest issues between the book trades of the United States and the UK. Most British publishers had agreed among themselves not to contract for any book from which the Australian and New Zealand rights were excluded, except in cases where the author was a resident of either country.[50] Britain's wartime paper and manpower shortages and difficulties with shipping to the most distant parts of the empire, however, meant that its publishers simply did not have the books with which to compete. American publishers did.[51]

But not all American publishers were as fastidious as Norton, who decided to stop shipping "even occasional orders" to British territories.[52] The New York firm of Macmillan had begun to consider direct sales to Australia within weeks of Britain's declaration of war against Germany, and the threat from the Yanks only grew as the war dragged on. "We all know that the Americans are determined to attack our overseas markets and their particular interest in Australia is beyond a doubt," Walter G. Harrap, of George G. Harrap & Company, Ltd., wrote Unwin in early 1945. Harrap was especially concerned that American publishers would expand their "dumping" of books in Australia, that is, unloading slow-selling titles at cut-rate prices. In truth, Americans, including staff members of both OWI and the State Department, were determined to attack British control over Australian publishing. An attaché in the Canberra legation noted that the British publishers "called the tune," but those days were numbered, if, as he thought, the United States could wring concessions on Australia out of the British.[53]

The Union of South Africa was another market that was particularly receptive to American books. As in Australia, there was increasing demand from booksellers, who had begun importing books from the United States "in defiance or ignorance of British copyrights and British-American market agreements."[54] In mid-1943, Allen & Unwin's agent in South Africa, Howard B. Timmins, informed Unwin that U.S. editions of British copyright books were arriving there. In this case, the importer was a Cape Town bookseller and book-club proprietor, who had apparently given an open order to his U.S. suppliers. Timmins, who represented other British publishers as well, asserted that the U.S. book-export firms should have known which books could and which could not be legitimately shipped to South Africa. He secured a pledge from the bookseller not to import "any further titles from America in which copyright might be involved," but asked Unwin to arrange for the president of the PA to send the bookseller a strong warning letter as well.[55] The problem persisted, in part because U.S. consular officials, who, according to Unwin, "don't understand anything about copyright, and assume that books can be handled like any other merchandise," were at best giving bad advice to South African booksellers or at worst actually encouraging them to import U.S. editions.[56] Eventually, the PA authorized Timmins and other South African agents of British firms "to take energetic action," which led to customs agents seizing American books imported illegitimately.[57]

In Timmins, Allen & Unwin and the other British publishers whom he represented could scarcely have found a more ardent defender of British publishing rights. He had entered the publishing trade in George Allen & Unwin's production department and demonstrated unswerving loyalty after his emigration to South Africa to set up his own agency business. Timmins observed the flow of American books into South Africa and did whatever he could personally to stop it.[58] The opening of a U.S. library in Cape Town was another sign of the U.S. publishers' and government's intentions "to establish their books in South Africa," with an eye toward the greater goal of using books to attract trade.[59]

Timmins got Unwin and the PA to underwrite a cooperative advertising campaign in various South African media.[60] But under the shabby circumstances of 1945, the campaign was left with one rather lame slogan out of four that Philip Unwin had suggested—"More British Books are on the way." Timmins, sadly, knew that one alternate slogan that said that British books were coming "soon" and the one that stated "There is no finer book than a British book" could not be used, if telling the truth was important. "Soon" could not be promised, and at that stage the appearance of American books, as Timmins knew full well, was "considerably superior." Meanwhile, he lamented, "the Yanks are doing their utmost to capture our trade."[61] Timmins preferred to think the worst of the competition, believing "that the majority of American publishers put 'money and trade' before any other sort of feeling." He wrote this the day after V-E Day, which encouraged him to anticipate a British publishing victory over the Americans: "When we once more have unlimited supplies we will give the U.S.A. a run for their money and prove that Britain can hold her own against their knavish tricks."[62] Unfortunately for the British publishers, the paper situation did not improve overnight and therefore neither did Britain's competitive position.

The application of the traditional British market agreement in India added occasional whiffs of censorship to the dispute, as may be illustrated by dilemmas the John Day Company faced in marketing some of its Asia-focused titles, especially the popular books of Lin Yutang. John Day was very eager to sell Lin's books in India, as well as Pearl Buck's. Obviously, there was much more money to be made at the end of World War II by selling American books to customers in the UK than could be earned at that time by selling to Indians—probably even when combined with Australians, New Zealanders, and South Africans. Losing the UK market for books by Lin, who was very popular there and whose books earned high royalties from British houses, would be unthinkable from the business point of view. The situation was even less satisfactory because Richard Walsh, of John Day, knew that not many copies of Lin's books published in London would actually make their way to India, even though lots more could be sold there. If he were willing to forego the UK market, he could deal directly with an Indian publisher. This was the case with respect to a book by Buck, who said she would rather have it read in India than in England.[63] Otherwise, he could sell rights to an India publisher only if no British publisher was interested in them at all.[64]

Even if an American publisher were willing to go along with the restraints placed by the PA, he could be disadvantaged if the British firm with which he contracted was slow to publish his edition. This happened when the British publisher Heinemann's edition of Lin's *Between Tears and Laughter* fell seriously behind schedule, for reasons that Walsh thought involved censorship. He complained to the London agent who handled the deal that the delay of nearly a year and a half in bringing out a British edition of a timely, best-selling book in the United States with strong potential readership in the empire as well as in the UK was costing the firm and the author dearly. Because of the commitment to Heinemann, John Day was unable to sell rights to an Indian publisher.[65] Walsh had been told secondhand that the British government wanted the firm to postpone the book indefinitely, but the reason for the delay was not clear. Possibly it did so as a means of rationing and prioritizing the republication of American books at a time of continuing scarcity of printing materials in Britain. More likely it was an act of government censorship, acquiesced in by the publisher, of content critical of British colonialism. Walsh was certainly convinced that "Heinemann held up this book for political reasons."[66]

The Heinemann incident was not the only one where censorship was suspected under cover of the policy on protecting British publications in their traditional market areas. Walsh also knew of another incident in which a British publisher shipped copies of an American book to Bombay. "At the moment of the arrival of the books in each store, the police walked in and <u>bought</u>, at full price, every copy." The publisher did not ship any more, so no Indian citizen got a copy. If an Indian publisher had published the book, Walsh added, "either it would have been kept in print there, or the government would have had to suppress it openly."[67] Britain's general wariness about any propaganda that might inspire independence movements in British colonies in Asia and elsewhere created some embarrassing situations for the United States, which was on record as espousing the "four freedoms." A small publisher like John Day might complain about the censorship of a book destined for India, but the U.S. government often acquiesced in Britain's efforts to limit libertarian propaganda in sensitive areas of the empire.[68]

In Canada, demand for American books was the strongest of all the dominions and Britain's position the weakest. As a book market, this nation of around 10 million people, including a sizable and rapidly growing minority of Francophones as well as increasing numbers of other, non-British ethnic groups, presented daunting challenges for any publisher. Its population spread thinly over an area larger than the United States, Canada was a difficult and expensive country for book travelers to service adequately. Having only relatively recently moved beyond the pioneering stage, Canada lacked a strong tradition of reading and book culture, or so said a British observer. There were few true bookstores. Most books were sold in department stores, and even these were restricted in number and locale. As a national book market, Canada failed to meet a rubric of the trade, that is, that "compressed centres of population make the best market for publishers; not empty spaces sparsely populated."[69]

Given these impediments, it was almost impossible for any single publishing house, Canadian or British, to secure an adequate volume of business without acting as an agency for many publishers, American and British. Culturally, the Canadians were caught between "two strong traditions—British and American," as well as divided into their own cultural and linguistic groups. "Canada was fundamentally British even though her people were American in ways and thought," according to representatives of the PA who met in London in October 1945 with delegates from the Canadian book trades.[70] Vast as the country was, the majority of its people lived in a narrow belt in close proximity to the U.S. border. An authority on Canadian publishing claimed that "Canada is, in fact, a forty-ninth state, more easily shipped to than Texas."[71] Communicating with a publisher in New York by phone was simpler and more efficient than sending a letter by post or, in special circumstances, dispatching a costly cable. With the growth and spread of popular media—magazines, newspapers, radio, and movies—in the twentieth century, how could the influence of the United States not have come to dominate?

British publishers may not have liked this U.S. cultural hegemony, but most understood it pragmatically and thus failed to defend the Canadian market as eagerly as they did their markets in Australia, New Zealand, and South Africa. Canada, said R. J. L. Kingsford, the wartime president of the PA, "was a market towards which before the war British publishers had been short-sighted and somewhat defeatist." Their inattentiveness was largely manifested in their willingness to throw Canadian rights in with U.S. rights when they sold British books to U.S. firms and to acquiesce in American publishers' retaining Canadian rights when they bought British books.[72]

The coming of the war, not surprisingly, solidified the predominance of American over British books in Canada. The sinking of three large shiploads of British books on their way to Canada in December 1942 was the Battle of the Atlantic's equivalent to the blitzing of book warehouses in London in 1940. The wartime shabbiness of those British books that did make their way to Canada compared most unfavorably with North American products, with their larger formats and more arresting graphics, especially on dust jackets. Thus, works by British authors in Canadian book outlets were more likely than not to be represented by their U.S. editions, sometimes with the permission of the British rights holder, but increasingly without his or her knowledge. By the end of the war, it seemed that for books from Britain "the Canadian market was all but lost" and, it was feared, it might take twenty years to win it back.[73]

British publishers faced competition from Americans in other areas of their traditional sales territories as well as in regions that were generally considered to be open markets. The demand for books after the defeat of the Axis powers in the Middle East, parts of which (Egypt, Palestine, and Iraq) were considered within the British market, was described as "phenomenal," but the number of British books going to the region, one observer noted, was "so fantastically low that it would not stock one bookshop more than about a week."[74] Both the British Council and the Ministry of Information responded by doing what they could to stimulate the export of British books to the Middle East, only to witness an "invasion" of the region, including Palestine, by American publishers, "who have now flooded it with their books."[75]

Latin America and the West Indies provided the setting for other competitive skirmishes. The British Council and the PA were actively seeking to market British books in Latin America, which was, according to Unwin, a "costly, and at present unremunerative, undertaking, but it is in the national interest that everything should be done to promote the knowledge of British life and literature in South America." He was concerned that George Brett, the head of Macmillan, "seems most anxious to take advantage of our difficulties in order to capture these particular [South American] markets, in which American publishers have shown much less interest in the past than we have done," and "to annexe the West Indies, which are still British colonies, and as such regularly supplied by us."[76]

The definition of rights for English-language publications on the continent of Europe was another problem for British publishers. For many years, the German firm of Tauchnitz dominated the market for books in English in Europe. The firm's famous series, Collections of British Authors, was launched in 1841 and later expanded to include works by U.S. writers. These rather squat, uniform paperbacks were aimed primarily at British and American travelers and the growing number of Europeans anxious and able to read British and American literature untranslated.[77] Unwin considered the effect of this German series on British book distribution on the Continent to have been "almost devastating."[78] The purchase by British interests of Albatross, a similar German series in pursuit of the same market, and its merger with Tauchnitz, and the rise of Penguin Books, rescued the Continental market for British literature from the Germans.[79]

It did not necessarily mean that British firms would automatically secure the European market after the war, however, for potent challengers arose, especially the Swedish firm Bonniers' line of paperback Zephyr Books.[80]

Unwin was particularly irate at what he considered the ignorance and insensitivity of some U.S. publishers in advancing their claims. For several months during the winter of 1943–44, Unwin engaged in a row with the U.S. firm Prentice-Hall over the terms of a rights contract, in which the U.S. publisher apparently unilaterally deleted Allen & Unwin's customary claim of European rights. A Prentice-Hall official was willing to consider Unwin's contention that his firm was particularly skilled in selling to the Continent and therefore better able to market the book there than the American publisher but, in order to evaluate the claim, he asked Allen & Unwin to provide him with full details of their sales methods in Europe, including a list of all of its customers.[81] To this naive request, Unwin responded, "I will do my best to be restrained, but the suggestion that I should hand over the complete list of accounts built up over forty years of personal visits to the Continent is one of the most amazing demands with which I have ever been confronted." But what concerned Unwin most was not so much the competition with U.S. firms for selling the same titles in Europe—he was confident that Allen & Unwin would prevail in any head-to-head battle—but rather that the U.S. firms would "dump" their editions in Europe by reducing the price and undercutting his firm.[82]

Trying to Understand the Other's Position

While Unwin was skirmishing with several American publishers, he was also engaging in an extended and more nuanced correspondence with Norton and Melcher, in which he laid out in great detail and with considerable passion how he regarded the issues of competition for markets with American publishers. In these letters, he emphasized his chief grievance, that American publishers were capitalizing on British publishing's war-imposed weakness to steal long-established British markets.

Unwin had become practiced at waving the "bloody shirt" at U.S. colleagues by recounting how hard and hazardous conditions were in wartime London, even as he, his staff, and his colleagues were soldiering through nerve-racking danger virtually every day. He gave Norton a detailed account of how close the war had come to his staff, to him, and to members of his family:

> Perhaps I feel unduly bitter because we are once again very much in the front line. My sister was blasted completely out of her house last week—not a ceiling or window left intact—and she regards herself as

lucky because two doors away there is nothing left of the house but rubble and the owner was killed by the "doodle-bug," as these flying bombs are called.... Many of our staff have suffered damage. Beard had his Sunday lunch covered with the plaster from his ceiling; his Baptist Chapel a door or two away saved him from worse trouble. Since then he has been blasted again, and this time it was his evening meal which got the plaster! He got no sleep when on duty last night, but turned up smiling this morning all the same.[83]

A convalescence from surgery gave Unwin plenty of time to ponder the impertinence of some American publishers, who, he wrote Melcher, "cannot apparently wait until the bombing has ceased" to poach on traditional British markets and pirate their books. He noted the unpleasant irony that "our principal allies, including the U.S.A., reserve the right to pirate our publications, whilst Germany is a most faithful adherent to the Berne Convention." He reminded Melcher how vital the export trade was to British publishers, who would "of necessity fight for it to the last gasp." He complained about U.S. hypocrisy and shortsightedness. U.S. publishers, for example, argued that Canada's proximity made it part of the U.S. market, but they failed to reciprocate by acknowledging that Britain's nearness to Europe made her a natural supplier of English-language books on the Continent. Few Americans, he said, have paid any attention to the Continental market and yet they think they can profit from it while selling the same books as British publishers. Unwin argued that they cannot. From all of his experience in foreign trade he knew that competition wouldn't succeed, because the European market "consists so largely of single copy business in hundreds of different centres in different countries with different languages, different currencies, different regulations, different requirements. There is no market so complex or troublesome," Unwin continued, "but the less people know about it the more glibly they talk." American publishers trying to sell in the Australian market "seem to picture us as wicked tyrants and themselves as gallant knights anxious to rescue the good lady from her thraldom, and a thraldom so appalling that they cannot wait till the war is over, but must start off next month if not next week to investigate it on the spot," wrote Unwin, in reference to the forthcoming visit Down Under by a delegation of American publishers.[84]

Melcher's response was clever. Playing the self-effacing provincial, he proclaimed himself in awe of the contributions of British literature and publishing to world history and of Unwin's place in the profession, especially for all he had done to help spread books in the English language throughout the world. "It means a lot to everyone in publishing," Melcher wrote, "that English, which has been the most widely printed language in the world, should become even more widely international in its use and with that situation come increased opportunities as well as responsibilities." What American publishers were trying to do, in other words, was nothing more than to pull their own weight in helping to spread the use of English, as British publishers had been doing for years. He "fumed," he said, that the United States had simply not done as much as it should have.[85] He admired the development in the UK of the National Book Council, the PA, and the British Council as instruments for spreading British books abroad, which put the United States to shame in contrast.

Melcher downplayed American intentions. What interest American publishers have shown in foreign markets, he said, has largely stemmed from external demand, rather than internal strategies for expansion. The Spanish civil war stimulated some activity in the United States, when new publishers in South America began to seek rights in American books. As Nazism took hold, engineers and other professional people outside Germany turned "from necessity" to American books. Similarly, "direct requests rather than invasionary efforts" stimulated demand from Canada, Australia, and other places. "Our relations to these markets," he told Unwin, "were far more casual than perhaps you in England seem to think." During the war, for example, orders for American books kept coming from Britain. One well-known English bookseller had been trying for several years to find a U.S. firm to handle his orders. "I had to beg one wholesaler to handle them and now he has given it up. That shows how export minded we are! It rather takes my breath away to hear from someone who thinks we are overdoing it."

More recently, Melcher admitted, American publishers *had* become more export-minded, but even here the incentives came from outside the U.S. book trade. First, American publishers had been impressed from reading accounts in *The Bookseller,* the British trade magazine, about all the inventive export activities that Unwin and others had stimulated. To this "blame the victim" explanation Melcher added another, that the publishers in the United States were responding to calls from their government, "which has begun to take books very seriously for their influence on international relationships." As for the failure of the United States to endorse the Berne convention on copyright, he reminded Unwin that the book publishers actually supported it. What had long stood in the way of joining Britain and much of the rest of the world was opposition from the more powerful music industry and from the printers and book manufacturers, who held fast to the manufacturing clause in the existing copyright law.[86]

In another exchange, Unwin acknowledged that there was little difference between the two of them over the general principles that the American had expounded. But, he added, Melcher had made "no reference to the application of those principles." Unwin claimed to have no objection to the desire of American publishers to export their books, but in practice, he said, they minimized the reasonable and legitimate opportunities to sell to British booksellers and to canvass

FIGURE 12.   Frederic G. Melcher (1879–1963), the influential, longtime editor of *Publishers' Weekly*. Photograph in *Frederic G. Melcher: Friendly Reminiscences of a Half Century among Books & Bookmen* (New York: Book Publishers Bureau, 1945). Photograph © Bachrach. Published by permission.

widely in adjacent Mexico, while allowing their books to be sold in South Africa, a member of the commonwealth, and "devoting their energy to supplying American books to Palestine which, for better or worse, is British mandated territory."[87]

From all of this, Unwin concluded that American publishers did not have the "patience or desire" to sell books abroad on a single-copy basis, which, Unwin maintained, constituted the bulk of the business. This being so, Unwin's U.S. colleagues should simply continue to use British publishers to handle these minute, occasional sales, just as they use jobbers to take care of small accounts at home. "Concentrating on a few best sellers," which is what Unwin judged U.S. publishers were really interested in, "merely hampers the activities of those anxious and willing to sell their whole list even though with the majority of titles a single copy is all that will be wanted."[88] This is much the same argument that full-service booksellers make today in criticizing discount chains, like Walmart, that sell huge quantities of a few best sellers, making it difficult for the regular trade to sell enough popular books to offset the inevitable losses incurred in handling a broad inventory.

Trying to Find Common Ground

The responses of Unwin and others to American publishers over incidents of encroachment, along with Unwin's complaints to U.S. colleagues Melcher and Norton, were tactical maneuvers, but efforts to deal strategically with the issues dividing the two greatest publishing nations were made through a series of mutual visits by delegates from both countries from 1942 to 1945. The first of these was the two-month-long solo visit to London that Hitchcock made at the end of 1942 as a representative of the Book Publishers Bureau, with sponsorship also from OWI. In the spring of 1943, delegates from Britain's Publishers Association—the three immediate past presidents, Walter Harrap (George G. Harrap), Geoffrey Faber (Faber & Faber), and Wren Howard (Jonathan Cape)—reciprocated with a seven-week trip throughout the United States and Canada, at the invitation of the BPB, with support from OWI. The British delegates came with the backing of the Ministry of Information.[89] Later, Edward M. Crane, president of D. Van Nostrand Co., was dispatched to London by the BPB in June 1945. In addition to these missions, two American publishers—Whitney Darrow (Scribner's) and Edward P. Hamilton (John Wiley)—visited Australia and New Zealand under the auspices of the bureau and OWI and, in September of that year, a delegation of five Canadian publishers, librarians, and trade officials journeyed to London to follow up the visit that the three British representatives had made to Canada two years earlier while also visiting the United States.[90]

None of these conferences produced any immediate solutions to the disagreements between the publishers in the United States and the UK over access to markets, but at least they kept the lines of communication open for more tangible results later. Publishers are known to be a gregarious lot, and the cocktail hours, dinner parties, and long speeches that were features of these missions helped soften the hard feelings that formed the background for the publishers' discussions. The meetings also inspired some fairly deep thinking—particularly among the British—about the relationship between a nation's book trade and its larger foreign economic and diplomatic policies. Real progress toward an understanding with the Americans, however, had to wait until after V-E Day.[91]

Hitchcock's meetings in London focused particularly on the disagreements between Britain and the United States over the Australian market, which had become the flash point of the controversy. Hitchcock asked British publishers to permit U.S. firms to supply books to Australia that they were unable to provide during the war emergency, but, looking to the future, he urged his British counterparts to modify their traditional understanding of rights and territories to allow Australian booksellers to import books directly from U.S. publishing houses, a change that would also respond to the claims of Australian booksellers and publishers for greater autonomy. The British publishers turned the Americans' argument around, asserting that it would actually be in the best interests of U.S. publishers to allow them, with their long experience selling around the globe, market U.S. imprints, best sellers and slow sellers alike. They asserted that publication in Britain usually produced a wider distribution of books throughout the world than could be achieved by publication in the United States alone. The consequence for Americans was that, if the British did not have the right to sell American books, including the strong sellers, to their traditional overseas markets, many good American titles would simply fail to find a British publisher, which would be far more of a loss than what would be gained from direct selling to Australia. The British publishers asked their U.S. colleagues to think not only of best sellers but of the whole business they do with Great Britain "and to be content, if needs be, to sacrifice these occasional plums for the good of the sale of the majority of American books."[92]

In his report to the bureau, Hitchcock painted an optimistic picture of how receptive British publishers were to U.S. works. He also took note of how nervous they were about U.S. designs "to grab while the grabbing is good."[93] It is not hard to see how Hitchcock's report, based on firsthand knowledge and coming only a year after the United States entered the war, could have opened the eyes of his fellow publishers to the opportunities that might lie abroad after the war, especially given the war-induced weakness of the British trade. Although he was certainly correct that American books would be in great demand after the war, both in a sophisticated literary and publishing community like Great Britain and in a less developed one like Australia, his optimism that Britain might be a weak competitor was rather misplaced. Nor did he see that the British trade's receptivity to American books could provide an alternate track to the world's bookshelves.

The reciprocal visit by publishers Harrap, Faber, and Howard occurred from mid-April through May 1943. Crossing the Atlantic in a British troopship, the delegates had time to prepare for the substantive discussions they expected to have with American publishers and government officials. For them, the two major issues were the familiar ones of separating Australian from British rights and of open markets on the Continent.

On the Australian question, the British publishers formally presented a compromise that had been informally discussed with Hitchcock the year before—namely, that if an American publisher had a book that he, perhaps on the insistence of his author, wanted to produce in Australia, he should require that the British publisher either produce the book in Australia himself or do his best to place it with a local publisher. In either case, the British publisher would pay 70 percent of the Australian royalties to the U.S. publisher. This would at least partially deflect the Americans' desire to deal directly with Australian entities. On the issue of open markets, the Britons chose not to suggest different approaches to extraterritorial markets in, say, Europe on the one hand and South America on the other. Instead, they proposed a "gentleman's agreement" on a code of practice to be mutually observed by publishers in both countries. It assumed that, in an open market, British and U.S. editions of the same title could freely compete, unless the contracting parties agreed in advance that one or the other would have exclusivity. To ease the British publishers' considerable fear of "dumping" by U.S. firms, the proposal included language to prevent price-cutting unless by mutual consent.[94]

The British attributed the lack of progress in negotiations to the absence of a unified position among the American publishers themselves and the unwillingness or inability of the BPB to bring them into line. While in the United States, they had learned how careful American publishers and the BPB were not to violate the Sherman Antitrust Act barring unlawful monopolies and restraints of trade. In Washington, they were surprised to hear government officials say that the BPB had less to fear from the Sherman Act than they thought. People at the State Department, in fact, would welcome a more strongly organized association of publishers because this would simplify their dealings with the book trade in spreading American books abroad.[95]

On returning to London, the three delegates drafted, and then published, a novella-length report on their mission to North America, which is remarkable not only for its clear analysis of the problems dividing the United States and Britain in international book-trade matters but also for its frank critique of U.S. society and politics generally. Despite sharing a language and "many similar habits and capacities," Harrap, Faber, and Howard discovered in their meetings with the Americans that "words and arguments...which seem on the surface to have the same meaning for both parties, are often loaded under the waterline with very different meanings and associations," all attributable to "very different mental and emotional attitudes, which often remain undisclosed simply because each side takes its own attitude for granted." They found Americans, however pleasant they might be, all too often to be oblivious to another party's position and even to facts. For example, many American publishers and others they encountered could not understand why the British considered it so vital to protect their traditional markets nor why they should feel that the Japanese occupation of British colonies in Asia should not make them as committed to the defeat of the Japanese as Pearl Harbor did for Americans.[96]

Perhaps most interesting was the delegates' sense of what drove the American people's attitudes toward business, politics, and international relations and their sense of how these both differed from and directly affected the future well-being of the UK in general and British publishing in particular. The core element they identified was how much Americans were in thrall to the values of business. For historical and cultural reasons, they wrote, "business, with us, however much it may absorb the interests and capacities of individuals, does not dominate the life of the country as it dominates the United States." That, combined with U.S. idealism, admirable as it might be in the abstract,

> is too apt to take the shape of supposing that what the rest of the world needs is what America can produce, and that America's principal duty is to spread the gospel of American material civilization. That American commerce would enormously benefit as a result is not stressed, but cannot be ignored. That British trade might well suffer is a consequence that has, perhaps, not occurred to Americans....Almost with the simplicity of a child the American has made himself believe that if by the freeing of all peoples from the yoke that he considers lies around their necks he gains a new market for his commercial products, it is a pure accident and nothing was further from his mind.[97]

In their observation of business and moral values in the United States, the delegates saw clear signs of an expansionist plan, not only in terms of books—through intentions to establish a chain of U.S. libraries throughout Europe and Latin America; in the dispatch of several publishers' missions, backed by government, to world capitals; and in the efforts of Pocket Books and other publishers to sell cheap U.S. editions throughout the world—but also in a far broader sense. "What is new," the delegates proclaimed, "is the appearance of a deliberate, collective drive towards the economic hegemony of the world. Stimulated by the war, this drive may soon pass far beyond its origins in business and may take on a definitely political and imperialist character. If this should happen—and signs of such a development are not wanting now—the idealism and the insensitivity we have been describing could easily become its very dangerous servants." If such aggressive expansionism goes forward "undeterred by any prospect of resistance, using American idealism to justify itself whenever resistance appears," the three publishers argued, "the United States may eventually find itself the most powerful country in the world—and the most disliked. No opportunity, therefore, ought to be lost now of enabling representative Americans to gauge the nature and strength of the forces which an all-out policy of world-wide business extension is likely to provoke."[98] In essence, the United States must grasp "that the business ethic which she has evolved for herself is not an ethic to be used as a method of pressure upon peoples, very differently circumstanced, least of all upon those peoples whose co-operation she must use both during and after the war; and that by her use of this business ethic she may soon bring her own motives under suspicion and spread alarm among her friends."

In describing what might be called the nascent "biblioimperialism" of the United States, the authors perhaps failed to see how much of what they wrote could also have described the imperialist business ethics that underlay the establishment of the British Empire, whose prerogatives they naturally defended. Astutely, however, they recognized that Americans' "freely expressed dislike of British imperialism" served to mask *American* imperialism from their consciousness. Perhaps, though, the Britons' distaste for U.S. expansion produced blinders to their own.[99]

By February 1944, several months after the PA delegates' report was issued, the Board of Trade had also become a believer in the dark designs that U.S. publishers had on British markets. Given the tremendous importance of British export trade, especially in books, Britain's relations with the world "would be very adversely affected if the world trade in books in English were to be controlled by America instead of being as heretofore very largely in British hands." A U.S. victory in the battle for the export trade in the dominions and elsewhere would present a grave threat "not only to the financial stability of British publishing but also to British prestige and cultural influence, and possibly even to the Imperial connection itself." The board was concerned not only about the introduction of American books in places where they had rarely gone but also about the apparent decrease in interest in British books in the United States.[100]

At the heart of the Americans' assault against the traditional British dominance, according to a PA white paper issued around the same time, was the transformation of the best seller into cult status, backed by new forms of "high-powered sales techniques." U.S. authors and their agents were increasingly pressuring their publishers to sell their Dominion rights separately to publishers in Australia and elsewhere and to secure a separate advance payment for them.

Meanwhile, those Dominion publishers were themselves becoming increasingly eager to buy U.S. best-seller rights directly from New York or Boston, rather than from London, and more resentful of any attempts by British houses to prevent them from doing so. Without the profits from U.S. best sellers to guard them from likely losses in the larger, less remunerative titles in their lists, UK publishers would find it difficult to sustain the kind of comprehensive trade they had long carried on throughout the empire and commonwealth.[101]

Two years after Faber, Harrap, and Howard's mission to North America and a month and a half after V-E Day, Edward M. Crane visited England as part of an itinerary that included stops on the Continent. Crane was chairman of both the D. Van Nostrand Company and USIBA, the nonprofit, quasi-governmental organization that American book publishers had recently set up to maintain and improve upon the activities of OWI in facilitating the export and sale of rights to American books abroad. Selling USIBA was a major objective of his tour, as was another attempt to settle long-standing disagreements. With the war in Europe over and with both nations' publishers eager to move forward in peacetime, it was at last possible for at least the two publishers' groups to come to an agreement.

The agreement divided world markets into two categories—home markets (exclusive markets within the United States and its dependencies and the British Empire and Commonwealth) and other markets (open markets in the rest of the world). Only Canada and Europe were to be considered exceptions in certain cases, generally to be decided by the contracting publishers on a title-by-title basis. For reasons of efficiency and proximity, the American publisher might have an exclusive market in Canada, perhaps for British works to which it owned rights as well as to its own, American titles. Similarly, a British publisher might gain exclusive access to the Continental market for its own books as well as the American books in which it was a rights holder. To achieve the agreement, both sides needed to compromise. In order to retain Continental rights, the British publishers had to water down the position they took with the visiting Canadian delegates in London not to sell Canadian rights to U.S. firms.[102] Although he could not have regarded it as an unalloyed triumph, Unwin was pleased with the agreement, which meant that "the Battle for Britain" had not been fought "in vain."[103]

Although the BPB and the PA had agreed to this compromise in principle, they were not able to adopt it formally because not all American publishers favored it and, even if there had been unanimity, the pact would likely have been illegal in the United States under the Sherman Act, however much the State Department might have desired more coordination. There remained considerable disagreement about what constituted the British Empire and Commonwealth for purposes of defining the British market. The British insisted that it should include the historical British Empire, including such territories that by the mid-1940s were no longer part of it, like Ireland and Palestine. Wisely if inconsistently, the British never argued that those former colonies that now constituted the United States should be included.[104]

With no restraint in Britain comparable to the Sherman Act, the British publishers, through the PA, could unilaterally assent to the British Traditional Markets Agreement in 1947, which became fully effective the next year.[105] The agreement, which was perfectly legal under British law, stipulated that each of the signatory publishers "will not...enter into any contract for the publication of any book written by any British or foreign author...unless the rights granted include the sole rights of publication and distribution in the British Publishers' Traditional Market," which consisted of seventy countries, from Aden to Zanzibar. Again, the only possible exception to the full force of the agreement was Canada, rights for which a British publisher could voluntarily cede to a U.S. contracting partner. The agreement generally worked well for the British, who maintained an impressive solidarity toward it, as well as for the Americans, who came to see enough benefit in it to make its coercive nature easier to swallow.

In effect, U.S. publishers came to accept the argument long made by Unwin and his colleagues that the maintenance of a financially healthy British publishing trade was key for U.S. prosperity as well, since it allowed British houses to buy rights to titles for publication in Britain and for effective distribution in the UK and in the seventy countries around the world that constituted the traditional market. In time, however, U.S. dissatisfaction with the cartelization of British publishing resurfaced. The Traditional Markets Agreement was eventually abandoned, some forty years after it was instituted officially.[106]

BOOKS FOR OCCUPIED GERMANY AND JAPAN

On entering the vanquished Third Reich, Allied troops and accompanying war correspondents found a country in absolute ruins, physically, psychologically, and morally. Janet Flanner (writing under the pen name Genêt) told her readers in *The New Yorker* that Cologne was "a model of destruction," whose people "have little to say. Dazed by a week of defeat, three years of bombings, and twelve years of propaganda, the old men and the women and children who now inhabit the city sound as if they had lost all ability to think rationally or to tell the truth."[1] Germany was an enemy country, a defeated nation—not like the countries that German soldiers had overrun and that the Allied forces had liberated in the wake of D-Day. The Allies established military governments, with plenary powers, each in its own zone at first. For Germany there was no negotiated armistice, only unconditional surrender. Although Flanner didn't say so explicitly, uncensored books, free of the razzle-dazzle of Nazi propaganda, might be just the prescription to heal the mental and moral incapacitation she observed among the Germans of Cologne and to speed their reentry into the company of civilized peoples.

The war against Japan ended more suddenly than the war against Germany did, but even so it took not one but two atomic bombs to persuade Emperor Hirohito and his warlords to surrender to the United States and its allies. As did Germany, Japan surrendered unconditionally. The defeat would bring an all-powerful military government to bear on the Japanese people, as in Germany. On the deck of the USS *Missouri*, the man who would be supreme commander, Gen. Douglas MacArthur, told the assembled enemy officials that the victors, no less than the vanquished, had responsibilities, that is, to free the Japanese people from a "condition of slavery" and to channel the citizenry's energies into constructive pursuits, allowing them to expand "vertically rather than horizontally."[2] For the Japanese, MacArthur's words must have been at least a bit reassuring and, though they could not have known it, they were certainly much different from the stern orders that the Joint Chiefs of Staff had given General Eisenhower for the military government of Germany.

The suddenness of the Pacific war's end, coming as it did without an invasion, and the far longer supply lines than those in continental Europe delayed the actual installation of military government in Japan. It was two weeks after the emperor had told his subjects in a nationwide broadcast on August 15, 1945, that the war was lost before the first major elements of the occupation forces went ashore in Japan. The atomic bombings had also thrown off the estimates of many wartime government planners, including those in the Office of War Information, that the conflict in the Pacific would likely last a year or more beyond V-E Day, leaving OWI officials unready to implement a book program for Japan. Anyone involved in a book program for Japan who read MacArthur's words, however, might have felt inspired. Implicit in his statement was the notion that occupation government would strive to enable Japan to grow through democracy, new ideas, inventiveness, and industriousness ("vertically") rather than by geographical expansion through conquest of others ("horizontally"). A solid book program, if successful, could help point the way, but that too would be delayed.

Occupation Government and U.S. Book Policy

Carrying out U.S. book policy for occupied Germany and Japan was a much different undertaking from what prevailed in the countries the Axis had overrun. Allied policy in the overrun nations was to assist in the reestablishment of the regular local channels of communication, including book publishing, as soon as possible. For Germany and Japan, the rehabilitation of local publishing was no less an ultimate objective, but it would be accomplished under the close direction of the military governments and under important restrictions.[3] That Germans were regarded as being historically highly influenced by books was both good news and bad. Having seen the power for evil that books had demonstrated during the ascendancy of Adolf Hitler, author of the best seller *Mein Kampf,* the Allies realized the necessity of neutralizing that kind of seductive power and replacing it with a more uplifting message.[4] Japan was also regarded as a bookish country, and might be more pliable.

The actual structures of the military governments during the occupation of Japan and Germany were quite different, however, directly affecting how book publishing was controlled in the two countries. In the realm of consolidation propaganda through books in Germany, the United States was sovereign only within its own zone, which complicated matters for American publishers wishing to do business with a German publisher in, say, the British zone. An alternative model shaped the occupation of Japan. This was entirely deliberate, for U.S. officials wished to avoid many of the problems arising from the quadripartite military rule in Germany. Given its dominant role in defeating Japan, the United States was able to run the occupation virtually single-handedly. Military government in Japan was unitary, exercising control over the whole of the country. Although the real power in the government in Japan was overwhelmingly American, the U.S. book program cooperated with the other Allied powers, especially Great Britain and the Soviet Union. When MacArthur's military government, SCAP (Supreme Command for the Allied Powers) assumed the responsibility of licensing the Japanese publication of foreign works in translation, it processed not only American titles, but British, Russian, and French books as well.[5]

The Psychological Warfare Division of SHAEF (later OMGUS, the Office of Military Government, United States), led by Brig. Gen. Robert A. McClure, set general policy for consolidation propaganda for Germany, as did the Psychological Warfare Branch of SCAP, under the command of Brig. Gen. Bonner F. Fellows, in Japan. At this point, consolidation propaganda meant the reeducation or reorientation of the German and Japanese populations away from their fascist and militaristic moorings. This transformation would include rehabilitated publishing industries to which the U.S. military governments would in time turn over control.

The first steps toward reeducation in each country, however, could not have differed more. In its own zone in Germany, the United States basically dismantled the existing structure of communications, including book publishing and bookselling, and then, at least theoretically, rebuilt it by purging people with Nazi connections and licensing firms whose principals had "clean" backgrounds ideologically. On the other hand, the Joint Chiefs of Staff had decided to govern Japan through the existing bureaucracy of the Japanese government, rather than to tear it down and rebuild it through purges and licensing, as was being done in Germany. The decision was made as a way of conserving U.S. forces and resources and as a pragmatic response to the reality that few Americans had the language and cultural skills to govern the country effectively themselves.[6] The occupation of Japan therefore necessarily placed considerably less emphasis on purging individuals from government posts or positions in the civilian economy than was the case with denazification in Germany.

This meant that the existing trade structure was not dismantled, with the result that book publishing in Japan at the start of the occupation was far more robust and lively than it was in Germany. To be sure, SCAP early on set out to overturn the most oppressive features of the imperial regime, including its system for censoring the printed word. This included an analysis of the effect of imperial purges from Japanese libraries, prompting a reluctance to remove too many more books from libraries so as not to "bring a charge of 'book-burning' against the Allies."[7] Still, the military government essentially left it to "the vanquished themselves to fill this new space."[8] Because Japanese publishers were allowed to go back to work immediately, it meant that an effective U.S. book program was not as necessary to provide the first books for an intellectually hungry populace as it was in Europe, including Germany.

Overseas Editions in Occupied Germany and Japan

On the whole, Overseas Editions played a smaller role in Germany than they did in other parts of Europe and almost no role in Japan. This constituted a problem for Germany but less of one for Japan, where indigenous publishing was never dismantled before being rehabilitated. Transatlantic Editions were never intended to be shipped to either country.

The German-language Overseas Editions were the last titles selected by the Office of War Information and produced by the Council on Books in Wartime's subsidiary Overseas Editions, Inc. They were also late in being distributed in Germany. Sales of the allotment of over eight hundred thousand copies of twenty-three titles through the local book trade at one mark each did not begin until 1946.[9] Little is known about how the books circulated, how many were bought, or what the German public thought of them. Almost certainly, though, they were among the first American books to reach German soil.

Some OEs reached Germany under other auspices than OWI and the U.S. Army. German prisoners of war repatriated from their camps in the United States brought them home, along with the Bücherreihe Neue Welt books they had purchased in the camp canteens. OWI had begun cooperating with the Office of the Provost Marshal General's Special Projects Division in its program of reorienting German (and Italian) POWs in December 1944.[10] OWI provided OEs in lots of ten thousand copies per title.[11] Chester Kerr, the chief progenitor of OEs, opposed any diversion of the stock of the German editions from their intended civilian readers in the German homeland. He had no choice but to acquiesce once higher-ups in OWI approved the arrangement, but he complained that the OPMG officers "had far too little notion of what they were doing" and that "the quantity of 10,000 of each Overseas Edition in German had always seemed absurdly high to me." He turned out to be right. About half of the OWI publications placed in the canteens, including the OEs, remained unsold as of early

November 1945, which irritated Kerr.[12] Perhaps the BNWs had already saturated the market when the OEs appeared in the camps, by which time many POWs had been shipped back home. In any case, the remainders were returned to OWI, which made plans for them to be shipped for use among the civilian populations in Germany and Austria, for whom they were originally intended.[13]

OEs played a negligible role in the reorientation of the Japanese population, in marked contrast to their usefulness in Europe. The planned production of Japanese-language editions of approved titles never took place, so the State Department (OWI having disbanded) decided to use English-language OEs instead, figuring that a satisfactory number of Japanese citizens, particularly among the elite, would be able to read them. Thirty-five hundred copies of each title were allocated for Japan, awaiting disposition as of late February 1946. It was the task of the Civil Information and Education Section of SCAP to arrange for their distribution by one or more Japanese book wholesalers. The division set several conditions for distribution of the books. Like the OEs for Europe, the books were to be sold rather than given away, with the proceeds, by law, returning to the U.S. Treasury. The retail price was to be ¥3.75, about twenty-five cents, the standard price for paperback books in the States. The wholesaler would have to agree to distribute the books nationwide and to safeguard against the diversion of copies into the black market as well as their purchase by occupation forces.[14]

Launched late, the OE operation for Japan may never really have gotten off the ground. It is not clear whether any wholesaler was engaged or that any significant distribution was actually carried out. Probably not, since two years after the OEs arrived in Japan, permission was granted to distribute the remaining copies for free. Even so, few if any of the books had been given away even six months after free distribution was authorized, judging by an inventory dated October 31, 1948, which showed that between twenty-five hundred and fifty-four hundred copies of twenty of the OEs remained on hand. If these figures were correct, the number of copies actually imported must have exceeded the thirty-five hundred of each title originally allocated to Japan. At this point, CIE was to turn the surplus books over to the army for final distribution, particularly to various Japanese agencies and institutions.[15]

A number of reasons may account for the failure of the OE program in Japan. It may have stemmed, at least in part, from ignorance and indifference within the occupation government. With OWI defunct and the military and civilian officials most aware of the OE program stationed in Europe, perhaps there was no one in Japan to push hard for the speedy distribution of the books that the New York office had produced with such great effort. Or it may simply have been that the books arrived too late and into a market that needed them less than the Europeans did, since Japanese publishers were able to bring out books much more quickly than their counterparts in Europe.[16]

Allied Book Policy for Germany

PWD/SHAEF's underlying principle was that Germans had to take responsibility for their conversion to democratic ways, which in turn had to rely on the re-creation of a communications system in which Germans spoke to Germans.[17] Nazis need not apply, of course, which determined the policy of screening individuals about their beliefs and activities during the years of the Third Reich, and then licensing or registering individuals who passed muster. Publishers were to be licensed; booksellers needed only to be registered, a simpler process. (Analogously, film producers needed to be licensed, while exhibitors of films had only to be registered.)[18] The screening process was vital to the long-term success of the U.S. book policy in Germany. Until local publishers could receive licenses and get back in business, there would be no new books available in Germany beyond the OEs and some other materials. Nor would American publishers be in a position to have their books translated and published in the new Germany.

A person who had actively resisted the Nazis and who had training or experience in publishing as well as adequate financial resources or backing was the ideal candidate for licensing. A publisher or bookseller who could show that the Nazis had shut down his enterprise, according to Edward C. Breitenkamp, the head of a regional Information Control Division (ICD) publications office during the occupation, possessed "the very best recommendation one could have next to having been an inmate of a concentration camp."[19]

Because consideration in licensing was given to an applicant's professional experience as well as his distance from Nazism, most of the earlier licensees were publishers who had flourished under the Weimar Republic but whose careers had suffered under the scrutiny of the Nazis. Some had worked in the underground; others had been put into concentration camps. Many, of course, were of advanced age and not particularly vigorous. The younger licensees, on the other hand, were far less experienced and sometimes had difficulties coping with the tough realities of occupied Germany's financial and political world.[20] At the higher levels of scrutiny, U.S. officials also considered the likelihood that the applicant's publishing plan would fill a real need.[21]

There was a great deal of pressure to license book publishers quickly, inasmuch as Germans were just as hungry for books as the citizens of the nations their forces had overrun. What was more, American publishers, eager as they were to supply its titles, could not do so until German publishing firms were licensed and in business. Furthermore, getting more books into the German marketplace sooner would help reduce social tensions and discourage the publication and distribution of underground publications.[22]

Obtaining a license conferred benefits beyond enabling individuals to engage in the business and, presumably, to earn a living once the new publisher had functioning presses, paper, the necessary labor, and texts to set in type, all of which could be some time distant. The most immediate benefit, rather, was that it enabled the lucky individual to obtain living quarters, increased food rations, a telephone, gasoline, coal, and a railroad pass, which, in the awful first year following the defeat, could make the difference between living and dying. One publisher called the license an "Open Sesame!" to a better life. To Breitenkamp, it seemed that virtually everyone in Germany who had not joined a Nazi organization at least considered applying.[23] The promised quick change in fortune and the future prospects of a lucrative career persuaded one of that multitude, the anonymous author of a riveting memoir of life after the fall of Berlin, to join with several acquaintances in obtaining a license and setting up shop. At least she had some publishing experience.[24]

Information Control in Germany

After SHAEF was disbanded on July 14, 1945, jurisdiction within occupied Germany was divided among the Americans, British, French, and Russians, each in its own zone. The task of reorganizing the communications structure in Germany was assigned to each power's information-control unit. For the United States, that outfit was the Information Control Division of OMGUS. Essentially, the staff of PWD/SHAEF, from Brig. Gen. Robert A. McClure on down, carried over to run the ICD. McClure's deputy, Col. William S. Paley, in civilian life the founder and chairman of the Columbia Broadcasting System, prepared a detailed manual to cover all phases of the U.S. effort to control the German information services, within the authority of the overall military-government regulations.[25] The reintroduction of books—which was the responsibility of the ICD's Publications Branch—would take place after the more immediate needs of calming and informing the population had gotten underway through the mass media of radio, newspapers, and magazines.[26]

The licensing program took longer to implement than OWI officials had expected. Several levels of approval were needed, from initial submission of the application at a local ICD office, to one of the five regional *Land* headquarters, all the way up to OMGUS in Berlin. Application forms (*Fragebogen*) became available in early July and the first license was granted on July 13. From then through the end of September, eight book publishers were licensed in the U.S. zone, half of them general trade publishers and half publishers of religious books. By the end of October, four thousand bookshops had been registered. By the end of November, the number of licensed publishers had grown to sixty-nine.

After the relatively quick early approvals, the process of licensing a publisher could take from three months to a year. For OMGUS, filling "this great literary void" remained a huge problem, especially since it slowed "an unrivaled opportunity to bring to bear upon the Germans the best influences of our culture" by having American books published there.[27] By July 1948, 387 book and periodical publishers had been licensed. They had published approximately 7,250 books and pamphlets and founded 383 periodicals. More than seventy of those firms had negotiated nearly three hundred contracts to publish American books.[28]

Surprisingly, few of the books were actually obtainable by the public. Of the standard maximum press run of five thousand copies of a book in the early period of the occupation, the publisher frequently sold only as many as he needed to finance his next book. The rest he held back against the time when the currency system would be reformed. Booksellers did the same thing with some of the stock they purchased from publishers. To favored customers they might sell a copy of the book they kept under the counter. This tendency to hoard goods of all kinds during the soft-money period was widespread throughout the economy.[29]

Conditions remained broadly uncongenial to the timely redevelopment of German publishing. Many publishers, of necessity, had been on the move. Bombed out of Leipzig or Berlin, they sought new locations to reestablish their businesses. In fact, after capturing Leipzig, the U.S. Army invited the leading anti-Nazi publishers to accompany U.S. forces when it withdrew from the city, which was to be in the Soviet zone.[30] Perhaps one-third of all publishers, it was estimated, changed their location in 1946. Breitenkamp noted that even some publishers "with internationally known names traveled about the country in freight trains or trucks with their knapsacks on their backs seeking a place to reestablish their firms." The fortunate ones who secured office space had difficulty finding a printer. Printing plants that were open had far more orders than they could fulfill. "It was looked upon as a true act of grace," Breitenkamp wrote, "when a printer agreed to accept work from a publisher." That assumed, of course, that the publisher had something to publish. Few new manuscripts by Germans were forthcoming. According to the ICD official, one writer told his publisher that it was still "more important to raise potatoes and cabbages than to write books." This shortfall of domestic literature made the acquisition of literary properties from abroad (or the reprinting of German classics) all the more important.[31]

Continuity of staffing within ICD was uncharacteristically high, all the way up to General McClure. Many individuals continued to work for the division for several years. Breitenkamp, a keen observer of the division's activities as head of the publications control branch in Marburg for a year beginning in June 1947, classified the U.S. personnel of the zonal ICD into the categories of career army; U.S.-born-and-bred university professors and educators; "and lastly persons of German or European birth or background, the majority of whom were refugees from the Nazi system and of Jewish race."

The career army people, he claimed, had little or no interest in the specific task to which the division was assigned and exerted only "slight" influence, unless they held general policymaking responsibilities. Many of the academics and other professionals, on the other hand, brought considerable skills and enthusiasm to their jobs. Among them were the publications chief for the entire U.S. zone, Douglas L. Waples, professor of social psychology at the University of Chicago, specializing in the sociology of libraries and "the social psychology of public influence by print,"[32] and Hellmut Lehmann-Haupt, a professor in the library school at Columbia, a contributor to *Publishers' Weekly*, and later a historian of U.S. publishing. In Breitenkamp's opinion, the refugees or émigrés in information control—to whom the U.S.-born staff members deferred—"exercised the greatest influence." Many of them, he noted, had worked in publishing or other media in Germany before fleeing. Of course they were fluent in German, unlike most of the native-born Americans. Many had strong connections with refugee communities throughout the world. Some also maintained ties to friends or family whose publishing or book-selling businesses the Nazis had confiscated. The émigrés on the ICD staff were particularly helpful to fellow refugees when they sought licenses upon their return to Germany. Nevertheless, Breitenkamp considered the émigrés in the ICD to be an essentially reactionary element, who managed to turn the clock back to the publishing culture of Weimar Germany.[33]

The ICD also employed a number of German civilians in secretarial or clerical positions. Despite the essentially menial nature of their jobs, the indigenous personnel, Breitenkamp wrote, "often exercised an influence far exceeding their positions." This form of power he attributed to the natives' natural fluency in German, familiarity with the local situation, and their ability to provide continuity when their U.S. bosses rotated in and out. Most were too young to have held any position of influence in the Nazi regime, and in any case they underwent screening to weed out those with suspect backgrounds. A number of the men had been prisoners of war in camps in the United States and had gone through the reeducation, or denazification, program that the OPMG had put into effect prior to repatriation.[34] The Americans' innate informality tended to encourage close personal relationships with their German underlings, despite official policies against fraternization. Working for the Americans had considerable attraction for ambitious Germans, not the least of which was having a hot lunch every day, when many of their compatriots were starving.[35] Karl Arndt, an ICD officer in the religious-affairs section, observed in handwritten annotations made in his copy of Breitenkamp's book that some baser instincts occasionally influenced the work of ICD. Applicants did not always succeed in getting licensed simply by making a good impression on the control officer, Arndt noted, but sometimes by offering bribes. Similarly, some German employees gained influence beyond their low status "when the US chief slept with the secretary or clerk, as was often the case."[36]

Anglo-American Competition and Cooperation

Despite the competitiveness that marked the publishing relationships between Britain and the United States during the war and the occupation period, the two nations' publishing-control authorities often cooperated with one another, out of both professional courtesy and the allied military-command structure. This was particularly important when information or advice was needed on matters that crossed between the U.S. and British zones. Information-control officers in both armies, of course, were not only looking after the reeducation programs of their military governments but also keeping an eye on their nations' book interests.

The British probably had the advantage, thanks to the close connection between Stanley Unwin and two key British officers, which proved useful for the British information-control effort and advantageous for the publisher's own postwar plans. As it happened, the man in charge of Britain's information-control effort in Germany was Col. R. H. Unwin, a relative of the publisher, though without any experience in book publishing of his own. Another staff member was Maj. Charles A. Furth, who in civilian life was head of educational publishing for Allen & Unwin.[37] A third member of the team, Capt. Spencer Curtis Brown, was a member of the family that controlled the prominent transatlantic literary agency Curtis Brown, Ltd., with which Unwin's firm had long done business. For his part, Stanley Unwin put his extensive knowledge of the German book trade at the service of the control commission. In turn, both Furth and R. H. Unwin performed useful favors for Stanley Unwin, particularly in providing information on the whereabouts of German publishers with whom Unwin had done business prior to the war or might wish to postwar.

Unwin carried on a correspondence directly with Waples, the U.S. control officer, also to mutual advantage. Since, of course, not all of the German publishers that Unwin wished to do business with were conveniently located in the British zone, Waples was occasionally able to help Unwin reestablish contact with publishers located within his jurisdiction. One particular time, Unwin wished to learn from Waples whether or not the publisher of the German edition of Unwin's textbook on publishing (*The Truth about Publishing*, or, in German, *Das wahre Gesicht des Verlagsbuchhandels*) resided in the U.S. zone. Unwin was eager that his new revision be translated and made available in Germany. Such a book "is badly needed in Germany," he wrote, "the more so because of the many young and inexperienced firms that have arisen." The firm had indeed survived the war and was willing to bring out the new edition, but to do so the publisher needed a guarantee of an adequate paper supply for the edition. For this Unwin sought Waples's intercession. The fact that a new German edition appeared in 1948

(Stuttgart: Poeschel Verlag) suggests that Waples was able to assist.[38] In other situations, Waples benefited from Unwin's help. From time to time, the Englishman provided useful advice on the political leanings of publishers he had known who found themselves in the U.S. zone.[39] He also responded sympathetically when Waples sought advice on whether there might be any postwar opportunities for him in London as a consultant on publishing on the Continent.[40]

In his letters home, Furth provided gripping details on the difficult logistics involved in finding enough information to issue licenses to the "white sheep," while giving closer scrutiny to the possible "black sheep," as well as on the physical and human costs of the devastation of Germany. Much the same could have been reported by the American, Waples, no doubt. Furth made it a point to visit all of the most important candidates himself. From makeshift headquarters in several houses in a remote village, he and his top aide drove over wretched roads to the would-be licensees' last-known addresses. By mid-July, he had visited twenty-five of them. The interviews were by turns depressing or hopeful. Of the firms visited, only one had escaped bombing. In one instance, "maneuver[ing] the car past piles of rubble [we] drew up before a bomb hole, which we identified as the address we were seeking. But if one climbed on into the ruins, one generally found, somewhere, four patched up walls, within which machines were running again." The owner of this shop happened to be "a bully and a swine," and for him and others like him "one has no sympathy. But it's difficult not to sympathise with the ordinary poor devils living in these ruins and picking their way over the broken pavements."

Furth, his British colleagues, and his counterparts in U.S. information control like Waples, Lehmann-Haupt, and Breitenkamp were witnesses to how much combat damage and cultural change had wrought on the most centralized and most stable book trade in the world. Now what was left of the trade was scattered throughout four zones of occupation, each administered by a military government, one of which, the Soviet zone, was increasingly at odds politically with the others. Furth believed that what had so characterized the German trade throughout history—the centrality of Leipzig—was likely gone for good. Still, he marveled that "the viability of some of the more stable German firms under total war and total defeat has been astonishing."[41]

In time, though, the optimism of both Allies and Germans that a new day for publishing beckoned with the defeat of Hitler gave way to much cynicism. Breitenkamp was not alone in becoming more pessimistic about what information control could accomplish. The conditions of the time and place—pervasive poverty, worthless money, shortages of materials and labor, and many other woes—helped limit the number of books that could be published and the number of copies that actually reached the public. This was frustrating enough; but adding to the uneasiness were concerns that the growing schism between the

Soviets and the Americans and their allies would make U.S. goals for rebuilding German book publishing increasingly important, as a counterweight to Soviet propaganda, even as it compromised their ability to reform it.

Publishing Books in Occupied Japan

The slow pace of licensing publishers and publishing books in Germany was averted in Japan, though the latter program had its own share of problems that particularly affected the influence of American books in that country. Just how quickly and efficiently the Japanese book trade resuscitated itself is revealed by the fact that, in the few months between surrender and the end of 1945, Japanese publishers issued nearly one thousand new books, many of which were titles on taboo subjects and other books that the militarists had suppressed.[42]

These thousand books appeared with no real impetus from the occupation government, although they were subject to its prepublication censorship. In fact, they were not published as part of the U.S. program governing consolidation propaganda in Japan. While the OE scheme was going nowhere, no alternate plan was ready to replace it, only the germ of one. In November 1945, just three months after the surrender, Japanese publishers had begun to request SCAP's permission to translate American books and to negotiate with the copyright holders. CIE was not quite ready to deal with them, but, within a month, SCAP had determined that American books could be translated and published by Japanese firms. Some twenty U.S. titles, preapproved by the State Department, were offered to Japanese publishers for translation and publication. These included Owen Lattimore's *Solution in Asia*, Charles A. Beard's *American Government and Politics* and *The Republic*, Ambassador Joseph Grew's *Ten Years in Japan*, Joseph F. Pennell's *The History of Rome Hanks*, Mary O'Hara's *My Friend Flicka*, and Ernest Hemingway's *For Whom the Bell Tolls*. The titles selected were mostly cut from the same cloth as the OEs and other books approved and stockpiled for use in Europe. Reading, or examination, copies of twenty other books, sent by American publishers, were to follow.[43]

The lack of a real program proved both frustrating to SCAP and members of the Japanese publishing trade and embarrassing to the military government.[44] It took another year before a formal program was announced and nearly two more years of desultory progress before it really got off the ground.[45] Deeply influencing such inaction were the unfortunate consequences of a copyright treaty that the United States and Japan concluded in 1906. The agreement specified that Japanese publishers could issue translations of U.S. works without permission or payment of fees or royalties. American publishers had the same freedom with regard to translations from the Japanese, a dubious right since in 1945, as in

1906, American books were far more valuable commodities in Japan than Japanese books were in the United States.[46] U.S. officials were anxious to ensure that the rights of U.S. copyright holders would be protected under any formal book program for American books in Japanese, a concern that favored hesitation over action.

Japanese publishers filled the cultural vacuum against formidable obstacles, even if a German-style dismantling of the industry before its reconstruction was not one of them. For years they had worked under a system that tightly controlled what they could and could not publish. MacArthur's proconsulship imposed some restraints of its own, particularly against publishing material that criticized the Allies or glorified Japanese militarism. Bombing had left many printing plants destroyed or heavily damaged. There was little capital to invest in new or revivified publishing enterprises and publishing continued to be a risky business financially. As in Europe, paper remained in short supply and highly regulated until the occupation ended in 1951. All things considered, the recovery of Japanese book publishing was astonishing. Because of the pent-up demand for books and other reading material, publishing was actually one of the first Japanese industries to recover. Some three hundred publishing houses survived the end of the war. Eight months later, there were almost two thousand firms, many of them, to be sure, short-lived. The peak came in 1948, with about forty-six hundred publishers, before a recession bankrupted many of them. Still, in 1951, about nineteen hundred firms remained, more than six times the number that existed on V-J Day.[47]

The rapid response of Japanese publishers was highly welcome locally. No less than Europeans, the Japanese public hungered for books after their own lengthy intellectual blackout. How else could one explain why a couple hundred people began lining up outside a Tokyo bookstore three days before a new edition of the collected works of philosopher Nishida Kitarō was to go on sale? The tastes of the Japanese reading public turned out to be catholic and eclectic. They longed for books representing their own cultural traditions, even as they were eager to reacquaint themselves as well with the high points of European literature.[48] They were also "burning to read American books," in the not entirely disinterested opinion of Capt. Charles Tuttle, who was serving in the CIE and later established in Tokyo an important Japanese-American bookstore (inside the Takashimaya department store) and publishing house. "The current Japanese craving for American books is perhaps unimaginable to anyone not in Japan," wrote Tuttle. "They are hungrier for print than for gum or chocoletto." Tuttle attributed this not only to the pragmatic notion that it would be useful to know something about the culture of their conquerors but also to a willingness to absorb the principles of U.S. liberalism and democracy.[49] But it proved difficult to gain anything approaching a dominant position for American books, in large part because of the structure and policies of the occupation government, or, perhaps, because of its inaction.

In charge of the administration of information control, including the book program, was the Press and Publications Branch of SCAP/CIE. Its supervisor and principal line of communications back home was the New York field office of the army's Civil Affairs Division. The process by which SCAP/CIE brought American—and other Western—books into occupied Japan evolved through several phases. After the failed attempt to sell the OEs, the efforts were based primarily on permitting Japanese publishers to issue the books immediately, rather than on importing books stockpiled elsewhere for the purpose—precisely the opposite of what occurred in Europe.

These haphazard early efforts involved licensing of foreign books and prior censorship of domestic titles but were governed by no particular master plan. It seems likely that many if not most of the books licensed during the first three years of occupation were titles in the public domain or those on which the rights holder was willing, perhaps even eager, to waive royalties.[50] The licensing process, which included the clearance of rights, was made more difficult by the demise of the United States International Book Association at the end of 1946, when the book program in Japan was still far from up to speed. With no other entity able to represent the foreign-trade goals of the American book publishers, the military had to take on much of the work itself, or contract it out.[51] In effect, the "United States of America" became the purchaser of sole rights to Japanese translations of American books, which they then resold to selected Japanese publishers.[52]

Efforts to encourage the publishing of Japanese translations of U.S. titles—as opposed to books from other allied nations—during the first two or three years of occupation, however, were not much more successful than the marketing of OEs. Few of the early reprints of foreign literature were American books. Books by U.S. authors in fact numbered only 104 (7.6 percent) of the 1,367 translations that Japanese publishing houses issued between November 1945 and April 1948. In a list that has been characterized as "genuinely cosmopolitan," U.S.-authored books were greatly eclipsed by titles of French authorship (350), German (294), Russian (251), and British (194). Trailing the U.S. figure were books by Chinese (43) and Italian (37) authors, with another 94 titles by authors of several other countries.[53]

The relatively poor showing of the United States on the master list is explainable, however. An examination of the titles on the list reveals a predominance of older works, many of them recognized classics of Western literature. To cite only a few examples, the accounting of U.S. authors includes Emerson, Hawthorne, Poe, Stowe, Twain, and Whitman. The British list names Bunyan, Carlyle, Defoe, Dickens, Doyle, Mill, Shakespeare, and Stevenson. Similarly, the likes of

Balzac, Baudelaire, Descartes, Dumas, Hugo, Maupassant, and Moliere appear on the French list. Such giants as Chekhov, Dostoyevsky, Pushkin, and Tolstoy may be found on the Russian list, as may Lenin and Stalin. The German section includes Engels and Marx among Goethe, Grimm, Hesse, Kant, and Nietzsche. Although the list does not indicate as much, most likely these were titles that Japanese publishers had published in translation before the war, which they wanted to bring back into print. There doesn't seem to be any other way these could have been produced so quickly. Because these books, including the pillars of Marxist thought, were known quantities (and the warmish glow regarding the Russian allies had not yet turned cold), the licensors at CIE would have faulted them only with difficulty.

Looked at in this way, American writers' fifth-place finish does not seem so surprising. After all, Britain, France, and Germany had much longer and more distinguished traditions of philosophy and literature than the United States, and their publishers had also cultivated foreign markets more strenuously and for a much longer time. Although Japanese translations of U.S. works in the public domain would produce no present or future revenues in Japan for American publishers, there was a chance that more-recent, copyrighted U.S. works translated into Japanese could earn some money for their American publishers. The state of war against Japan had technically rendered null and void the 1906 copyright treaty between the United States and Japan, which permitted publishers of each country to translate each other's literary works without authorization, but American publishers were determined to control their rights unambiguously in the future.[54] As increased opportunities for publishing newer U.S. titles arose, therefore, the United States hoped to be able to gain an inside track onto Japanese bookshelves as well as elsewhere in the world.

But this would take some time. Even U.S. popular literature failed to find an instant audience in occupied Japan, where the people seemed eager for a cosmopolitan reading list of serious books. Early postwar best sellers included a short guide to English-language conversation, works by Japanese writers that the militarist government had banned, non-Japanese books like Jean-Paul Sartre's *Nausée,* André Gide's *Intervues Imaginaires,* Erich Maria Remarque's *Arc de Triomph,* and T. H. Van de Velde's popular manual on marital sex. Not until an authorized translation of Margaret Mitchell's *Gone With the Wind* appeared in 1949 did a U.S. author appear on the top-ten best-seller list in Japan.[55]

The books that represented high points of the Western intellectual tradition, including the works of Marx, Engels, and Lenin, spoke to Japanese readers' response to defeat and the resulting culture of remorse, as well as to their own serious yearnings to embrace democratic thought. This intellectual flowering caught U.S. occupation officials, even the liberal New Dealers among them, completely off guard. Not only that, the ideas that the intelligentsia read in newly translated books radiated outward to much wider audiences through the mass media. To their credit, the U.S. censors and book licensers did not, at least at first, arbitrarily block the publication of key works of French existentialism like those of Sartre and Gide, Van de Velde's sex manual, or the foundation stones of Marxism, even though such books were out of the mainstream of U.S. thought. While the more left-leaning among the SCAP officials encouraged the ferment, just as their counterparts in the U.S. military government in Germany did in their bailiwick, watchful anticommunists among their colleagues took note of their names on blacklists and discredited them during the height of cold-war fever.[56]

While SCAP's licensing of 1,367 titles of foreign authorship between November 1945 and April 1948 was no mean feat, the 104 U.S.-authored works fell far short of meeting the objectives of a U.S. book program for Japan. Many additional, and newer, American books, like those being licensed around the same time by publishers in the liberated countries of Europe and, in due course, in Germany itself, would be needed there as well.

SCAP/CIE worked closely with the appropriate private-sector organization, the Japan Publishers' Association. The JPA was established on October 10, 1945, following the dissolution of the wartime publishers' organization that Prime Minister Hideki Tojo had set up and controlled. Perhaps most important among the association's responsibilities was allocating to its membership the paper made available to the industry as a whole.[57] SCAP assigned it responsibility for processing the applications of Japanese publishers to reprint foreign books.[58] The association was also given the responsibility of depositing royalties in "blocked" yen (meaning funds not immediately convertible to dollars) due foreign publishers into the custody account of SCAP in the Bank of Japan.[59] Relationships between SCAP officers, including Captain Tuttle, and JPA officials included dinner and conversation to discuss issues of mutual interest.[60] Despite such cordiality, numerous applications for translation and publishing rights quickly formed a bottleneck at the offices of JPA, pending the establishment of a formal program.[61]

With the collapse of USIBA late in 1946 and the inability or unwillingness of the American Book Publishers Council to assume its functions, the War Department engaged the services of the *Infantry Journal* as its procurement and contractual agent for the government's book programs in both occupied Germany and Japan. The duties involved the clearing of German and Japanese translation rights for approved American books as well as the procurement of U.S. books in English for export into the two countries. During 1947, *Infantry Journal* purchased for the government option rights on "many carefully selected titles for Japan," but the options on many titles lapsed in the absence of a real program.[62] In short, the Japanese book program was not going well.

Problems for Books in Germany

Things weren't going very well in Germany either. The geopolitical situation there was changing rapidly. These early stages of the cold war prompted shifts in information-control policy as well. Over time, the need to get the full range of media in Germany, including books, operating as quickly as possible in order to provide pro-U.S. material and to counter the influence of Soviet propaganda encouraged the taking of shortcuts in the licensing process, which approved a number of individuals with less-than-spotless wartime records. One of the most prominent was the house of Bertelsmann, a firm still very much in business and in fact the owner of many important U.S. publishing houses.[63] (The still-thriving firm of Kodansha provided a Japanese analogy.)[64] By 1948, staffing in the ICD suffered from a gradual loss of personnel, making it even more difficult to do a thorough job of weeding out the bad apples. Consequently, ICD officers had to rely heavily on the use of German civilians to staff all of the bureaucracies, with the result that it was even easier to wink at the compromised past of an otherwise competent and useful official.

The Soviet blockade of Berlin in 1948 made clear, if nothing else had, that the Soviet Union was becoming a foe. This brought about a major shift in policy toward the Germans. As the IDC officer Breitenkamp put it, "It suddenly became expedient to shut up about the 'criminally militaristic Germans' and urge the necessity of rearming against the Communist threat."[65] The ongoing ideological and administrative contests with the Soviet Union meant that it was more important than ever to keep denazification from interfering with the swift re-creation of a strong, friendly western Germany that could be an ally against communism. More often than not, this depended on the reinstatement of conservative businessmen, bankers, and even book publishers.[66] Walter L. Dorn, a U.S. civilian working in the denazification program, characterized this phenomenon as "driv[ing] out the communist devil with the aid of the Nazi Beelzebub."[67]

For American and British book publishers, the most eagerly anticipated benefit of the work of the control agencies was that licensing German book publishers would pave the way for them to sell translation rights to their books. Occupation officials spent much time facilitating and brokering such transactions, as they did in the liberated countries. An important part of the U.S. effort was to provide translations of American books for the use of German publishers, a task that fell to the Book Translations Unit of OMGUS, which had begun operations in Bad Homburg in 1945 before transferring to the ICD in Berlin in April 1946. Aiding in the promotion of American books in translation was the publication of *Bücher aus Amerika*, a monthly newsletter distributed to the German book trade, which explained the procedure for acquiring translation rights and carried reviews of current U.S. books that had been screened for their suitability for publication in Germany.[68]

Unfortunately for the publishers, the kind of frenzied buying and selling of translation rights that had followed in the wake of the liberation of France, Belgium, the Netherlands, and other countries did not occur in occupied Germany.

Formulating a Viable Program for Japan

At last, in May 1948, SCAP implemented a structured program for the "commercial" translation and publication of licensed books in occupied Japan. The key to the initiative was both greater oversight of the selection process and the utilization of an auction system through which Japanese publishers would bid for translation rights of SCAP-approved books. The chief criterion for approval of books for Japan was how well they advanced the purposes of the occupation, namely reorienting the Japanese toward democracy and fostering the development of an economically self-sufficient nation. Exactly what this meant, of course, was a matter of debate. While general trade books had dominated OWI's emergency selection of titles for Europe, educational, scientific, and technical books seemed equally able to meet the objectives of the occupation, particularly since Congress intended that appropriated funds should be used to translate "a representative group of American books about America."[69]

SCAP believed that it had considerable discretion in selecting titles on the basis of how much they were needed in Japan, but determining the ratio between technical and nontechnical books spawned arguments within the military government and among publishers watching developments from home.[70] One could certainly argue that, since the United States had put a great deal of pressure on the Japanese to reform their systems of education and health care, books necessary to bring the Japanese up-to-date in those fields should not be barred. Nor should books that helped increase the technological know-how of the people—a "means toward the end of a self-supporting Japan"—be excluded when an important result of the supreme commander's economic-stabilization program could be the reduction of the cost to the U.S. taxpayer of economic aid to Japan. But there was encouragement also for "the printing of recommended contemporary [i.e., trade] books," which, in the zero-sum game of paper rationing, necessitated "greater selectivity" in other areas, including technical books and titles in the public domain or otherwise offered royalty free.[71]

CIE gathered suggestions of various U.S. titles that "may be of value in the reorientation of the Japanese people or in the reconstruction of the Japanese economy" from various sections of SCAP as well as from reviews in U.S. periodicals. CIE also received recommendations of American books from Japanese publishers and from U.S. publishers promoting their own titles.[72] Staff in appropriate sections of SCAP (e.g., the Economic and Scientific Section) evaluated technical and professional books. CIE staff scrutinized titles of general interest. Consideration was given as to whether or not the possible Japanese demand for a title, especially a professional or technical book, was likely to be high enough to warrant translation. Selecting books upwards of three hundred pages in length for translation was discouraged owing to paper shortages, "unless their content is of special value." For titles that were judged affirmatively, CIE requested a firm contract from the U.S. publisher if it was confident that some Japanese publisher would be interested.[73]

At this point in the process, the U.S. government was the owner of nonexclusive Japanese translation rights to the titles. In most cases, acceptable titles were then put up for bid (in lots of around thirty to one hundred). To stimulate publishers' interest, the JPA put a copy of each title on display in Tokyo, Osaka, and Kyoto, along with pertinent "reviews." Writing these was one of the services that *Infantry Journal* provided SCAP. Their purpose was "to tell a prospective Japanese publisher in clear, simple language what the book is about." This was important because not all would-be rights purchasers could actually view, let alone read, a copy of the book. The commissioned descriptions were supposed to quote from or summarize reviews of the books published in U.S. newspapers and magazines. CIE frankly told the contractor, "As the function of the review is to interest Japanese publishers in bidding for a book which is considered desirable for reasons of reorientation, it is preferred that adverse [U.S. magazine or newspaper] reviews be minimized unless balanced by favorable reviews." In 1949, Noble and Noble, a publisher of educational books, apparently replaced (or possibly complemented) the *Infantry Journal* as the contractor for clearing rights. CIE became displeased with the quality of Noble and Noble's reviews, which probably explains why *Infantry Journal* seems to have regained the contract for 1950.[74]

The publisher bidding the highest advance against royalty prevailed when bids were otherwise identical. The government's contract for each title was then assigned to the successful Japanese publisher. In the case of works of non-U.S. authorship that successfully passed the review process, CIE arranged for rights through the appropriate nation's representative, for example, the United Kingdom Liaison Mission in Japan and the French Mission in Japan.[75]

The review process to select the books for auction seems to have been undertaken just as seriously as the system governing the books destined for European civilians. Fewer people likely had a hand in it, however, since this program was aimed mainly at the citizens of one country, while the European plan had to cover several nations and other contingencies. Some reviews extant in the archives are rather lengthy; others (perhaps summarizing the conclusions of full reviews) are brief. With such an eclectic group of books reviewed, the range and basis of opinions varied widely. For example, while responding negatively to one U.S. manual on writing business letters, a reviewer noted that there was great interest in Japan in knowing how to communicate with Americans for business and so recommended that one or another of two "superior" handbooks on the subject be published.[76] A book called *Education after School* was thought to be "a very good description of the process of group work among youth. The role of the leader; the relationship of group life to the community; the method of acquiring facilities; the financing of such work; and the problems of administration are all matters that need to be known by Japanese youth workers."

With most if not all of the evaluations dating from 1948 and later, the specter of the Soviet Union and the ideological skirmishes of the cold war were reflected in some reviews. In the negative evaluation of Paul B. Anderson's *People, Church, and State in Modern Russia,* the reviewer noted that, when the book was published (in 1944), "the rosy glow concerning Russia had still not been dispelled, and the last chapters undoubtedly depict a much more favorable circumstance concerning religious freedom than actually exists. It is therefore considered both unrealistic and undesirable."[77]

CIE scrutinized Soviet recommendations particularly carefully. After reading English translations of books of Russian origin submitted by the Soviet Liaison Mission in Tokyo, the book officer rated one book about the siege of Leningrad as "Acceptable" and another as "Unacceptable." Nikolai Tikhonov's *Leningrad,* "a fairly straight report of the sufferings and exertions of besieged Leningrad," could be published in translation because its "references to Communism and Communist government are without emphasis." On the other hand, a book of documents, sketches, and stories, *Heroic Leningrad,* merited rejection because "it is liberally larded with Communist propaganda."[78] A. A. Gromov, the trade representative of the USSR in Japan, complained to CIE's chief about the fact that only two of ten Soviet books submitted for approval in a particular round were recommended for translation.[79]

Communism, of course, could be contested not only defensively, as these rejections suggest, but offensively as well, by publishing American books critical of socialism and of the Soviet Union. Such a stance was apparently encouraged by anticommunists at home, who thought the government was not doing enough on that score through the book program or, as the chief of the Information Division put it, "Apparently the grouchers regard as piddling our efforts to include in the translation program books which combat Communism." Still, he bowed to the pressure and pushed the expediting of firm contracts on a number of such titles, including David Dallin's *The Real Soviet Russia,* Louis Fisher's *Men and Politics,* Max Eastman's *Marx, Lenin, and the Science of Revolution,* and Arthur Koestler's *The Yogi and the Commissar.*[80]

The first auction closed on June 5, 1948. Up for bid were ninety-eight titles, twenty-three of which were British. About three-quarters of the total were works for the general reader. Even so, it would be fair to characterize most of the titles on the list as rising somewhat above the middlebrow level exhibited by the books chosen for the Overseas and Transatlantic editions. Examples include *Animal Farm* by George Orwell, *Economic Policy and Full Employment* by Alvin H. Hansen, *The Humanities and the Common Man* by Norman Foerster, *Penicillin: Its Practical Application* by Sir Alexander Fleming, and *When Democracy Builds* by Frank Lloyd Wright. Only one book on the list, David E. Lilienthal's *TVA: Democracy on the March,* had been published in the OE and TE programs. Two hundred thirty-eight Japanese publishers placed a total of 1,012 bids on ninety-one of the ninety-eight titles. The new rights holders planned editions totaling 2,237,000 copies. Incredibly, the winning bids ranged from 5.5 to 36 percent in royalties, with an average of 15 percent.[81]

Royalty rates continued to range widely, even wildly, in the early months of the program, with some publishers specifying terms far higher than was common for the sale of translation rights internationally. The bids generated by the second group of approved titles ranged from a minimum of 5 percent to 35.5 percent. The highest rate was offered for *Fun with Science,* an illustrated science book for children by Mae and Ira Freeman. Offers of 32 and 28 percent were also registered, for Pearl Buck's *Water Buffalo Children* and Mary O'Hara's *My Friend Flicka,* respectively. The average rate proposed was 13.9 percent. One hundred thirty-three publishers entered a total of 439 sealed bids on fifty-eight titles in this second round. Forty-eight participated in the bidding for Pearl Buck's entry. Offers of advances on royalties totaled ¥1,060,000, three hundred thousand yen of which was for Bob Considine's *The Babe Ruth Story,* predicted to make a hit with the baseball-mad Japanese. The average royalty was slightly down from the bids in the first auction. Advances offered were much higher during the first round, which included about a third more books—¥6,793,709. In the first auction, the would-be Japanese publisher of Joseph C. Grew's *Ten Years in Japan* offered an astounding advance of ¥1,184,000. Forty-six publishing firms bid on George Orwell's *Animal Farm* in the inaugural auction.[82] Actually, the excessive bids during the first several auctions displeased CIE because "old-line publishers consider [them] destructive."[83]

By the June 1949 round, overenthusiastic bidding seems to have been curbed somewhat. In that competition, the 22 percent royalty for the rights to Walt Disney's book of *Snow White and the Seven Dwarfs* was the highest offered. The two other American children's books did well also: 17 percent on Brown and Ylla's *Sleepy Little Lion* and 13.6 percent on Dr. Seuss's *The 500 Hats of Bartholomew Cubbins.* The deal for *Snow White* was for a straight, rather than graduated, advance against royalties of 17 percent, or twenty-two thousand yen for the proposed twenty thousand copies to be sold at one hundred yen each. The advance for *Sleepy Little Lion* was higher (thirty-six thousand yen), but the advance for *Bartholomew Cubbins* was lower (thirteen thousand six hundred yen). Textbooks and other books of practical significance tended to command royalties in the 8–10 percent range. One was significantly higher as well as graduated: 15 percent on the first ten thousand copies of Franklin M. Kreml's useful if prosaic *Accident Investigation Manual,* and 20 percent thereafter.[84]

Obtaining the translations of foreign books for the Japanese program was the responsibility of the local publisher. The competency of the translation would be judged by the U.S. government as represented by CIE, with the advice of the Japan Publishers' Association's Translation Committee.[85] In practice, the opinion of the JPA committee was vital to the understaffed CIE. Data sheets on the contracted books record the name of the translator, along with his or her age and affiliations or qualifications. Thus Tsutomu Ikuta, age thirty-seven and a graduate (in architecture) of and professor at Tokyo University, was the translator of volume one of Lewis Mumford's *The Condition of Man.* The translator of George B. De Huszar's *Practical Application of Democracy* was forty-eight-year-old Binnosuke Kagatani, a graduate of Yamaguchi Commercial College, a teacher, author of a the highly relevant books *How to Translate Japanese into English* and *Modern English Grammar,* and the translator of selections by Mark Twain.[86]

Although the auction process was considered the "official" program for the sale of translation rights to Japanese publishers, U.S. and foreign rights owners wishing to enter the market for books in translation could apply to SCAP/CIE for a no-fee blanket license to deal directly with Japanese publishers regarding any and all titles on which it controlled rights. Most major U.S. publishers received blanket licenses, as did several major British houses, like George Allen & Unwin and Jonathan Cape.[87] Licensees included not only publishing companies but also other rights holders, like agents and authors. Among the authors who obtained licenses were Erskine Caldwell, Margaret Mitchell, Pearl Buck, Samuel Eliot Morison, Vicki Baum, Thomas Mann, and Graham Greene.[88]

SCAP continued to censor books under this plan, so having a blanket license was no guarantee of publication. This alternate approach made it possible for the owners of rights to books that had been rejected through the "official" process to gain a second chance of entering the market. For some rights holders, it was the preferred way, at least in certain circumstances. For others, like William Sloane Associates, however, direct negotiations seemed a considerable waste of time.[89] Among the earliest titles that licensed rights holders successfully pitched directly to Japanese publishers were Winston Churchill's *The Gathering Storm,* Margaret Mitchell's *Gone With the Wind,* John Hersey's *Hiroshima,* James Hilton's *Random Harvest,* and Cordell Hull's *Memoirs.* Contracts were pending for Dwight D. Eisenhower's *Crusade in Europe,* Churchill's *Their Finest Hour,* Pearl Buck's *The Good Earth,* and Stefan Heym's *The Crusaders.*[90]

Under both methods, the non-Japanese rights holders could receive royalty payments only in "blocked" yen, that is, in Japanese currency held in an account in Japan that could not be converted to dollars until some undetermined time in the future, which turned out to be April 1949 when a fixed exchange rate of 360 yen to the dollar was promulgated.[91]

In May 1949, CIE expressed pride in the "creditable record" of the translation and publication program to that point. Between June 1, 1948, and March 15, 1949, CIE put up six lots of U.S. titles for bidding by Japanese publishers. The total number of translation rights assigned by then was 823. This figure was made up of 295 titles approved under the "official" program, sixty-five titles under the alternate method, 339 works to which royalties were waived (by such authors as Upton Sinclair; P. G. Wodehouse; John Dewey; Albert Einstein; Stefan Zweig; and, through the Soviet government, Lenin and Stalin; and such institutions as the American Council of Learned Societies and the Association for the Study of American Education), and 124 noncopyrighted "books and pamphlets of governmental agencies, SCAP staff sections, and state and municipal authorities."

The titles selected made for a very eclectic list. A substantial number of them were non-American books, particularly among those whose personal or institutional authors had waived royalties. The American books were, in fact, quite representative of the U.S. book trade as a whole. They included many books of fiction and nonfiction in the humanities, social sciences, and public policy, some of them recently published (for example, David E. Lilienthal's *TVA: Democracy on the March;* John Dewey, *Quest for Certainty;* Willa Cather, *My Antonia;* Upton Sinclair, *World's End*); titles in technology, science, and education (Ronald King, *Electromagnetic Engineering;* Kenneth Chester, *Nature and Prevention of Plant Disease;* James Bryant Conant, *Education for One World*); publications of associations (American Council of Learned Societies, *Conference on the Character and State of Studies in Folklore*); and a scattering of children's books (Laura Ingalls Wilder, *Little House in the Big Woods*).[92]

The record of actual publication of the approved titles, however, was less "creditable." By May 1949, apparently only the first twenty-five recommended titles had reached the Japanese public, in print runs totaling 327,815 copies. CIE reported that, after rights were assigned, six to eight months were required for the translation, plus another two months for typesetting, printing, and distribution. Delays plagued the program in Japan, as they had in Germany. It took some time before non-American publishers began to submit applications under the official program, for example. Perhaps the most important reason was that the Japanese publishing industry, faced with shortages, could absorb only about eighty titles every eight weeks from the SCAP book program.[93] Unfortunately, a considerable number of titles that were at long last approved for translation and publication were not issued because their Japanese publishers defaulted on the contracts they had made with SCAP/CIE. A steep downturn in the Japanese book trade beginning in 1948 and extending until at least 1950 made matters even worse.[94]

Copies of virtually all of the books, along with most pamphlets, newspapers, and magazines published during the first four years of the occupation, are preserved in McKeldin Library at the University of Maryland thanks to the perspicacity and finesse of Gordon W. Prange, a naval staff member in the occupation forces before joining MacArthur's historical staff as a civilian in 1946, best known now for his history of Pearl Harbor. When censorship was lifted in 1949, Prange arranged for the hundred thousand or so copies of books and other publications in the files of the Civil Censorship Detachment (CCD) to be acquired by his university's library.[95] The collection constitutes a treasure house of information about Japan's transition from an aggressively militaristic nation to a prosperous democracy.

Judged by a small sampling of books of U.S. and other foreign authorship from the Prange Collection, the books that Japanese publishers issued were surprisingly nice looking. The low-quality paper used in the paperbound books particularly betrays their occupation-era origin, but it was not much worse than the paper stock used for the Armed Services and Overseas editions in the United States. Otherwise, the graphic design of the volumes is generally striking. Most books examined have title pages or other elements printed in two colors, occasionally even more. Some bear nice woodcuts or other illustrations. For example, an edition of Matthew Arnold's *Discourses in America* [*Amerika bunmeiren*] bears a cover printed in black and red, with a frontispiece portrait of the author. On the multicolored paper covers of André Maurois's *America* is a line drawing of a female nude, perhaps oddly reflecting its Gallic origins more than its U.S. subject matter. Other books achieve their full graphic impact through use of colors. The covers of Ralph Waldo Emerson's *The American Scholar and Other Addresses* [*Amerika no gakusha*], for example, bear black type over an orange-ink wash. The title is in Japanese on the cover, in English on the verso of the title page. There is one edition of Louisa May Alcott's *Little Women* [*Wakakusa monogatari*], with an attractive multicolored floral-pattern paper cover and the title rendered in green ink in both languages on the title page. Another edition of the book carries green and scarlet paper covers. In the back matter of an edition of *My Friend Flicka*, by Mary O'Hara, are advertisements for other books recommended to Japanese readers by SCAP.

These books are very much in a Japanese style, of course. The only book in English in the sampling—James A. B. Scherer, *America: Pageants and Personalities* (Tokyo: The Houseido Press, 1948)—looks like an American book. It is a rare hardcover, bound in blue over flexible boards, with the spine stamped in gold. The dust jacket is in red, white, and blue with an illustration of young women dressed in naval uniforms holding a model of a ship. It appears to be what in the United States would be a book for children, but perhaps it was aimed as well at Japanese adults, who might find its simple text useful in their study of the English language.

Although most of SCAP's efforts at introducing American books to Japan were focused on the translation program, pressures mounted to make an effort to promote the commercial importation of American books, in English, as well. In October 1947, a number of prominent Japanese intellectuals formed a "Committee for Prompting the Importation of Overseas Publications," which sought the assistance of UNESCO. The petition centered its argument that "the new Japan...is truly democratic and sincerely peace-loving," and that the expansion of the knowledge of English in the country calls for a steady flow of books in that language. In London, Stanley Unwin obligingly persuaded the Publishers Association to refer the matter to the Secretary of State for Foreign Affairs.[96]

It was not that the importation of books from the United States or elsewhere had been prohibited. One simply needed a license from SCAP to conduct the business.[97] It just had not been done on a large-scale basis, owing to currency restrictions and shipping shortages. The government and various philanthropies had sent American books for use in CIE's seventeen libraries for Japanese nationals. From the beginning of the occupation, CIE had refrained from asking for any of the limited dollar resources in the SCAP trust fund to be spent to assist in the importation of American books for sale to individuals while they might be better spent on food and other necessities of life. By September 1948, however, CIE officials had concluded that "arrangements for the importation of American books no longer can be delayed without serious embarrassment to SCAP." The Economic and Scientific Section of SCAP had particularly lobbied CIE to oversee the importation of publications that might "help to improve Japanese industrial techniques." CIE was at last willing to go along, though it rejected the notion that SCAP trust funds should be employed solely for books aimed at improving Japanese technology and sought assurances that such limitations would not be imposed. As Col. Donald R. Nugent, CIE's chief, put it, "SCAP has other missions of considerable importance to world peace and the welfare of the American people, and not the least among them is the mission of reorienting Japan." Nugent was hopeful that a system of barter could be implemented for the importation of SCAP-approved American books, paid for in yen, which could then be used to buy Japanese publications for export to the United States. By stimulating the sale of Japanese books abroad, it was argued, more dollars would be available for American books to be purchased in Japan.[98]

Missions to Germany

As in Japan, the slow and inefficient flow of titles through ICD's licensing system in occupied Germany, a prerequisite for deals between U.S. and German publishing houses, was a major disappointment. This time the close public/private partnership between American publishers and the government was not going especially well. Both the government and the publishers were deeply concerned that the U.S. book program for Germany might not succeed.

Accordingly, former OWI and USIBA officer Sidney Sulkin and his wife and assistant, Edith, undertook a six-week inspection tour of the U.S. zone in early 1947 at the invitation of General McClure. The army wanted the visitors to study the problems of publishing in the U.S. zone as they related to the overall effectiveness of the program to reeducate German civilians toward free thought and democracy. On returning home, the Sulkins reported the obvious—that among the difficulties that lay in the way were the devastated physical conditions in the zone and the poor literary quality of books being published in Germany.

As the Sulkins learned, the War Department blamed key players within the U.S. publishing trade for being uncooperative. Despite the army's efforts to obtain translation rights of appropriate American books, too many publishers, agents, and authors were more eager to sell German-language rights to Swiss publishers, who would pay more than the $250 flat rate offered by the War Department. Army officials maintained that American publishers had a necessary stake in assisting their effort to reeducate the German citizenry. According to Sidney Sulkin, "The important thing is to recognize that the re-education program may stand or fall on how many good American books can get translated and published in Germany."[99] Little if anything changed immediately. Perhaps the publishers' seeming lack of cooperation stemmed from their flight from solidarity with the government on the larger national interest in the uses of books in cultural diplomacy, so vividly underscored with the demise of USIBA.

The publishers in turn became deeply frustrated with the efforts of OMGUS to reactivate the German book industry. Harry F. West, head of the American Book Publishers Council, which had succeeded the BPB as the principal trade organization, noted that some 300 million textbooks and other books had already appeared in the Soviet zone and some 8 to 12 million volumes had been published in the British zone, while production in the U.S. zone was a paltry 2.5 million books. This worked out to only 1.3 textbooks per capita, while the Soviets had produced nearly six times as many. Moreover, the system in which the government acquired translation rights to selected U.S. titles for resale to German publishers had bogged down. The government had engaged the *Infantry Journal,* still under the leadership of Colonel Greene, to serve as its agent in the process, but he had managed to acquire rights to fewer than three hundred titles, of which only thirty-eight had actually appeared under a German publisher's imprint by early spring 1948. West wisely recognized that more than U.S. business interests were threatened. With the flood of books in the Soviet zone, the ability of the United States to counter with its own books-as-bullets in a new war of ideology was very much at risk.[100]

The government was no less troubled by the slow progress, West told Robert de Graff, of Pocket Books, in inviting him on behalf of the ABPC to join another, larger, more blue-ribbon visiting committee to report and advise on the situation in the U.S. zone. West emphasized the public-service aspect of the mission. "It isn't often that our industry is called upon by the government to provide the benefit of its advice and experience, and I should like personally to see us discharge the moral responsibility, if I may call it that, which has been thrust upon us in this regard. If you ask me, publishing conditions in Germany urgently require study at first hand by qualified experts." It thus seemed apparent that the Sulkins' mission the previous year was unproductive or at least unsatisfactory to both the government and the trade.

Joining de Graff on the visiting committee as nominees of the ABPC were William Sloane, president of William Sloane Associates, and H. Stahley Thompson, director of production and research at Rinehart and the man who had come up with the ideas for the design and production of the Armed Services Editions while serving as a graphic-arts specialist with the Army's Special Services Division. The other major book-industry association, the American Textbook Publishers' Institute, which the army had also solicited for nominations, selected George P. Brett Jr., president of Macmillan, and Edward M. Crane, president of D. Van Nostrand. The committee members chose Crane as chairman.[101] Crane understood the magnitude of the committee's task. Not only would it examine the "very practical matters" of publishing and the distribution of books, but it would deal "also with the broader and more important area embraced with the cold war of ideas."[102]

Once again, a delegation of prominent American publishers was going overseas to advance both the industry's and the government's goals for books in international markets. While meeting in New York before departure, the delegates were able to speak with General McClure, who was on a stateside visit. McClure drafted the mission statement, which asked the visiting committee to advise him on the soundness of the army's present policy toward reestablishing "the German book publishing industry as a part of the German domestic economy," and, more specifically, to judge whether the ICD was operating efficiently and whether or not controls on German publishers and booksellers were being relaxed too rapidly. Omitted from the statement were two questions that nevertheless came up frequently: What should be the role of a vigorous, independent publishing industry in Germany in the face of the emerging cold war with the Soviet Union? And how might the German readers become better customers for American books?[103]

The group arrived in Germany on June 20, 1948. It spent five weeks there, one week in Austria, and several days in Switzerland before returning home. As had become customary during the various missions abroad that publishers had made during and after the war, the travelers worked hard in the service of the trade and the nation, while temporarily neglecting their own businesses. Unlike previous publishers' delegations overseas, however, this committee was not studying an independent national publishing system, be it British, Chinese, or Australian, but rather a system that was in transition from three years of absolute control by the occupying powers to one that would soon be run by Germans. The group found much to lament or to criticize about the state of publishing in Germany. This time, agreement on what the delegates had learned and wished to recommend was not easy to achieve.

Differences of opinion on just how a democratic book industry could be established for a democratizing Germany divided the committee members, in ways that are not entirely clear from the documentary record. The visiting publishers did agree on some fundamentals. One was that "a sound, free, and effective democratic publishing industry is, in the final analysis, the product of a democratic society, not its cause, but that publishing can also have a revolutionary effect upon a society in ferment," citing the cases of Diderot and Harriet Beecher Stowe as proof. The committee worried that it would take quite a while longer for the German book trade to function well, a situation that doomed, among other things, an early and steady stream of American books into the country. The situation would be worse, they felt, if the government abandoned its German translation program. It would still be necessary for the United States to guide the process by which German publishers became acquainted with American books, preventing German publishers from taking a "hit or miss" approach to publishing American books. What they feared most was that, if left uncontrolled and undirected, German publishers would issue "many American books which do not present us at our best and which would damage our prestige in much the same way that films do nowadays in many parts of the world."[104] The legacy of Goebbels's effective propaganda and the negative images projected by Hollywood films, it appeared, had not been completely eradicated.

Sloane was assigned to draft the delegation's final report, incorporating material supplied by colleagues based on their expertise (for example, de Graff on books for the German mass market). Sloane found writing the "damn report" to be one of the hardest tasks he had ever undertaken.[105] A number of personal and professional problems also weighed on him. He had left Henry Holt in 1946 after the firm was taken over by the Texas oilman Clint Murchison, whose politics and vision of publishing he found incompatible with his own. Taking some key Holt staff members and half of its authors with him, he started a small publishing house, William Sloane Associates.[106] He soon ran into serious personal financial difficulties. It is surprising that he agreed to absent himself from the office for a couple of months when the firm and he were experiencing such difficulties, though the handsome per diem offered to the delegates might have helped. On returning home, he found it difficult to complete the report because of other personal matters: illness, jury duty, continued crises in his own office, and a general downturn in the U.S. publishing business.[107] But mostly he was stymied by disagreements among the committee members, mainly between him and his colleagues. When Sloane had nearly completed the draft, he wrote, "the others wished to change so much of it, to which I was unwilling to subscribe, that the whole job had to be done over."[108] Sloane labored through at least two more drafts. It is not clear exactly what the nature of the disagreements was, but it is likely that they had to do with his belief that the best interests of American publishers in general and the national interests of the United States and even Germany should trump narrower interests of individual American publishers or small groups of them.[109] Sloane ultimately got the job done, primarily by tempering or qualifying some of the points on which he disagreed. "There's a good deal of double-talk in it," he confessed.[110] Waples, the ICD officer, sympathized with the difficulties Sloane faced in drafting the report and agreed entirely with Sloane that the task of bringing American books to Germany was a long-term one and "correspondingly important." "I had a line with my SHAEF superiors," Waples said, "that ours was the slowest and most difficult weapon to detonate, but all the more devastating in its effects on non-democratic ideologies."[111]

The committee's report was formally submitted to the military governor, Gen. Lucius D. Clay, in December 1948. Although attention will be paid here primarily to the recommendations related to American publishers' access to German markets, most had to do with strengthening the German publishing industry itself and its supporting contexts. Some of the latter were, interestingly, also helpful to the former objective, including one that recommended that the German constitution outlaw or heavily restrict state-subsidized publishing in educational and other areas. The goal was to bring the level of translation and publication of books in the U.S. zone up to a total of fifty to seventy-five per year. Other recommendations pertinent to access to the market included encouraging and facilitating the importation of low-priced British and American books; appropriating dollar funds to bid on German rights for American books, up to two thousand dollars per title; urging the relaxation of restrictions on the conversion of blocked marks in order to encourage the sale of rights to U.S. literary properties; putting more emphasis on books for children and "a more representative selection of current American fiction"; and exploring ways to increase trade in American books with the Soviet zone.[112]

The timing of the publishers' German mission was auspicious, as the Marshall Plan, the massive infusion of U.S. financial aid to avert an economic calamity in Europe, was just being implemented. In April 1948 Congress passed, and President Truman signed, the Economic Cooperation Act, which was the Marshall Plan's legislative foundation. The act established the Economic Cooperation

Administration to administer the program. For publishers, the Marshall Plan, through the ECA, held promise that hastening Europe's recovery might in due course help them in their quest for new markets. Although it was not yet so apparent as it would become, the Marshall Plan helped frame the early stages of the cold war, which re-created some of the "emergency" incentives that had fostered the strong public/private partnership of the Second World War.

But at least one ICD official, Laurence P. Dalcher, who had advocated for the German visiting committee's mission, felt that American publishers were themselves making "a horrible mess" by not taking full advantage of the opportunities available to them for exporting books to Germany under the ECA. Dalcher believed that the "American book publishing trade has not brought to the government its particular knowledge of the problems confronted in sending American ideas abroad." He in effect criticized the industry for failing to even make the arguments that the wartime publishers had won, that is, that books were "the most enduring propaganda of all," and that the industry should continue to play its special role, in close partnership with the government. Instead, book publishers had been overshadowed by the greater successes of the newspaper and magazine industries as the voice of American ideas overseas, while the efforts of individual publishers were seen as "nothing more than requests for favors." As it was, both the periodical press and book publishers were disadvantaged in competing for ECA support because all such proposals were judged along with applications regarding "steel rails or fertilizers."[113] What was needed, therefore, was for the industry to offer the government its assistance in making the best use of the ECA for the dissemination of American ideas overseas, so that books would not be lumped together with fertilizer, except, perhaps, in the sense that books made ideas flower.

Once again much was at risk. Since strict currency restrictions were expected to continue in many European countries for some time to come, Dalcher noted, "the Government must assist, and must assist with the knowledge that it is making an investment in ideas and not merely granting a subsidy to the book trade."[114] Sloane offered to help, but the economic well-being of his industry was at least as important in his mind as an investment in ideas. Unless the book trade brought its own ideas on how to export U.S. ideas, he told Dalcher, "the magazine boys will get all the dough."[115]

Some actions to solve the problems of gaining access to ECA funds were simultaneously under way. The three major book-trade associations—the American Book Publishers Council, the American Textbook Publishers Institute, and the Association of American University Presses—were working together to make their concerns known in Washington. Certain roadblocks made it particularly difficult to make optimum use of ECA funds. First, books had to be furnished to ECA "at cost, with no allowance for profit," according to Sloane. Although this might make sense when books were seen as advancing national cultural diplomacy, several major publishers (mostly specializing in technical books), including McGraw-Hill, Macmillan, Van Nostrand, and Wiley, were disinclined to participate in the Marshall Plan if, ironically, they were not treated the same as other industries. McGraw-Hill and Macmillan, at least, felt that they were big enough to secure a good share of foreign business through their own devices. To make matters worse, Time, Inc., and the Readers' Digest Co. had managed to interpret "at cost" in a manner favorable to the magazine industry but not to book publishers. Second, there was a tremendous amount of red tape involved. Sloane cited the case of a European country that requested eight hundred thousand dollars from ECA funds to buy American books, but found that it would take some forty thousand separate purchase orders to accomplish.[116] These doings may well have signaled the magazine and newspaper publishers' determination to become greater factors internationally, having gained some experience during the war with producing editions of their publications for U.S. forces all over the world.[117]

Currency reform in 1948, which accompanied the Marshall Plan, was a watershed event for the German publishing industry, as it was for German life in general, but it also produced some disadvantages for American and German publishers. Once the currency was stabilized, books that publishers and booksellers had hoarded against that day were put on sale. Government controls on commodities like paper were eliminated. Publishers were free to satisfy the desires of readers, not just to please their local information-control officers. Demand increased for light fiction, travel, and other entertaining books, at the expense of more serious types of literature. Political works were a drag on the market. One publisher sold only twenty thousand of a press run of one hundred thousand copies of Arthur Koestler's *Darkness at Noon*. Most discouragingly, the public seemed more reluctant in general to buy books after currency reform than they were before.[118] One reason was that the elimination of controls also made many other consumer items and entertainment choices available.[119] A more hopeful sign, however, was the return of some émigré authors after the mark was stabilized, brightening the prospects for new German works to publish.[120] Although this would certainly be good for the rebirth of German culture, it would produce more competition for American literature. If anything, though, the changed circumstances strengthened the case for U.S. governmental assistance in getting good American books into cold war Germany.

Another piece of legislation enacted in 1948 improved the chances of that. The legislation was not nearly so monumental as the law that created the Marshall Plan, but it was vital to the continuation of U.S. information activities overseas and to the continuation in some form of public/private cooperation in the circulation of American books abroad. This was the Smith-Mundt Act (formally, the U.S. Information and Educational Exchange Act), which President Harry Truman signed in late January 1949. The law authorized the continuation of an overseas information program in peacetime, providing validation and a semblance of permanence for the interim programs that Truman had authorized following the abolition of OWI and CIAA. Smith-Mundt was the legislative basis for the establishment of the United States Information Agency, which became the platform for U.S. propaganda and public diplomacy for a half century.[121] But it would be another five years before USIA was established.

The book programs instituted under the military governments of Germany and Japan fell far short of the success that Americans had hoped for them. Many of the same factors that applied in Europe kept the U.S. book program in Japan from achieving all of its goals. Poverty was abundant. Shortages of paper, machinery, labor, capital, and hard currency prevented German and Japanese publishers and the general public from purchasing as many American books as U.S. publishers and the government desired. Once consumer markets began to return to normal, booksellers had to compete with other forms of entertainment and enrichment for their customers' marks and yen. In both countries, the necessity of tight U.S. military government oversight of publishing frustratingly postponed the open, unrestricted buying and selling of rights between American and foreign publishers that had occurred in the overrun nations. Book officers in Germany had to contend with a country divided into four zones. Their counterparts in the unitary, U.S.-administered Japan ironically had to assist their allies in promoting their books in Japan, in competition with American titles. Nonetheless, the United States succeeded overall in introducing a freer, more democratic system of publishing in Japan as it had in Germany, and in making both countries on the whole good friends and reliable allies for the ensuing cold war.

AMERICAN BOOKS ABROAD
AFTER 1948

The "inside track to the world's bookshelves" that American books took after the Second World War was frequently obstructed by hurdles, potholes, water hazards, and competitors' elbows. It soon became clear that the race was a marathon, not a sprint. Despite the enthusiastic and dogged wartime efforts of both the government and the publishers to lay the groundwork for increasing overseas business, the impediments to the export of physical books or publishing rights owing to trade barriers, currency difficulties, and the general poverty of the world outside North America were daunting. Progress was especially slight, early on, in the occupied countries where the military was most fully in charge of the process and the constraints on improvisation the greatest. In Germany, the U.S. military government was slow to get the German book-publishing industry on its feet and to put a wide array of American books into the hands of citizens. SCAP, General MacArthur's proconsulship in Japan, did no better.

With the dire emergency that was World War II successfully concluded, not all American book publishers were as willing to maintain the close ties with the government they had forged during the heady days of the Council on Books in Wartime and the Office of War Information. That said, the publishers' interest in foreign markets that the war had stimulated was not about to be extinguished. The international reach of American books continued, in general, to expand, and even the public/private partnership in promoting books abroad, while not robust, was far from dormant.

Exports and Rights Sales after 1948

Both exports of American books and the sale of foreign rights grew substantially after 1948, albeit with occasional peaks and valleys. Certainly publishers' interest in foreign business grew, as did their efforts. Effort alone, however, was not always enough. More than domestic business, foreign trade succeeds or fails depending on many extrinsic factors. Conditions in overseas markets, like the value of foreign currencies against the dollar, tariffs, censorship, and shifting tastes, could—and did—foil high-mindedness, determination, and hard work.[1]

Many publishers took steps to institutionalize, professionalize, and expand their efforts to export books and sell foreign rights, even after the feeding frenzy of the mid-1940s had subsided. Those that persevered in the face of continuing problems with currency, tariffs, and foreign cartels often found considerable success. The strongest foreign revenues from the 1950s on tended to be earned by firms that published textbooks and technical publications. Among them were specialist firms like John Wiley and Sons and McGraw-Hill, which continued to refine their ability to sell to foreign customers. A more traditional trade house, albeit with a strong technical program, Harper & Brothers, was a pacesetter in overseas marketing.

By the mid-1950s, McGraw-Hill's international efforts had grown considerably. There were either branch offices of its Export Department or full-time representatives in Australia, Brazil, France, Germany, India, Cuba, Japan, Chile, Mexico, the Philippines, Denmark, Sweden, and Norway, and part-time stringers in twenty-three other lands. The company had succeeded in having about thirteen hundred textbooks adopted for use in forty-one foreign countries. Total export sales annually reached about 1 million copies of about thirty-five hundred different titles.[2]

Although Wiley put plans to open a London operation on hold, the firm continued to look strategically overseas. At the end of the 1940s, the financial incentives of the Marshall Plan brightened the prospects of doing business in Europe efficiently and profitably, while money earmarked for the rebuilding of Europe's infrastructure increased demand for the very kind of practical books on engineering that Wiley published. By the mid-1950s, after several years of stagnant domestic income, foreign business had become "the star of the show," in the words of the author of an official company history. Until 1956, the company's gross sales had lagged behind the record set in 1948. But the overseas share of that business had grown to 21 percent of total sales, and 49 percent of sales for its educational books, all highly concentrated in English-speaking countries. A few years later, in 1960, the firm followed through on its goal of establishing a foreign branch by chartering John Wiley & Sons, Ltd., and opening its offices and a warehouse in England.[3]

The establishment of branches or subsidiaries on various business models in Mexico City, Rio de Janeiro, Sydney, Tokyo, and New Delhi helped Wiley sell their books in Australasia and Latin America. By the early 1960s, Wiley had set up "complete stocking facilities" in Australia, which allowed them to be more competitive on price there and throughout the southwestern Pacific than before, thereby at least partially solving the pricing dilemma that Edward Hamilton had observed on a publishers' mission in 1945. Also interesting was the development of Wiley International Editions, low-cost reprints of several hundred standard textbooks intended for university students in developing countries, in direct imitation of a British publishing-and-marketing innovation. In the late 1970s, the company began a new line of translations and original publications in Arabic, called Arabooks. It also made its first steps toward gaining a foothold in China.[4]

One of the most ardent seekers after foreign business following the war was the venerable firm of Harper & Brothers, founded in 1817. The company, which became Harper & Row through a 1962 merger, published textbooks and professional technical materials as well as trade books. In the 1950s, Harper's was especially interested in cultivating markets in Asia and the Pacific. It did so primarily through close financial connections with an entity called Pacific Book & Supply Corporation, with headquarters in New York and an office in Jakarta, Indonesia, where it formed an alliance with a local firm. Pacific Book envisioned a large potential market in Southeast Asia for American books of all kinds and viewed Indonesia as an entrée. Altruism mixed with the profit motive, as evidenced by the company manager's belief that "American books can help this new, ambitious young nation grow."[5] The president of Harper's, Cass Canfield, was actively involved as the principal outside member of the board of directors. Later, Pacific Books's interests expanded beyond Indonesia to Thailand, Burma, India, and Pakistan, where Britain's control on distribution was showing signs of weakness.[6]

Just as the Good Neighbor Policy had fueled dreams of Latin American markets for publishers and other businesses during the Roosevelt administration, so too did President John F. Kennedy's Alliance for Progress and the U.S. Agency for International Development in the early 1960s. These initiatives helped stimulate Harper's interests south of the Rio Grande, as well as elsewhere. Harper & Row set up an international division in 1963 to handle its foreign trade in exports and rights. A British corporation, Harper & Row, Ltd., was established in London to sell the firm's titles in Britain not published by UK houses as well as its entire list in Europe and the Middle East not subject to competing territorial rights. In addition, the firm established a distribution and promotion center in Australia, an affiliated company in Tokyo, and a distribution center in Mexico. To gain markets in poor, emerging nations, these centers distributed copies of Harper International Series books, inexpensive paperbound editions of selected Harper's titles, in English, catering to local needs. Another fixture was the export trade in scientific and technical books in English.

Harper's set up a department devoted to managing its growing traffic in foreign rights, that is, both English-language reprint rights for British publishers and translation rights for other countries.[7] Internal reorganization and new procedures were instituted to optimize the returns from such transactions. Oversight of the process was given to a single staff member in order to improve on former, rather lax lines of responsibility and communication. For instance, editors were cautioned not to promise rights in a particular title to the first foreign publisher who expressed interest, but rather to encourage solicitations from several firms and "wait on the best combination of financial offer and publisher we can get for the particular work." They were also strongly cautioned that the rights manager had to be informed of even tentative proposals. She kept detailed, centralized records of the status of a myriad of combinations and permutations of rights, a responsibility designed to prevent confusions when company staff dealt with agents, publishers, and translators. Such records had long been kept in card files, but they never fully prevented embarrassing and sometimes costly gaffes, like selling a foreign publisher rights that it actually did not own or—the bane of Stanley Unwin's existence—selling its own books in territories from which it was restricted. By 1972, Harper's had computerized these rights files. The system even had the capability of automatically canceling an order for a title from a country in which the firm did not hold the rights.[8]

Although the figures on Harper's foreign-rights sales contain gaps and display figures in dollars not adjusted for inflation, they reveal a steady rise in activity, sales, and income over the period 1960–1975 (the years in which figures for both British and foreign translation rights are available, with a gap in 1968–70). Total income from foreign-rights sales increased by more than 800 percent during that period, from $62,702 to $216,070. The proportion of the total income represented by transactions with British publishers ranged from about a quarter to nearly 40 percent. The firm's share of the income (after agents, authors, and other rights holders took their cuts) varied between 20 and 37 percent. That share in 1975 was more than six times what it had been in 1963. The activity in the firm's rights office, as measured by the number of contracts signed annually, also rose over the period, if unspectacularly. In 1975 the staff negotiated 290 contracts, more than twice the number in 1962.[9]

It is difficult to compare Harper's income from rights sales to that of the trade as a whole. No industry-wide statistics on the value of the sale of U.S. publishing rights abroad were available until the Department of Commerce began tracking them in 2001 (though figures have not yet been released beyond 2003), and they are susceptible to undercounting. They show that rights sales decreased over the three-year period: $298 million in 2001, $274 million in 2002, and $230 million in 2003. It is not clear whether the assignment of foreign rights to an American book within the various national imprints of international publishing conglomerates is taken account of in Commerce's numbers, but an authority on publishing-industry statistics thinks this might be a factor in the relatively low, and decreasing, figures that the department has published.[10] Only estimates are available for earlier periods. These showed a trajectory boldly upward, ranging from about $17 million in 1970 to some $300–400 million in 1990.[11]

At Harper's, the amount of translation-rights income, arranged by language from Afrikaans to Yugoslavian, varied considerably from year by year. For example, French rights brought in only about fifteen hundred dollars in 1959 and 1960, but ten thousand in 1961. Until 1967, only the familiar European languages and Japanese were tallied separately, with "other" languages being lumped together, usually in an amount well under 10 percent of the total. Of these, German was usually the language with the largest revenues. By the early '70s, the foreign-rights department displayed all languages separately, including less familiar languages, like Afrikaans, Arabic, Bengali, Hebrew, Korean, Thai, and Vietnamese. It is likely that the greater detail came in response, not so much to increased business from the third world, but rather to events, like the war in Vietnam, as well as to the firm's wish to demonstrate its commitment to assisting in the cold-war battle for hearts and minds in the developing world, along with governmental and quasi-governmental agencies such as the United States Information Agency and Franklin Book Programs, a nonprofit corporation providing translations and publishing assistance to publishers in unaligned nations.

Harper's was one of many companies selling rights to USIA and Franklin Book Programs for titles used in their translations of American books meant for nonaligned nations. Harper's sold rights to at least forty-eight—perhaps more—of its titles to USIA and seven to Franklin.[12] About a quarter were for editions in English, primarily for India. About five were in Spanish or Portuguese, more likely for the Latin American market than the Iberian. The rest were in the critical languages of the developing world. The topics of the books were in the predictable fields of U.S. history, politics, international relations, and social thought.

Statistics on exports of American books in the postwar period are best seen at the industry-wide level, as compiled by the Commerce Department. From 1945 to 1955, export values increased by about 150 percent, from at least $12.5 million to $31 million.[13] For a later period, 1970 to 2005, exports grew from $174.9 million to $1.9 billion, an increase of nearly 1,000 percent. Fluctuations in annual figures were influenced by changing values of world currencies.[14] Here too, exports are likely undercounted owing to many small shipments of books overseas by post or express carriers that eluded or were exempt from Commerce's tabulations. Export figures should be increased by around 50 percent to compensate for undercounting.[15] All in all, considering growing competition from the Internet and cable and satellite television, U.S. book exports totaling nearly $1.9 billion in 2005 is hardly an insignificant amount.

The Vicissitudes of the Government/Publisher Relationship

The earliest of the publishers' postwar efforts to rationalize and institutionalize their marketing efforts overseas accompanied a revival in governmental support that took place in the 1950s, on the heels of the Marshall Plan and the establishment of USIA. Propaganda and cultural diplomacy related to the ideological struggle with the Soviet Union, more than the promotion of the U.S. publishing business abroad, was the principal objective for the government, meaning there was less in it for the publishers in the pure marketing sense. That and the fact that the cold war, at least for publishers, never seemed to rise to the level of emergency that was World War II created considerable skepticism in their ranks.[16] The relationship between government and publishers, in short, has run hot and cold from the 1950s to the present.

Chief among the cold-war collaborations was Franklin Book Programs, which sponsored translations and underwrote publication of books intended for people in nonaligned nations in the Middle East, Asia, and Africa.[17] Set up as a nonprofit corporation in 1952 at the instigation of the International Information Agency (USIA's immediate predecessor), Franklin received government funding in the form of contracts as well as support from the book trade, U.S. foundations, and governments of the countries in which it operated branches. The U.S. Agency for International Development later played a significant funding role.

There are interesting similarities and differences between the Franklin effort and the Office of War Information's work with Overseas Editions during the war. Unlike the OEs, Franklin's books were geared toward the third world, not the countries at the core of European civilization emerging from their Nazi nightmare. OWI selected the titles for the OEs, based on very specific propaganda objectives. Franklin, on the other hand, allowed groups in the countries to which they were directed to choose the books for translation, in order to meet "the needs and aspirations of people whom the US is trying to aid in many other ways," according to Franklin's draft statement of policy. This nonimperialistic approach to selection—one that could easily result in publications abroad that strayed from USIA orthodoxy—irked the agency, which in time reduced its funding. Like OWI's, the focus of Franklin's scheme was in large part on the local elites, but primarily as the intellectual driving force in selection and translation rather than as the main prospective purchasers. Another difference lay in Franklin's desire to aid in the modernization of the countries involved by assisting in the development of indigenous book industries. Although encouraging the early restoration of the local trade in European and Asian countries was an objective of OWI, the agency had not been on a mission of modernization. Whatever elements of an "indigenous development" approach there were in the OWI program was more incidental than central, more self-serving than altruistic.

Financial woes led to the formal dissolution of Franklin Book Programs in 1979, after more than a quarter century of existence. The organization left a mixed legacy. It probably did little to modernize publishing in its client countries. Although it is unclear how many books Franklin managed to bring to its audiences, at the very least Franklin did help make some important American books available in translation in sensitive areas. In all, the program oversaw the translation and publication of more than three thousand titles. The corporation spent more than $100 million, mostly in foreign currencies, during its life span. Nearly 80 percent of the money had come from contracts with foreign governments and from earned income. U.S. government sources contributed most of the rest. Franklin's demise halted a stream of significant, though rarely commercially viable, American books in translation into its host countries. The program of translations into Arabic, Farsi, and Urdu, targeted for countries like Afghanistan, Egypt, Saudi Arabia, Iraq, Iran, and Pakistan was, of course, a victim of Franklin's liquidation, with what early twenty-first-century consequences one can only speculate.

Franklin's principal patron, the USIA, kept the government's hand in using books for cold-war public diplomacy, though with varying degrees of effort and success and frequently with its own continued existence a subject of congressional debate. At some level, according to a veteran of U.S. cultural diplomacy, USIA competed with commercial media, including book publishers, but the private sector "generally acquiesced in this arrangement, while maintaining an arm's-length relationship with USIA activities to avoid public identification with government propaganda."[18] Through USIA in particular, Uncle Sam was a very good customer for American book publishers. Between 1950 and 1969 alone, the agency was responsible for the distribution of 100 million copies of more than thirteen thousand titles.[19] With the postwar shift in the government's propaganda focus from Europe and Japan to the poorer, nonaligned nations, publishers were mostly content to let government supplement and often underwrite their efforts in those areas. The publishers could not envision large and enduring markets in areas with soft currencies and customers who could afford only the cheapest of books, at least not without government aid. As one scholar has put it, "The cultural Cold War was won for the free market, but it was not won by the free market," because "the USIA operated only where the commercial US media saw no profit."[20]

Another federal entity, the Central Intelligence Agency was, more notoriously, involved covertly in various book programs, including a large undertaking that echoed OEI's marketing strategy by putting subtly anticommunist books in the hands of elites in the states behind the iron curtain. The CIA also clandestinely funded the publication by existing houses, like Frederick Praeger, of books deemed useful in the ideological struggle. The agency supported much of its covert work through various real and dummy foundations. One of the latter was the Farfield Foundation, on whose "rubber-stamp board of directors" sat Cass Canfield, the president of Harper's.[21] The World War II alliance between the government and publishers had been more overt and founded on a mutual confidence in the cultural value of books. From time to time, studies were conducted, resulting in calls to strengthen the government/publisher relationship.[22] Having gone largely underground during the cold war, the partnership quickly lost relevance and urgency once the Soviet empire collapsed.

The Internationalization of U.S. Book Publishing

The progression from the time when army trucks and jeeps carried millions of American books over rutted roads to eager newly liberated civilians to a time when American books could indeed be found everywhere on the world's bookshelves was not as direct and emphatic as the architects of the program in OWI and CBW desired or anticipated. Too many obstacles—protracted poverty in many of the customer nations (particularly in the unaligned third-world countries so important for cold-war propaganda), business recessions, currency restrictions, trade barriers, geopolitics—stood in the way of an unstoppable, upward movement of international business that seemed so likely during the high-minded euphoria sparked by the brisk postliberation trade in international rights. Even when conditions abroad improved, the complexities of dealing with exports and foreign-rights sales (which had caused many a prewar publisher to pray that the odd overseas order would blow out his office window and save him from having to fill it) remained for years, though the rise of computer technology and instantaneous worldwide communication has surely made such work easier and less prone to gaffes.

Nevertheless, the marketing of American books abroad grew impressively after 1948. A number of factors account for this. The introduction of Overseas and Transatlantic editions was certainly one of them, as were other manifestations of the paperback revolution such as the Armed Services Editions (many of which were left behind to be read by the locals) and the general success and increased prestige of U.S. paperback series, like Pocket Books, Ballantine, and the New American Library. There is no straight line of progress from the OEs and TEs to the strength of the American book presence abroad, but the wartime public/private partnership awakened the aspiration for international business that publishers have never lost. Robust demand for new kinds of U.S. college textbooks abroad also contributed. These joint products of U.S. academics and publishers had received a giant boost domestically from the explosive growth of U.S. higher education thanks in large part to the GI Bill. As higher education abroad began to emulate U.S. models, including the growth and democratization of student bodies and the introduction of new curricula, demand for U.S. text-books and works in science, medicine, and technology grew with it. The rise in American studies programs overseas, themselves benefiting from U.S. govern-ment assistance in many cases, also created demand for books in U.S. history, literature, and kindred disciplines. The expansion of English as an international tongue made much of this possible. The language's advocates during and just after the war, like Stanley Unwin and Frederic Melcher, deserve some credit for that. Similarly, there was growth in university and other libraries abroad, also increasing demand for American books.

The dissolution of the British Traditional Markets Agreement in 1978 removed a substantial impediment against U.S. marketing in both the historically English-speaking countries, like Australia, and developing countries, like India, where Brit-ish colonizers had planted the English language even more firmly than the Union Jack. The end of the 1947 agreement, which Unwin had defended so long, came as a result of a lawsuit the U.S. Department of Justice filed, fittingly, in the year celebrating the bicentennial of the United States' independence from Great Britain. This change made it easier for U.S. publishers to issue often expensive, copublished editions in English for the entire world, for which no single market could justify the cost. As more American publishers attended the Frankfurt Book Fair, successor to Leipzig's, complex projects like these could be worked out face-to-face. Frank-furt also was an important venue for buying and selling foreign translation and other rights, which was particularly important to trade publishers, even if non-trade books garnered the majority of international sales from the 1950s on.[23]

The wartime book programs contributed to the long-term expansion of American books abroad, even if they did not fully cause it. The rise of the United States to superpower status after the war, along with the economic and cultural hegemony it produced, no doubt propelled American books all over the world, alongside American music, movies, and television, to say nothing of Levi's, McDonald's, and Miller Lite.

Moreover, the landscape of U.S. publishing in general changed drastically, be-ginning with the first great round of modern mergers in the 1960s, followed by the construction of vast international communications conglomerates, which, though increasingly controlled overseas, in a sense validated the importance and profit-ability of American books abroad that the publishers and government propagan-dists of the 1940s predicted for them. It is ironic that today a handful of foreign media giants control much of U.S. trade publishing, as Germany's Bertelsmann owns Random House, which had earlier incorporated Knopf as well as other lead-ing U.S. imprints. To paraphrase the old Remington shaver TV commercial, Ber-telsmann must have liked American books so much, he bought the company.

At another level, however, the growth of the global economy has altered the landscape of book publishing to such a degree that the very notion of what constitutes an American book is moot. So too are notions of exports and imports. The geography of U.S. book publishing now includes U.S.-owned firms operating internationally as well as foreign corporations publishing books in the United States. Changes also skew data gathering. How and to which country's credit are the values attributed for separate editions of a novel by an American published by various national components of, say, Bertelsmann? Since the copyright law of 1978 dropped the requirement of U.S. manufacture, the value of books published by a U.S. house but printed in, say, China, has been counted as an import.[24]

The people of the Council on Books in Wartime and the Office of War Information would likely not feel much at home in today's publishing world, with its stress on profitability and corporate synergies more than on distinction and cultural value and its emphasis on marketing to the masses at the expense of a more discriminating and influential clientele. One of the first instances of conglomeratization forced William Sloane to leave Henry Holt in 1946 to establish his own firm. When the Texas oil tycoon Clint Murchison bought Holt, Sloane found he could not work for someone who "had a very black record and absolutely no publishing interests whatsoever." When he later headed up Rutgers University Press, he despaired that even university presses were beginning to compromise the highest values of publishing.[25] Chester Kerr too left trade publishing and found his true life's work in university-press publishing, at Yale. In our day, even after multiple waves of conglomerating mergers and takeovers, some publishers lament the world that had been and has mostly been lost. Similarly titled books on publishing in the second half of the twentieth century by Jason Epstein (*Book Business: Publishing Past, Present, and Future,* 2001) and André Schiffrin (*The Business of Books: How International Conglomerates Took Over Publishing and Changed the Way We Read,* 2000) project the values that the publishers, booksellers, and librarians of the 1940s treasured.

At its best, the wartime collaboration between government and the publishing industry, along with similar partnerships during the cold war, provided a vital backstop to the shortcomings of the free market. Historically, government has served publishing best when it has been willing to subsidize American books of high cultural-diplomacy value, which likely would not otherwise have reached foreign shores, and when it has tried to act as a "fixer" for publishers wishing to do business abroad, or, as a trade official put it in the 1950s, by assisting publishers "in surmounting the manifold barriers to book exports."[26] As Lawrence P. Dalcher, an official in the U.S. book program in Germany, noted in 1948, the government had to keep its hand in the export of American books abroad "with the knowledge that it is making an investment in ideas and not merely granting a subsidy to the book trade."[27]

Has the dissemination of American books abroad succeeded in winning hearts and minds and blunting the propaganda of others? Probably yes and no. Perhaps results would have been better if the stereotypes of U.S. culture promulgated abroad hadn't too often had at least some truth to them. One recalls the strongly voiced views of the three British publishers visiting the United States in 1943 that Americans were tone-deaf to the opinions of others and that the aggressiveness of U.S. publishers in expanding their international markets masked a larger imperialism that could make Americans hated around the world. In the years since the Second World War, the reputation of the United States abroad seems to have suffered most when the country has been engaged in wars that people in many other countries wanted no part of. But perhaps the absence of American books abroad would have made matters worse, particularly if much of the worst of other forms of U.S. culture flowed freely internationally.

The current conflicts in the Middle East have raised troubling questions about the image of the United States abroad that may be just as significant as those that preceded and followed World War II—many of the kind of images that troubled the three British publishers. The widespread sympathy and support for the United States in the wake of the September 11 terrorist attacks on the World Trade Center and the Pentagon were short-lived, suffering grievous blows after the invasion of Iraq. Just as Goebbels had fostered powerful propaganda based on his view of the crassness and cultural inferiority of U.S. society, many people abroad since then have remained suspicious of U.S. motives and contemptuous of American mores and culture.

The George W. Bush administration floundered in its halfhearted attempts to revive public diplomacy. Even Defense Secretary Donald Rumsfeld told the Army War College in 2006, "If I were grading, I would say we probably deserve a 'D' or a 'D-plus' as a country as to how well we're doing in the battle of ideas that's taking place in the world."[28] Richard T. Arndt, a former USIA career officer and president of the U.S. Fulbright Association, exhaustively revisited the rise and fall of this diplomatic style in his 2006 book *The First Resort of Kings: American Cultural Diplomacy in the Twentieth Century.* A call for a restoration of U.S. "soft power" through diplomacy has come also from columnists like Nicholas D. Kristof, of the *New York Times,* who, after noting that the "United States has more musicians in its military bands than it has diplomats," argues that the result of overinvesting in military tools and underinvesting in diplomacy "is a lopsided foreign policy that antagonizes the rest of the world and is ineffective in tackling many modern problems."[29]

Such is a shame, if not a scandal. Of course, books are only part of a program of cultural diplomacy, but historically they have been an important part. Among the most lamented results of the U.S. retreat in this field has been the closing of USIS libraries throughout the world, where local publishers as well as readers could sample some of the United States' best books, perhaps with an eye to purchasing rights or importing copies. Programs to put subsidized U.S. books into foreign marketplaces expired even earlier, but there are signs of a possible revival of both kinds of book programs.

The demise of Franklin Book Programs in the late 1970s cut off an important source of books in Arabic for the Middle East. During the first decade of the twenty-first century, however, several private initiatives have begun to try to remedy the situation. The Sabre Foundation, for example, has collected publisher-donated books—mostly but not exclusively science and technology titles—and shipped them to universities in Iraq.[30] Sabre has had some federal support, but its program does not answer the need for books in translation representing high points of U.S. thought and culture to be read by ordinary citizens. However, the Global Americana Institute, established by Juan Cole, a University of Michigan professor of Middle East studies, is attempting to do just that through his organization's Americana Translation Project. Cole founded the organization after concluding, in view of the virtual defunding of USIA and its being folded into the State Department, as well as the closing of USIA libraries in the Middle East, "Frankly, we have been failed by our government and foundations in getting the message of what America really is out to the rest of the world."

Cole's plan is to translate and publish several key works of U.S. political and social thought, including works of the founding fathers and of such later figures as Abraham Lincoln, Susan B. Anthony, John Dewey, W. E. B Dubois, and Martin Luther King, for sale in the Middle East. The Franklin Books Program, minus the work of modernizing indigenous publishing industries, served as a model for Cole's program. Progress has been slow. As of October 2009, he had in hand a completed translation of an anthology of Thomas Jefferson's writings but still needed to find a publisher for it in the Middle East.[31] One might question how effective such a program could be, particularly in an age in which books are viewed as lagging behind the electronic media as molders of international opinion. Still, it might be useful for at least the opinion makers in developing and crisis-ridden countries to have available to them translations, in book form, of some of the representative works of the American democratic tradition, particularly since Internet access is more sketchy in the region. The markets may hardly be robust enough for this to be a purely commercial venture in most parts of the Middle East. So, just as the government assisted American book publishers in providing books for the people of war-torn Europe and Asia who couldn't afford them at the time, so too might it be a good idea for programs of subsidized books for areas of low commercial potential—as a stopgap by Juan Cole's foundation, but eventually with the support of a governmental agency.

In the complex and tense world of the early twenty-first century, the public/private model for the export of representative American books might still prove useful. President Barack Obama and his secretary of state, Hillary Rodham Clinton, are on record for increasing the channels of soft power in the nation's diplomacy. Shouldn't books be part of the nation's tool kit and become, once again, weapons in the war of ideas?

OVERSEAS AND TRANSATLANTIC EDITIONS

Appendix A. Overseas and Transatlantic Editions. (Shaded rows denote Transatlantic Editions; unshaded rows denote Overseas Editions.)

AUTHOR	TITLE	LANGUAGE	SERIES	NUMBER	COPYRIGHT DATE(S)	PUBLISHER OF ORIGINAL	IN ASE?
Agar, Herbert	Keerpunt der Tijden	Dutch	TE	USBK/H/54	1942	Little, Brown	A-21
Agar, Herbert	A l'échelle de l'époque	French	TE	USBK/F/54	1942	Little, Brown	A-21
Basso, Hamilton	Mainstream	English	OE	E-2	1943	Reynal & Hitchcock	No
Becker, Carl L.	How New Will the Better World Be?	English	OE	E-7	1944	Alfred A. Knopf	No
Becker, Carl L.	Quel sera le monde de demain?	French	OE	F-7	1944	Alfred A. Knopf	No
Becker, Carl L.	Die Welt von Morgen	German	OE	G-7	1944	Alfred A. Knopf	No
Benét, Stephen Vincent	America	English	OE	E-21	1944	Farrar and Rinehart	N-3
Benét, Stephen Vincent	Amérique	French	TE	USBK/F/50	1944	Farrar and Rinehart	N-3
Benét, Stephen Vincent	Amerika	German	OE	G-19	1944	Farrar and Rinehart	N-3
Benét, Stephen Vincent	America	Italian	OE	I-5	1944	Farrar and Rinehart	N-3
Bowen, Catherine Drinker	Yankee from Olympus	English	OE	E-15	1943–44	Little, Brown	P-32
Bowen, Catherine Drinker	Olympien d'Amérique	French	OE	F-15	1943–44	Little, Brown	P-32
Bowen, Catherine Drinker	Der Yankee vom Olymp	German	OE	G-15	1943–44	Little, Brown	P-32
Brogan, D. W.	Politische Kultur	German	OE	G-23	1945	Alfred A. Knopf	No
Brown, Harry	A Walk in the Sun	English	OE	E-18	1944	Alfred A. Knopf	No
Brown, Harry	Promenade au soleil	French	OE	F-18	1944	Alfred A. Knopf	No
Brown, Harry	Ein Marsch in der Sonne	German	OE	G-18	1944	Alfred A. Knopf	No
Burns, Eugene	Et s' il n'en reste qu'un . . .	French	OE	F-1	1944	Harcourt, Brace	No
Chinard, Gilbert	Thomas Jefferson	French	OE	F-20	1939	Little, Brown	No
Dulles, Foster Rhea	The Road to Teheran	English	OE	E-1	1944	Princeton University Press	No
Dulles, Foster Rhea	Le chemin de Téhéran	French	OE	F-4	1944	Princeton University Press	No

Author	Title	Language	Type	Code (TE)	Code (OE)	Year	Publisher	
Dulles, Foster Rhea	Der Weg nach Teheran	German	OE		G-1	1944	Princeton University Press	No
Fast, Howard	Citizen Tom Paine	English	OE		E-14	1943	Duell, Sloan & Pierce	No
Fast, Howard	Le citoyen Tom Paine	French	OE		F-14	1943	Duell, Sloan & Pierce	No
Fast, Howard	Il cittadino Tom Paine	Italian	OE		I-4	1943	Duell, Sloan & Pierce	No
Fortune, Editors of	Japan	English	OE		E-11	1944	Time, Inc.	No
Fortune, Editors of	Le Japon	French	OE		F-11	1944	Time, Inc.	No
Fortune, Editors of	Japan	German	OE		G-11	1944	Time, Inc.	No
Furnas, J. C.	Schetsen uit het Amerikaansche familieleven	Dutch	TE	USBK/H/63		1941–44	Henry Holt	No
Furnas, J. C.	How America Lives	English	OE		E-6	1940–44, 1945	Henry Holt	No
Furnas, J. C.	Comment vit l'Amérique	French	OE		F-6	1940–44, 1945	Henry Holt	No
Grew, Joseph C.	Rapport uit Tokio	Dutch	TE	USBK/H/60		1942	Simon & Schuster	A-2
Grew, Joseph C.	Mission à Tokyo	French	OE		F-21	1942	Simon & Schuster	A-2
Grew, Joseph C.	Bericht aus Tokio	German	OE		G-10	1942	Simon & Schuster	A-2
Hemingway, Ernest	For Whom the Bell Tolls	English	OE		E-19	1940	Charles Scribner's Sons	No
Hersey, John	Descente dans la vallée	French	TE	USBK/F/51		1942	Alfred A. Knopf	No
Hersey, John	Dentro la vallata	Italian	OE		I-1	1943, 1944	Alfred A. Knopf	No
Hilton, James	De geschiedenis van Dr. Wassell	Dutch	TE	USBK/H/53		1943	Little, Brown	D-91
Hilton, James	L'histoire du Dr. Wassell	French	TE	USBK/F/53		1943	Little, Brown	D-91
Holt, Rackham	George Washington Carver	English	OE		E-5	1943	Doubleday, Doran	A-25
Holt, Rackham	George Washington Carver	French	OE		F-5	1943	Doubleday, Doran	A-25
Holt, Rackham	George Washington Carver	German	OE		G-5	1943	Doubleday, Doran	A-25
Hough, Donald	Captain Retread	English	OE		E-9	1944	W. W. Norton	S-17
Hough, Donald	Le capitaine requinqué	French	OE		F-9	1943, 1944	W. W. Norton	S-17

(Continued)

Appendix A. *(Continued)*

AUTHOR	TITLE	LANGUAGE	SERIES	NUMBER	COPYRIGHT DATE(S)	PUBLISHER OF ORIGINAL	IN ASE?
Hough, Donald	*Nach fünfzwanzig Jahren*	German	OE	G-9	1944	W. W. Norton	S-17
Huxley, Julian	*De wonder-vallei "TVA"*	Dutch	TE	USBK/H/52	1943	Architectural Press	No
Huxley, Julian	*La Vallée du miracle "TVA"*	French	TE	USBK/F/52	1943	Architectural Press	No
Jaffe, Bernard	*Men of Science in America*	English	OE	E-16	1944	Simon & Schuster	809
Jaffe, Bernard	*Savants américains*	French	OE	F-16	1944	Simon & Schuster	809
Jaffe, Bernard	*Männer der Forschung in Amerika*	German	OE	G-16	1944	Simon & Schuster	809
Kazin, Alfred	*On Native Grounds*	English	OE	E-17	1942	Reynal & Hitchcock	No
Kazin, Alfred	*Der amerikanische Roman*	German	OE	G-17	1942	Reynal & Hitchcock	No
Lilienthal, David E.	*Construit pour le peuple: "TVA"*	French	TE	USBK/F/57	1944	Harper & Brothers	No
Lilienthal, David	*TVA: Democracy on the March*	English	OE	E-4	1944	Harper & Brothers	No
Lilienthal, David	*Die Tennessee-Stromtal-Verwaltung*	German	OE	G-4	1944	Harper & Brothers	No
Lippmann, Walter	*Amerika en internationale samenwerking*	Dutch	TE	USBK/H/62	1943–44	Little, Brown	C-73 (U.S. Foreign Policy)
Lippmann, Walter	*U.S. Foreign Policy & U.S. War Aims*	English	OE	E-8	1943, 1944	Little, Brown	C-73 (U.S. Foreign Policy)
Lippmann, Walter	*Buts de guerre des États-Unis*	French	OE	F-8	1944	Little, Brown	C-73 (U.S. Foreign Policy)
Marshall, Gen. George, Adm. Ernest J. King, Gen. Henry H. Arnold	*Rapport du haut commandement américain*	French	OE	F-12	NA	[Original]	No

Author	Title	Language	OE/TE	Code	Year	Publisher	Last
Marshall, Gen. George, Adm. Ernest J. King, Gen. Henry H. Arnold	Der Bericht des amerikanischen Oberkommandos	German	OE	G-8	N/A	[Original]	No
Marshall, Gen. George, Adm. Ernest J. King, Gen. Henry H. Arnold	Relazione del comando supremo americano	Italian	OE	I-2	N/A	[Original]	No
Miller, Max, Lt. Cmdr.	Daybreak for Our Carrier	English	OE	E-12	1944	Whittlesey House	No
Nevins, Allan, & Henry Steele Commager	The Pocket History of the United States	English	OE	E-20	1942	Little, Brown	No
Nevins, Allan, & Henry Steele Commager	Petite histoire des Etats-Unis	French	OE	F-22	1942	Little, Brown	No
Nevins, Allan, & Henry Steele Commager	Die Geschichte der Vereinigten Staaten	German	OE	G-21	1942	Little, Brown	No
Pratt, Fletcher	Front de mer: Pacifique, 1941–1942	French	TE	USBK/F/58	1942–44	Harper & Brothers	No
Pratt, Fletcher	Amerikas Flotte im Kriege	German	OE	G-12	1942	Harper & Brothers	No
Pratt, Fletcher	Zeeslagen in den Grooten Oceaan, 1941–1942	Dutch	TE		1942	Harper & Brothers	No
Pyle, Ernie	G.I. Joe	English	OE	E-10	1942–44	Henry Holt	F-170/P-30
Pyle, Ernie	G.I. Joe	French	OE	F-10	1942–44	Henry Holt	F-170/P-30
Ratcliff, John D.	Aus der Welt der Wissenschaft	German	OE	G-20	1945	Doubleday, Doran	M-9
Rourke, Constance	Audubon	French	OE	F-3	1936	Harcourt, Brace	No
Saroyan, William	The Human Comedy	English	OE	E-3	1943	Harcourt, Brace	A-15
Saroyan, William	La commedia umana	Italian	OE	I-3	1943	Harcourt, Brace	A-15
Sherrod, Robert	De strijd om Tarawa	Dutch	TE	USBK/H/64	1942	Duell, Sloan & Pierce	No
Sherrod, Robert	Tarawa	French	OE	F-2	1944	Duell, Sloan & Pierce	No
Sherrod, Robert	Tarawa	German	OE	G-2	1944	Duell, Sloan & Pierce	No
Steffens, Lincoln	L'enfant à cheval	French	OE	F-17	1931, 1935	Harcourt, Brace	No

(Continued)

Appendix A. *(Continued)*

AUTHOR	TITLE	LANGUAGE	SERIES	NUMBER	COPYRIGHT DATE(S)	PUBLISHER OF ORIGINAL	IN ASE?
Steffens, Lincoln	*Ritt ins Leben*	German	OE	G-22	1931, 1935	Harcourt, Brace	No
Steinbeck, John	*Lâchez les bombes!*	French	OE	F-13	1942	Viking	No
Stettinius, Edward L.	*Le Prêt-bail: arme de victoire*	French	TE	USBK/F/55	1944	Éditions de la Maison Française and Macmillan	No
Stimson, Henry	*Vorspiel zur Invasion*	German	OE	G-3	1944	Public Affairs Press	No
Trumbull, Robert	*34 dagen op een reddingsvlot*	Dutch	TE	USBK/H/65	1942	Henry Holt	No
Trumbull, Robert	*The Raft*	English	OE	E-22	1942	Henry Holt	No
Trumbull, Robert	*Le radeau*	French	OE	F-19	1942	Henry Holt	No
Trumbull, Robert	*Das Floss*	German	OE	G-6	1942	Henry Holt	No
Van Doren, Carl	*Benjamin Franklin*	French	TE	USBK/F/56	1938	Viking	K-30
Van Doren, Carl	*Benjamin Franklin*	English	OE	E-13	1938	Viking	K-30
Van Doren, Carl	*Benjamin Franklin*	German	OE	G-13	1938	Viking	K-30
White, E. B.	*Au fil des jours*	French	TE	USBK/F/59	1938–44	Harper & Brothers	P-26
White, E. B.	*Des anderen Brot*	German	OE	G-14	1938–44	Harper & Brothers	P-26
No author	*Vrede en oorlog*	Dutch	TE	USBK/H/61	1943	U.S. Government Printing Office	No

TITLES IN THE BÜCHERREIHE NEUE WELT SERIES

The titles are listed in their numerical order within the series. Two titles were published in two volumes, each with its own number.

1. Stephen Vincent Benét, *Amerika*
2. Wendell Willkie, *Unteilbare Welt*
3. Joseph Conrad, *Der Freibeuter*
4. Ernest Hemingway, *Wem die Stunde schlägt*
5. Franz Werfel, *Das Lied von Bernadette*
6. Eve Curie, *Madame Curie*
7. Joseph Roth, *Radetzskymarsch*
8. Leonhard Frank, *Die Räuberbande*
9. Alfred Einstein, ed., *Die schönsten Erzählunger deutscher Romantiker*
10. Thomas Mann, *Achtung, Europa! Aufsätze zur Zeit*
11. Carl Zuckmayer, *Der Hauptmann von Köpenick*
12. Alfred Einstein, ed., *Briefe deutsche Musiker*
13. Erich Maria Remarque, *Im Westen nichts Neues*
14. Thomas Mann, *Der Zauberberg,* erster Band (vol. 1)
15. Thomas Mann, *Der Zauberberg,* zweiter Band (vol. 2)
16. Heinrich Heine, *Meisterwerke in Vers und Prosa*
17. Franz Werfel, *Die vierzig Tage des Musa Dagh,* erster Band (vol. 1)
18. Franz Werfel, *Die vierzig Tage des Musa Dagh,* zweiter Band (vol. 2)

---

*The source of the information in this appendix is Robert E. Cazden, *German Exile Literature in America, 1933–1950* (Chicago: American Library Association, 1970), 193–94.

19. Arnold Zweig, *Der Streit um den Sergeanten Grischa*
20. Vicki Baum, *Liebe und Tod auf Bali*
21. Thomas Mann, *Lotte in Weimar*
22. Carl Zuckmayer, *Ein Bauer aus dem Taunus*
23. John Scott, *Jenseits des Ural*
24. William Saroyan, *Menschliche Komödie*

Notes

Abbreviations for archival sources can be found in the bibliography.

PREFACE AND ACKNOWLEDGMENTS

1. This scheme follows the Council on Books in Wartime's division of the proposal for the program into sections on "The Problem" and "The Solution." "Council on Books in Wartime Overseas Book Project," July 6, 1944, CBW Records, box 32, folder 8, Princeton.
2. Travis, "Books As Weapons," 353–99.

INTRODUCTION

1. *Psychological Warfare Division*, 66–68.
2. Richard Hollander, draft of history of Allied psychological warfare in northwestern France, Paris, Oct. 10, 1944, 60–61, 331/87/16, NACP. (References to the National Archives in College Park, Maryland, are given as follows: 331/87/16 denotes record group 331/entry 87/box 16.) See also François, *Normandy*, 14, 196, 273, and Wieviorka, *Normandy*, 222–26.
3. Tebbel, *Between Covers*, 280–81.
4. Cheney, *Economic Survey;* Tebbel, *Between Covers*, 280–81.
5. Dave Wilson to Washington Review Board, Nov. 30, 1944, 208/415/807, NACP.
6. "British Public Opinion and the United States," Feb. 23, 1942, INF 1/102, TNA; Wallace Carroll to Edward W. Barrett, June 14, 1945, Harper & Row, Series II, Columbia.
7. Travis, "Books As Weapons," 362.
8. Ballou, *Council,* 358.
9. Simon to Roosevelt, December 8, 1941, Simon Papers, Columbia.
10. Winkler, *Politics of Propaganda,* 55, 110–11.
11. Kerr to Norton, Apr. 26, 1944, CBW Records, box 32, folder 8, Princeton. See also Ballou, *Council,* 83–94, esp. 83–87.
12. A. Ben Candland to Arthur Myers, Feb. 4, 1944, 208/465/2953, NACP.
13. Kerr to Norton, Apr. 26, 1944, CBW Records, box 32, folder 8, Princeton. See also Ballou, *Council,* 83–94, esp. 83–87. Issues of mistrust between British and U.S. staff within PWD SHAEF are addressed in Garnett, *Secret History of PWE.*
14. Mildred E. Allen to E. Trevor Hill, Aug. 14, 1944, 208/6B/4, NACP.
15. Kerr to Norton, Apr. 26, 1944, CBW Records, box 32, folder 8, Princeton.
16. Draft of Operational Memorandum for Books, n.d. [ca. Aug. 1944], 208/464/2949, NACP; "Take a Bow: Harold Guinzburg," *PW,* Feb. 3, 1945, 634–36.
17. "Revised Draft of Operational Memorandum for Books," ca. Aug. 1944, 208/464/2949, NACP.
18. Green, *American Propaganda Abroad,* 67–68; Saunders, *Cultural Cold War,* 18–19; Benjamin, *U.S. Books Abroad,* 24–27.
19. See Laville and Wilford, eds., *U.S. Government, Citizen Groups, and the Cold War.*

CHAPTER 1

1. See James L. W. West III, "The Expansion of the National Book Trade System," in Kaestle and Radway, eds., *Print in Motion,* 78–89, on these and other points in this chapter.

2. Cheney, *Economic Survey,* 233–50. For an interesting gendered analysis of the Cheney report, see Travis, "Reading Matters," 41–51.

3. *Report by the Three Delegates,* 44.

4. Cheney, *Economic Survey,* 321–37.

5. Tebbel, *Between Covers,* 280–81.

6. Satterfield, *World's Best Books,* 25–27.

7. Ibid., 135.

8. Rubin, *Middlebrow Culture,* 92–147; Radway, *A Feeling for Books,* esp. 154–86.

9. Rubin, *Middlebrow Culture,* 101; Radway, *A Feeling for Books,* 182.

10. Satterfeld, *World's Best Books,* 27–28.

11. Davis, *Two-Bit Culture,* 31–39.

12. Ibid., 50–60.

13. Ibid., 59–63.

14. Dizard, *Strategy of Truth,* 32; Dizard, *Inventing Public Diplomacy,* 10, 13.

15. Friedman, *Nazis and Good Neighbors,* 2–3; Pilgert, 3.

16. Reich, *Nelson Rockefeller,* 208–9; Fleming, *New Dealers' War,* 132.

17. "Our Relations with South America," *PW,* Dec. 9, 1939, 2148.

18. On the French, see Nettelbeck, *Forever French* and Mehlman, *Émigré New York.*

19. Davie, *Refugees in America,* esp. 37–46.

20. "Exiled Writers and America," *PW,* Oct. 4, 1941, 1376–79.

21. Cazden, *German Exile Literature,* 90–93; Pfanner, *Exile in New York,* 115–16.

22. Cazden, *German Exile Literature,* 94.

23. Nettelbeck, *Forever French,* 58–61; *PW,* May 31, 1941, 2170–72.

24. *PW,* Sept. 6, 1941, 804–5; Hanna Kister, "Books and the Peace," *PW,* Mar. 25, 1944, 1283–85; *Time,* June 26, 1944; *PW,* Nov. 25, 1944, 2075.

25. Affadavit of support, n.d., and Mildred Adams, Emergency Rescue Committee, to Walsh, Oct. 16, 1940; both John Day Company Archives, Editorial Correspondence, box 150, folder 35, Princeton.

26. Tebbel, *Between Covers,* 276–84.

27. Tebbel, *Between Covers,* 276–84, and West, "Expansion of the National Book Trade System," in Kaestle and Radway, eds., *Print in Motion,* 80.

28. Charles A. Seavey with Caroline F. Sloat, "The Government as Publisher," in Kaestle and Radway, eds., *Print in Motion,* 471–73.

29. James P. Danky, "Reading, Writing, and Resisting: African American Print Culture," in Kaestle and Radway, eds., *Print in Motion,* 356–57.

CHAPTER 2

1. Annual report to the stockholders [1942], Henry Holt and Company Archives, Box 161, folder 15, Princeton; "Revised Draft of Operational Memorandum for Books," [ca. Aug. 1944], 208/464/2949, NACP.

2. Minutes of board of directors, Feb. 28, 1945, Henry Holt and Company Archives, Box 198, Princeton; Benjamin W. Huebsch to Jonathan Cape, Nov. 14, 1944, Huebsch Papers, Box 4, LC; James L. W. West III, "The Expansion of the National Book Trade System," in Kaestle and Radway, eds., *Print in Motion,* 81.

3. OWI, Overseas Branch, "Draft of Operational Memorandum for Books," n.d. [ca. Aug. 1944], 208/464/2949, NACP. See also Butler, ed., *Books and Libraries in Wartime,* 101–2, and Greco, *Book Publishing Industry,* 21.

4. *Time,* Dec. 18, 1944, 104.

5. Bennett Cerf to Donald S. Klopfer, August 25, 1943, in Cerf and Klopfer, *Dear Donald,* 107.

6. Cerf to Klopfer, Jan. 7, 1944, ibid., 127.

7. Cerf to Klopfer, Mar. 21, 1944, ibid., 145–46.

8. Klopfer to Cerf, Jan. 12, 1944, ibid., 130.

9. Tebbel, *Book Publishing* 4: 9–10.

10. *PW,* May 13, 1944, 1840–41, and Dec. 16, 1944, 2311.

11. Ibid., Sept. 29, 1945, 1538–40.

12. Ibid., Oct. 30, 1943, 1705.

13. Tebbel, *Book Publishing* 4: 9.

14. *PW,* Jan. 13, 1945, 142; ibid., May 13, 1944, 1854; ibid., June 10, 1944, 2180–81.

15. R. V. B. Sinclair, Bennington, Vt., Bookshop, Letter to the editor, ibid., June 10, 1944, 2169–70.

16. Ibid., June 20, 1942, 2263; ibid., Aug. 25, 1945, 734.

17. National Publishers Association, "Bulletin No. 797," Jan. 29, 1943, Publishers' Weekly Collection, box 1, Princeton.

18. Circular letter, Donald L. Geddes et al. to literary organizations, Mar. 26, 1943, Publishers' Weekly Collection, box 7, Princeton.

19. "The Essentiality of Books," *PW,* Sept. 18, 1943, 974–77.

20. Minutes of the board of directors meeting, Macmillan Company (New York), July 2, 1947, Macmillan Publishing Archives, MSS 54877, British Library.

21. *PW,* Feb. 7, 1942, 661.

22. *Report by the Three Delegates,* 15.

23. Melville Minton, Edward M. Crane, Norman V. Donaldson, and Lawrence Saunders to board of directors and [Book Publishers] Bureau subscribers, July 27, 1943, Publishers' Weekly Collection, box 1, Princeton.

24. *PW,* Mar. 4, 1944, 1021–22. On the campaign to gain "essential" status, see "The Essentiality of Books," *PW,* Sept. 18, 1943, 974–77; Badmington, ed., *Books Are Indispensable;* "Editorial: No. 1 Critical War Material," *PW,* May 13, 1944, 1837; and "The Essentiality of Books," ibid., Aug. 12, 1944, 489–90.

25. Ibid., Mar. 28, 1942, 1248.

26. Ibid., May 9, 1942, insert between 1740 and 1741.

27. Kingsford, *Publishers Association, 1896–1946,* 113–14.

28. William G. Corp, "The British Book Trade during 1938," *PW,* Jan. 21, 1939, 193.

29. *PW,* Apr. 25, 1942, 1572.

30. Feather, *British Publishing,* 215; Calder, *People's War,* 511; Gardiner, *Wartime,* 484–86. On the general subject, see also Calder-Marshall, *The Book Front,* 30–41, and Unwin, *Publishing in Peace and War.*

31. Kingsford, *Publishers Association,* 162.

32. Unwin, *Truth about a Publisher,* 393; Kingsford, *Publishers Association,* 158; Feather, *British Publishing,* 215–16; Gardiner, *Wartime,* 485–87.

33. Kingsford, *Publishers Association,* 172, 185.

34. Waller, *London 1945,* 95.

35. Kingsford, *Publishers Association,* 207; Gardiner, *Wartime,* 485; Hodges, *Gollancz,*146; Holman, *Print for Victory,* 244, 248–49.

36. Kingsford, *Publishers Association,* 171; Unwin, *Truth about a Publisher,* 392–93; Munby and Norrie, *Publishing and Bookselling,* 400.

37. *Bookseller,* Jan. 18, 1945, 38.

38. Kingsford, *Publishers Association,* 181; Holman, *Print for Victory,* 75–82.

39. Calder, *People's War,* 511.

40. Gardiner, *Wartime,* 484.

41. "Confidential to the Publishing Industry—Not for Publication Dec. 28, 1942," CBW Records, box 5, folder 11, Princeton. See also Feather, *British Publishing,* 214–15.

42. Calder, *People's War,* 512, citing S. Nowell Smith, *The House of Cassell* (London: Cassell, 1958), 225.

43. *PW,* May 9, 1942, 1745.

44. Klopfer to Cerf, Feb. 17, 1944, Cerf Papers, box 6, Columbia. On the Excess Profit Tax, see Holman, *Print for Victory,* 238–39.

45. Feather, *British Publishing,* 216.

46. Unwin, *Truth about a Publisher,* 252–53, 278; Feather, *British Publishing,* 216.

47. Stanley Unwin to David S. Unwin, November 8, 1940, AUC 101/5, Reading. (AUC denotes George Allen & Unwin, Ltd., Records, Correspondence.)

48. *PW,* Feb. 1, 1941, 624–27.

49. Pamphlet issued by the Book Manufacturers' Institute, Inc., n.d., in Publishers' Weekly Collection, box 7, Princeton.

50. Unwin, *Truth about a Publisher,* 252.

51. Ziegler, *London at War,* 256; Calder, *People's War,* 511; Gardiner, *Wartime,* 486, 491–92; Hewison, *Under Siege,* 22.

52. "Editorial: In Sympathy and Admiration," *PW,* Feb. 1, 1941, 617.

53. Ibid., May 9, 1942, 1760–61.

54. Walsh to Cape, Dec. 30, 1940, box 149, folder 24, editorial correspondence, John Day Archives, Princeton.

55. R. J. L. Kingsford, The Publishers Association, circular letter to members, Dec. 2, 1941, CW 91/22, Reading. (CW denotes Chatto & Windus, Ltd., Records.)

56. Cape to Walsh, Dec. 6, 1940, box 149, folder 24, editorial correspondence, John Day Archives, Princeton.

57. See, for example, Unwin to Mrs. M. A. Hamilton, M.P., Oct. 2, 1944, AUC 193/10, Reading. See also Brophy, *Britain Needs Books,* 31–33, 41.

58. Brett to Macmillan, Nov. 16, and Dec. 2, 1939, both Macmillan Publishing Archives, BL.

59. Walsh to W. G. Cousins, May 27, 1940, box 148, folder 19, John Day Archives, Princeton.

60. "Confidential to the Publishing Industry—Not for Publication Dec. 28, 1942," CBW Records, box 5, folder 11, Princeton. See also *Bookseller,* Apr. 1, 1943, 283. On the background of the mission, see *PW,* Oct. 3, 1942, 1435–36, 1444.

61. Paraphrased in John Carter, "A Bookseller's Day in London," *PW,* Nov. 2, 1940, 1764. See also Waller, *London 1945,* 94.

62. Calder, *People's War,* 513; *Bookseller,* Aug. 5, 1943, 203–4.

63. *PW,* Oct. 23, 1943, 1609.

64. Ibid., May 9, 1942, 1747.

65. "Confidential to the Publishing Industry—Not for Publication Dec. 28, 1942," CBW Records, box 5, folder 11, Princeton.

66. See, for example, Unwin to Sir William Beveridge, June 11, 1943, AUC 157/16, Reading.

67. Letter to the editor, *PW,* Nov. 6, 1943, 1777.

68. "Revised Draft of Operational Memorandum for Books," n.d. [ca. Aug. 1944], 208/464/2949, NACP.

69. *PW,* June 12, 1943, 2230–33.

70. Ibid., Dec. 15, 1945, 2616–20.

71. Ibid.

72. Ibid.

73. "Draft of Operational Memorandum for Books," n.d. [ca. Aug. 1944], 208/464/2949, NACP.

74. Brooks, *Prisoners of Hope,* 114–15, 132.

75. Ibid., 185–92.

76. Ibid., 192–93.

77. Hanna Kister, "Books and the Peace," *PW,* Mar. 25, 1944, 1283.

78. *PW,* Sept. 6, 1941, 804–5; Ibid., Dec. 28, 1946, 3404–5.

79. S. O. Gregory, "Books in the Far East after the War," *PW,* Dec. 29, 1945, 2771–73.

80. William M. Sloane, "War and China's Publishing Industry," n.d., Sloane Papers, box 7, unnumbered folder, Princeton. See also "Take a Bow: William Sloane," *PW,* Aug. 21, 1943, 574–75.

81. Sloane, "To Chungking," unpublished memoir, n.d. [ca. 1944], p. 25, Sloane Papers, box 6, unnumbered folder, Princeton.

82. Sloane to Johnson, Dec. 13, 1944, Sloane Papers, box 2, folder 1; Stanley Hunnewell, Book Publishers Bureau, to Sloane, June 29, 1943, Sloane Papers, box 2, folder 2; both Princeton.

83. *PW,* Aug. 21, 1943, 568. See also Sloane, "Confidential Memorandum to Mr. Malcolm Johnson [Book Publishers Bureau] Regarding the New Copyright Treaty with China," July 14, 1943, Sloane Papers, box 2, folder 2, Princeton.

84. *PW,* Aug. 21, 1943, 568.

85. "From James T. Ruddy's letter of July 9, 1943," Sloane Papers, box 2, folder 2, Princeton.

86. Sloane to Henry Blundin, OWI, Aug. 6, 1943, and David H. Stevens, Rockefeller Foundation, to Charles A. Thomson, Department of State, Aug. 6, 1943; both Sloane Papers, box 2, folder 2, Princeton.

87. Sloane, "To Chungking," p. 10, Sloane Papers box 7, unnumbered folder, Princeton.

88. Sloane to Johnson, Jan. 1, 1944, Sloane Papers, box 2, folder 1, Princeton.

89. Sloane to Kerr, "Memorandum of Kunming Book Situation," n.d., Sloane Papers, box 2, folder 1, Princeton.

90. Sloane to Malcolm Johnson, Nov. 17, 1943, and Sloane to Johnson, Jan. 1, 1944; both Sloane Papers, box 2, folder 1, Princeton.

91. Sloane to Johnson, Nov. 27, 1943, Sloane Papers, box 2, folder 1, Princeton.

92. Ibid.

93. Ibid.

94. Sloane to Johnson, Dec. 11, 1943, and Sloane to Johnson, Dec. 18, 1943; both Sloane Papers, box 2, folder 1, Princeton.

95. Sloane to Johnson, Jan. 1, 1944, Sloane Papers, box 2, folder 1, Princeton.

96. "China Book Week," Northwestern University on the Air, *Of Men and Books,* Mar. 25, 1944, transcript of broadcast over the Columbia Broadcasting System.

97. Dachin Yih to Li Soh-Ming, n.d., ca. Mar. 1944, Sloane Papers, box 2, folder 2, Princeton.

98. Benjamin H. Stern, Stern & Reubens, to Sloane, Aug. 2, 1944, Sloane Papers, box 2, folder 2, Princeton; "Statement of Marybeth Peters, the Register of Copyrights, before the Subcommittee on Intellectual Property, Committee of the Judiciary," United States Senate, May 25, 2005, 4, http://www.copyright.gov/docs/regstat052505.html.

99. *PW,* July 27, 1946, 382.

100. Kurt Bernheim, "The Swedish Book Trade Carries On," *PW,* July 25, 1942, 234–36.

101. *PW,* Feb. 2, 1947, 1256; Fischer, *My European Heritage,* 116–32; *PW,* Sept. 16, 1944, 996–97; British Publishers Guild, "Memo on Visit to Sweden," ca. June 1945, CW 98/17, Reading.

102. British Publishers Guild, quarterly circular no. 2, Aug.-Nov. 1945, CW 98/17, Reading.

103. Harrap to Jonathan Cape and Harold Raymond, Sept. 6, 1944, CW 98/17, Reading.

104. Hellmut Lehmann-Haupt, "The German Booktrade in 1945. Part 1. Bookselling and Publishing under National Socialism," *PW,* Nov. 24, 1945, 2332.

105. *German Book Publishing,* 14.

106. "Exiled Writers and America," *PW,* Oct. 4, 1941, 1376–79.

107. "Revised Draft of Operational Memorandum for Books," ca. Aug. 1944, 208/464/2949, NACP.

108. Emil Lengyel, "The Sad Plight of Books in Germany," *PW*, Jan. 11, 1939, 676.

109. H. J. Krould to Jackson et al., Feb. 28, 1945, 208/464/2950, NACP; Lehmann-Haupt, "The German Booktrade in 1945, Part 1: Bookselling and Publishing under National Socialism," *PW*, Nov. 24, 1945, 2332–34.

110. Edgar Bielefeld, Hans Brockhaus, Georg Petermann, and Th. Volckmar-Frentzel, "The German Book-Trade at the Time of Occupation by the Allied Military Government: Situation, Problems, Hopes," May 8, 1945, 260/16(A1)18/258, NACP. This was a document written by German members of the book trades at the request of the occupying authorities. See also *PW*, Aug. 19, 1944, 578–80.

111. Lehmann-Haupt to Maj. Douglas Waples, Mar. 1, 1945, 260/16(A1)18/258, NACP.

112. *PW*, Dec. 11, 1943, 2157.

113. Reichmann, "The First Year of American Publishing Control in Germany," *PW*, Nov. 16, 1946, 2810–12.

114. Lehmann-Haupt, "German Booktrade in 1945," 2333–34.

115. *German Book Publishing*, 4–15.

116. Melcher, "A Report on the Japanese Book Market," *PW*, May 3, 1947, 2295, and *PW*, Oct. 23, 1948, 1815.

117. Capt. Charles E. Tuttle, "Japan Wants American Books," *PW*, Mar. 9, 1946, 1518–19; Shillony, *Wartime Japan*, 148–51.

118. Melcher, "Japanese Book Publishing Today," *PW*, Sept. 20, 1947, 1261.

119. Morris, *Traveller from Tokyo*, 59–60, 141–46.

120. Shillony, *Wartime Japan*, 110.

121. Melcher, "Japanese Book Publishing Today," *PW*, Sept. 20, 1947, 1256.

122. Morris, *Traveller from Tokyo*, 61–62; Shillony, *Wartime Japan*, 120–22.

123. Shillony, *Wartime Japan*, 112–18, 126–29.

124. Melcher, "Japanese Book Publishing Today," *PW*, Sept. 20, 1947, 1256.

CHAPTER 3

1. Lingeman, *Don't You Know There's a War On?*

2. Reynolds, *Rich Relations*, xxiv.

3. The following draws substantially on Travis, "Books As Weapons." On the term "bookmen," see her "Reading Matters," 6–8.

4. Ballou, *Council*, 3–6, 32–53; Travis, "Books As Weapons," 358. Norton took credit for originating the slogan. See Norton to Stanley Unwin, Apr. 13, 1945, AUC 233/1, Reading. The trade accepted his authorship of the phrase. See *PW*, Dec. 2, 1944, 2158. Benjamin Disraeli's epigram "A book may be as great a thing as a battle" reflected much the same sentiment. See Saunders, *Cultural Cold War*, 21–22.

5. Ballou, *Council*, 3–5.

6. Travis, "Books As Weapons," 356.

7. Ibid., 366–68.

8. Ibid., 359, 368–71.

9. Ibid., 363–65, 373.

10. Ibid., 384, 393–95.

11. Melcher to Stanley Hunnewell, July 3, 1942, CBW Records, box 12, folder 11, Princeton; Feather, *British Publishing*, 191; Unwin, *Truth about a Publisher*, 370–71.

12. Tebbel, *Book Publishing*, 25–26.

13. See letterhead in CBW Records, box 32, folder 9, Princeton.

14. Minutes of the special board of directors meeting, Apr. 14, 1943, box 2, folder 5; Archibald Ogden to J. Kendrick Noble, Noble and Noble, Dec. 19, 1944, box 3, folder 6;

and Noble to Ogden, Jan. 26, 1945, box 2, folder 9; all CBW Records, Princeton. On the textbook association, see Tebbel, *Between Covers*, 343, 441.

15. Ballou. *Council*, 11–19.

16. "Report of the Reorganization Committee," Jan. 28, 1943, CBW Records, box 1, folder 9, Princeton.

17. Kerr to Norton, Jan. 26, 1943, CBW Records, box 14, folder 2, Princeton.

18. Davis to Norton, Jan. 26, 1943, CBW Records, box 14, folder 2, Princeton.

19. "Proceedings, Luncheon Meeting, Council on Books in Wartime, Inc.," Feb. 2, 1943, p. 29, CBW Records, box 1, folder 9, Princeton.

20. Johnson to Norton, Oct. 13, 1943, CBW Records, box 3, folder 3, Princeton.

21. Ballou, *Council*, 46–48; Travis, "Reading Matters," 61–68.

22. Kerr to Gardner Cowles Jr., Apr. 9, 1943, 208/339/1695, NACP; Ballou, *Council*, 55–59.

23. Ballou, *Council*, 65; Jamieson, *Books for the Army*, 142; Cole, ed., *Books in Action*, 3.

24. Minutes of the board of directors meeting, Oct. 19, 1944, CBW Records, box 2, folder 7, Princeton; George G. Harrap to Stanley Unwin, Jan. 15, 1945, AUC 224/3; and Unwin to Howard Timmins, Mar. 12, 1945, AUC 241/5, Reading.

25. Poster in the collection of the author.

26. Jamieson, *Books for the Army*, 60–63, 285.

27. Ibid., 60–62.

28. "Manual for State and Local Directors, Victory Book Campaign, Number 1, Jan. 1942," p. 6, Publishers' Weekly Papers, box 2, Princeton.

29. "Final Reports, Victory Book Campaign 1942–1943," 1944, p. 19, Publishers' Weekly Papers, Box 2, Princeton.

30. Canceled check, box 2, Publishers' Weekly Papers, Princeton.

31. Lee Barker to Melcher, June 19, 1942, Publishers' Weekly Papers, box 2, Princeton, and Miller, *Books Go to War*, 6. See also *PW*, July 11, 1942, 112.

32. Ballou, *Council*, 75; "Armed Services Editions," memo issued by the Army Library Branch, July 1945, Publishers' Weekly Collection, box 1, Princeton.

33. Jamieson, *Books for the Army*, 156–57.

34. Minutes of the board of directors meeting, Apr. 20, 1944, CBW Records, box 2, folder 7, Princeton; Tebbel, *Book Publishing* 4: 31; Ballou, *Council*, 64–82. A complete list of the ASEs (both by number and alphabetically by author) appears in Jamieson, *Editions for the Armed Services*, 35–139, and (alphabetically by author only, but with corrections and revisions from the previous title) in Cole, ed., *Books in Action*, 33–78. The final 144 books, intended for occupation forces, were printed in the more traditional upright format. Jamieson, *Editions for the Armed Services*, 23–24.

35. Lewis Gannett, "Books," in Goodman, ed., *While You Were Gone*, 460.

36. *PW*, Apr. 25, 1942, 1579–80; Col. Joseph I. Greene, "Military Books for the General Reader," *PW*, July 24, 1943, 254–61.

37. Greene, ed., *Infantry Journal Reader*, v–xi.

38. C. B. Boutell to Ivan Veit, May 9, 1942, CBW Records, box 1, folder 2, Princeton.

39. Greene, "Standard Military Books," *PW*, Jan. 31, 1942, 424–26; *PW*, June 5, 1943, 2143–44.

40. Enoch, *Memoirs*, 157–58; Lewis, *Penguin Special*, 213.

41. *PW*, Apr. 25, 1942, 1579–80.

42. Tebbell, *Book Publishing* 4: 75; Davis, *Two-Bit Culture*, 60–63, 102; Lewis, *Penguin Special*, 214.

43. Minutes of the Executive Committee meeting, July 21, 1943, CBW Records, box 3, folder 5, Princeton.

44. Davis, *Two-Bit Culture*, p. 78–79; Michael Hackenberg, "The Armed Services Editions in Publishing History," in Cole, ed., *Books in Action*, 19–20.

45. Ballou, *Council*, 27–31.

46. *PW,* June 14, 1947, 2937–38.

47. Schlesinger, *A Life in the Twentieth Century,* 288.

48. Warburg, *Unwritten Treaty,* 88–89. See also Dizard, *Strategy of Truth,* 34.

49. Robert Bruce Lockhart, Minutes, Aug. 28, 1944, INF 1/907, TNA.

50. Warburg, *Unwritten Treaty,* 55.

51. Winkler, *Politics of Propaganda,* 110–11.

52. Donaldson, *Archibald MacLeish,* 363–64.

53. Winkler, *Politics of Propaganda,* 63–65; Schlesinger, *A Life in the Twentieth Century,* 289–93; Dizard, *Strategy of Truth,* 34.

54. Winkler, *Politics of Propaganda,* 64, 156–57,

55. Ibid., 154–57.

56. Ibid., 55, 110–11. For evidence of the OWI overseas book program's goal to help oppose fascism "wherever it raises its head," see "Revised Draft of Operational Memorandum for Books," n.d. [ca. Aug. 1944], 208/464/2949, NACP.

57. *Psychological Warfare Division,* 25. See also Lerner, *Psychological Warfare against Nazi Germany.*

58. Minutes of a Meeting…with Representatives of O.W.I., July 31, 1942, FO 898/102, TNA.

59. Winkler, *Politics of Propaganda,* 113–14.

60. Garnett, *Secret History of PWE,* 251, 327, 350–51.

61. Tebbel, *Between Covers,* 428–30. See also Weybright, *Making of a Publisher.*

62. Stacks, *Scotty,* 74–76.

63. Weybright, *Making of a Publisher,* 129–30.

64. Davis, *Two-Bit Culture,* 250–51.

65. Oscar Schisgall to Harold S. Latham, Apr. 7, 1944, CBW Records, box 14, folder 3, Princeton; "Book and Magazine Bureau," Feb. 1945, 208/339/1695, NACP.

66. Minutes of the Executive Committee meeting, Feb. 23, 1944, CBW Records, box 3, folder 7, Princeton; Elmer Davis to W. W. Norton, Mar. 31, 1944, Norton to Davis, Apr. 6, 1944, and Kerr to Norton, Apr. 17, 1944; all CBW Records, box 14, folder 3, Princeton. See also Ballou *Council,* 59.

67. Kerr to Davis, and file memo, both Apr. 29, 1944, 208/464/2949, NACP.

68. Grace Hogarth to David Unwin, May 28, 1945, AUC 225/4, Reading.

69. See Madison, *Jewish Publishing in America.*

70. Travis, "Reading Matters," 34.

71. http://www.freedomhouse.org/template.cfm?page=2 and http://infoshare1.prince ton.edu/libraries/firestone/rbsc/finding_aids/FH/; and "Agar Called to Navy," *NY Times,* Aug. 17, 1942.

72. See CBW Records, box 11, folder 5, Princeton.

73. *PW,* June 9, 1945, 2289.

74. Schlesinger, *A Life in the Twentieth Century,* 114.

75. Kerr, brief biographical sketch, Chester Brooks Kerr Papers, Princeton.

76. Ibid.

77. "Mr. Kerr's remarks at organization luncheon of Council on Books in Wartime." 208/339/1695, NACP.

78. Kerr to Fredric G. Melcher, Mar. 6, 1944. Publishers' Weekly collection, box 1, Princeton; Kerr to W. W. Norton, July 16, 1943, Chester Brooks Kerr Papers, Princeton. See also *PW,* Mar. 18, 1944, 1217.

79. Kerr, brief biographical sketch, ca. Apr. or May 1944, ibid.

80. Kerr to Ferris Greenslet, Houghton Mifflin, Nov. 5, 1943, ibid.

81. Melcher, "Editorial," *PW,* Aug. 21, 1943, 553; also 569.

82. See chapter 10.

83. Barbara [possibly Barbara McClure White] to Kerr, Apr. 23, 1944, Chester Brooks Kerr Papers, Reese Co.

84. Chester Kerr to Richard L. Simon, Jan. 22, 1945, 208/464/2951A, NACP; Tebbel, *Book Publishing* 4: 635–37; obituary of Kerr in the *NY Times,* Aug. 26, 1999; obituary of Kerr in the Yale Bulletin & Calendar, Sept. 6–13, 1999, http://www.yale.edu/opa/v28.n3/story10.html.

85. Obituary of Col. H. A. Guinzburg, *NY Times,* Nov. 17, 1928.

86. *NY Times,* May 22, 1938.

87. "Take a Bow: Harold Guinzburg," *PW,* Feb. 3, 1945, 634–36; Tebbel, *Between Covers,* 157, 221, 253–55, 292, 392; obituary of Harold K. Guinzburg, *NY Times,* Oct. 19, 1961.

88. Mahl, *Desperate Deception,* 64–65. Guinzburg is not cited in the index of William Stevenson, *A Man Called Intrepid: The Secret War* (New York: Harcourt Brace Jovanovich, 1976).

89. *PW,* Apr. 17, 1943, 1576.

90. Dizard, *Inventing Public Diplomacy,* 28.

91. "A Man of Integrity," *NY Times,* Oct. 20, 1961.

92. See quotation by Melcher in "Books for Our Fighting Men," the transcript of the broadcast of *Northwestern University on the Air: Of Books and Men,* Columbia Broadcasting System, Sept. 11, 1943, 3.

93. *PW,* Jan. 2, 1943, 27.

94. Ibid., Sept. 26, 1942, 1235.

95. "Conferences between Representatives of Council on Books in Wartime, OWI and Public Relations Bureaus of the Government," Sept. 17, 1942; Washington Committee of the Council on Books in Wartime, "Report on Government Agencies and their Relation to Books in Wartime, Dec. 1942, 2–5; both Publishers' Weekly Archives, box 7, Princeton. See also Ballou, *Council,* 54–55.

CHAPTER 4

1. For an example of the slogan's use in Britain, see Stanley Unwin, "Status of Books in War-Time England," *PW,* Dec. 27, 1941, 2288–91.

2. Ibid., May 9, 1942, 1752. See also Ryback, *Hitler's Private Library.*

3. MacLeish, "The Strongest and the Most Enduring Weapons," *PW,* May 16, 1942, 1810.

4. "Guidance Notes, Part II. Consolidation Activities in Liberated Areas," June 14, 1944, 331/87/11, NACP.

5. "Joint M.O.I. and P.W.B. Plan for Liberated France," July 20, 1944, FO 898/393, TNA.

6. Cruickshank, *The Fourth Arm,* 40.

7. Psychological Warfare Branch, COSSAC, "Composition, Functions and Relations to Other Agencies or Departments," Dec. 22, 1943, FO 898/385, TNA.

8. "Revised Draft of Operational Memorandum for Books," n.d. [ca. Aug.-Sept. 1944]. 208/464/2949, NACP.

9. The term "paper bullets" appeared in *Sea Bee,* May 23, 1945, 13; copy in 208/356/1721, NACP.

10. Melcher, "Editorial," *PW,* Oct. 13, 1945, 1755.

11. Gen. McChrystal, PWB SHAEF, to Barrett and Bernard, [ca. mid-1944], 208/464/2951A, NACP.

12. Minutes of the Executive Committee meeting, May 12, 1943, CBW Records, box 3, folder 4, Princeton.

13. "China Book Week," Northwestern University on the Air, *Of Men and Books,* Mar. 25, 1944, transcript of broadcast over the Columbia Broadcasting System; Charles S. Miner, "Postwar Gains in Book Trade Seen by Sloane," *Shanghai Evening Post and Mercury* (U.S. edition), Mar. 31, 1944, in Sloane Papers, box 7, Princeton.

14. Brooks, *Prisoners of Hope,* 52.

15. *PW,* Jan. 12, 1946, 172–73.

16. Dower, *Embracing Defeat,* 180–81, 186.

17. Edward Barrett to Pat Allen, June 8, 1944, 208/464/2949, NACP.

18. Stanley M. Rinehart Jr. to Archibald Ogden, Apr. 2, 1945, quoting Irwin Ross citing M. Monnet, director of the Cercle de la Librarie, Paris, CBW Records, box 8, folder 2, Princeton. See also Bishop, "Overseas Branch," 147.

19. Cruickshank, *Fourth Arm,* 136.

20. A. Ben Candland to Arthur Myers, Feb. 4, 1944, 208/465/2953, NACP.

21. Minutes of the Executive Committee meeting, Apr. 19, 1944, box 3, folder 7, and Kerr to Norton, Apr. 26, 1944, box 32, folder 8, both CBW Records, Princeton; "Basic Plan for Books," Sept. 20, 1944, 208/480/2997, NACP.

22. "Report upon Methods of Increasing Trade in British Books Overseas," BW 70/1, TNA.

23. Unwin, *Truth about Publishing,* 215–16; Unwin, *Truth about a Publisher,* 422.

24. Minutes of the meeting of the Books and Periodicals Committee, June 12, 1941, BW 70/1, and minutes of the meeting of the Books and Periodicals Committee, Feb. 12, 1942, BW 70/2; both TNA.

25. Minutes of the meeting of the Books and Periodicals Committee, July 31, 1941, BW 70/1, TNA.

26. Minutes of the meeting of the Books and Periodicals Committee, Apr. 9, 1942, BW 70/2, TNA.

27. On the British wartime book trade generally, see Holman, *Print for Victory.*

28. Evans, "English Books in War—& After," *Times* (London), May 27, 1944, in CBW Records, box 14, folder 5, Princeton.

29. E. Sykes, "Annual Report on Books and Periodicals," Feb. 16, 1942, BW 70/2, TNA.

30. Minutes of the meeting of the Books and Periodicals Committee, July 9, 1942, BW 70/2, TNA.

31. Minutes of the meeting of the Books and Periodicals Committee, July 9, 1942, and minutes of the meeting of the Books and Periodicals Committee, Sept. 10, 1942; both BW 70/2, TNA.

32. Minutes of the meeting of the Books and Periodicals Committee, Sept. 9, 1943, BW 70/2, TNA.

33. John Lehmann, "An International Writers' Conference," typescript, n.d. ca. Apr. 1943, of an article commissioned by the Ministry of Information for its Russian-language magazine, *Britanski Soyuznik,* and Marris Murray to John Lehmann, Apr. 26, 1943; both Lehmann Family Papers, box 35, folder 11, Princeton.

34. Minutes of the meeting of the Books and Periodicals Committee, Nov. 12, 1942, BW 70/2, TNA.

35. Ulich, *Can the Germans Be Reeducated?,* 3; "U.S. Takes School Planning Part for Europe, Asia in Post-War Era," *NY Times,* Oct. 2, 1943; "The United Nations Educational, Scientific and Cultural Organization (UNESCO): Creation," http://www.nationsencyclopedia.com/United-Nations-Related-Agencies/The-United-Nations-Educational-Scientific-and-Cultural-Organization-UNESCO-CREATION.html.

36. "Educators Urge World Committee," *NY Times,* Oct. 9, 1943; "U.S. To Help Build War-Torn Schools," *NY Times,* Apr. 1, 1944.

37. "U.S. Takes School Planning Part for Europe, Asia in Post-War Era," *NY Times,* Oct. 2, 1943.

38. "Remembering Jack Fobes," http://auhighlights.blogspot.com/2006/10/jack-fobes-lien-link-memorial-articles.html, consulted Nov. 15, 2006; Donaldson, *Archibald MacLeish,* 376; "Fulbright Will Head Talks on Education," *NY Times,* Apr. 7, 1944.

39. "Historical Context," http://portal.unesco.org/education/en/ev.php-URL_ID=9021&URL_DO=DO_TOPIC&URL_SECTION=201.html.

40. Pat Allen to Edward Barrett, June 8, 1944, 208/464/2949, NACP.

41. M. R. D. Foot, "Political Warfare Executive," in I. C. B. Dear, ed., *The Oxford Companion to World War II* (Oxford and New York: Oxford University Press, paperback edition, 2001), 709.

42. Cruickshank, *Fourth Arm,* 149.

43. Sylvain Mangeot to Col. Sutton, Apr. 20, 1943, FO 898/435, TNA.

44. Mr. Paniguian to Mangeot, Apr. 21, 1943, FO 898/435, TNA.

45. West, "Books for Liberated Europe," 3–6; reported in *PW,* Mar. 4, 1944, 1022ff.

46. Minutes of the meeting of the Books and Periodicals Committee, May 14, 1942, BW 70/2, TNA.

47. Rinehart to Norton, Mar. 9, 1944, referencing an earlier letter to Kerr, W. W. Norton II Papers, box 2, Columbia; minutes of the Executive Committee meeting, Mar. 29, 1944, CBW Records, box 3, folder 7, Princeton.

48. Paraphrase of cable from Gen. McChrystal to Barrett and Bernard, n.d. [1943], 208/464/2951A, NACP.

49. Fred Schwed Jr. to Joseph Barnes, Apr. 13, 1943, 208/6B/5, NACP; Bishop, "Overseas Branch," 81–82.

50. "Work of the Book Section," Apr. 30, 1943, and "Operational Procedures for Books," Oct. 27, 1943; both 208/6B/5, NACP.

51. A. Ben Candland to George Snell, Dec. 18, 1943; Joseph Barnes to all bureau chiefs, Dec. 21, 1943; both 208/6B/5, NACP.

52. Col. Ray L. Trautman, in "Third Annual Meeting of the Council on Books in Wartime," Feb. 1, 1945, CBW Records, box 1, folder 15, Princeton.

53. Vincenzo Petrullo and Trevor Hill to Edward Barrett, Apr. 5, 1944, 208/415/806, NACP.

54. See *OWI in the ETO,* 18.

55. Petrullo and Hill to Barrett, Apr. 5, 1944, 208/415/806, NACP. See also Gerson and Michon, eds., *History of the Book in Canada* 3: 201–2.

56. Petrullo and Hill to Barrett, Apr. 5, 1944, 208/415/806, NACP.

57. Samuel T. Williamson to all bureau division chiefs, Mar. 18, 1944, 208/465/2953, NACP.

58. First draft, "History, Bureau of Publications, Overseas Branch, Office of War Information," Nov. 1944, 208/6H/1, NACP.

59. "Book Operations Plan April to June 30, 1944," Apr. 12, 1944, 208/464/2949, NACP.

60. Petrullo and Hill to Edward Barrett, Apr. 5, 1944, 208/415/806, NACP. See also minutes of the meeting of the Advisory Committee on Books for France, Apr. 20, 1944, 208/415/806, NACP.

61. "Book Operations Plan, April to June 30, 1944," Apr. 12, 1944, 208/464/2949, NACP. See also Mildred E. Allen to members of the New York Review Board, Apr. 10, 1944, and Apr. 18, 1944, "copying a report of the Book Section of the London Office dated April 5th and distributed by the Outpost Bureau on April 17th"; both 208/415/806, NACP. See also minutes of the Executive Committee meeting, Apr. 12, 1944, CBW Records, box 3, folder 7, Princeton. For a view challenging the need to match the British program, while advocating relying largely on commercial publishers, see T. L. Barnard to Barrett, Apr. 16, 1944, 208/464/2951, NACP.

62. Copy of a memorandum from Williamson, Apr. 15, 1944, in Mildred E. Allen to members of the New York Review Board, Apr. 16, 1944, 208/415/806, NACP.

CHAPTER 5

1. "Book Operations Plan, April to June 30, 1944," Apr. 12, 1944, and Chester Kerr to W. W. Norton, Apr. 17, 1944; both CBW Records, box 14, folder 3, Princeton; "Monthly Progress Report," May 6, 1944, 208/464/2949, NACP.

2. Mildred E. Allen to New York Review Board, Apr. 10, 1944, copying a letter from Ronald Freelander in London to Samuel Williamson, Apr. 1, 1944, 208/415/806, NACP; Kerr to Norton, Apr. 26, 1944, CBW Records, box 32, folder 8, Princeton.

3. Memorandum by Williamson, Apr. 15, 1944, quoted in memorandum from Mildred E. Allen to New York Review Board, Apr. 16, 1944, 208/415/806, and Williamson to Washington Review Board, Aug. 14, 1944, 208/415/807; both NACP.

4. Ballou, *Council*, 85.

5. Minutes of the Executive Committee meeting, Apr. 19, 1944, CBW Records, box 3, folder 7, Princeton.

6. Minutes of the Executive Committee meeting, Mar. 15, 1944, CBW Records, box 3, folder 7, Princeton; Ballou, *Council*, 83–84.

7. Minutes of the Executive Committee meeting, Mar. 22, 1944, CBW Records, box 3, folder 7, Princeton.

8. Minutes of the Executive Committee meeting, Mar. 29, 1944, CBW Records, box 3, folder 7, Princeton.

9. Minutes of the Executive Committee meeting, Apr. 5, 1944, CBW Records, box 3, folder 7, Princeton.

10. Minutes of the Executive Committee meeting, Apr. 19, 1944, CBW Records, box 3, folder 7, Princeton.

11. Kerr to Norton, Apr. 20, 1944, 208/464/2951A, NACP.

12. On consolidation propaganda, see Thomson, *Overseas Information Service*, 106–7.

13. Minutes of the Executive Committee meeting, Apr. 26, 1944, CBW Records, box 3, folder 7, Princeton.

14. Excerpts from a letter from Norton to Elmer Davis, May 19, 1944, 208/464/2951A, NACP.

15. Kerr to Norton, Apr. 26, 1944, CBW Records, box 32, folder 8, Princeton. Kerr was present at the meeting on Apr. 26, when CBW considered his proposal. Minutes of the Executive Committee meeting, Apr. 26, 1944, CBW Records, box 3, folder 7, Princeton. See also Ballou, *Council*, 83–94. On Stern, see Tebbel, *Between Covers*, 344–45.

16. Ballou, *Council*, 86.

17. Davis to Norton, Apr. 26, 1944, 208/464/2951A, NACP; minutes of the Executive Committee meeting, Apr. 26, 1944, CBW Records, box 33, folder 4, Princeton; Kerr to N. Locker, June 23, 1944, 208/464/2951A, NACP; minutes of the Executive Committee meeting July 5, 1944, CBW Records, box 3, folder 8, Princeton.

18. Rinehart, Best, and Sloane to Norton, May 3, 1944, CBW Records, box 32, folder 8, Princeton.

19. "Basic Plan for Books," Sept. 20, 1944, 208/480/2997, NACP.

20. "Book Section Monthly Progress Report," June 19, 1944, 208/464/2951, and Williamson to Edward W. Barrett, July 17, 1944, 208/6B/3, both NACP; minutes of the Executive Committee meeting, July 12, 1944, and minutes of the Executive Committee meeting, Aug. 9, 1944, both CBW Records, box 3, folder 8, Princeton.

21. Guinzburg to Kerr, Apr. 29, 1944, 208/464/2949, NACP. See also Althea Chantre to Vincenzo Petrullo for Kerr, Apr. 26, 1944, copying cable from Guinzburg-Freelander in London, 208/464/2949, NACP.

22. De Graff to Kerr, May 9, 1944, 208/464/2951A, NACP.

23. Ballou, *Council*, 89.

24. Because OWI was prohibited by law from making payments to its contractors in advance of delivery, it needed a source of start-up funds. "Report to the Chairman, Council on Books in Wartime from the Committee on Overseas Editions," May 3, 1944, box 33, folder 12, and minutes, Management Committee meeting, Aug. 30, 1944, box 33, folder 6. The agreement was contained in a letter from the chairman of OEI to de Graff, Sept. 14, 1944, box 32, folder 8. All CBW Records, Princeton.

25. Mildred E. Allen to members of New York Review Board, Apr. 10, 1944, copying letter from Freelander to Williamson, Apr. 1, 1944, 208/415/806, and minutes of the Executive Committee meeting, Apr. 26, 1944, CBW Records, box 33, folder 7, Princeton.

26. Kerr to Althea Chantre, text for cable to Guinzburg, Apr. 20, 1944, 208/464/2949, NACP.

27. Chantre to Kerr, Apr. 26, 1944, copying cable from Guinzburg-Freelander to Vincenzo Petrullo, 208/464/2949, NACP.

28. Lehmann-Haupt et al., *Book in America*, 409.

29. Allen to members of New York Review Board, Apr. 10, 1944, copying letter from Freelander to Williamson, Apr. 1, 1944, 208/415/806; Kerr to Chantre, cable to Guinzburg, London, Apr. 20, 1944, 208/464/2949; Chantre to Petrullo for Kerr, cable #24755 April from Guinzburg-Freelander in London, Apr. 26, 1944, 208/464/2949; all NACP.

30. Chantre to Petrullo for Chester Kerr, cable #24755 April from Guinzburg/Freelander in London, Apr. 26, 1944, and Norton to Davis, May 19, 1944; both 208/464/2951A NACP.

31. *NY Times,* May 22, 1944.

32. "Extracts from Hearings before the Subcommittee of the Committee on Appropriations…June 1, 1944," 208/6B/4, NACP.

33. Ballou, *Council,* 87–89; Cowan/Williamson/Kerr to Hamblet/Guinzburg/Freelander, June 3, 1944; and Chantre to Hill, June 9, 1944, transmitting text of cable from Cowan/Williamson/Kerr to Hamblet/Guinzburg/Freelander, all 208/464/2949, NACP. See also minutes of the Management Committee meeting, OEI, Aug. 30, 1944, box 33, folder 6; "Notes of meeting held in Pocket Books' office," Sept. 7, 1944, box 33, folder 7; and chairman, OEI, to de Graff, Sept. 14, 1944, box 32, folder 8; Sloane to de Graff, Oct. 5, 1944, box 32, folder 9; all CBW Records, Princeton.

34. Chantre to Hill, Aug. 15, 1944, transcribing cable from Guinzburg in London, 208/464/2949, NACP.

35. Williamson to Washington Review Board, Aug. 14, 1944, 208/415/807, NACP.

36. Williamson to Eva Polak, New York Review Board, Sept. 11, 1944, 208/464/2951A, NACP.

37. Kerr to Sloane, Oct. 4, 1944, 208/464/2949; "Special Report on Overseas Book Program," in "Monthly Progress Report, October 1–November 1, 1944," 208/413/2201, both NACP.

38. "Monthly Progress Report—May 6th, [1944]," 208/464/2949, NACP.

39. Memorandum, Chantre to Williamson and Hill, Aug. 4, 1944, transcribing cable from Hamblet/Guinzburg, 208/464/2949, NACP.

40. "Revised Draft of Operational Memorandum for Books," [ca. Aug.–Sept. 1944], 208/464/2949, NACP.

41. Hill to Allen, Aug. 14, 1944; memo, n.d.; both 208/464/2939, NACP.

42. "Plan for Belgian Publications," n.d. [ca. Aug. 1944], 208/464/2949, NACP.

43. Webber, London, to Williamson and Hill, Sept. 22, 1944, 208/464/2949, NACP.

44. This would explain why Transatlantic Editions are not mentioned in Ballou's official history of the Council on Books in Wartime and its subsidiaries.

45. Ronald Freelander to Kerr, July 6, 1944, 208/464/2949, NACP. On the use of the USIS name for OWI overseas, see Bishop, "Overseas Branch," 272, and Green, *American Propaganda Abroad,* 17.

46. The English-only imprint was "for uniformity." Kerr to Freelander, Aug. 30, 1944, 208/464/2949, NACP.

47. Hill to Guinsburg, July 10, 1944, 208/464/2949, NACP. See also Mahl, *Desperate Deception,* 64–65, 171, 195.

48. Guinzburg to Jean Parket, text for cable to Hamblet, Sept. 5, 1944, 208/464/2949, NACP; Ballou, *Council,* 88–89.

49. "Monthly Progress Report, November 28th to December 29th, 1944," 208/413/2201, NACP.

50. Agenda and minutes, P.W.E./O.W.I./PWD Tripartite Committee, Overlord Plan FO 898/375, TNA.

51. Freelander to Hill, Apr. 3, 1945, 208/464/2949, NACP, and Kerr to Ogden, Apr. 30, 1945, CBW Records, box 33, folder 1, Princeton.

52. Kerr to Milton MacKaye, Feb. 13, 1945, 208/464/1749, NACP.

53. Minutes of the Board of Directors meeting, Aug. 9, 1945, CBW Records, box 2, folder 10, Princeton.

CHAPTER 6

1. Kerr to Rex Stout, Dec. 9, 1944, 208/44/2949, NACP.

2. Samuel T. Williamson to Kerr, May 28, 1944, 208/464/2949, NACP; Ballou, *Council,* 92; "Special Report on Overseas Book Program," ca. Oct. 1944, 208/413/2201, NACP.

3. Minutes of the Executive Committee meeting, Mar. 28, 1945, box 3, folder 10, CBW Records, Princeton. A list of OEs and TEs is in appendix A.

4. Ballou, *Council,* 92; handwritten memo, Kerr to Williamson, May 28, [1944]; cable, Cowan/Williamson/Kerr to Hamblet/Guinzburg/Freelander, June 3, 1944; cable, Hamblet/Guinzburg/Freelander to Trevor Hill, June 9, 1944; all 208/464/2849, NACP. See also minutes of the annual meeting of the CBW, Jan. 30, 1946, CBW Records, box 1, folder 16, Princeton.

5. I was fortunate to acquire a complete set of the Overseas Editions and Transatlantic Editions, which had belonged to Chester Kerr.

6. "Revised Draft of Operational Memorandum for Books," n.d. [ca. Aug. 1944], 208/464/2949, NACP.

7. Handwritten annotations on Kerr to A. Ben Candland, Feb. 13, 1945; "List of OWI Materials for Italian Prisoners of War" and "List of OWI Materials for German Prisoners of War," ca. winter 1945, all 208/467/2060; "German Committee Minutes," May 4–5, 1945, 208/404/803. All NACP. See chapter 11.

8. Dave Wilson to Washington Review Board, Nov. 30, 1944, 208/415/807, NACP.

9. Ibid.

10. "British Public Opinion and the United States," Ministry of Information, Home Intelligence, Special Report No. 8, Feb. 23, 1942, INF 1/102, TNA.

11. Wieviorka, *Normandy,* 110.

12. Wallace Carroll to Edward W. Barrett, June 14, 1945, Harper & Row, Series II, Columbia.

13. Warburg, *Unwritten Treaty,* 99; Winkler, *Politics of Propaganda,* 59; and Koppes and Black, *Hollywood Goes to War,* 91–93.

14. Dizard, *Inventing Public Diplomacy,* 21–22.

15. *PW,* June 2, 1945, 2191–92.

16. Dave Wilson to Washington Review Board, Nov. 30, 1944, 208/415/807, NACP.

17. Williamson to Barrett, May 10, 1944, 208/415/807, NACP.

18. "Procedure for Selection of Books for Inclusion in Overseas Editions Series," May 31, 1944, 208/464/2949, NACP.

19. Rubin, *Making of Middlebrow Culture,* 110–47; Radway, *A Feeling for Books,* 176–83.

20. Barrett to Wallace Carroll, May 13, 1944; Althea Chantre to Williamson, quoting teletype #606 May from Carroll in Washington; both 208/415/2949, NACP. Kerr to Philip Van Doren Stern, June 1, 1944, 208/464/2951A; "Members of Outside Advisory Committee Serving OWI in Selection of Overseas Editions," 208/464/2949; both NACP.

21. Kerr to E. Trevor Hill, Aug. 16, 1944, 208/464/2949, NACP.

22. "Procedure for Selection of Books for Inclusion in Overseas Editions Series," 208/464/2949, NACP; Kerr to Stern, Aug. 15, 1944, CBW Records, box 14, folder 4, Princeton.

23. Ferdinand Kuhn Jr. to Senator James M. Mead, June 5, 1944, 208/464/2951A; Barrett to Pat Allen, June 8, 1944, 208/464/2949; both NACP.

24. Cable, Kerr to Freelander, June 3, 1944, 208/464/2949, NACP.

25. Robert Hollander, draft of history of Allied psychological warfare in northwestern France, 58–59, 331/87/16, NACP.

26. Kerr to Rex Stout, Dec. 9, 1944, 208/44/2949, NACP.

27. Williamson to Louis G. Cowan, May 24, 1944, 208/467/2060, NACP.

28. Sidney Sulkin, "The OWI and Book-Hungry Europe," *NY Times Book Review,* Oct. 28, 1945.

29. S. Spencer Scott, "Memorandum on Royalties," Nov. 29, 1944, CBW Records, box 3, folder 8, Princeton.

30. Carol Lunetta to Capt. K. Carrick, Jan. 13, 1945, 208/6B/3; "Extracts from Hearings before the Subcommittee of the Committee on Appropriations…June 1, 1944," 208/6B/4; both NACP.

31. De Graff to Kerr, May 9, 1944, 208/464/2951A, NACP.

32. "Leaflets, Publications and Books: Instructions on Policy and Practice," ca. mid-1943, FO 898/435, TNA.

33. Chantre to Hill, quoting cable from Cowan/Williamson/Kerr to Hamblet/Guinzburg/Freelander, June 9, 1944, 208/464/2949; Memorandum, Mar. 24, 1945, "Minutes of the German Committee Meeting on March 23, in New York," 208/404/803; both NACP.

34. Kerr to J. C. Furnas, Oct. 10, 1944, 208/464/2949, NACP; Furnas, *How America Lives* (New York: Overseas Editions, Inc., 1945), vii–xi.

35. Chester Kerr to Philip Van Doren Stern, Oct. 30, 1944, 208/464/2949, NACP. Van Doren's *Benjamin Franklin* also was published in the Éditions Transatlantique series, with no indication of abridgment.

36. Minutes of the Overseas Branch Review Board Book meeting, June 22, 1944, 208/415/807, NACP.

37. Minutes of the Overseas Branch Review Board Book meeting, June 22, 1944, 208/415/807, NACP.

38. "Books Currently Being Considered for Overseas Editions," July 5, 1944, CBW Records, box 32, folder 6, Princeton.

39. Natalie Gammon to Susan Klein, July 15, [1944], CBW Records, box 35, folder 10, Princeton.

40. "Recommendations of Subcommittee on Books Herewith Submitted for Review Board's Approval," n.d., 208/464/2951, NACP.

41. July 23, 1944, 208/464/2949, NACP.

42. See Allen to Barrett, June 8, 1944, and Lehmann-Haupt to Guinzburg, Nov. 9, 1944; both 208/464/2949; and "Books in German," Dec. 11, 1944, 208/404/803; all NACP.

43. "British Public Opinion and the United States," Ministry of Information, Home Intelligence, Special Report No. 8, Feb. 23, 1942, INF 1/102, TNA.

44. Upton Sinclair to Benjamin W. Huebsch, Viking Press, June 12, 1944; and Sinclair to Ryo Namikawa, Apr. 12, 1948, both box 1, Viking Press Manuscripts, Lilly.

45. Review Branch, OPMG, Washington, to Review Branch, New York, June 20, 1945, 389/459A/1646, NACP.

46. Press release, July 27, 1945, CBW Records, box 33, folder 2, Princeton.

47. Mildred E. Allen, New York Review Board, to Alice Curran, Washington Review Board, Aug. 6, 1944; M. J. van Schravan to Wallace C. Carroll, [ca. Aug. 1944]; both 208/415/807, NACP.

48. David Wilson to Washington Review Board, Apr. 18, 1945, 208/6E/2, NACP.

49. Chantre to Williamson and Hill, Aug. 4, 1944, transcribing cable from Hamblet and Guinzburg in London; Williamson to Barrett and Bernard, Aug. 5, 1944; Chantre to Hill, Aug. 15, 1944, transcribing cable from Guinzburg in London; all 208/464/2949, NACP.

50. Hill to Allen, Aug. 14, 1944, 208/464/2949, NACP.

51. See appendix A for a list of the titles.

52. "Working Plan for P.W.D. in Holland [draft]," June 12, 1944, 331/87/11, NACP.

53. Notes on meeting between Davis and book publishers at the New York Public Library, Nov. 3, 1943, CBW Records, box 14, folder 3, Princeton.

54. "Revised Draft of Operational Memorandum for Books," n.d. [ca. Aug. 1944], 208/464/2949, NACP. Another document indicated five thousand copies as the run in London for the Dutch titles; 208/464/2949, NACP. Still another indicates fifteen thousand copies; 208/413/2201, NACP.

55. Book Section, London, "Monthly Progress Report," May 6, and June 5, 1944, 208/415/807, NACP; *PW,* Oct. 9, 1943, 1442–43.

56. See Claude A. Buss, OWI, San Francisco, to Monroe E. Deutsch, University of California, July 13, 1944, and Barrett to Buss, June 18, 1944; both 208/488&489/3104, NACP.

57. Buss to John K. Fairbank, June 2, 1944, and Buss to David MacDougall, British Political Warfare Executive Mission, San Francisco, Apr. 4, 1944; both 208/488&489/3104, NACP.

58. See chapter 2.

59. "Publications Plan for China," Sept. 14, 1944, 208/464/2951, NACP.

60. Ibid.

61. W. L. Holland and Catherine Porter to Hill or Kerr, Nov. 8, 1944, 208/464/2949, NACP.

62. "Publications Plan for China," Sept. 14, 1944, 208/464/2951, NACP.

63. Sloane, "To Chungking," pp. g-nn, box 6, Sloane Papers, Princeton; minutes of the Executive Committee meeting, Mar. 8, 1944, CBW Records, box 3, folder 7, Princeton.

64. The best sellers were Carl Van Doren's *Benjamin Franklin* (on the lists in 1938), Hemingway's *For Whom the Bell Tolls* (1940–41), William Saroyan's *The Human Comedy* (1943), Walter Lippmann's *U.S. Foreign Policy* (1943), Ernie Pyle's *Here Is Your War* (1943), the same author's *Brave Men* (1944–45), and Catherine Drinker Bowen's *Yankee from Olympus* (1944). Korda, *Making the List,* 72, 88–89. All but the Van Doren biography of Franklin also appear as "Best Sellers" or "Better Sellers" on lists compiled on a different basis in Mott, *Golden Multitudes,* 314–15. Lippmann's best seller was paired with his *U.S. War Aims* in the Overseas and Transatlantic versions; both of Pyle's best sellers were published together by OEI under the title *G.I. Joe.*

65. Among BOMC selections were Constance Rourke's *Audubon* and the books by Van Doren, Hemingway, Saroyan, and Bowen. List of BOMC selections, 208/464/2949, NACP.

66. D. F. Fleming, *NY Times Book Review,* Apr. 9, 1944.

67. Orville Prescott, *NY Times,* Oct. 30, 1942.

68. Frederick L. Schuman, *NY Times Book Review,* Nov. 28, 1945.

69. Stegner, *NY Times Book Review,* Feb. 28, 1943; Commager, *NY Times Book Review,* Oct. 9, 1938.

70. *NY Times Book Review,* Nov. 29, 1942.

CHAPTER 7

1. Quoted in Hitchcock, *Bitter Road to Freedom,* 170.

2. Dower, *Embracing Defeat,* 39–40.

3. "Draft Operational Plan for Germany," fourth draft, n.d., 389/459A/1627, NACP.

4. Marlene J. Mayo, "Civil Censorship and Media Control in Early Occupied Japan: From Minimum to Stringent Surveillance," in Wolfe, ed., *Americans as Proconsuls,* 285.

5. A French Gallup poll named the United States as the "nation that will help France rise again after the war." Jackson to McClure, ca. Sept. 1944, FO 898/391, TNA.

6. See chapter 12.

7. "Operational Plan for Germany," third draft, Jan. 16, 1945, 208/404/803, NACP; William Harlan Hale, PWD/SHAEF, to Col. William S. Paley and Mr. Schneider, June 18, 1945, 260/16(A1)16/254, NACP.

8. McClure to the director-generals of the British PID and MoI and the directors of the London offices of the U.S. OWI and OSS, Aug. 8, 1944; Oliver [illeg.] to Sir Cyril Radcliffe, MoI, Sept. 4, 1944; both INF 1/987, TNA. See also memorandum, Sub-Committee to Deal with Books for Germany to the Joint Publications Committee, Sept. 6, 1944, U.S. copy, 208/464/2949, NACP, British copy, FO 898/471, TNA; and PWD/SHAEF to Chief of Staff, "Prohibition of Publication in and Importation to Germany by Allied and Neutral Nationals, of Newspapers, Books, and Periodicals," Apr. 1945, 331/6/3, NACP.

9. "London—Monthly Progress Report—May 6th—Book Section," May—June 1944, 208/415/807, NACP.

10. Summary of policy toward purchasing books from Sweden and Switzerland, n.d., 260/16(A1)16/254, NACP; Packard, *Neither Friend Nor Foe,* 155; Leitz, *Sympathy for the Devil,* passim.

11. Mildred E. Allen to Wallace Carroll et al., "Minutes of German Committee Meeting on February 17th in Washington," Feb. 20, 1945, 208/404/803, NACP.

12. Allen to members of the German Committee, Mar. 3, 1945, 208/404/803, NACP.

13. Agwar/Marshall to SHAEF PWD/Eisenhower, May 16, 1945, 331/6/3, NACP.

14. PWD/SHAEF to Chief of Staff, "Prohibition of Publication in and Importation to Germany by Allied and Neutral Nationals, of Newspapers, Books, and Periodicals," Apr. 1945, 331/6/3, NACP.

15. "Points on Which Recommendations Are Required by PID and OWI in Connection with Books for Germany," Mar. 15, 1945, 260/16(A1)/254; "Minutes of German Committee Meeting on February 17th in Washington," Feb. 20, 1945, 208/404/803; Maj. Douglas Waples to C. D. Jackson, Mar. 29, 1945, and Paley to Gen. Robert A. McClure, Apr. 4, 1945; both 260/16(A1)16/254; all NACP.

16. Waples to Jackson, Mar. 29, 1945, 260/16(A1)16/254, NACP.

17. "Operational Plan for Germany," second draft, Jan. 2, 1945, 208/464/2949, NACP.

18. "Operational Plan for Germany," third draft, Jan. 16, 1945; "Book List to Implement the Long-Range Directive of Dec. 4, 1944," draft, Feb. 28, 1945; both 208/404/803, NACP.

19. Norman Cousins to Harold Guinzburg, Apr. 20, 1945, 208/404/803, NACP. On the policy of unconditional surrender, see Fleming, *New Dealers' War,* 180–88, and Goedde, *GIs and Germans,* 12–13, 60.

20. "Draft Operational Plan for Germany," fourth draft, 389/459A/1627, NACP.

21. "De-Nazifying Reich Is Tough OWI Job," article by Associated Press correspondent Trudi McCullough, *Milwaukee Journal,* June 10, 1945, clipping in 208/356&357/1721, NACP.

22. Allen to Wallace Carroll et al., "Minutes of the German Committee Meeting on March 23 in New York," Mar. 24, 1945, 208/404/803, NACP.

23. Kerr to Allen, Oct. 5, 1944, 208/464/2949, NACP.

24. "Overseas Editions for Germany," minutes of the German Committee meeting, Apr. 6, 1945, 208/404/803, NACP.

25. "Statement Prepared for German Committee Meeting, New York, Apr. 20, 1945," 208/404/803, NACP.

26. "Operational Plan for Germany," fourth draft, n.d., 208/459A/1627, NACP.

27. Hellmut Lehmann-Haupt to Guinzburg, Nov. 9, 1944, 208/464/2949, NACP.

28. "Operational Plan for Germany," fourth draft, n.d., 389/459A/1627, NACP.

29. Minutes of the Joint PWD/OWI/MOI/PID Publications Committee meeting, Aug. 10, 1944, FO 898/471, TNA; "Draft Operational Plan for Germany," fourth draft, n.d., 389/459A/1627, NACP.

30. Psychological Warfare Division, "Report on the Books 'Sub-Committee,'" [ca. fall 1944], FO 898/471, TNA.

31. See, for example, Allan Nevins and Henry Steele Commager, *Die Geschichte der Vereinigten Staaten* (New York: Overseas Editions, Inc., n.d.) and Bernard Jaffe, *Männer der Forschung in Amerika* (New York: Overseas Editions, Inc., n.d.).

32. Fiedler, *Enemy among Us,* 6, 11.

33. Keefer, *Italian Prisoners of War,* 28.

34. Robin, *Barbed-Wire College,* 6.

35. Ibid., 18.

36. Cazden, *German Exile Literature,* 122.

37. Robin, *Barbed-Wire College,* 18.

38. Ibid., 22–23.

39. Krammer, *Nazi Prisoners of War,* 194–95.

40. Ibid., 195.

41. Keefer, *Italian Prisoners,* 52–54; Davison to Italian service units, Aug. 22, 1945, 389/459A/1647, NACP.

42. The unit began as the Special Projects Branch (SPB), but was upgraded to a division in December 1944. See Lt. Col. Edward Davison to Col. Joseph I. Greene, Dec. 14, 1944, 389/459A/1645, NACP. The name Special Projects Division (SPD) is used here throughout.

43. *PW,* Feb. 10, 1945, 749.

44. "Final Reports, Victory Book Campaign 1942–1943," (1944), 19, Publishers' Weekly Papers, box 2, Princeton.

45. Simmons, *Swords into Plowshares,* 20.

46. Waters, *Lone Star Stalag,* 13, 37–38.

47. Robin, *Barbed-Wire College,* 91–92.

48. Davison, "Criteria for the Selection of Books," Oct. 20, 1944, 389/459A/1647, NACP. See also Robin, *Barbed-Wire College,* 92.

49. Krammer, *Nazi Prisoners,* 207. One list of unapproved titles covered eleven pages and included works by Thomas Carlyle, Houston S. Chamberlain, Friedrich Nietzsche, Romain Rolland, Oswald Spengler, Alfred von Tirpitz, and Emperor Wilhelm I. 389/459A/1645 NACP. Another list, 196 pages long, is in 389/459A/1648.

50. See list in appendix B.

51. "These were printed in cooperation with the 'Infantry Journal' although its name is not used." Ben Gedalecia to Guinzburg, June 11, 1945, 208/407/2192, NACP. Within OWI, the BNW books were known as "Infantry Journal books." Gedalecia to Robert Paxton, Nov. 16, 1945, 208/406/2191.

52. Krammer, *Nazi Prisoners,* 79, 83–84.

53. Lt. (later Capt.) Walter Schoenstedt to Lt. Col. Edward Davison, Oct. 19, 1944, 389/459A/1648, NACP.

54. Robin, *Barbed-Wire College,* 46–48.

55. Greene to Davison, Nov. 2, 1944, 389/459A/1648, NACP.

56. Davis, *Two-Bit Culture,* 20–25, 58–59; Lewis, *Penguin Special,* 212; Enoch to Norton, Dec. 10, 1942, CBW Records, box 4, folder 1, Princeton. See also Enoch, *Memoirs.*

57. Greene to Davison, Feb. 8, 1945, 389/459A/1648, NACP.

58. Davis, *Two-Bit Culture,* 56–63; Lewis, *Penguin Special,* 212–13.

59. Cazden, *German Exile Literature,* 10.

60. Schoenstedt to Davison, Feb. 5, 1945; Davison to Greene, Feb. 6, 1945; Greene to Davison, Feb. 8, 1945; all 389/459A/1648, NACP.

61. Lerch to Chief, Army Exchange Service, Dec. 12, 1944, 389/459A/1648, NACP.

62. Davison to Greene, Dec. 14, 1945, 389/459A/1648, NACP.

63. Enclosure, Davison to Chief, Materials and Distribution Branch, and Chief, Field Services Branch, Dec. 14, 1944, 389/459A/1645, NACP.

64. Paul Mueller, Schoenhof Publishers, to Davison, Aug. 18, 1945, 389/459A/1647, NACP.

65. "Justification of the Selection for the First Series of the Buecherreihe Neue Welt," Apr. 3, 1945, 389/459A/1645, NACP.

66. Davison, "Statement for Press Concerning Publication of Buecherreihe Neue Welt," to General Bryan, May 10, 1945, 389/459A/1648, NACP.

67. In discussing Bücherreihe Neue Welt in his book on the reeducation of German POWs in the United States, Ron Robin quotes from the brief statements about the titles taken from the "Justification for the First Series" document. He also provides deft readings of the contents of many of the books, noting the ways in which their texts might have sounded various themes that OPMG wanted German POWs to hear. There is no evidence, however, that deliberations anywhere near as sophisticated as Robin's analyses actually took place within the SPD. If Robin noted the second document (the press release), he makes no reference to it. In fact, he makes no mention of Bermann-Fischer and his contributions to the project at all. By missing the complex publication history of Bücherreihe Neue Welt, Robin failed to realize how constrained strategically and operationally the officers of SPD actually were in choosing books for the program. Whatever the foundation of the program was—pragmatism perhaps, even opportunism—it was not "the endorsement of the 'Great Books' tradition" that the peacetime humanities professors who ran the program had brought along, as Robin asserts. Robin, *Barbed-Wire College*, 96–105.

68. For a prosopography of the refugee writers, see Davie, *Refugees in America*, 333–44. See also Krammer, *Nazi Prisoners*, 207.

69. See list in Leonidas E. Hill, "The Nazi Attack on Un-German Literature, 1933–1945," in Rose, ed., *Holocaust and the Book*, 13. See also Krammer, *Nazi Prisoners*, 207.

70. Greene to Davison, Nov. 2, 1944, and Schoenstedt to Davison, Nov. 3, 1944; both 389/459A/1648, NACP.

71. It was the only one of the twenty-four titles not on the list of books ready for production. Greene to Bermann-Fischer Verlag, Jan. 9, 1945, 389/459A/1648, NACP.

72. Maj. Gen. J. A. Ulio to Commanding Generals, Jan. 23, 1945, 389/459A/1648, NACP; "Re-Education of Enemy Prisoners of War," Historical Monograph, OPMG, Office of the Chief of Military History, 1945, 87–88, copy in the Center for Military History, Fort McNair, Washington, D.C.

73. Lerch to Chief of Army Exchange Service, Dec. 12, 1944; Davison to Greene, Dec. 18, 1944; Maj. McKnight to Maj. Gemmill, Dec. 26, 1944; all 389/459A/1648, NACP.

74. Greene to Bermann-Fischer, Jan. 9, 1945, 389/459A/1648, NACP.

75. Ulio to commanding generals, Jan. 23, 1945; Greene to Erich Maria Remarque, June 9, 1945; both 389/459A/1648, NACP.

76. Davison to Greene, Feb. 17, 1945, 389/459A/1648, NACP.

77. Bermann-Fischer to Schoenstedt, Mar. 22, 1945, 389/459A/1648, NACP.

78. McKnight to Capt. Richards and Capt. Banke, June 4, 1945, 389/459A/1648, NACP.

79. Ulio to commanding generals, Jan. 23, 1945, 389/459A/1648, NACP.

80. Lt. Charles G. Stefan, to SPD, June 8, 1945, 389/459A/1646; Robin, *Barbed-Wire College*, 105.

81. Maj. Maxwell S. McKnight, acting director, SPD, to Gen. Bryan, June 6, 1945, 389/459A/1646, NACP.

82. Davison to Greene, Jan. 20, 1945, 389/459A/1645, NACP.

83. Cazden, *German Exile Literature*, 72.

84. Krammer, *Nazi Prisoners*, 208–9; Jones, *Autobiography*, 217–18.

85. Capt. Robert F. Richards to Greene, Apr. 25, 1945, 389/459A/1645, NACP.

86. Richards to Greene, July 13, 1945, 389/459A/1646, NACP.

87. Lt. Col. W. L. Wolcott to SPD, June 25, 1945; Davison to director, Prisoner of War Operations Division, Sept. 21, 1945; both 389/459A/1647, NACP.

88. ASF circular, No. 383, Oct. 11, 1945, 389/459A/1647, NACP.

89. Richards to Chiefs, Transportation, Apr. 4, 1946, 389/459A/1648, NACP.

90. Richards to Chief, Army Exchange Division, June 17, 1946, 389/459A/1648, NACP.

91. Greene to Davison, Nov. 2, 1944, 389/459A/1648, NACP.

92. A preliminary description based on an examination of four titles in the series in the possession of the author: number one, Stephen Vincent Benét, *Amerika;* number ten,

Thomas Mann, *Achtung, Europa!;* number twenty-two, Carl Zuckmayer, *Ein Bauer aus Dem Taunus;* and number twenty-three, John Scott, *Jenseits des Ural.* I am indebted to Babette Gehnrich for the translation of the motto on the Benét cover.

93. Krammer, *Nazi Prisoners,* 208.

94. Robin, *Barbed-Wire College,* 106.

95. Krammer, *Nazi Prisoners,* 207–8; Robin, *Barbed-Wire College,* 105–6.

CHAPTER 8

1. Blanche Knopf to Harry Brown, May 18, 1945, Alfred A. Knopf Papers, Series III, Blanche Knopf, box 686, folder 6, HRC.

2. Archibald G. Ogden to W. B. Schnapper, Public Affairs Press, Nov. 28, 1944, CBW Records, box 36, folder 22, Princeton.

3. See contracts in title-by-title production files, CBW Records, boxes 33–38, Princeton. Sample contract is in 208/464/2951A, NACP.

4. O. W. Riegel to Edward J. Barrett, Aug. 2, 1944, 208/415/807, NACP.

5. W. Kenward Zucker to J. E. French, H. O. Houghton & Co., May 11, 1945, box 39, folder 15, CBW Records, Princeton.

6. Sanford Greenburger to Archibald Ogden, Dec. 8, 1944; Ogden to Greenburger, Dec. 12, 1944; both CBW Records, box 14, folder 9, Princeton.

7. http://www.frencheuropean.com/French%20Books/EMF.htm; Nettelbeck, *Forever French,* 58–66. See Okrent, *Great Fortune,* 192, 277, 411, 432.

8. Chester Kerr to C. Raymond Everitt, Little, Brown, and Co., Dec. 4, 1944, CBW Records, box 38, folder 5, Princeton.

9. Davie, *Refugees in America,* xvi. See also Coser, *Refugee Scholars.*

10. See various letters and curricula vitae, CBW Records, box 40, folder 7, Princeton.

11. Ballou, *Council,* 92.

12. Contract, Oct. 31, 1944, CBW Records, box 40, folder 6, Princeton.

13. Salary figures are in 208/480/2997&2999, NACP.

14. Memorandum, 208/6B/3, NACP.

15. See Charles Schulz to Zucker, Nov. 21, 1944, CBW Records, box 40, folder 7, Princeton.

16. Elizabeth Porter to Ogden, Sept. 26, 1944; Marian G. Canby to Ogden, Nov. 21, 1944; Canby to Ogden, Dec. 7, 1944, and Dec. 13, 1994; all CBW Records, box 40, folder 7, Princeton.

17. In many cases, the foreign origins of translators are explicit in their letters and curricula vitae, where available. In other cases, their handwriting, writing style, vocabulary, spelling, and punctuation style point to their European roots. Their names, by themselves, are strong, if not definitive, clues. See, for example, curricula vitae of Peter de Scandiano and Lucy Tal, and Inga Tuteur to Irene Rakosky, Oct. 25, 1944, and Frida Friedberg to CBW, Oct. 26, 1944; all CBW Records, box 40, folder 7, Princeton.

18. Kenneth T. Jackson, ed., *The Encyclopedia of New York City* (New Haven: Yale University Press and New York: New-York Historical Society, 1995), s.v. "Kew Gardens," 635.

19. Rochedieu to Ogden, Oct. 9, 1944, CBW Records, box 37, folder 7, Princeton. See also Roger Picard to Ogden, Nov. 25, 1944, CBW Records, box 40, folder 7, Princeton.

20. David to Rakosky, May 23, 1945, CBW Records, box 35, folder 2, Princeton.

21. Irene Rakosky to Kerr, Feb. 19, 1945, CBW Records, box 36, folder 9, Princeton.

22. Anderson, ed., *Hitler's Exiles,* 154; Fry, *Surrender on Demand,* photo between 114–15 and 187; Karina von Tippelskirch, "Hans Sahl: A Profile," www.logosjournal.com/issue_4.2/sahl_profile.htm; Varian Fry, "What Has Happened to Them Since," *PW,* June 23, 1945, 2436.

23. Aldo Caselli to CBW, July 15, 1944, CBW Records, box 35, folder 31, Princeton.

24. See, for example, Dow to Ogden, July 10, 1944, box 37, folder 27; Kerr to Ogden and Ogden to Caselli, both Aug. 3, 1944, box 35, folder 31; all CBW Records, Princeton.

25. Ogden to Boorsch, Aug. 28, 1944, CBW Records, box 37, folder 23, Princeton.

26. www.yalealumnimagazine.com/issues/2006_3/milestones.html.

27. Pinthus to Ogden, Feb. 24, 1944, CBW Records, box 35, folder 13, Princeton.

28. Pinthus to Ogden, March 10, 1945, and Ogden to Pinthus, Mar. 5, 1945, and Mar. 12, 1945; all CBW Records, box 36, folder 5, Princeton.

29. Telegram, Pinthus to Ogden, Mar. 27, 1945, CBW Records, box 36, folder 5, Princeton.

30. Grace Ernestine Ray, "*Books Abroad* in Wartime," *PW*, Mar. 22, 1941, 1291–94. On Pinthus, see www.ushmm.org/museum/exhibit/online/bookburning/author_detail. php?content=bbpinthu.xml.

31. A. Ben Candland to W. W. Norton, Aug. 4, 1944, CBW Records, box 40, folder 6, Princeton.

32. Kerr to Ogden, July 5, 1944, and Ogden to Paul E. Jacob, July 6, 1944; both CBW Records, box 38, folder 6, Princeton.

33. Kerr to Ogden, July 5, 1944, CBW Records, box 35, folder 22, Princeton.

34. Kerr to Ogden, Oct. 26, 1944, CBW Records, box 36, folder 14, Princeton.

35. *NY Times,* Oct. 6, 1981; Fry, *Surrender on Demand,* esp. 48–53; Fry, "What Has Happened to Them Since," *PW,* June 23, 1945, 2436.

36. Ogden to Possony, Jan. 5, 1945, CBW Records, box 40, folder 7, Princeton.

37. Obituary by Wolfgang Saxon, *NY Times,* May 2, 1995.

38. Gammon to Klein, July 13, 1944, box 37, folder 30; Ogden to Elbau, Oct. 31, 1944, box 36, folder 3; and Ogden to Pinthus, Nov. 14, 1944, box 36, folder 5; all CBW Records, Princeton.

39. Kerr to Ogden, Oct. 26, 1944, CBW Records, box 38, folder 2, Princeton.

40. Jacob to Ogden, July 10, 1944, CBW Records, box 38, folder 6, Princeton.

41. "In Memoriam: Domenico Vittorini," *Italica* 35 (1958): 77–82; Vittorini to Ogden, Sept. 10, 1944, and April 22, 1945, both CBW Records, box 35, folder 22, Princeton.

42. Rochedieu to Ogden, Aug. 30, 1944, CBW Records, box 37, folder 7, Princeton.

43. Ogden to Picard, Nov. 22, 1944, CBW Records, box 36, folder 8, Princeton.

44. Denkinger to Ogden, June 19, 1945, CBW Records, box 40, folder 6, Princeton.

45. Rakosky to Kerr, May 23, 1945, CBW Records, box 36, folder 2, Princeton.

46. Hill to Williamson and Kerr, Sept. 7, 1944, 208/464/2949, NACP.

47. Ogden to M. E. Coindreau, Nov. 9, 1944, and Coindreau to Ogden, Nov. 9, 1944; both CBW Records, box 36, folder 13, Princeton.

48. Kerr to Milton MacKaye, Feb. 13, 1945, 208/464/1749, NACP.

49. Ibid.

50. Norton to Harry F. West, June 7, 1944; J. Joseph Whalan to George A. Hecht, Oct. 6, 1944; both CBW Records, box 40, folder 3, Princeton.

51. Ballou, *Council,* 87.

52. Jack W. Powell, Bermingham & Prosser Co., to Zucker, Nov. 29, 1944; Zucker to Ogden, n.d. [late 1944]; and untitled chart of paper supplies, n.d. [late 1944]; all CBW Records, box 40, folder 3, Princeton. On the production aspects of OEs generally, see Ballou, *Council,* 90–92.

53. Minutes of the Board of Directors meeting, Nov. 16, 1944, CBW Records, box 2, folder 7, Princeton; *NY Times,* Jan. 14, 1946.

54. Ballou, *Council,* 90–92; Candland to Thomas Carroll, Oct. 18, 1944, 208/465/2954, NACP.

55. Minutes of the Executive Committee meeting, Oct. 29, 1944, CBW Records, box 3, folder 8, Princeton; Glick to Kerr, Oct. 15, 1944, CBW Records, box 32, folder 9, Princeton.

56. See book dealers' quotes, CBW Records, box 32, folder 8, Princeton.

57. "Report of Work to Date—Mar. 28, 1945," CBW Records, box 40, folder 5, Princeton.

58. J. E. French to Zucker, Nov. 27, 1944, CBW Records, box 37, folder 10, Princeton.

59. Zucker to Ogden, Feb. 14, 1945, CBW Records, box 33, folder 6, Princeton.

60. C. Holmes, Secretary, Association Provinciale des Maitres Imprimeurs du Québec, to Charles Chartier, Quebec Trade Bureau, New York City, May 11, 1944, in response to letter from Stern, CBW Archives, box 14, folder 3, Princeton. See also Gerson and Michon, eds., *History of the Book in Canada* 3:201–2.

61. Ballou, *Council,* 89–92. See W. F. Hall letterheads, CBW Records, box 40, folder 10, Princeton.

62. Untitled, undated text, enclosed with Ranald Savery to Zucker, Apr. 17, 1945, box 33, folder 1; Zucker to French, Feb. 20, 1945, box 39, folder 15; Zucker to H. A. Wisotzkey Jr., Dec. 13, 1944; all CBW Records, box 40, folder 2, Princeton.

63. The quantities and costs appear in the title-by-title production records in boxes 33–38, CBW Records, Princeton.

64. See Zucker to M. B. Wall, Apr. 10, 1945, CBW Records, box 34, folder 33, Princeton.

65. Ogden to Kerr, Jan. 8, 1945, CBW Records, box 37, folder 24, Princeton.

66. Gammon to Annie Von Wasserman, Jan. 30, 1945, CBW Records, box 37, folder 31, Princeton.

67. "Operational Plan for Germany," third draft, Jan. 16, 1945, 208/404/803, NACP.

68. Ballou, *Council,* 90. However, trim size is given as 4¼ x 6¼ in "Physical Specifications for Overseas Editions," June 15, 1944, CBW Records, box 32, folder 8, Princeton.

69. The identity of the cover stock, along with many other details, is noted in the cost sheets of the OEs. See, for example, the cost sheet for the English edition of *G.I. Joe* in CBW Records, box 34, folder 32, Princeton.

70. Stern to Office of Emergency Management, Oct. 20, 1944; H. J. Revere, to OEI, Dec. 12, 1944; and Zucker to Kerr, Mar. 20, 1945; all CBW Records, box 40, folder 3, Princeton.

71. Glick to Kerr, Jan. 4, 1945, 208/464/2951A, NACP.

72. Ogden to Kerr, Dec. 19, 1944, CBW Records, box 39, folder 6, Princeton. The care taken in designing and producing the books may be seen generally in the title-by-title production files, CBW Records, boxes 33–38.

73. See, for example, Andre Leveque, n.d., box 40, folder 6, and miscellaneous order no. 95, issued to Elsie Lumley, Feb. 3, 1945, box 35, folder 10; both CBW Records, Princeton.

74. Glick to Kerr, Jan. 4, 1945, 208/464/2951A, NACP.

75. Minutes of the Executive Committee meeting, Aug. 24, 1944, CBW Records, box 3, folder 8, Princeton; Milton B. Glick to Chester Kerr, Jan. 4, 1945, 208/464/2951A; and cable, Hamblet/MacKaye to Williamson/Candland/Foulke/Kerr/Hill, Jan. 25, 1945; and cable, Cowan to Williamson, Jan. 25, 1944; both 208/464/2949; all NACP.

76. "Report of Work to Date—January 24, 1945," CBW Records, box 40, folder 5, Princeton.

77. "Report of Work to Date—April 19, 1946," CBW Records, box 40, folder 5, Princeton.

78. "Report of Work to Date—September 12, 1945," CBW Records, box 40, folder 5, Princeton.

79. Ogden to Zucker, Aug. 28, 1945, CBW Records, box 14, folder 10, Princeton.

CHAPTER 9

1. *OWI in the ETO,* 5, 22.

2. *Psychological Warfare Division,* 65.

3. Richard Hollander to Commanding General, PWD/SHAEF, Feb. 6, 1945; Gen. Robert A. McClure to Chief of Staff, 6th Army Group, Feb. 23, 1945; both 331/87/11, NACP.

4. See Wieviorka, *Normandy,* 323–55.

5. See Paul Brooks, "Books Follow the Jeep," *PW,* Dec. 8, 1945, 2528–30. On the staff composition of PWD/SHAEF for the consolidation-propaganda effort, see "Guidance Notes, Part II. Consolidation Activities in Liberated Areas," June 14, 1944, and "The

Authorities for the Conduct of Psychological Warfare Consolidation Propaganda by SHAEF in Rear of the Combat Zone," n.d.; both 331/87/11, NACP.

6. *Psychological Warfare Division,* 65.

7. Ibid.

8. Kerr to Alfred McIntyre, Little, Brown, Apr. 26, 1945, 208/464/2949, NACP.

9. *Psychological Warfare Division,* 65; "House of Hachette Never Collaborated with Nazis," *PW,* Oct. 21, 1944, 1642. On Hachette's monopoly position, see Assouline, *Gaston Gallimard,* 189–90.

10. See Wieviorka, *Normandy,* 217–26.

11. *OWI in the ETO,* 18.

12. Richard Hollander, draft of history of Allied psychological warfare in northwestern France, Oct. 10, 1944, 331/87/16, NACP.

13. *Psychological Warfare Division,* 65; *OWI in the ETO,* 23.

14. *Psychological Warfare Division,* 65–66.

15. Ibid., 66.

16. Ibid., 66–67.

17. *OWI in the ETO,* 32.

18. *Psychological Warfare Division,* 65–66.

19. Hollander, draft of history of Allied psychological warfare in northwestern France, Oct. 10, 1944, 331/87/16, NACP.

20. *Psychological Warfare Division,* 68. See also Sugarman, *My War,* a rare eyewitness account of the operations on the invasion beaches for the four months from D-Day to the closing of the beaches by a young U.S. naval officer.

21. *Psychological Warfare Division,* 67–68.

22. Flora Russell to William Bourne, Sept. 20, 1945, 208/464/2951, NACP.

23. Minutes of the Board of Directors meeting, Aug. 9, 1945, CBW Records, box 2, folder 10, Princeton.

24. Minutes of the Board of Directors meeting, Sept. 20, 1945, CBW Records, box 2, folder 10, Princeton.

25. Brooks, "Books Follow the Jeep," 2529.

26. Sulkin, "The OWI and Book-Hungry Europe," *NY Times Book Review,* Oct. 28, 1945.

27. A copy of the issue of May 5, 1945, is in 208/464/2951, NACP.

28. Sulkin, "America's Position in World Publishing," lecture before Anglo-American Society, Leeuwarden, the Netherlands, Jan. 23, 1946, 260/16(A1)16/254, NACP.

29. Sulkin, "The OWI and Book-Hungry Europe."

30. *Psychological Warfare Division,* 92.

31. Ballou, *Council,* 93–94.

32. Theodotos to OEI, Dec. 19, 1945, CBW Records, box 33, folder 12, Princeton.

33. The lack of such letters regarding OEs, compared to missives from readers of ASEs, is understandable. Europeans would likely not have known whom to write to. Even if they had, most of the OEs would have come into the possession of individuals who read the books not long before both SHAEF and OWI were disbanded, meaning that there would have been nobody left in the agencies to receive, answer, and file the letters.

34. Press release, July 27, 1945, 208/464/2951, NACP.

35. Cruickshank, *Fourth Arm,* 159–175.

36. *PW,* Oct. 14, 1944, 1577.

37. Ingeborg Anderson to Blanche Knopf, Oct. 10, 1945, Alfred A. Knopf, Inc., Papers, Series III, box 4, folder 2, HRC.

38. *PW,* Mar. 24, 1945, 1282–83.

39. Laurence Pollinger to Albert H. Walsh, July 24, 1945, John Day Archives, box 206, folder 1, Princeton.

40. G. C. Lang to Charles Scribner's Sons, New York, June 21, 1945, Charles Scribner's Sons Archives, Foreign Rights, box 9, folder 28, Princeton.

41. Albert Walsh to P. A. Gruenais, Nov. 8, 1945, box 198, folder 36; Albert Walsh to Édition Nagel, Dec. 14, 1945, box 205, folder 10; and Richard Walsh Jr. to Mildred C. Smith, Dec. 20, 1945; all John Day Archives, Princeton.

42. *PW,* Feb. 9, 1946, 999.

43. *PW,* Jan. 26, 1946, 607–8.

44. *PW,* Jan. 25, 1947, 442.

45. *PW,* June 1, 1946, 2904.

46. *PW,* Feb. 8, 1947, 880.

47. See, for example, Albert Walsh to Charles Muller Publishing Company, Budapest, Oct. 3, 1945, John Day Archives, box 205, folder 8, Princeton. On USIBA, see chapter 10.

48. See, for example, A. Cleyman, American Compensation Corp., Antwerp, to the John Day Company, Oct. 23, 1945, John Day Archives, box 198, folder 1, Princeton.

49. Marguerite Bogatko, Translation Department, USIBA, to Albert Walsh, Sept. 25, 1945, John Day Archives, box 205, folder 8, Princeton.

50. Frederic Melcher, editorial, *PW,* Sept. 30, 1944, 1397; Mildred C. Smith, editorial, *PW,* Oct. 21, 1944, 1637.

51. See Elizabeth Pryor, "The John Day Company," in Dzwonkoski, ed., *Dictionary of Literary Biography* 46: 104–6.

52. Korda, *Making the List,* 65–66.

53. *PW,* Jan. 20, 1945, 234–35; Richard J. Walsh to Stanley Unwin, Apr. 23, 1945, John Day Archives, box 198, folder 23, Princeton.

54. Flora B. Luddington, report on India, Jan. 7, 1947, Chester Brooks Kerr Papers, Princeton.

55. On this, see chapter 11.

56. Richard Walsh Jr. to Lt. Commander Leo Monteleoni, Jan. 26, 1945, John Day Archives, box 198, folder 46, Princeton.

57. Albert Walsh to Margaret Landon, Mar. 23, 1945, box 203, folder 31; Richard Walsh to William D. Ten Broeck, Apr. 23, 1945; both John Day Archives, Princeton.

58. Mike Meyer, "Pearl of the Orient," *NY Times Book Review,* Mar. 5, 2006.

59. See various agreements in John Day Archives, box 199, folder 13, Princeton.

60. Richard Walsh Jr. to Dr. Ragussi, Bompiani & Co., Jan. 18, 1945, John Day Archives, box 198, folder 46, Princeton.

61. John Day Archives, boxes 198–203, Princeton.

62. John Day Archives, boxes 199, 204, Princeton.

63. Richard Walsh to Laurence Pollinger, June 25, 1945, John Day Archives, box 206, folder 1, Princeton.

64. Pearl S. Buck to David Lloyd, Nov. 13, 1944, David Lloyd Agency Papers, box 49, folder 8, Princeton.

65. "Memorandum of Agreement," Mar. 13, 1945, John Day Archives, box 198, folder 46, Princeton.

66. Albert Walsh to Sonia Chapter, Sept. 26, 1945, John Day Archives, box 199, folder 13, Princeton.

67. Tebbel, *Book Publishing* 4: 144–52; Herbert H. Johnson and Margaret Becket, "Alfred A. Knopf," in Dzwonkoski, ed., *Dictionary of Literary Biography* 46: 202–8.

68. Ambassador Henri Bonnet to Blanche Knopf, Sept. 30, 1949, Alfred A. Knopf Papers, Series III, box 690, folder 6, HRC.

69. "Our Relations with South America," *PW,* Dec. 9, 1939, 2148; Melcher, "Editorial: To Learn About Our Neighbors," *PW,* June 29, 1940, 2391.

70. Blanche Knopf, "South America—1942," Alfred A. Knopf Papers, Series III, box 696, folder 11, HRC.

71. Blanche Knopf to Sumner Welles, Feb. 13, 1945; Welles to Blanche Knopf, Feb. 17, 1945; Herbert Weinstock to Blanche Knopf, June 8, 1945; all Alfred A. Knopf Papers, Series III, box 697, folder 4, HRC.

72. Blanche Knopf, "'43 Trip to England," Alfred A. Knopf Papers, Series III, box 696, folder 8, HRC.

73. Maj. Walter R. King to Capt. Donald Reap, June 12, 1946, Alfred A. Knopf Papers, Series III, box 696, folder 7, HRC.

74. Kerr to Lt. Col. Richard G. Elliott, July 17, 1946, 208/464/2949, NACP.

75. Blanche Knopf, untitled, undated reminiscence of trip to Berlin, Jan. 1949, Alfred A. Knopf Papers, Series III, box 696, folder 7, HRC.

76. Grace Hogarth to Stanley Unwin, Feb. 5, 1945, George Allen & Unwin, Ltd., Records, 225/4, Reading.

77. Blanche Knopf, untitled, undated observations of publishing in Britain and Europe, ca. summer 1946, Alfred A. Knopf Papers, Series III, box 696, folder 9, HRC.

78. Tebbel, *Book Publishing* 4: 235–39; Margaret Becket, "Charles Scribner's Sons," in Dzwonkoski, ed., *Dictionary of Literary Biography* 46: 412–19.

79. Charles Kingsley to Charles Scribner, Oct. 13, 1939, Charles Scribner's Sons Archives, London Office, box 18, folder 6, Princeton.

80. Kingsley to Scribner, Jan. 15, 1940, Charles Scribner's Sons Archives, London Office, box 18, folder 7, Princeton.

81. Carter's career is detailed in Dickinson, *John Carter.*

82. Kingsley to Scribner, Mar. 8, 1940; Scribner to Kingsley, Mar. 20, 1940; both Charles Scribner's Sons Archives, London Office, box 18, folder 7, Princeton.

83. Carter, "Memorandum of Plans Made for the Conduct of the Rare Book Department During the War," Sept. 13, 1939, Charles Scribner's Sons Archives, London Office, box 18, folder 6, Princeton; Carter, "A Bookseller's Day in London," *PW,* Nov. 2, 1940, 1764–65.

84. Kingsley to Scribner, Oct. 15, 1939, Charles Scribner's Sons Archives, London Office, box 18, folder 6, Princeton.

85. Carter to Scribner, Oct. 16, 1940, Charles Scribner's Sons Archives, London Office, box 19, folder 1, Princeton. See picture of Carter and his staff with the British and U.S. flags flying over the entrance to the London office, *PW,* Dec. 27, 1941, 2291.

86. Dickinson, *John Carter,* 141–42.

87. Scribner to Arthur Dust, May 11, 1945, Charles Scribner's Sons Archives, London Office, box 19, folder 6, Princeton.

88. See chapter 11.

89. Carter to Scribner, May 13, 1945; Scribner to Carter, Dec. 13, 1945; both Charles Scribner's Sons Archives, London Office, box 19, folder 6, Princeton.

90. Scribner to Carter, Dec. 13, 1945, Charles Scribner's Sons Archives, London Office, box 19, folder 6, Princeton.

91. A 1946 Publishers Association survey of its members indicated that the queue of books waiting to be produced amounted to some forty thousand out-of-print books and over eight thousand manuscripts ready to go. This was the equivalent of the entire output of British printers and binders for the previous three and a half years. John Carter to Charles Scribner, Jan. 11, 1946, Charles Scribner's Sons Archives, London Office, box 19, folder 7, Princeton.

92. Burlingame, *Endless Frontiers,* 251–53, 377–82; Carole B. Michaels-Katz and Martha A. Bartter, "McGraw-Hill," in Dzwonkoski, ed., *Dictionary of Literary Biography* 46: 231–34.

93. Burlingame, *Endless Frontiers,* 324.

94. See chapter 10.

95. "McGraw-Hill's Foreign Department Expands," *PW,* Apr. 14, 1945, 1560; Walter A. Bara to Archibald Ogden, Mar. 9, 1945, CBW Records, box 5, folder 13, Princeton.

96. "Proposed Trip to India and Russia," Sept. 19, 1945, 59/1559/179, NACP.

97. Kenji Arakawa, Tokyo, to GHQ, SCAP, n.d. (ca. fall 1949), 331/ 1664/ 5256, NACP.

98. Cazden, *German Exile Literature,* 10–11; Fischer, *My European Heritage,* 111.

99. Cazden, *German Exile Literature,* 10–11; Fischer, *My European Heritage,* 117–23.

100. Hendrik Willem Van Loon to Mr. and Mrs. Gottfried Bermann-Fischer, Aug. 5, 1940, S. Fischer Verlag Papers, Lilly. Courtesy Lilly Library, Indiana University, Bloomington.

101. Cazden, *German Exile Literature*, 10–11; Fischer, *My European Heritage*, 125–35.

102. A. I. Ward, U.S. embassy, Moscow, to Van Loon, June 12, 1940; Gottfried Bermann-Fischer to Van Loon, July 10, 1940; Bermann-Fischer to Van Loon, July 20[?], 1940; all in S. Fischer Verlag Papers, Lilly.

103. Fischer, *My European Heritage*, 134–37.

104. *PW*, Oct. 9, 1943, 1442–43.

105. Notice on page opposite title page of Brooks, *Prisoners of Hope*.

106. Cazden, *German Exile Literature*, 11–12, 97–98; Fischer, *My European Heritage*, 143.

107. *PW*, Nov. 23, 1940, 1968; cited in Cazden, *German Exile Literature*, 98.

108. Cazden, *German Exile Literature*, 98–100.

109. See chapter 7.

110. *PW*, Sept. 16, 1944, 996–97.

111. Fischer, *My European Heritage*, 163–66, 200.

112. Cazden, *German Exile Literature*, 167; Fischer, *My European Heritage*, 165–67.

113. Cazden, *German Exile Literature*, 167; Fischer, *My European Heritage*, 201, 213–15.

114. Cazden, *German Exile Literature*, 124.

115. Ibid.

116. See chapter 7.

117. Cazden, *German Exile Literature*, 103–5, 192–93.

118. Krammer, *Nazi Prisoners*, 206; Cazden, *German Exile Literature*, 103–6, 121–23, 134n144. See also *PW*, July 14, 1945, 139.

119. Werner Herzfelde to Karl Burger, Mar. 15, 1946; Capt. David J. Coleman to Herzfelde, Apr. 24, 1946; both 260/16(A1)16/242, NACP; Cazden, *German Exile Literature*, 106, 124.

120. Interview with Emanuel Molho (Isaac's son and current owner of the business), New York City, May 17, 2007; Nettelbeck, *Forever French*, 58–65; *PW*, May 31, 1941, 2170–72; *NYTimes*, Sept. 2, 2009; www.frencheuropean.com.

121. *PW*, Mar. 10, 1945, 1125.

122. *PW*, June 9, 1945, 2288–89.

123. Jacques Michon, "Book Publishing in Quebec," in Gerson and Michon, eds., *History of the Book in Canada* 3: 202.

CHAPTER 10

1. On the first "summit" meeting, in Sept. 1942, see chapter 3.

2. Kerr to Samuel T. Williamson, Aug. 18, 1944, 208/464/2949; Llewellyn White to Williamson, Aug. 28, 1944, 208/6E/2; White to Edward W. Barrett, Sept. 11, 1944, 208/6E/2; all NACP.

3. Williamson to Edward W. Barrett, Aug. 28, 1944, 208/6E/2, NACP.

4. "Revised Draft of Operational Memorandum for Books," ca. Aug.-Sept. 1944, 208/464/2949, NACP.

5. "Memorandum on OWI Overseas Book Operations for Consideration at Book Conference Held at Office of War Information, October 3, 1944," n.d., CBW Records, box 38, folder 26, Princeton.

6. "Book Activities of the Division of Cultural Cooperation, Department of State," n.d., before Oct. 3, 1944, CBW Records, box 38, folder 26, Princeton.

7. "Distribution of U.S. Books Abroad," Oct. 2, 1944, 208/464/2949, NACP.

8. Ibid.

9. Untitled, undated minutes of the meeting of Oct. 3–4, 1944, CBW Records, box 38, folder 26, Princeton.

10. *PW*, June 12, 1943, 2236; Macmahon, *Postwar International Information Program*, 89–91.

11. *Report by the Three Delegates,* 62.

12. Kerr to Edward Klauber, Dec. 16, 1944, 208/464/2950, NACP.

13. Reich, *Nelson Rockefeller,* 208–9; Fleming, *New Dealers' War,* 132; Hilton, *Hitler's Secret War in South America,* 201.

14. David Loth to Don Francisco, Mar. 21, 1944, 229/127/1467, NACP.

15. Reich, *Nelson Rockefeller,* 261.

16. Kerr to Klauber, Dec. 16, 1944, 208/464/2950, NACP.

17. Kerr to Crane, Nov. 17, 1944, 208/6E/2, NACP.

18. *PW,* Dec. 2, 1944, 2151.

19. "Prospectus for the United States International Book Association," Feb. 15, 1945, CBW Records, box 20, folder 6, Princeton.

20. *PW,* Jan. 26, 1946, 603.

21. Kerr to Klauber, Dec. 16, 1944, 208/464/2950, NACP.

22. *NY Times,* Jan. 19, 1946.

23. Crane, "The Formation of an American Book Export Organization," *PW,* Dec. 2, 1944, 2137–40.

24. Melcher, editorial, *PW,* Feb. 3, 1945, 621.

25. *PW,* Sept. 1, 1945, 859.

26. "Prospectus for the United States International Book Association," Feb. 15, 1945, CBW Records, box 20, folder 6, Princeton.

27. http://www.teachmefinance.com/Financial_Terms/Webb-Pomerene_Association. html.

28. In addition to Crane, the board members were Donald C. Brace (Harcourt Brace), George P. Brett Jr. (Macmillan), Melville Minton (Putnam's), Burr L. Chase (Silver Burdett), Hugh Gibson (Doubleday Doran), Edward P. Hamilton (John Wiley), Curtice N. Hitchcock (Reynal & Hitchcock), Malcolm Johnson (Van Nostrand), John O'Connor (Grosset & Dunlap), Lawrence Saunders (Saunders), M. Lincoln Schuster (Simon & Schuster), Charles Scribner (Scribner's), and James Thompson (McGraw-Hill). "Prospectus for the United States International Book Association," Feb. 15, 1945, CBW Records, box 20, folder 6, Princeton.

29. Ibid.

30. Reynal, address to USIBA annual meeting, Jan. 18, 1946, 59/1559/183, NACP.

31. "Confidential to the Publishing Industry—Not for Publication Dec. 28, 1942," CBW Records, box 5, folder 2, Princeton.

32. "Prospectus for the United States International Book Association," Feb. 15, 1945, CBW Records, box 20, folder 6, Princeton.

33. Ibid.

34. Ibid.

35. Crane to Raymond Everitt, Feb. 23, 1945, 208/464/2950, NACP.

36. *PW,* Apr. 20, 1946, 2186–91.

37. "The United States International Book Association, Inc.," Sept. 24, 1945, 260/16(a1)16/254, NACP; *PW,* Nov. 9, 1946, 2725.

38. Carroll to Kerr, Dec. 1, 1945, Chester Brooks Kerr Papers, Princeton.

39. Philip H. Hiss, "United States International Book Association Activities in Holland," Feb. 2, 1946, 208/356&357/1721, NACP; *PW,* July 27, 1946, 368–75.

40. Reynal, address to USIBA annual meeting, Jan. 18, 1946, 59/1559/183, NACP.

41. Reynal, "New Horizons for the Book Business," *PW,* Feb. 2, 1946, 851–54.

42. *PW,* July 27, 1946, 372.

43. *NY Times,* Dec. 16, 1946.

44. *PW,* Nov. 9, 1946, 2725; *NY Times,* Dec. 16, 1946.

45. Kerr to Crane, Sept. 17, 1946, Chester Brooks Kerr Papers, Princeton.

46. Kerr to Sulkin, Oct. 26, 1946, ibid.

47. Kerr to Crane, Sept. 16, 1946, ibid.

48. Thompson to Kerr, Oct. 23, 1946, ibid.

49. Tebbel, *Book Publishing* 4:504.

50. Kerr to Brett, Sept. 26, 1946, Chester Brooks Kerr Papers, Princeton.

51. Thompson to Kerr, Oct. 23, 1946, ibid.

52. Kerr to Ronald Freelander, Oct. 31, 1946, ibid.

53. *PW*, Dec. 21, 1946, 3295–97.

54. *NY Times*, Dec. 16, 1946. See also *Bookman*, Jan. 4, 1947, 8.

55. Anne Perlman, *NY Herald Tribune*, Jan. 9, 1947.

56. *NY Herald Tribune*, European edition, Jan. 8, 1947; reprinted in *NY Herald Tribune*, Jan. 9, 1947.

57. *PW*, Dec. 31, 1946, 3279.

58. Crane to Richard Heindel, Jan. 10, 1947, 59/1559/183, NACP.

59. Heindel to William Benton et al., Jan. 14, 1947, 59/1559/183, NACP.

60. Heindel to William T. Stone, Dec. 19, 1946, 59/1559/183, NACP; *PW*, Dec. 31, 1946, 3295.

61. Melville Minton to council members, ABPC, Apr. 18, 1947, and Kerr to Crane [letter not sent], both Chester Brooks Kerr Papers, Princeton.

62. Bound, *A Banker Looks at Book Publishing*, 52.

63. Draft of a letter from the seven publishers to their European accounts, n.d., Chester Brooks Kerr Papers, Princeton.

64. Hazel Ferguson to Mr. Rose et al., June 18, 1947, draft of a letter from the seven publishers to their European accounts, n.d., ibid.; "New Expor[t] Services Organized for Europe Following Dissolution of USIBA," *PW*, Jan. 28, 1947, 402–5.

65. *PW*, Nov. 16, 1946, 2821.

66. "Points in Russak's Jan. 13th Letter Answered in HKG's Letter of Jan. 23rd," Chester Brooks Kerr Papers, Princeton.

67. Johnson to Reynall, Jan. 31, 1947, ibid.

68. *PW*, Jan. 4, 1947, 57; *PW*, Jan. 11, 1947, 177.

69. "New Expor[t] Services Organized for Europe Following Dissolution of USIBA," *PW*, Jan. 28, 1947, 402–5.

70. See chapter 3.

CHAPTER 11

1. *Report by the Three Delegates*, 60.

2. Kingsford, *Publishers Association*, 187; Bryant, "English Language Publication and the British Traditional Market Agreement," 374–75.

3. Kingsford, *Publishers Association*, 162, 178, 187; Unwin, *Truth about Publishing*, 337; Brophy, *Britain Needs Books*, 17.

4. Frederic G. Melcher, "Editorial: Our Imports from England," *PW*, Aug. 10, 1940, 391.

5. F. D. Sanders, circular letter to members of the PA, Dec. 29, 1943, AUC 176/4, Reading; Kingsford, *Publishers Association*, 187.

6. Matons of INLE, Barcelona, to Wendy Simpson, British Council, n.d. (circa Nov. 1945), AUC 213/15, Reading.

7. Unwin to Simpson, Oct. 1, 1945, Nov. 15 and 19, 1945; all AUC 213/15, Reading

8. Simpson to Unwin, Sept. 23, 1945, AUC 213/15, Reading.

9. Walter Starkie, British Institute, Madrid, to B. Kennedy Cooke, British Council, Dec. 13, 1945; Starkie to Unwin, Mar. 6, 1945; both AUC 213/15, Reading.

10. Kingsford, *Publishers Association*, 163; Unwin, *Truth about a Publisher*, 392.

11. Unwin, *Truth about a Publisher*, 395–96.

12. On the tax, see Calder, *People's War*, 114.

13. *Bookseller*, Mar. 15, 1945, 353–54.

14. *Bookseller*, Mar. 22, 1945, 372; OWI, "Basic Plan for Books," Sept. 20, 1944, 208/480/2997, NACP.

15. Kingsford, *Publishers Association,* 168–69, 176, 183; Unwin, *Truth about a Publisher,* 393.

16. Unwin, "Are Books a Necessity?" in Hopkins, ed., *Battle of the Books,* 11–12.

17. Kingsford, *Publishers Association,* 162, 166–67.

18. Ibid., 162–65.

19. Ibid., 159–86, passim; John Carter, Charles Scribner's Sons, Ltd., to Charles Scribner III, Jan. 11, 1946, Charles Scribner's Sons Archives, London–New York office correspondence, box 19, folder 7, Princeton.

20. Kingsford, *Publishers Association,* 159–97, passim.

21. Memo from president of the PA to members of both houses of Parliament, in *Bookseller,* Jan. 11, 1945, 24.

22. Brophy, *Britain Needs Books,* 17, 28–39, 44. See also Feather, *British Publishing,* 215–16.

23. Weybright, "On Viewing Some Books from Britain," *Bookseller,* Nov. 14, 1946.

24. Unwin, *Truth about a Publisher,* 295.

25. Brophy, *Britain Needs Books,* 42–43; John Hampden, "Envoys Extraordinary," in Hopkins, ed., *Battle of the Books,* 31.

26. "Confidential to the Publishing Industry—Not for Publication. Dec. 28, 1942," CBW Records, box 5, folder 11, Princeton.

27. Unwin to Juliet O'Hea, Dec. 21. 1945, AUC 215/3, Reading.

28. Biographical information is taken from S. Unwin, *Truth about a Publisher* and P. Unwin, *Publishing Unwins.*

29. Unwin, *Truth about a Publisher,* 112–13.

30. P. Unwin, *Publishing Unwins,* 73, quoting Munby in *Publishing and Bookselling.*

31. P. Unwin, *Publishing Unwins,* 90, 105.

32. Unwin, *Truth about a Publisher,* 368–69; P. Unwin, *Publishing Unwins,* 80–81; Unwin to Frederic Melcher, Jan. 28, 1946, AUC 275/6, Reading.

33. Unwin, *Truth about a Publisher,* 200–1; P. Unwin, *Publishing Unwins,* 80–81.

34. D. Unwin, *Fifty Years with My Father,* 106.

35. Unwin, *Truth about a Publisher,* 368; P. Unwin, *Publishing Unwins,* 64.

36. Crane to Unwin, Feb. 24, 1948, AUC 380/10; P. Unwin, *Publishing Unwins,* 94–95.

37. See the chapter titled "How to Make a Nuisance of Oneself," in Unwin, *Truth about a Publisher,* 335–54.

38. Unwin, *Truth about a Publisher,* 388–89.

39. White, *British Council,* 1, 30–31.

40. Unwin, "Confidential Report to the Council of the Publishers Association" (draft, corrected by hand), n.d., AUC 203/10, Reading.

41. Holman, *Print for Victory,* 20.

42. Unwin, *Truth about a Publisher,* 394, 416–39, esp. 416–17, 422; White, *British Council,* 6; P. Unwin, *Publishing Unwins,* 140.

43. Kingsford, *Publishers Association,* 63, 118; Feather, *British Publishing,* 204; Bryant, "British Traditional Market Agreement," 375.

44. Bryant, "British Traditional Marketing Agreement," 372–73.

45. Richard Walsh to Padumai Padippaham, Ltd., Mar. 26, 1945, John Day Archives, box 203, folder 49, Princeton.

46. H. P. Wilson, W. W. Norton & Company, to W. N. Beard, Allen & Unwin, Dec. 1, 1944, AUC 201/5, Reading.

47. Memo from president of the PA to members of both houses of parliament, in *Bookseller,* Jan 11, 1945, 24.

48. *PW,* Nov. 28, 1942, 2185–86.

49. Page, *Australian Bookselling,* xi, 95–96.

50. Kingsford, *Publishers Association,* 191.

51. Holman, *Print for Victory,* 200.

52. Wilson to Beard, Dec. 1, 1944, AUC 201/5, Reading.

53. L. C. Z., Dec. 12, 1944, enclosure in Canberra legation to secretary of state, Jan. 24, 1945, 59/1559/183, NACP.

54. Memo from president of the PA to members of both houses of parliament, in *Bookseller,* Jan 11, 1945, 24.

55. Timmins to Unwin, extracted in Unwin to F. D. Sanders, Publishers Association, June 18, 1943, AUC 176/3, Reading.

56. Unwin to Harrap, Sept. 7, 1944, AUC 193/8; Unwin to Melcher, Apr. 27, 1945, AUC 236/6; both Reading.

57. Sanders to Unwin, Oct. 2, 1944, AUC 203/10. See also Kingsford, *Publishers Association,* 190.

58. Timmins to Union Booksellers, Pretoria, May 23, 1945; Timmins to F. D. Sanders, July 7, 1945; Timmins to Unwin, Feb. 10, 1945; Timmins to Unwin, May 17, 1945; Timmins to Unwin, July 18, 1945; all AUC 241/5, Reading.

59. Timmins to Unwin, Mar. 1, 1945, AUC 241/5, Reading.

60. Timmins to Unwin, May 17, 1945, AUC 241/5, Reading.

61. Timmins to P. Unwin, Nov. 21, 1945; Unwin to Timmins, Dec. 28, 1945; both AUC 241/5, Reading.

62. Timmins to Unwin, May 8, 1945, AUC 241/5, Reading.

63. Richard Walsh to Melville Minton, Book Publishers Bureau, Apr. 24, 1945, John Day Archives, box 201, folder 10, Princeton.

64. Richard Walsh to William D. Ten Broeck, International Book House, Ltd., Bombay, Apr. 23, 1945, John Day Archives, box 203, folder 3, Princeton.

65. Richard Walsh to Juliet O'Hea, Curtis Brown, Ltd., London, Jan. 20, 1945, John Day Archives, box 199, folder 13, Princeton.

66. O'Hea to James Walsh, Dec. 22, 1945, box 199, folder 13; O'Hea to Richard Walsh, July 6, 1945, box 199, folder 13; Richard Walsh to Melville Minton, July 2, 1945, box 204, folder 23; and Curtis Brown to John Day Co., July 20, 1945, box 199, folder 13; all John Day Archives, Princeton.

67. Richard Walsh to Minton [publ. assn.], Apr. 24, 1945, John Day Archives, box 201, folder 10, Princeton.

68. Winkler, *Politics of Propaganda,* 83–84; Cruickshank, *Fourth Arm,* 41–42.

69. Lovat Dickson, "Anglo-Canadian Publishing: The Chance before Us," *Bookseller,* Aug. 2, 1944, 58–61.

70. Kingsford, *Publishers Association,* 120, 190–91; minutes of meetings between representatives of the Canadian book trade and the PA, Oct. 2, 8, 10, 16, 1945, AUC 236/4, Reading.

71. Dickson, "Anglo-Canadian Publishing," 58.

72. For example, see W. G. Low, Charles Scribner's Sons, to Braby & Waller, London, Apr. 20, 1945. Charles Scribner's Sons Archives, foreign rights, box 9, folder 2, Princeton.

73. Kingsford, *Publishers Association,* 190, 194; Dickson, "Anglo-Canadian Publishing," 58–61; minutes of meetings [between British and Canadian publishers], Oct. 2, 8, 16, 1945, AUC 236/4, Reading; "Publishers' Odyssey," *Bookseller,* Oct. 21, 1943, 431–34.

74. Copy of letter, dated June 9, 1943, from British Council to president of the PA, AUC 176/3, Reading.

75. Ann Brown, MoI, to P. Unwin, May 18, 1944, AUC 199/6/1, Reading.

76. Harrap, circular letter to members of the PA, May 12, 1941, CW 91/22; Sir William Beveridge to Unwin, May 21, 1943, and Unwin to Beveridge, June 11, 1943; both AUC 157/16, Reading.

77. Feather, *British Publishing,* 172–73.

78. Unwin, *Truth about Publishing,* 75–76.

79. Feather, *British Publishing,* 208–9; Lewis, *Penguin Special,* 75–78.

80. British Publishers Guild, "Report on Visit to Sweden," ca. June 1945, CW 98/17, Reading.

81. Lyle Fowler McInnes, Prentice-Hall, to Juliet O'Hea, Curtis Brown, Dec. 13, 1943, and Dec. 31, 1943, both AUC 186/9, Reading.

82. Unwin to O'Hea, Jan. 29, 1944, and Feb. 18, 1944, both AUC 186/9, Reading. Allen & Unwin published the book, in several editions.

83. Unwin to Norton, Mar. 8, 1945, AUC 245/11, Reading.

84. Unwin to Melcher, n.d. [probably Dec. 1944], AUC 203/12.

85. Melcher made this argument publicly as well, in an editorial in *PW,* Dec. 4, 1943, 2081.

86. Melcher to Unwin, Mar. 16, 1945, AUC 236/6, Reading.

87. Unwin to Melcher, Feb. 27, 1945, and Melcher to Unwin, Mar. 22, 1945; both AUC 236/6, Reading.

88. Unwin to Melcher, Apr. 27, 1945, AUC 236/6, Reading.

89. B. W. Fagan, circular letter, Apr. 14, 1943, AUC 176/3, Reading.

90. These conferences and meetings are briefly described in Kingsford, *Publishers Association,* 191–97.

91. Ibid., 195–96.

92. "Australia and New Zealand," position paper by Walter Harrap, dated July 12, 1942, copied as memo from the BPB, Jan. 18, 1943, Random House Papers, box 135, Columbia; Kingsford, *Publishers Association,* 192–93.

93. "Confidential to the Publishing Industry—Not for Publication Dec. 28, 1942," CBW Records, box 5, folder 11, Princeton.

94. "Publishers' Odyssey," *Bookseller,* Oct. 21, 1943, 422–24; Kingsford, *Publishers Association,* 193–94; *PW,* Aug. 7, 1943, 397–400.

95. "Publishers' Odyssey," 429.

96. *Report by the Three Delegates,* 36, 50–51, 55–56, 59.

97. Ibid., 56–58.

98. Ibid., 58–60; Holman, *Print for Victory,* 136.

99. *Report by the Three Delegates,* 63.

100. "Memorandum of British-American Publishing Problems and Their Effect on the Export Trade in Books," Feb. 1944, BT 11/2026, TNA.

101. Ibid.; Holman, *Print for Victory,* 137.

102. Kingsford, *Publishers Association,* 196–97; Bryant, "British Traditional Market Agreement," 376–77; "Minutes of a Meeting between Representatives of the Canadian Book Trade and of the Publishers Association," Oct. 16, 1945, AUC 236/4, Reading.

103. Unwin to O'Hea, Dec. 21, 1945, AUC 215/3, Reading.

104. See Canfield, *Up and Down and Around,* 74.

105. Sanders, circular letter to members of the PA, August 3, 1948, AUC 370/1, Reading.

106. Bryant, "British Traditional Market Agreement," 376–78. The countries in the British Traditional British Market, defined as of 1948, are listed on 394–95. See also Richard Abel, "The Internationalization of the US Book Trade: The World's Rediscovery of America," in Graham and Abel, eds., *The Book in the United States Today,* 91.

CHAPTER 12

1. Janet Flanner, "Letter from Cologne," Mar. 19, 1945; reprinted in *Reporting World War II: Part Two, American Journalism, 1944–1946* (New York: Library of America, 1995), 662.

2. Dower, *Embracing Defeat,* 39–43.

3. Mayo, "American Wartime Planning," in Wolfe, ed., *Americans as Proconsuls,* 286.

4. *Psychological Warfare Division,* 219.

5. Dobbins et al., *America's Role in Nation-Building,* section on Japan, 30–32, 39.

6. Dower, *Embracing Defeat,* 27.

7. Central Liaison Office, Tokyo, to imperial Japanese government, Jan. 1946, and memo for the chief of staff, Jan. 23, 1946; both 331/1651/5116; and Nugent, "Confiscation of Books," Sept. 9, 1946, 331/1647/5061; all NACP.

8. Dower, *Embracing Defeat,* 175.

9. Reichmann, "Reorganization of the Book Trade in Germany," 196. See also "Proposed Statement Opening the Meeting of the Börsenverein," Sept. 27, 1945, 260/16(A1)18/258, NACP.

10. Ben Gedalecia to Ferdinand Kuhn, Director, Interim Information Service, Nov. 6, 1945, 208/406/2191, NACP.

11. Ibid.; "List of OWI Materials for German Prisoners of War," ca. late 1945, 208/467/2060, NACP.

12. Kerr to J. Robert Paxton, Nov. 7, 1945, and Lt. Col. Edward Davison, Director, Special Projects Division, to Gedalecia, Nov. 2, 1945; both 208/406/2191, NACP.

13. Davison to Gedalecia, Nov. 2, 1945, 389/459A/1647; Gedalecia to Robert Paxton, Nov. 16, 1945, 208/406/2191; Gedalecia to Davison, Nov. 16, 1945, 389/459A/1647; all NACP.

14. Donald R. Nugent, "Reprints of American Books," Feb. 27, 1946, and Nugent, "Reprints of American Books," Mar. 22, 1946; both 331/1647/5061, NACP.

15. "Release of Army Books," Oct. 30, 1948, 331/1647/5069, NACP.

16. Dower, *Embracing Defeat,* 182.

17. Brig. Gen. Robert A. McClure to the director-generals of the British PID and MoI and the directors of the London offices of the U.S. OWI and the OSS, Aug. 8, 1944; Sub-Committee to Deal with Books for Germany to the Joint Publications Committee, Sept. 6, 1944; both 208/464/2949, NACP.

18. *Psychological Warfare Division,* 192.

19. Breitenkamp, *Information Control Division,* 37–40.

20. Pilgert, *Press, Radio and Film,* 19–21.

21. Breitenkamp, *Information Control Division,* 40–41.

22. *Psychological Warfare Division,* 99, 102, 219–20; *German Book Publishing,* 21; Ziemke, *U.S. Army in the Occupation,* 374–75; Mildred E. Allen to Harold Guinzburg, June 7, 1945, copying memorandum from Ronald Freelander to Raymond Everitt, May 31, 1945, 208/404/803, NACP; "Report of the Military Governor, U.S. Zone, 20 Aug. 1945, No. 1," Sloane Papers, box 2, folder 9, Princeton.

23. Breitenkamp, *Information Control Division,* 59–60, 68.

24. Anonymous, *Woman in Berlin,* 237–60.

25. Paley, *As It Happened,* 176–77; Clay, *Decision in Germany,* 282.

26. "Short-Range German Information Plan," July 30, 1945, 331/87/6, NACP.

27. "Report of the Military Governor, U.S. Zone, No. 5, 20 December 1945," Sloane Papers, box 2, folder 9, Princeton; Pilgert, *Press, Radio and Film,* 19–21.

28. *German Book Publishing,* 111.

29. Breitenkamp, *Information Control Division,* 71.

30. "Semi-monthly Report, Publications Branch," OMGUS, Jan. 20, 1949, Sloane Papers, box 2, folder 9, Princeton.

31. Breitenkamp, *Information Control Division,* 45–47.

32. Review of Waples et al., *What Reading Does to People* (Chicago: University of Chicago Press, 1941), in *NY Times Book Review,* Mar. 2, 1941, 33.

33. Breitenkamp, *Information Control Division,* 41–44; Lehmann-Haupt, "The German Booktrade in 1945, Part 1: Bookselling and Publishing under National Socialism," *PW,* Nov. 24, 1945, 2332–34; Part 2: "After V-E Day," *PW,* Dec. 8, 1945, 2531–34; Part 3: "Problems of Reconstruction," *PW,* Dec. 22, 1945, 2684–86.

34. On this, see chapter 7.

35. Breitenkamp, *Information Control Division,* 40–44.

36. Arndt spent much of his postwar career as a professor of German at Clark University in Worcester, Mass. His annotated copy of Breitenkamp's *Information Control Division* is in Clark's Robert H. Goddard Library. See pp. 40, 44.

37. Unwin, *Truth About a Publisher,* 239–40.

38. Unwin to Waples, Jan. 5, 1946; Unwin to Waples, June 16, 1947; Unwin to Waples, Oct. 28, 1947; all AUC 282/15, Reading. See also Unwin to Waples, Dec. 5, 1946, and Waples to Unwin, Feb. 12, 1946; both AUC 282/15, Reading.

39. Unwin to Waples, Mar. 4, 1946, and Unwin to Waples, Apr. 9, 1946; both AUC 282/15, Reading.

40. Waples to Unwin, May 1, 1946; Unwin to Waples, May 9, 1946; both AUC 282/15, Reading.

41. Furth to Unwin, Sept. 12, 1945, and July 30, 1945; both AUC 221/14, Reading.

42. Dower, *Embracing Defeat,* 182.

43. Weekly Report for 1–8 December 1945, 331/1651/5116, NACP.

44. CIE to Public Health & Welfare Section, Apr. 8, 1946, 331/1647/5061, NACP.

45. Odette Jensen, "Japan Needs and Wants American Books," *PW,* May 22, 1948, 2159–60.

46. Capt. Charles E. Tuttle, "Japan Wants American Books," *PW,* May 9, 1946, 1520.

47. Dower, *Embracing Defeat,* 180–81.

48. Ibid., 185–86.

49. Tuttle, "Japan Wants American Books," 1518–20; *PW,* July 24, 1948, 309; T. C. Morehouse, Macmillan, report to the ABPC et al., ca. 1949.

50. Nugent to chief, Civil Affairs Division, Special Staff, Jan. 2, 1948, 331/1647/5062, NACP.

51. Nugent to Ginn and Company, Nov. 6, 1948, 331/1664/5257; Nugent to Shigetaro Yamanaka, Mar. 7, 1946, 331/1647/5061; both NACP.

52. "Translation Rights License," July 7, 1947, 331/1647/5062, NACP.

53. Lt. S. Scheuer and Anthony Cornell, "Foreign Books Translated into Japanese" [subsequent to November 1945], Apr. 8, 1948, 331/1664/5256, NACP; Dower, *Embracing Defeat,* 182.

54. Tuttle, "Japan Wants American Books," 1520.

55. Dower, *Embracing Defeat,* 163, 188–90; Memorandum re "Die vollkommene Ehe—The perfect marriage" by Van de Velde, Sept. 17, 1948, 331/1664/5256, NACP.

56. Dower, *Embracing Defeat,* 237–39.

57. "The Japan Publishers Association Inc.," May 18, 1948, 331/1647/5069, NACP.

58. Weekly Report for 1–8 December 1945, 331/1651/5116, NACP.

59. SCAP to Japanese government, "Application of Directives to Copyright," Sept. 9, 1948, 331/1664/5256, NACP.

60. Tuttle, "Japan Wants American Books," 1519.

61. Lt. Col. Harold Fair to commanding general, 8th Army, Jan. 26, 1946, 331/1647/5061, NACP.

62. Melcher, "A Report on the Japanese Book Market," and "Infantry Journal to Act as Procurement and Contractual Agent for War Department," both *PW,* May 3, 1947, 2295 and 2297; Col. Joseph I. Greene to Maj. Gen. Paul J. Mueller, Far East Command, Dec. 13, 1948, 331/1647/5072, NACP.

63. Furth to Unwin, July 30, 1945, George Allen & Unwin, Ltd., Records, 221/14, Reading.

64. Dower, *Embracing Defeat,* 175.

65. Breitenkamp, *Information Control Division,* 94–95.

66. Peterson, *American Occupation of Germany,* 351; Dobbins et al., *America's Role in Nation-Building,* section on Germany, 13–14.

67. Walter L. Dorn, "The Unfinished Purge of Germany: An Examination of Allied Denazification Policy," unpublished typescript, chap. 1, p. 27, box 13, Dorn Papers, Columbia.

68. Pilgert, *Press, Radio and Film*, 60–61.

69. Greene to Mueller, Dec. 13, 1948, 331/1647/5072, NACP.

70. Ibid., and Mueller to Greene, Jan. 6, 1949, both 331/1647/5072, NACP.

71. Book officer to chief, Information Division, July 29, 1948, 331/1664/5257, and memorandum for record, "Translation Program for Japan," Jan. 1, 1949, 331/1647/5072; both NACP.

72. ESS to CIE, Mar. 31, 1949, 331/1664/5256, NACP.

73. CIE to NY field office, CAD, "Translation and Publication," Feb. 25, 1949, 331/1647/5072; Nugent to chief, Special Staff, CAD, Aug. 6, 1948, 331/1647/5066; both NACP.

74. CIE to NY field office, CAD, "Translation and Publication," Feb. 25, 1949, 331/1647/5072, NACP.

75. Nugent to Noble and Noble, Feb. 15, 1949; Michael Weyl, chief, Libraries and Book Rights Section, to chief, CIE, June 1, 1949; and CIE to NY field office, CAD, "Translation and Publication," Feb. 25, 1949; all 331/1647/5072, NACP.

76. Nugent, "Shurter's *Effective Letters in Business*," July 18, 1949, 331/1664/5257, NACP.

77. W. K. Bunce, chief, Religion and Cultural Resources Division, to Mr. Wheeler, Press & Publications Branch, Information Division, Aug. 13, 1949, 331/1664/5256, NACP.

78. Book officer, Press and Publications Branch, to chief, Information Division, July 20, 1948, 331/1664/5257, NACP.

79. A. A. Gromov to chief, CIE, Nov. 23, 1948, 331/1647/5072, NACP.

80. Donald Brown to book officer, Press and Publications Branch, Feb. 20, 1949, 331/1664/5257, NACP.

81. SCAP, "Summation No. 32. Non-Military Activities, Japan, for the Month of May 1948," Foreign Office Records, 371/69897, and "Summation No. 33. Non-Military Activities, Japan, for the Month of June 1948" FO 371/69898; both TNA.

82. "Japanese Publishers Granted Translation Rights to 58 Foreign Books," Oct. 25, 1948, 331/1664/5256, NACP.

83. Book officer, Press & Publications, to chief, Information Division, Aug. 23, 1948, 331/1664/5257, NACP.

84. "Successful Bidders for Translation Rights," July 13, 1949, 331/1664/5257, NACP.

85. See representative "Contract for Assignment of Translation Rights," dated Aug. 18, 1948, 331/1647/5072, NACP.

86. Data sheets in 331/1664/5256, NACP.

87. John Jamieson, H. W. Wilson Co., to Harriet Rourke, CAD, Oct. 20, 1949; and Nugent to Kenneth Roberts, Nov. 25, 1949; both 331/1664/5257; Benjamin O. Warren to CIE, July 18, 1949, 331/1647/5072; all NACP.

88. The principal documents relating to licensing and other matters relating to the book translation and publication program may be found in 331/1664/5256, NACP.

89. Col. G. P. Lynch to chief, CIE, Mar. 21, 1950, 331/1664/5257, NACP.

90. Nugent to chief, NY field office, CAD, May 3, 1949, 331/1647/5072; and Col. G. P. Lynch, chief, Reorientation Branch, to chief, CIE, 331/1664/5257; both NACP.

91. Book officer and magazine officer, Press and Publications Unit, CIE, to OIC, Press and Publications Unit, CIE, May 27, 1948; and Nugent to Frederick A. Praeger, Nassau Distributing Co., Sept. 10, 1949; both 331/1664/5257, NACP; and Maj. A. J. Rehe, assistant adjutant general, to Alfred A. Knopf, Inc., Dec. 31, 1948, 331/1664/5256, NACP; *PW,* June 25, 1949, 2458–59. On setting the exchange rate, see Dower, *Embracing Defeat,* 540.

92. Nugent to chief, NY field office, CAD, May 3, 1949; plus enclosed lists of titles, ca. same date; all 331/1647/5072, NACP.

93. Ibid.

94. Edited translation of article in *Nippon Dokusho Shimbum,* June 28, 1950, 331/1664/5257, NACP.

95. http://lib.umd.edu/prange/index.jsp.

96. "Petition for Importation of Overseas Publications," Oct. 17, 1947; Maruzen Company, Ltd., to Unwin, Jan. 15, 1948; and Unwin to Maruzen Co., Mar. 31, 1948; all AUC 361/15, Reading.

97. "Telecon Items," May 7, 1948, 331/1664/5256, NACP.

98. "Proposed Barter of Scientific Books," Sept. 20, 1948, 331/1664/5256; and CIE to ESS/ST, Oct. 13, 1948, 331/1647/5069; both NACP.

99. "Problems Confronting Publication Control in Germany," *PW,* Mar. 29, 1947, 788–91.

100. West to Robert F. de Graff, Mar. 9, 1948, and a list of the books already published or to be published when there was sufficient paper; both Sloane Papers, box 7, Princeton.

101. *German Book Publishing,* 3–4. On Thompson, see Jamieson, *Books for the Army,* 144, 149.

102. Crane to Sloane, Mar. 24, 1948, Sloane Papers, box 2, folder 4, Princeton.

103. *German Book Publishing,* 3–11; Sloane to Crane, Mar. 22, 1948, Sloane Papers, box 2, folder 4, Princeton.

104. Visiting committee to Waples and Laurence Dalcher, June 28, 1948, Sloane Papers, box 7, Princeton.

105. Sloane to Maj. Thomas W. Simpson, Nov. 22, 1948; Sloane to Ralph Lewis, U.S. Information Center, Feb. 1, 1949; both Sloane Papers, box 2, folder 5, Princeton.

106. Tebbel, *Between Covers,* 387–88, 411–12.

107. Sloane to Gilbert Loveland, Feb. 19, 1948, box 2, folder 11; West to de Graff, Mar. 9, 1948, box 7, unnumbered folder; Sloane to Crane, Mar. 22, 1948, box 2, folder 4; Sloane to Simpson, Nov. 10, 1948, box 2, folder 5; all Sloane Papers, Princeton.

108. Sloane to Fritz Wolcken, Nov. 22, 1948, box 2, folder 5, Sloane Papers, Princeton.

109. Sloane to Crane, Dec. 4, 1948, Sloane Papers, box 2, folder 4, Princeton.

110. Sloan to Dalcher, Dec. 13, 1948, Sloane Papers, box 2, folder 4, Princeton.

111. Waples to Sloane, Aug. 17, 1948, 260/16(A1)18/259, NACP.

112. *German Book Publishing,* 36, 64, 72, 92, 133, 142–43, 162.

113. Sloane to Dalcher, Feb. 17, 1949, Sloane Papers, box 2, folder 4, Princeton.

114. Dalcher to Sloane, Dec. 1, 1948, Sloane Papers, box 2, folder 4, Princeton.

115. Sloane to Dalcher, Dec. 13, 1948, Sloane Papers, box 2, folder 4, Princeton.

116. Sloane to Dalcher, Dec. 24, 1948, Sloane Papers, box 2, folder 4, Princeton.

117. Jamieson, *Books for the Army,* 128–41.

118. Breitenkamp, *Information Control Division,* 92–93.

119. Philip H. Hiss, "United States International Book Activities in Holland," Feb. 2, 1946, 208/356&357/1721, NACP.

120. Breitenkamp, *Information Control Division,* 95.

121. Dizard, *Strategy of Truth,* 37–38; Dizard, *Inventing Public Diplomacy,* 176.

EPILOGUE

1. For a summary of these problems in the 1950s, see Jennison, "Distribution of American Books Abroad," in Grannis, ed., *What Happens in Book Publishing,* 274–95, especially 276–77.

2. Burlingame, *Endless Frontiers,* 381–82.

3. Moore, *Wiley,* 168, 174.

4. Moore, *Wiley,* 174–75, 181–87, 191–94, 237–42.

5. Alvin Grauer to Cass Canfield, May 17, 1951, box 222, Harper & Row Papers, Series II, Columbia.

6. Grauer to Canfield, Sept. 9, 1953, box 222, Harper & Row Papers, Series II, Columbia.

7. Exman, *House of Harper,* 292–93.

8. R. B McAdoo to all editors, Aug. 3, 1966, box 196, and Tom Yodice to distribution list, July 21, 1972, box 226; both Harper & Row Papers, Series II, Columbia.

9. Box 196, Harper & Row Papers, Series II, Columbia.

10. E-mail from Albert N. Greco to author, July 25, 2008.

11. Lofquist, "United States Statistics on Exports and Imports," 30.

12. Box 196, Harper & Row Papers, Series II, Columbia.

13. Jennison, "Distribution of American Books Abroad," in Grannis, ed., *What Happens in Book Publishing,* 275.

14. Greco, "Market for U.S. Book Exports and Imports, 2005," 524–25; Greco, Rodriguez, and Wharton, *Culture and Commerce of Publishing,* 53.

15. Jennison, "Distribution of American Books Abroad," in Grannis, ed., *What Happens in Book Publishing,* 275; Richard Abel, "The Internationalization of the US Book Trade: The World's Rediscovery of America," in Graham and Abel, eds., *The Book in the United States Today,* 97.

16. Evan Dubrule to Evan Thomas, Sept. 6, 1962, box 196, Harper & Row Papers, Series II, Columbia.

17. Much of the following account of Franklin Book Programs is drawn, with the author's permission, from Amanda Laugesen, "The Creation of a Global Modern Publishing Culture in the Cold War: Franklin Book Programs, Translation, and Modernization in the Developing World, 1952–1968," unpublished paper delivered at the annual conference of the Society for the History of Authorship, Reading and Publishing (SHARP), Oxford, England, June 2008; from the same author's "Books for the World: American Book Programs in the Developing World during the Cold War, 1948–1968," in Gregory Barnhisel and Cathy Turner, eds., *Pressing the Fight: Print, Propaganda, and the Cold War* (Amherst: University of Massachusetts Press, forthcoming); and from Benjamin, *US Books Abroad,* 24–27.

18. Dizard, *Inventing Public Diplomacy,* 6–7.

19. Henderson, *United States Information Agency,* 75–77.

20. Nicholas J. Cull, "Public Diplomacy and the Private Sector," in Laville and Wilford, *US Government, Citizen Groups, and the Cold War,* 222.

21. Saunders, *Cultural Cold War,* 135–37.

22. Benjamin, *U.S. Books Abroad,* and Childs and McNeil, eds., *American Books Abroad.*

23. Richard Abel, "The Internationalization of the US Book Trade," in Graham and Abel, eds., *The Book in the United States Today,* 85–99.

24. Luey, "Organization of the Book Publishing Industry," in Nord, Rubin, and Schudson, eds., *A History of the Book in America,* vol. 5: *The Enduring Book.*

25. Gilbert, ed., *House of Holt,* 196; Sloane to Horace G. Butler, Apr. 12, 1946, box 2; Sloane to Herbert S. Bailey Jr., Princeton University Press, Aug. 4, 1966, box 1, folder 5; all Sloane Papers, Princeton.

26. Jennison, "Distribution of American Books Abroad," in Grannis, ed., *What Happens in Book Publishing,* 280.

27. Dalcher to Sloane, Dec. 1, 1948, box 2, folder 4, Sloane Papers, Princeton.

28. Fred Kaplan, "Barnes & Noble Goes to Baghdad," *Slate,* posted Apr. 28, 2006, http://www.slate.com/id/2140682/.

29. Kristof, "Make Diplomacy Not War," Week in Review, *NY Times,* Aug. 9, 2008.

30. "Sabre Foundation Ships More than 50,000 New Books and CD-ROMs to Iraqi Universities in New Program," Dec. 31, 2007, http://sabre.org/publications/PressRelease_Iraq_12%2031%2007.pdf.

31. Cole, "Americana in Arabic," posted Apr. 17, 2006, http://www.juancole.com/2006/04/americana-in-arabic-challenge-to.html; http://www.globam.org/; email from Cole to author, Oct. 14, 2009.

Bibliography

ARCHIVAL SOURCES

Alfred A. Knopf, Inc., Papers. Harry Ransom Humanities Research Center, University of Texas, Austin [HRC]

Cerf, Bennett A., Papers. Rare Book and Manuscript Library, Columbia University, New York, N.Y.

Charles Scribner's Sons Archives. Manuscripts Division, Department of Rare Books and Special Collections, Princeton University Library, Princeton, N.J.

Chatto & Windus, Ltd., Records. Special Collections Services, Reading University, Reading, England [CW]. By permission of The Random House Group Ltd.

Council on Books in Wartime Records, 1942–1947. Public Policy Papers, Department of Rare Books and Special Collections, Princeton University Library, Princeton, N.J. [CBW].

David Lloyd Agency Papers. Manuscripts Division, Department of Rare Books and Special Collections, Princeton University Library, Princeton, N.J.

Dorn, Walter Louis, Papers. Rare Book and Manuscript Library, Columbia University, New York, N.Y.

D. Van Nostrand Company Collection of Edward M. Crane. Manuscripts Division, Department of Rare Books and Special Collections, Princeton University Library, Princeton, N.J.

George Allen & Unwin, Ltd., Records, Correspondence. Special Collections Services, Reading University, Reading, England [AUC]. By permission of the Estate of Sir Stanley Unwin.

Harper & Row, Series II. Rare Book & Manuscript Library, Columbia University, New York, N.Y.

Henry Holt and Company, Archives. Manuscripts Division, Department of Rare Books and Special Collections, Princeton University Library, Princeton, N.J.

Huebsch, Benjamin W., Papers. Manuscript Division, Library of Congress, Washington, D.C. [LC].

John Day Company, Archives. Manuscripts Division, Department of Rare Books and Special Collections, Princeton University Library, Princeton, N.J.

Kerr, Chester Brooks, Papers. Public Policy Papers, Department of Rare Books and Special Collections, Princeton University Library, Princeton, N.J.

Lehmann Family Papers. Manuscripts Division, Department of Rare Books and Special Collections, Princeton University Library, Princeton, N.J.

Macmillan Publishing Archives. Department of Manuscripts, British Library, London [BL].

National Archives (UK), Kew, England [TNA].

> Board of Trade Records [BT].
> British Council Records [BW].
> Central Office of Information Records [including Ministry of Information] [INF].
> Colonial Office Records [CO].
> Foreign Office Records [FO].

National Archives (U.S.), College Park, Md. [NACP]. (Example of form of references in notes: 208/44/2949 denotes record group 208/entry 44/box 2949).

> Record group 59, general records of the Department of State.
> Record group 208, records of the Office of War Information.
> Record group 229, records of the Office of Inter-American Affairs.
> Record group 260, records of U.S. Occupation Headquarters, World War II.
> Record group 331, records of Allied Operational and Occupation Headquarters, World War II (SHAEF).
> Record group 389, records of the Office of the Provost Marshal General.

Publishers' Weekly Collection. Manuscripts Division, Department of Rare Books and Special Collections, Princeton University Library, Princeton, N.J.
Random House Papers. Rare Book & Manuscript Library, Columbia University, New York, N.Y.
S. Fischer Verlag Papers. Lilly Library, Indiana University, Bloomington [Lilly].
Simon, Richard L., Papers. Rare Book & Manuscript Library, Columbia University, New York, N.Y.
Sloane, William M., Papers. Manuscripts Division, Department of Rare Books and Special Collections, Princeton University Library, Princeton, N.J.
Viking Press Manuscripts. Lilly Library, Indiana University, Bloomington [Lilly].
W. W. Norton & Co., Norton Collection, Series II. Rare Book & Manuscript Library, Columbia University, New York, N.Y.

SECONDARY SOURCES

Anderson, Mark M., ed. *Hitler's Exiles: Personal Stories of the Flight from Nazi Germany to America*. New York: New Press, 1998.
Anonymous. *A Woman in Berlin: Eight Weeks in the Conquered City*. New York: Metropolitan/Holt, 2005.
Arndt, Richard T. *The First Resort of Kings: American Cultural Diplomacy in the Twentieth Century*. Washington, D.C.: Potomac Books, 2006.
Assouline, Pierre. *Gaston Gallimard: A Half Century of French Publishing*. San Diego: Harcourt Brace Jovanovich, 1984.
Badmington, Barbara Leslie, ed. *Books Are Indispensable*. New York: Book Publishers Bureau, 1943.
Ballou, Robert O. *A History of the Council on Books in Wartime, 1942–1946*. From a working draft by Irene Rakosky. New York, 1946.
Benjamin, Curtis G. *U.S. Books Abroad: Neglected Ambassadors*. Washington, D.C.: Library of Congress, 1984.
Bishop, Robert Lee. "The Overseas Branch of the Office of War Information." PhD diss., University of Wisconsin, 1966.
Bound, Charles F. *A Banker Looks at Book Publishing*. New York: Bowker, 1950.
Breitenkamp, Edward C. *The U.S. Information Control Division and Its Effect on German Publishers and Writers, 1945 to 1949*. Grand Forks, N.Dak.: privately printed, 1953.
Brooks, Howard L. *Prisoners of Hope: Report on a Mission*. New York: L. B. Fischer, 1942.
Brophy, John. *Britain Needs Books*. London: National Book Council, 1942.
Bryant, Mary Nell. "English Language Publication and the British Traditional Market Agreement." *Library Quarterly* 49 (Oct. 1979): 374–75.
Burlingame, Roger. *Endless Frontiers: The Story of McGraw-Hill*. New York: McGraw-Hill, 1959.
Butler, Pierce, ed. *Books and Libraries in Wartime*. Chicago: University of Chicago Press, 1945.

Calder, Angus. *The People's War: Britain, 1939–1945*. New York: Pantheon, 1969.

Calder-Marshall, Arthur. *The Book Front*. London: Bodley Head, 1947.

Canfield, Cass. *Up and Down and Around: A Publisher Recollects the Time of His Life*. New York: Harper's Magazine Press, 1971.

Cazden, Robert E. *German Exile Literature in America, 1933–1950: A History of the Free German Press and Book Trade*. Chicago: American Library Association, 1970.

Cerf, Bennett, and Donald Klopfer. *Dear Donald, Dear Bennett: The Wartime Correspondence of Bennett Cerf and Donald Klopfer*. New York: Random House, 2002.

Cheney, O. H. *Economic Survey of the Book Industry, 1930–1931*. New York: National Association of Book Publishers, 1931.

Childs, William M., and Donald E. McNeil, eds. *American Books Abroad: Toward a National Policy*. Washington, D.C.: Helen Dwight Reid Educational Foundation, 1986.

Clay, Lucius D. *Decision in Germany*. Garden City, N.Y.: Doubleday, 1950.

Cole, John Y., ed. *Books in Action: The Armed Services Editions*. Washington, D.C.: Library of Congress, 1984.

Coser, Lewis A. *Refugee Scholars in America: Their Impact and Their Experiences*. New Haven, Conn.: Yale University Press, 1984.

Cruickshank, Charles. *The Fourth Arm: Psychological Warfare, 1938–1945*. Oxford: Oxford University Press, 1981.

Davie, Maurice R. *Refugees in America: Report of the Committee for the Study of Recent Immigration from Europe*. New York: Harper, 1947.

Davis, Kenneth C. *Two-Bit Culture: The Paperbacking of America*. Boston: Houghton Mifflin, 1984.

Dickinson, Donald C. *John Carter: The Taste & Technique of a Bookman*. New Castle, Del: Oak Knoll, 2004.

Dizard, Wilson P., Jr. *Inventing Public Diplomacy: The Story of the U.S. Information Agency*. Boulder, Colo., and London: Lynne Rienner Publishers, 2004.

——. *The Strategy of Truth: The Story of the U.S. Information Service*. Washington, D.C.: Public Affairs Press, 1961.

Dobbins, James, John G. McGinn, Keith Crane, Seth G. Jones, Rollie Lal, Andrew Rathmell, Rachel M. Swanger, Anga R. Timilsina. *America's Role in Nation-Building: From Germany to Iraq*. Santa Monica, Calif.: RAND, 2003. http://www.rand.org/pubs/monograph_reports/MR1753/.

Donaldson, Scott. *Archibald MacLeish: An American Life*. Boston: Houghton Mifflin, 1992.

Dower, John W. *Embracing Defeat: Japan in the Wake of World War II*. New York: Norton and The New Press, 1999.

Dzwonkoski, Peter, ed. *Dictionary of Literary Biography*. Vol. 46, *American Literary Publishing Houses, 1900–1980: Trade and Paperback*. N.p.: Gale Group, 1986.

Enoch, Kurt. *Memoirs of Kurt Enoch*. N.p.: privately printed by Margaret M. Enoch, ca. 1984.

Epstein, Jason. *Book Business: Publishing Past, Present, and Future*. New York: Norton, 2001.

Exman, Eugene. *The House of Harper: One Hundred and Fifty Years of Publishing*. New York: Harper & Row, 1967.

Fairbank, John King. *Chinabound: A Fifty-Year Memoir*. New York: Harper Colophon, 1983.

Fairbank, Wilma. *America's Cultural Experiment in China, 1942–1945*. Washington, D.C.: Government Printing Office, 1976.

Feather, John. *A History of British Publishing*. London: Routledge, 1988.

Fiedler, David. *The Enemy among Us: POWs in Missouri during World War II*. St. Louis: Missouri Historical Society Press, 2003.

Fischer, Brigitte B. *My European Heritage: Life among the Great Men of Letters*. Boston: Branden, 1986.

Fleming, Thomas. *The New Dealers' War: Franklin D. Roosevelt and the War within World War II.* New York: Basic Books, 2001.

François, Dominique. *Normandy: Breaching the Atlantic Wall: From D-Day to the Breakout and Liberation.* Minneapolis: Zenith, 2008.

Friedman, Max Paul. *Nazis and Good Neighbors: The United States Campaign against the Germans of Latin America in World War II.* New York: Cambridge University Press, 2003.

Fry, Varian. *Surrender on Demand.* Boulder, Colo.: Johnson, 1997.

Gardiner, Juliet. *Wartime: Britain 1939–1945.* London: Review, 2004.

Garnett, David. *The Secret History of PWE: The Political Warfare Executive, 1939–1945.* London: St. Ermin's, 2002.

German Book Publishing and Allied Subjects: A Report by the Visiting Committee of American Book Publishers. Munich, 1948.

Gerson, Carole, and Jacques Michon, eds. *History of the Book in Canada.* Vol. 3, *1918–1980.* Toronto: University of Toronto Press, 2007.

Gilbert, Ellen D., ed. *The House of Holt, 1866–1946: A Documentary Volume.* Detroit: Thomson Gale, 2003.

Goedde, Petra. *GIs and Germans: Culture, Gender, and Foreign Relations, 1945–1949.* New Haven, Conn.: Yale University Press, 2003.

Goodman, Jack, ed. *While You Were Gone: A Report on Wartime Life in the United States.* New York: Simon and Schuster, 1946.

Graham, Gordon, and Richard Abel, eds. *The Book in the United States Today.* New Brunswick, N.J.: Transaction, 1996.

Grannis, Chandler B., ed. *What Happens in Book Publishing.* New York: Columbia University Press, 1957.

Greco, Albert N. *The Book Publishing Industry.* Boston: Allyn and Bacon, 1997.

———. "The Market for U.S. Book Exports and Imports, 2005: Dynamic Changes." In *Library and Book Trade Almanac, 2006.* 51st ed. Medford, Mass.: Information Today, 2006.

Greco, Albert N., Clara E. Rodriquez, and Robert M. Wharton. *The Culture and Commerce of Publishing in the 21st Century.* Stanford, Calif.: Stanford Business Books, 2007.

Green, Fitzhugh. *American Propaganda Abroad.* New York: Hippocrene Books, 1988.

Greene, Col. Joseph I., ed. *The Infantry Journal Reader.* Garden City, N.Y.: Doubleday, Doran, 1943.

Henderson, John W. *The United States Information Agency.* New York: Praeger, 1969.

Hewison, Robert. *Under Siege: Literary Life in London 1939–1945.* New York: Oxford University Press, 1977.

Hilton, Stanley E. *Hitler's Secret War in South America: German Military Espionage and Allied Counterespionage in Brazil, 1939–1945.* Baton Rouge: Louisiana State University Press, 1981.

Hitchcock, William I. *The Bitter Road to Freedom: A New History of the Liberation of Europe.* New York: Free Press, 2008.

Hodges, Sheila. *Gollancz: The Story of a Publishing House, 1928–1978.* London: Victor Gollancz, 1978.

Holman, Valerie. *Print for Victory: Book Publishing in England, 1939–1945.* London: British Library, 2008.

Hopkins, Gerard, ed. *The Battle of the Books.* London: Allan Wingate, 1947.

Jamieson, John. *Books for the Army: The Army Library Service in the Second World War.* New York: Columbia University Press, 1950.

———. *Editions for the Armed Services, Inc.: A History.* New York: Editions for the Armed Services, Inc., n.d.

Jones, Howard Mumford. *An Autobiography.* Madison: University of Wisconsin Press, 1979.

Kaestle, Carl F., and Janice A. Radway, eds. *Print in Motion: The Expansion of Publishing and Reading in the United States, 1880–1940*. Vol. 4 of *A History of the Book in America*. Chapel Hill: University of North Carolina Press, 2009.

Keefer, Louis E. *Italian Prisoners of War in America, 1942–1946*. New York: Praeger, 1992.

Kingsford, R. J. L. *The Publishers Association, 1896–1946*. Cambridge: Cambridge University Press, 1970.

Koppes, Clayton R., and Gregory D. Black. *Hollywood Goes to War: How Politics, Profits, and Propaganda Shaped World War II Movies*. New York: Free Press, 1987.

Korda, Michael. *Making the List: A Cultural History of the American Bestseller 1900–1999*. New York: Barnes and Noble, 2001.

Krammer, Arnold. *Nazi Prisoners of War in America*. Lanham, Md.: Scarborough House, 1996.

Laville, Helen, and Hugh Wilford, eds. *The US Government, Citizen Groups, and the Cold War: The State-Private Network*. London: Routledge, 2006.

Lehmann-Haupt, Hellmut. *The Book in America: A History of the Making and Selling of Books in the United States*. In collaboration with Lawrence C. Wroth and Rollo G. Silver. 2nd ed. New York: Bowker, 1952.

Leitz, Christian. *Sympathy for the Devil: Neutral Europe and Nazi Germany in World War II*. New York: New York University Press, 2001.

Lerner, Louis. *Psychological Warfare against Nazi Germany: The Sykewar Campaign, D-Day to VE-Day*. Cambridge, Mass.: MIT Press, 1971.

Lewis, Jeremy. *Penguin Special: The Life and Times of Allen Lane*. London: Viking, 2005.

Lingeman, Richard R. *Don't You Know There's a War On?: The American Home Front, 1941–1945*. New York: Putnam's, 1970.

Lofquist, William S. "United States Statistics on Exports and Imports." *Publishing Research Quarterly* 8 (Fall 1992): 30.

Luey, Beth. "Translation and the Internationalization of Culture." *Publishing Research Quarterly* 17 (Winter 2001): 41–49.

Macmahon, Arthur W. *Memorandum on the Postwar International Information Program of the United States*. Washington, D.C.: Department of State, 1945.

Madison, Charles A. *Jewish Publishing in America: The Impact of Jewish Writing on American Culture*. New York: Sanhedrin, 1976.

Mahl, Thomas E. *Desperate Deception: British Covert Operations in the United States, 1939–44*. Dulles, Va.: Brassey's, 1999.

Mehlman, Jeffrey. *Émigré New York: French Intellectuals in Wartime Manhattan, 1940–1944*. Baltimore: Johns Hopkins University Press, 2000.

Miller, Daniel J. *Books Go to War: Armed Services Editions in World War Two*. Charlottesville, Va: Book Arts Press, 1996.

Moore, John Hammond. *Wiley: One Hundred and Seventy Five Years of Publishing*. New York: Wiley, 1982.

Morris, John. *Traveller from Tokyo*. London: Book Club, 1945.

Mott, Frank Luther. *Golden Multitudes: The Story of Best Sellers in the United States*. New York: Macmillan, 1947.

Munby, Frank Arthur, and Ian Norrie. *Publishing and Bookselling in the 20th Century*. 5th ed. London: Jonathan Cape, 1974.

Nettelbeck, Colin W. *Forever French: Exile in the United States, 1939–1945*. New York: Berg, 1991.

Nord, David, Joan Shelley Rubin, and Michael Schudson, eds. *A History of the Book in America*. Vol. 5, *The Enduring Book: Print Culture in Postwar America*. Chapel Hill: University of North Carolina Press, 2009.

Okrent, Daniel. *Great Fortune: The Epic of Rockefeller Center*. New York: Viking, 2003.

OWI in the ETO: A Report on the Activities of the Office of War Information in the European Theatre of Operations, January 1944–January 1945. London: U.S. Office of War Information, 1945.

Packard, Jerrold M. *Neither Friend nor Foe: The European Neutrals in World War II.* New York: Scribner's, 1992.

Page, Roger. *Australian Bookselling.* Melbourne: Hill of Content, 1970.

Paley, William S. *As It Happened: A Memoir.* Garden City, N.Y.: Doubleday, 1979.

Peterson, Edward N. *The American Occupation of Germany: Retreat to Victory.* Detroit: Wayne State University Press, 1977.

Pfanner, Helmut F. *Exile in New York: German and Austrian Writers after 1933.* Detroit: Wayne State University Press, 1983.

Pilgert, Henry P. *Press, Radio and Film in West Germany, 1945–1953.* With the assistance of Helga Doggert. N.p.: Historical Division, Office of the Executive Secretary, Office of the U.S. High Commissioner for Germany, 1953.

The Psychological Warfare Division, Supreme Headquarters, Allied Expeditionary Force: An Account of Its Operations in the Western European Campaign, 1944–1945. Bad Homburg, Germany, 1945.

Radway, Janice A. *A Feeling for Books: The Book-of-the-Month Club, Literary Taste, and Middle-Class Desire.* Chapel Hill: University of North Carolina Press, 1997.

Reich, Cary. *The Life of Nelson Rockefeller: Worlds to Conquer, 1909–1958.* New York: Doubleday, 1996

Reichmann, Felix. "The Reorganization of the Book Trade in Germany." *Library Quarterly* 17 (July 1947): 196.

Report by the Three Delegates of the Publishers' Association Sent to North America… 1943. London: Publishers' Association, 1944.

Reynolds, David. *Rich Relations: The American Occupation of Britain, 1942–1945.* London: HarperCollins, 1996.

Robin, Ron. *The Barbed-Wire College: Reeducating German POWs in the United States during World War II.* Princeton, N.J.: Princeton University Press, 1995.

Rose, Jonathan E., ed. *The Holocaust and the Book: Destruction and Preservation.* Amherst: University of Massachusetts Press, 2001.

Rubin, Joan Shelley. *The Making of Middlebrow Culture.* Chapel Hill: University of North Carolina Press, 1992.

Ryback, Timothy W. *Hitler's Private Library: The Books That Shaped His Life.* New York: Knopf, 2008.

Satterfield, Jay. *The World's Best Books: Taste, Culture, and the Modern Library.* Amherst: University of Massachusetts Press, 2002.

Saunders, Frances Stonor. *The Cultural Cold War: The CIA and the World of Arts and Letters.* New York: New Press, 1999.

Schiffrin, André. *The Business of Books: How International Conglomerates Took Over Publishing and Changed the Way We Read.* London: Verso, 2000.

Schlesinger, Arthur M., Jr. *A Life in the Twentieth Century: Innocent Beginnings, 1917–1950.* Boston: Houghton Mifflin, 2000.

Shillony, Ben-Ami. *Politics and Culture in Wartime Japan.* Oxford: Clarendon Press, 1981.

Simmons, Dean B. *Swords into Plowshares: Minnesota's POW Camps during World War II.* St. Paul, Minn.: Cathedral, 2000.

Stacks, John F. *Scotty: James B. Reston and the Rise and Fall of American Journalism.* Boston: Little, Brown, 2003.

Sugarman, Tracy. *My War: A Love Story in Letters and Drawings.* New York: Random House, 2000.

Tebbel, John. *Between Covers: The Rise and Transformation of American Book Publishing.* New York: Oxford University Press, 1987.

——. *A History of Book Publishing in the United States.* Vol. 4, *The Great Change, 1940–1980.* New York: R. R. Bowker, 1981.

Thomson, Charles A. H. *Overseas Information Service of the United States Government.* Washington, D.C: Brookings Institution, 1948.

Travis, Patricia Ann (Trysh). "Reading Matters: Book Men, "Serious" Readers, and the Rise of Mass Culture, 1930–1965." PhD diss., Yale University, 1998.

Travis, Trysh. "Books As Weapons and 'The Smart Man's Peace': The Work of the Council on Books in Wartime." *Princeton University Library Chronicle* 60 (1999): 353–99.

Ulich, Robert. *Can the Germans Be Reeducated?* G.I. Roundtable Series, no. 26. Washington, D.C.: American Historical Association, 1945.

Unwin, David. *Fifty Years with My Father: A Relationship.* London: Allen & Unwin, 1982.

Unwin, Philip. *The Publishing Unwins.* London: Heinemann, 1972.

Unwin, Stanley. *Publishing in Peace and War.* London: Allen & Unwin, 1944.

——. *The Truth about a Publisher.* London: Allen & Unwin, 1960.

——. *The Truth about Publishing.* New York: Macmillan, 1960. First published in 1927 by Houghton Mifflin.

Waller, Maureen. *London 1945: Life in the Debris of War.* New York: St. Martin's, 2005.

Warburg, James P. *Unwritten Treaty.* New York: Harcourt, Brace, 1946.

Waters, Michael R. *Lone Star Stalag: German Prisoners of War at Camp Hearne.* College Station: Texas A&M University Press, 2004.

Weiskopf, F. C. "German Publishers Have Their Problems." *Books Abroad* 21 (1947): 9.

West, Rebecca. "Books for Liberated Europe." *English-Speaking World* 26 (Dec. 1943–Jan. 1944): 3–6.

Weybright, Victor. *The Making of a Publisher: A Life in the 20th Century Book Revolution.* New York: Reynal, in association with William Morrow, 1967.

White, A. J. S. *The British Council: The First 25 Years 1934–1959.* London: British Council, 1965.

Wieviorka, Olivier. *Normandy: The Landings to the Liberation of Paris.* Cambridge, Mass.: Harvard University Press, 2008.

Winkler, Allan M. *The Politics of Propaganda: The Office of War Information 1942–1945.* New Haven, Conn.: Yale University Press, 1978.

Wolfe, Robert, ed. *Americans as Proconsuls: United States Military Government in Germany and Japan, 1944–1952.* Carbondale: Southern Illinois University Press, 1984.

Ziegler, Philip. *London at War.* Knopf, 1995.

Ziemke, Earl F. *The U.S. Army in the Occupation of Germany, 1944–1946.* Honolulu: University Press of the Pacific, 2005.

Index

Italic page numbers refer to illustrations.